Outdoor
Design

A Handbook for the Architect and Planner

Outdoor Design

A Handbook for the Architect and Planner

Olwen C. Marlowe
ARIBA, DipLD (Dunelm), DipTP (Birm)

Whitney Library of Design
an imprint of Watson-Guptill Publications
New York

First published in Great Britain 1977 by Crosby Lockwood Staples

First published in the United States of America in 1977
by the Whitney Library of Design,
an imprint of Watson-Guptill Publications
a division of Billboard Publications, Inc.
1515 Broadway, New York, New York 10036

Library of Congress Cataloguing in Publication Data
Marlowe, Olwen C.
Outdoor design

Bibliography : p.
Includes index
1. Landscape architecture. I. Title
SB472.M345   1977   712   77–3706
ISBN 0–8230–7405–6

Printed in Great Britain

Foreword

Professor Anthony S. Travis, BA(Hons), FRTPI, FRSA
Director, Centre for Urban and Regional Studies
Faculty of Commerce and Social Science, University of
Birmingham

It is just over a century since William Robinson, then Horticultural Correspondent of *The Times*, made his eventful
study visit to Paris to evaluate the state of outdoor design
there. The direct result was the publication of his book,
*The Parks, Promenades and Gardens of Paris, Described
and Considered in Relation to the Wants of Our Own Cities,
and of Public and Private Gardens*. It is from such sources
that the landscape philosophy of his subsequent seminal
work, *The English Flower Garden*, evolved.

Robinson's commentaries on the work of the French
landscapist Alphand gave this country a new landscape
design vocabulary which not only catered for the detailed
design, construction and maintenance of urban parks but,
more importantly, suggested a concept of conscious
humanisation and improvement of the landscape throughout the town. The need was seen for outdoor landscape
design to burst beyond the confining park railing into the
areas of need – the landscape of housing, of industry, of
roads and of leisure.

The nineteenth-century revolution in landscape design,
heralded by Robinson, is now almost taken for granted.
The later international influences of Olmsted in North
America, of Blom in Sweden, of Siren in Denmark, have
given way to further generations of ideas – the romantic
use of native plants by Burle Marx in Brazil, the formalism
of Eckbo in the USA, the ecological concepts of people like
McHarg, and the inventive individualism of a Fairbrother in
Britain. Olwen Marlowe's entry into this wide and constantly changing realm of writing on outdoor design is especially
welcome and timely. She brings to this field her long
experience and her concern for broad synthesising design,
practicality and attention to detail, which link us to the
essence of the Robinsonian tradition.

Why is such a work timely? I believe that, in a period of
local government reorganisation and of concern about environment, ecology and conservation, Society's expecta-
tions of architects, planners and landscape designers grow
apace: from diminished resources they are expected to
deliver 'more and better'. A major book addressing design
and maintenance of the hard and soft landscapes is much to
be welcomed. It is the landscape floor of the town and of
the region which provides the continuous plane on which
most of us spend much of our lives – living, working,
playing and travelling on or across landscapes which may
be hard and inert or soft, living and dynamic.

Since World War II, the emphasis of outdoor design has
shifted. Now may be seen extensive work on the after-use
of urban wasteland and derelict areas and on pedestrian-
isation of old city centres, while multiple-use building com-
plexes have greatly extended the realm and range of

technical problems involved in urban outdoor design. Concepts of landscape resources, both quantitative and qualitative, are very much a product of the last decade: familiar planting and design skills have been extended into conservation and restoration activities; new building types and forms have made greater demands on the designer attempting the planned integration of buildings and landscape. Design for energy conservation raises new challenges in terms of choice of surface materials, means and costs of landscape maintenance, if life is (in Geddes' terms) 'to be made more abundant' as a result of ingenious design.

With cost-yardstick building ever evident, it increasingly becomes necessary for landscape design to soften and humanise our surroundings, and give them an acceptable and desirable identity. 'The Nature in the City' movement may widen further the life-horizons of the town-dweller who seeks, in the new low-cost, low-maintenance urban landscape, diversity not only in plants but in bird, insect and even animal life, appropriate to specific locations and needs.

Thus this book not only considers the 'what' and the 'why' of outdoor landscape design, but also firmly focuses on the key question of 'how' to achieve the right sort of designed landscape. For this, one needs to know about the ingredients or component-elements of design, as well as the tools, construction, specific skills and personnel involved. It is noteworthy that the 'gestation period' of this landscape-design book coincided with European Archi-tectural Heritage Year, when particular attention was being paid to our urban landscape, as well as to our architectural heritage. The conservation and restoration of historic gardens, together with new settings for old buildings, indeed for whole city centres and for walled historic cities, demands from the urban designer a heightened sensitivity to place, time and ethos – whether in Chester or Nuremberg, York or Jerusalem, Edinburgh or Birmingham. Such a design process, moreover, includes project implementation, management and maintenance.

The author is most appropriately equipped by education and experience to fulfil the demanding brief she has set herself. Educated at the University of Durham and the Birmingham Planning School, Olwen Marlowe's working life has characterised the range and scope of modern practice – bridging architecture, landscape and planning; local government and private practice; the landscape of housing, of industry, of education and of town centre. The book thus reflects a wealth of practical experience on a sound academic base, and will be especially useful to architects, planners, surveyors and engineers in practice, as well as to students in these disciplines – not forgetting, too, that large gardening public whose leisure is found on modest allotment or leisure garden, suburban half-acre or spacious estate.

University of Birmingham
March 1976

Acknowledgements

In writing this book it has been necessary for me to consult many sources of information. I have been assisted by a number of individuals and organisations to whom I am greatly indebted for the help and advice which they have freely given. Without their co-operation, and continuous encouragement from friends, my task would have been tedious and difficult. In particular, I should like to express my warmest appreciation to the following:

Mr Jeffrey Bernhard, JP, Jeffrey Bernhard & Sons Ltd
Miss Audrey Bond, Solicitor
Mr Derek Bradshaw
Building Research Establishment
Mrs W. J. Carroll
Cadbury Schweppes Ltd
Cement and Concrete Association
C. M. Churchouse Ltd
City Architect, Birmingham
Civic Trust
Miss W. G. Constable, Architectural Press Ltd
Miss Gladys Danks
Comptroller, Her Majesty's Stationery Office
Mr Henry Southwell Eades, Midlands Arts Centre for Young People
Mr Roy Ellis, Engineer
Mr John English, OBE, Director, Midlands Arts Centre for Young People
Federation of Coated Macadam Industries
Mr C. Vernon Hackett, MSc, CEng, FIMechE
Miss Laura Hicks, Civic Trust
Mrs F. R. Hignell
Miss F. Hodson, Sand and Gravel Association Ltd
Ibstock Building Products Ltd
Miss Sue Matthews, Cement and Concrete Association
Mr Colin McCall, Deputy Editor, *The Architect*
Mr George Perkin, ARIBA, Editor, *Concrete Quarterly*

Mr Rattigan, Redland Group
Royds Midland Ltd, Royds Advertising Group
Mr I. H. Seeley, BSc, FRICS, MIMunE, FIQS, FIArb
Mr R. L. C. Tate, Thorn Lighting Ltd
Mr Michael J. Thorp
Mr Arthur Thorpe, NDD
Thorn Lighting Ltd, Thorn Group
Miss Barbara Trigg, Deputy Editor, *Lighting Equipment News*
TTC Services Ltd
Mr Colin Wilkinson, FRIBA
West Midlands Regional Health Authority

I am most grateful to Professor Anthony Travis for his kindness in contributing the Foreword. I should also like to thank all those who so kindly provided me with photographs, and the following for their courtesy in granting permission to reproduce those listed below:

Architects Journal: Plate 4
Mr Derek Bradshaw : Plates 13 and 19
Cadbury Schweppes Ltd : Plate 11
Blakedown Landscapes Ltd : Plate 18
Cement and Concrete Association : Plates 3, 8, 9 and 17
Civic Trust : Plate 7
Director, Midlands Arts Centre for Young People : Plates 6 and 20
Redland Group : Plates 2 and 5
Sand and Gravel Association Ltd : Plates 1, 10 and 12
Thorn Lighting Ltd : Plates 14, 15 and 16

Finally, but most important, my deepest gratitude goes to Mrs Michael Thorp who, with cheerful fortitude and patience, has expended considerable effort in transcribing my manuscript into a most commendably presented typescript.

O.C.M.

Contents

Introduction

Concern for the quality of the environment has been a fashionable topic of discussion ever since Plato and Socrates expounded their theories. Throughout the ages man has made his mark—for better or for worse—on his surroundings. Most of us, caught up in the whirl of urban life, tend to forget that the beginnings of our landscape lie buried deep beneath millions of years of solid geology, and that the land form that we see today is the result of its transformation by geological developments and by the activities of man from Pre-Cambrian times onwards. The adaptation of that form by man for his survival and pleasure has resulted in a succession of landscapes, each reflecting the economic, social and aesthetic values of its period. Civilised man has always been actively concerned with his immediate surroundings—records reveal that thought and energy have been devoted to the subject of garden design throughout history.

In the British Isles the factors responsible for the development of the landscape are many and varied. The royal forests which we enjoy today were originally hunting grounds formed under the Forest Law introduced by the Norman kings. Some of the finest buildings preserved in our city centres are legacies of the skills of guilds of merchants and craftsmen. In rural areas, the aftermath of the Black Death brought about the disintegration of the feudal system and the rise of the yeoman farmer whose prosperity from the upsurge in sheep-farming indirectly provided a rich endowment of ecclesiastical architecture. The demise of the long-bow as a weapon of war, and the setting up of a professional army, saw the abandonment of keep and castle in favour of the country house, which, by the end of the sixteenth century, had transformed the English landscape.

John Evelyn's *Sylva*, published in 1678, provided the impetus for the planting of trees on a large scale in the two centuries that followed. The influence of other writers of the period, together with the infiltration of ideas from France and Holland following the restoration of the monarchy (Charles II had spent his exile in France), heralded a new concept of garden and landscape design.

Prior to the middle of the eighteenth century enclosure of land had made slow progress. The spate of legislation during the reigns of George II and George III resulted in a gradual transformation: a landscape was created whose design reflected both the influence of contemporary poetry, essays and paintings and the practical needs of farming techniques such as those advocated by Jethro Tull, 'Turnip' Townsend, 'Coke of Norfolk', and Robert Bakewell.

The enormous spate of canal-building effected a great change in eighteenth-century landscape and communications. Stretches of water were introduced where previously there had been none, resulting in changes in the flora and fauna and influencing the growth of towns, some of which (e.g. Stourport) were established as a direct result of the new waterway system. The advent of steam-power, which relied upon coal, made it essential for industry to be located close to the waterways that provided the means of transporting the raw material. The effect of this new form of transport was seen, indirectly, in building construction, which no longer relied upon indigenous materials but was able to tap resources far afield, e.g. roofing slate from Wales and the North of England. Before the end of the century new road construction techniques, formulated by John L. Macadam and Thomas Telford, were introduced, resulting in much better roads.

The impact of the Railway Age on nineteenth-century landscape was even greater than that of canals in the previous century. The severe limitations imposed by necessarily shallow railway gradients resulted in vast amounts of earthworks with the creation of huge cuttings and embankments up and down the country. This new, rapid form of transport was responsible for the further growth of towns and the establishment of important railway centres, such as Crewe. It opened up new horizons for industry and brought increasing prosperity to the country as a whole.

This, briefly, is the history of our inheritance, of which we, like others before us, are the trustees. What we, in our turn, make of our environment will be our legacy for tomorrow.

In the present century the Jet Age is but a further step in the development of communications. Motorised transport has graduated from a red-flagged menace to embrace a network of motorways which, like the canals and railways that preceded it, has made further inroads into the landscape and created problems in town and city. Intense mechanisation of agriculture is eliminating much of the flora and fauna whose habitat is the hedgerows now fast disappearing in the creation of larger units of farmland. Rationalisation of tree-planting is depriving the landscape of much of its small-scale intimacy. Recreational use of land is in competition with the demands of power production and industrial progress—generating stations, nuclear reactors, cooling towers, oil refineries and a host of engineering artifacts, linked by a skyscape of wires and pylons.

In town and city centre the developer's dream has materialised—often assisted by blinkered authorities. 'Obsolete' buildings which once contributed to the intimate character of so many of our older towns have been swept away wholesale only to be replaced, in many instances, by slums for the twenty-first century and monotonously repeated commercial 'developments'. But the blame does not lie solely at the door of commerce. Although there are many enlightened public authorities and other bodies, such as the Civic Trust and the Design Council, who are making a valuable contribution to the execution and encouragement of good environmental design, there are, regrettably, others whose attitude and endeavours fall far short. Criticism of some aspects of our town-planning legislation may be justified; it must nevertheless be conceded that without the enforcement of such laws there would be little hope of achieving the kind of environment for which we are striving.

It is a sad fact that all too often insufficient forethought is given to what lies beyond the manholes and drainage runs on the perimeter of a building: the means whereby the assets of the site may be further enhanced, or the detrimental features overcome, are ignored. When cuts in expenditure have to be made, the external works are always the first to suffer, even though the saving is usually little more than one or two per cent of the total cost of the contract. It is seldom appreciated just how much can be achieved for a comparatively small outlay.

Environmental design embraces a wide field of activity within the ambit of the outdoor scene, embodying those concepts concerned not only with the visual impact of man's immediate physical surroundings, and the pattern into which they fit within the broad dimensions of the landscape, but also their psychological effect. The environmental designer is, by definition, a person of many parts, since his expertise must range from architecture, town planning, civil engineering, law and surveying, to agriculture, horticulture, forestry, botany, ecology, geology and pedology. A sensitive eye and a keen sense of design must be complemented by some understanding of human psychology. From the nature of his training, it is the landscape architect who is best fitted for this role, working within a team of other specialists whose knowledge and advice he may call upon as necessary. Unfortunately, at the present time there is a shortage of qualified persons and the output of graduates each year is only small. Although architectural students receive some instruction in landscape design and appreciation this, of itself, does not make an environmental designer.

Except in a few instances, e.g. in new towns, the general impact of good contemporary design has yet to be felt. Not until there is universal demand for an improvement in standards will environmental quality be recognised and ultimately accepted as the norm. A project is judged not solely upon good design in its broadest sense, but upon the attention that has been paid to detail in carrying it out.

This book does not pretend to supply a ready answer to every problem that may be encountered; basically, it attempts to convey the rudiments and practical realities of environmental design in a form that may be readily understood and applied by the environmentally-conscious architect. It is hoped that it will also serve as a helpful manual for those actively engaged in the planning and building of our environment.

One Site Clearance

TREE FELLING AND REMOVAL

Survey of existing trees

A survey plan of the site should show the existing trees, hedges and larger shrubs within the site and also the trees adjoining the site boundaries. It should also include a description of the species, size, condition and age of the trees and the advantages or otherwise of their location on the site.

Development of a site involving the removal of a number of trees is likely to affect the microclimate and, perhaps, the supply of surface water to those trees remaining. Another factor to be taken into account is the proximity of trees to the proposed buildings; branches may overhang and obstruct the daylight to windows and tree roots may cause damage to foundations or interfere with drainage or engineering services.

The root system of the trees should also be borne in mind where the proposed development is likely to include multi-storey buildings. Wind velocities in the vicinity of tall blocks can create considerable problems and shallow-rooted trees are liable to be uprooted, and others severely damaged, by wind. The subsoil should also be studied in relation to the tree species and their root systems. Poplars and elms can cause considerable damage to foundations and drainage where sited in clay soils. Trees to be removed for transplanting elsewhere should receive adequate preparation.

Marking and numbering trees

The marking and numbering of all trees to be retained should be recorded on the site layout drawings before any demolition work is begun. Those trees which it is intended to cut down should be marked with suitably clear markings so that no mistakes are made.

Sale of timber

Where the timber has any commercial value, a specialist should be called in to give a valuation. Owing to the different conditions under which timber may be sold, it is difficult to draw up a model agreement clause; each case must be treated on its merits, depending upon such factors as access, ground contours, quality of the timber, etc.

Tree felling

There are three methods of felling:
(a) *By hand.* This involves the use of an axe, saw or combined application of both. It is used for trees of up to 460 mm girth, measured at ground level.
(b) *By power.* A power-driven saw or mechanical equipment is employed to fell or extract the tree.
(c) *By explosive.* In this country, the use of explosive (gelignite) is usually confined to the removal of tree stumps. Before explosives can be used a permit must be obtained from the local Superintendent of Police and if more than 4·50 kg is to be stored a special magazine must be constructed. It is advisable in such cases to employ specialists to carry out the work.

The first stage in felling is the 'laying-in' (also called rounding-up, facing, setting-up, or daubing) whereby the swellings around the base of the trunk (buttresses, toes, spurs or claws) are cut away with the axe. Next comes the process of undercutting when the 'sink' (kerf, dip or birdsmouth) is formed by using the axe to make a gap on the 'front'—the side towards which it is intended the tree

Fig. 1   Tree felling

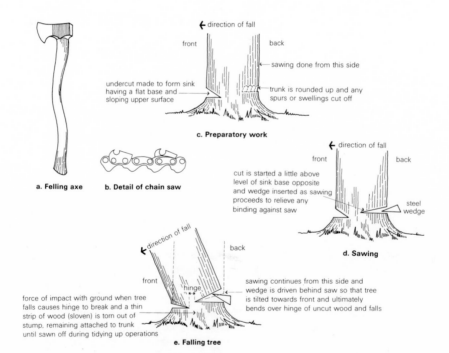

a. Felling axe

b. Detail of chain saw

c. Preparatory work

direction of fall
front
back
sawing done from this side
undercut made to form sink having a flat base and sloping upper surface
trunk is rounded up and any spurs or swellings cut off

d. Sawing

direction of fall
front
back
cut is started a little above level of sink base opposite and wedge inserted as sawing proceeds to relieve any binding against saw
steel wedge

e. Falling tree

direction of fall
front
back
hinge
force of impact with ground when tree falls causes hinge to break and a thin strip of wood (sloven) is torn out of stump, remaining attached to trunk until sawn off during tidying up operations
sawing continues from this side and wedge is driven behind saw so that tree is tilted towards front and ultimately bends over hinge of uncut wood and falls

shall fall. The third stage is to saw down the tree from the 'back'—the side opposite to the sink—until it topples over (Fig.1). The tree should be cut as near to ground level as practicable and the stump left with a clean horizontal surface, if it is to remain. Where a tree has been attacked by the honey fungus (*Armillaria mellea*), the stump and roots must be removed and burned. BS 3998 :1966 includes recommendations for tree removal. Methods of removing stumps are described below.

Where a tree is leaning away from the vertical, special care needs to be taken; if it is felled in the normal way there is a risk that it may split along the centre and thus ruin the timber. To prevent this a stout claw is put at the 'back' of the tree at the laying-in stage and the saw cut is commenced at the 'front' (i.e. on the side which is leaning towards the ground), not at the 'back' as in normal practice. The saw cut is only carried to just over halfway through the trunk. It is usually necessary to use wedges, which means that the blade cannot be lifted clear in the usual way but must be withdrawn to one side. The claw at the back is cut away with the axe, thus allowing the tree to topple over in the direction of the lean without splitting the timber. After felling, the tree is 'snedded' (trimmed out) by cutting away the side branches so that the timber can be moved.

Felling precautions

Trees on steep slopes should not be felled uphill because of the risk of the butt 'jumping' back and causing injury to both the felling operators and the timber. Felling in a high wind can be dangerous. Trees should not be felled across banks, walls, or other trees since damage may result when they fall. A large tree near to a building or in a confined space should be taken down in sections. Claims for third-party risks are the responsibility of the contractor.

It is important that the contractor should be given a date after which felling of timber may commence so as to avoid damage to adjacent crops or disturbance to shooting.

Extraction, loading and stacking of timber

A map should be prepared showing the routes (preferably with alternatives) which may be used to extract the felled timber and areas where it may be loaded and stacked.

If the timber is to be taken off the site it is first of all 'tushed' or 'snigged' (drawn butt end foremost) by a rope or chain pulled by a tractor and then loaded onto a pole waggon (tug or drag) and thence transported by road to its destination.

Felling of trees not marked for removal

It is necessary that the trees to be retained should be safeguarded by including a clause in the specification stating that if any tree not intended for felling is cut down the contractor is liable to pay a penalty. The exact sum would depend upon the circumstances, type and value of the tree.

Damage

All the interested parties should be safeguarded by a clause covering such items as gates, fences, hedges, walls, roads, bridges, streams, etc., damage to crops and grassland and livestock. A further point to be remembered is the risk of damage by rabbits where protective fencing is likely to be disturbed or damaged by felling operations; this applies especially to areas where young trees are growing in the locality of felling operations.

Where vehicles and machinery are likely to cause disturbance to ground surfaces the contractor should be required to level off all wheel tracks and leave such areas clean and tidy and free from heaps of sawdust and bark. The remains of all bonfire rubbish should also be cleared from the site.

HEDGING AND DITCHING

A hedge forms a demarcation line; a ditch acts as a drainage channel to carry away surplus surface water. Quite often a ditch forms the boundary of a site and there are many examples of ditches with a hedge running parallel to the boundary.

Neglected hedges soon become untidy and overgrown; ditches, too, become silted up and fail to function properly. Hedges and ditches to be retained should be put in good order at the start of site operations; by presenting an orderly appearance at the beginning of the contract they are less likely to suffer damage and abuse by operatives carrying out subsequent works on the site.

Although hedging and ditching are two operations which seem to go hand in hand, the former requires considerably skilled operatives to carry out a satisfactory job.

Clearing hedges

The first operation is to clear out rubbish and grub up all the unwanted plant material which, if left, would ultimately choke the hedge plants. All dead and diseased wood should be cut out and burned along with the unwanted herbage and rubbish. Dead tree stumps should also be removed, especially where they are sited in the vicinity of fruit trees, since they may be a host to the honey fungus which is liable to kill fruit trees.

Treatment of hedges

The two most satisfactory ways of dealing with a hedge are either by simple pruning or trimming or by cutting and laying. The second method can be used to produce a good hedge where it has become thin and open near the ground through neglect. Where there are farm crops the best time for carrying out the work is from July onwards, between hay and corn harvest, or in early autumn. The flush of growth is over by July and secondary growth after trim-

ming is not likely to spoil the tidiness of a well-trimmed hedge.

Hedge trimming

To keep hedges trim and neat and within reasonable bounds they need to be correctly trained from the start (Fig.2).

(a) *Formal hedges*. Trimming may be necessary once, twice or several times a year depending upon the types of shrub planted. Such hedges should be well furnished with growth right down to the base and trimmed so that the top is slightly narrower than the base (or with perpendicular sides) to prevent damage by snow and wind.

The treatment of a formal hedge depends very much on the plants forming it and their previous treatment or neglect. Where only light trimming is required, about a quarter of the length of new growth should be removed. Neglected hedges and those that require cutting back hard need to have more than half or three-quarters of the length of new growth removed.

(b) *Informal hedges* (*flowering*). These are pruned or trimmed to remove old and dead wood but must not be cut

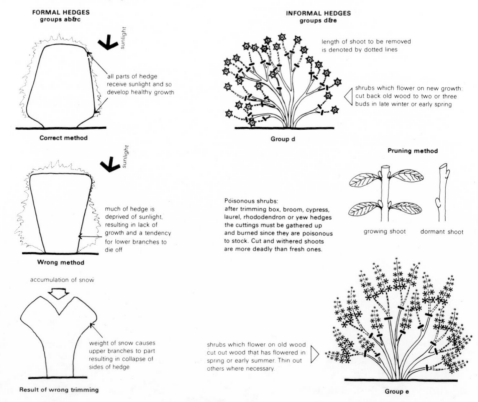

Fig. 2 Trimming of hedges

Table **1**
The trimming of established formal hedges

	Botanical name	Common name	Remarks
Hedges which require trimming once a year (in autumn, unless otherwise stated)	Aucuba japonica Variegata Berberis darwinii Berberis stenophylla Elaeagnus pungens Laurus nobilis Prunus laurocerasus Prunus lusitanica	Variegated or spotted laurel Barberry (in spring after flowering) Oleaster or wild olive Bay laurel Common or cherry laurel Portuguese laurel	Laurel and barberry should be trimmed with secateurs, not shears. Barberry is also grown as an informal flowering hedge.
Hedges which require trimming twice a year (July/August and October)	Berberis buxifolia Nana Buxus spp. Carpinus betulus Chamaecyparis lawsoniana and vars. Corylus avellana Cotoneaster simonsii Cupressus spp. Cupressocyparis leylandii Escallonia spp. Euonymus japonicus and vars. Fagus sylvatica and F.s. purpurea Ilex aquifolium and vars. Juniperus spp. Pyracantha spp. Rosmarinus officinalis Symphoricarpus spp. Tamarix gallica Taxus baccata and vars. Thuja plicata Viburnum tinus and vars.	Dwarf barberry Box Hornbeam Lawson's cypress Hazel Cotoneaster Cypress Leyland's cypress Chilean gum box Spindle tree Beech and purple beech Holly Juniper Firethorn Rosemary Snowberry Tamarisk Yew Western red cedar Laurustinus	Some of these plants may only require trimming once a year; the object of a second trimming is to remove any secondary growth made since the first trimming.
Hedges which require trimming several times a year	Crataegus oxycantha and vars. Ligustrum ovalifolium and vars. Lonicera nitida Prunus cerasifera Prunus spinosa Ulex europaeus and vars.	Hawthorn or quick Privet Bush honeysuckle Myrobalan Blackthorn or sloe Gorse	These hedges grow fairly quickly and require several trimmings a year in order to keep their formal shape.

back or clipped in the same way as a formal hedge. Flowering is an important consideration in the pruning or trimming operation and in order to ensure flowers for the following season the hedge must be cut back at the right time of year.

Flowering shrubs flower in one of the following ways:
(i) On young wood formed in the same year (i.e. on the ends of new growth)—prune in winter or early spring.
(ii) On wood formed during the previous year—prune immediately after flowering.
(iii) On spurs or side shoots—these require very little attention except for thinning out and shaping the hedge. Details of correct pruning for hedge shrubs is given in Tables 1 and 2.

Cutting and laying hedges
A cut and laid (plashed) hedge is one in which branches are kept long so that they can be bent over and wound in and out between stakes. The hedge height is kept to approximately 1050 mm. Cutting and laying (plashing) is a highly skilled operation and the method differs slightly from region to region (Fig.3).
(a) *Method.* The principle of hedge laying is to cut out many of the growths at the base; the remaining stems are half-severed at the base and then bent over at an angle of 45° to the ground and intertwined around stakes. The stakes are driven into the hedge in a straight line 150–200 mm from the centre line of the hedge to allow plenty of room for new growths springing from the base of the cut-back stools (i.e. base of shoots).

Table 2
The trimming of established informal hedges

	Botanical name	Common name
Hedges which require their flowering shoots to be cut back to two or three buds in late winter or early spring	Acer negundo and vars.	Box elder
	Atriplex halimus	Tree purslane
	Buddleia davidii and vars.	Buddleia
	Cistus spp.	Rock rose
	Fuchsia spp.	Fuchsia
	Hydrangea arborescens Grandiflora	Hydrangea
	Hydrangea paniculata Grandiflora	Hydrangea
	Hypericum patulum and vars.	Hypericum
	Lavandula spp.	Lavender
	Olearia haastii	Daisy bush
	Potentilla fruticosa	Shrubby cinquefoil
	Rosa pimpinellifolia	Scotch or burnet rose
	Rosa rubiginosa	Sweet briar
	Rosa rugosa	Ramanas rose
	Sambucus nigra Aurea	Golden-leaved elder
	Santolina chamaecyparissus and S. virens	Lavender cotton
	Spiraea japonica and vars.	Spiraea
	Tamarix pentandra	Tamarisk
Hedges which require trimming after flowering, their shoots cut back to within 150–200 mm of their base and thinned out as necessary	Amelanchier canadensis	Snowy mespilus
	Berberis darwinii	Barberry
	Berberis stenophylla	Barberry
	Buddleia alternifolia	Buddleia
	Ceanothus dentatus	Californian lilac
	Chaenomeles japonica	Quince or japonica
	Cytisus spp.	Broom
	Deutzia spp.	Deutzia
	Erica spp and vars.	Heather
	Forsythia spp.	Golden bell bush
	Hippophae rhamnoides	Sea buckthorn
	Kerria japonica	Jew's mallow
	Mahonia aquifolium	Oregon grape
	Osmanthus delavayi	Osmanthus
	Philadelphus spp.	Mock orange
	Prunus blireana	Purple-leaved flowering plum
	Prunus cerasifera Pissardii	Copper-leaved flowering plum
	Ribes sanguineum and vars.	Flowering currant
	Rosa moyesii	Rose
	Spiraea thunbergii	Spiraea
	Viburnum opulus Sterile	Snowball bush
	Weigelia spp.	Weigelia
Hedges which require little or no trimming except for cutting back long untidy growths in autumn or spring	Arundinaria japonica	Bamboo
	Berberis thunbergii Atropurpurea	Purple barberry
	Cotoneaster franchettii	Cotoneaster
	Cotoneaster frigida	Cotoneaster
	Cotoneaster microphylla	Cotoneaster
	Hebe traversii	Speedwell
	Kalmia latifolia	Calico bush
	Lonicera fragrantissima	Bush honeysuckle
	Phillyraea decora	Mock privet
	Rhododendron spp. and vars.	Rhododendron and azalea
	Rosa spp.	Rose species and musk roses
	Skimmia japonica	Skimmia

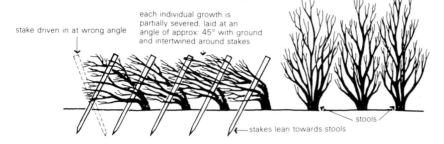

stake driven in at wrong angle

each individual growth is partially severed, laid at an angle of approx: 45° with ground and intertwined around stakes

stools

stakes lean towards stools

a. Stakes driven in at an angle

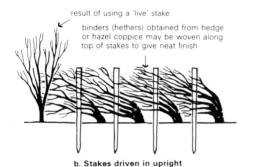

result of using a 'live' stake

binders (hethers) obtained from hedge or hazel coppice may be woven along top of stakes to give neat finish

b. Stakes driven in upright

The practice of planting hedges for setting out the boundaries of farms was introduced towards the end of the 17th century. Such hedges are often cut and laid – a method adopted to reclaim old or neglected hedgerows. Where the hedge is alongside a ditch the latter is normally cleaned out after cutting and laying is completed.

Fig. 3   Cutting and laying a hedge

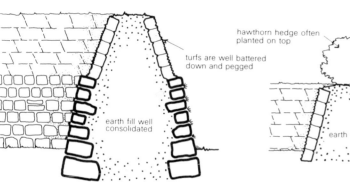

turfs are well battered down and pegged

earth fill well consolidated

a. Stone and turf

Lower part of hedge is constructed with stones, using thin sods to form the joints. Thicker sods are laid to the same batter to form the upper part. Height may vary.

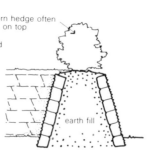

hawthorn hedge often planted on top

earth fill

b. Turf

Constructed with sods cut from site of hedge

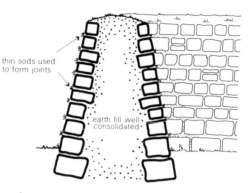

thin sods used to form joints

earth fill well consolidated

c. Stone and turf

Stones are generally laid at right angles to the bedding plane and built up in diminishing courses. Thin sods are placed between the individual stones. When established the grass eventually grows over the stones giving the appearance of a turf hedge.

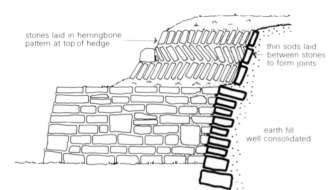

stones laid in herringbone pattern at top of hedge

thin sods laid between stones to form joints

earth fill well consolidated

d. Stone and turf

Another form of this type of hedge found in parts of Cornwall. The stones may be laid horizontally or at right angles to the batter (about 1:6)

Fig. 4   Turf and stone-faced hedges

(b) *Use of stakes.* Although the use of live upright stakes is likely to produce a mass of bushy growth at the top, spoiling the appearance of the hedge, it is claimed that hedges thus laid with no dead stakes to rot are true living fences.

Cut stakes of alder, beech, sweet chestnut or oak should be about 1·50 m in length and 38–76 mm diameter (if only thicker stakes are available they should be split longitudinally), spaced at 450–900 mm intervals and driven into the ground either upright or at an angle leaning towards the base of the layered shoots so that they are at right angles to them.

(c) *Finishing operation.* The layers, of fairly long growth, are intertwined around the stakes as in basket work. The stakes should be level and bound together at the top with binding (hethering) rods of hazel, willow or thorn and interwoven. This latter process is not vital but adds a finishing touch.

(d) *Hedges adjacent to ditches.* Where there is a ditch on one side, the best method of laying a hedge is to work from the ditch side so that, after the work is completed, the ditch can be cleaned out and spoil from the bottom used to make up any low places at the base of the hedge.

Fig. 5 Dealing with neglected ditches

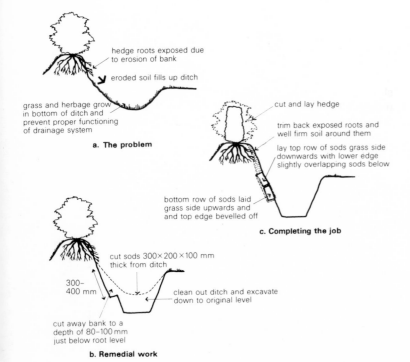

hedge roots exposed due to erosion of bank

eroded soil fills up ditch

grass and herbage grow in bottom of ditch and prevent proper functioning of drainage system

a. The problem

cut and lay hedge

trim back exposed roots and well firm soil around them

lay top row of sods grass side downwards with lower edge slightly overlapping sods below

bottom row of sods laid grass side upwards and and top edge bevelled off

c. Completing the job

cut sods 300×200×100 mm thick from ditch

300–400 mm

clean out ditch and excavate down to original level

cut away bank to a depth of 80–100 mm just below root level

b. Remedial work

Turf hedges

Turf hedges are banks of earth built up to a height of approx. 1·82 m with a width at the base of 1·30–2·45 m, sometimes crowned with a hedge of thorn, beech, ash or gorse and faced with turf. The sides of the turf walls are battered 150 mm in every 900 mm so that a hedge, say, 1·82 m high with a crown width of 760 mm would be 1·37 m at the base (Fig.4b).

The traditional time for carrying out the construction or repair work is during the winter months, but not during a spell of dry weather, otherwise the sods are likely to crumble. On the other hand, if there is rain during the period of construction the walls may swell and the turfs open up; this can be counteracted by pegging the turfs as work proceeds.

Soil and turfs from fields on either side of the proposed hedge site are taken off to a depth of approximately 300 mm for a distance of about 3·65–4 m back from the base of the hedge. The site is marked off with parallel lines set 1·52–1·82 m apart to denote the width of the base of the hedge. Sods are cut from this area and placed to one side for use. Stakes are then driven in at the ends of the hedge and nailed to cross-pieces to give the correct batter and shape of the hedge. This guide is repeated at approximately 20 m intervals and guiding lines are stretched between the stakes to assist in the construction. The size of sods used varies from county to county, e.g. :

Devon and Cornwall	300×300 mm
Carmarthenshire	380×180 mm
Pembrokeshire	230×100 mm

As the turfs are built up in bonded courses the centre is filled with earth, rammed well down, and the turfs well battered down (and often pegged) as the work proceeds. At corners and gateways the hedge is faced with stone to give it extra strength. Sometimes a protecting fence is fixed along the top instead of a hedge. Rabbits and rats are the worst enemies of this type of hedge and can soon ruin it if allowed to make a few holes. When repairing and rebuilding, all gaps and breaks in the hedge should be cut out down to a solid base.

Stone-faced hedges

In some parts of the country turf hedges give place to those faced on each side with stone or a combination of stone and turf (Fig.4a, c, d). The type of stone varies from square or rectangular granite blocks to thin shale or slates. Where stone and turf are used the stone blocks are built to a height of approximately 900–1200 mm and then turfs used for the rest, constructed to a similar size and shape as for turf hedges. The bottom stone course is built with the largest pieces, buried for up to half their height to form a firm foundation, with stones sloping inwards at an angle of 38–50 mm in every 300 mm and well firmed at the back with well-rammed soil as the construction proceeds. No mortar or cement is used; the hedge is built in the same manner as a dry wall with each course bedded down and well firmed. The top may be crowned with turf or planted with a hedge. A tonne of stone is sufficient to construct 2·7–3·34 m² of completed wall surface, assuming 150 mm thickness.

When this type of hedge is in need of repair (often due to the wall slipping or falling to pieces after a long period of neglect) it should be taken down to a firmly bedded course and rebuilt.

Cleaning out ditches and repairing banks

Where a hedge is planted on a bank adjacent to a ditch there is a tendency for soil to be washed down the bank into the ditch, which eventually becomes filled up. This eroding of the bank also exposes the root tips of the hedge and weakens the vitality of the plants, allowing strong winds to rock the hedge. To counteract the effects of this erosion the hedge bank should be covered with grass sods cut from the ditch (sodded) (Fig.5). This operation is carried out by cutting the bank away from just below the root level to a depth of 80–100 mm–the cut extending down the bank for 300–400 mm.

The sods, 100 mm thick × 300 mm long × 200 mm wide, are cut from the ditch and laid with the grass side uppermost along the lower edge of the cut, well beaten down and the top edge bevelled off. Sods of similar size to the first but slightly narrower in width are then set (grass side facing downwards) on top of the first sods so that the bottom edge slightly overlaps the sods beneath, and then well beaten down. Soil from the ditch is then placed on the bank and well firmed around the roots.

Forming new ditches

If a new ditch is to be made on sloping ground and a hedge planted beside it, the ditch should be sited between the hedge and the higher ground so that water draining off the latter will be collected before reaching the hedge (Fig.6b).

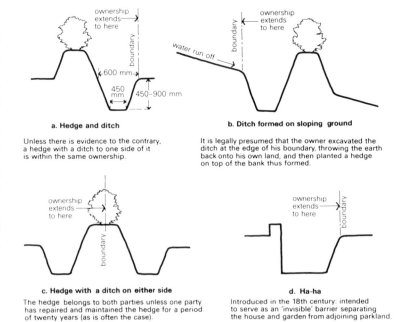

a. Hedge and ditch

Unless there is evidence to the contrary, a hedge with a ditch to one side of it is within the same ownership.

b. Ditch formed on sloping ground

It is legally presumed that the owner excavated the ditch at the edge of his boundary, throwing the earth back onto his own land, and then planted a hedge on top of the bank thus formed.

c. Hedge with a ditch on either side

The hedge belongs to both parties unless one party has repaired and maintained the hedge for a period of twenty years (as is often the case).

d. Ha-ha

Introduced in the 18th century: intended to serve as an 'invisible' barrier separating the house and garden from adjoining parkland.

Fig. 6   Formation of ditches

Ditches are usually dug 450–900 mm deep and about 600 mm wide at the top, tapering down to 450 mm at the bottom. The depth depends upon the level required to obtain an even fall to the lowest level so that the water can drain away easily to an outlet, e.g. a stream or local watercourse. Where dug in light soils the sides require a shallower slope than those in clayey soils. Although an excavating machine can be used for this work (the method often used for excavating trenches for the laying of drainage pipes) it is necessary for the sides of the trench to be cut back to form a batter, since the excavator cuts vertical but not sloping sides. Excavated soil is heaped up into a bank alongside the ditch, spread and levelled over the adjacent land or carted away, depending upon site circumstances and the quantity of material excavated (Fig.6a, c, d).

DEMOLITION AND CLEARING THE SITE

The method employed in clearing the site depends, to a large extent, on what is to be retained and the type of development proposed, but generally speaking the demolition of buildings and felling of trees are the first site clearance operations to be carried out. Some of these operations are executed in conjunction with excavation activities but for purposes of simplification and clarity are discussed here under their respective headings.

Protection of trees, shrubs and other landscape features

The location of existing large trees or those of desirable species often determines the siting of buildings or other permanent features and helps to play an important part in the overall design of the layout. Such trees are liable to destruction or damage from various causes during the course of the site operations (branches may be broken or scraped and roots dug away by excavating machines). Approximately 25 per cent of a tree's feeding roots are within the top 150 mm of the soil and need protection from damage due to soil compaction or waterlogging. It is essential, therefore, that all trees marked for retention are adequately protected before building or engineering operations begin. Protection may be effected in several ways, depending upon the conditions prevailing on site.
(a) *Groups of trees and shrubs.* Where a group of trees or shrubs is to be retained in the development, a stout temporary fence 1·52 m high around the perimeter of the group should be erected and no trespass permitted inside it.
(b) *Specimen trees.* Ideally, trees to be retained should be protected by fencing which extends beyond the spread of their branches so that crane jibs and other similar equipment do not foul the branches and cause damage to the trees. Sometimes a compromise has to be accepted and a fence of lesser radius erected, but it is inadvisable for this to be less than 3 m radius from the trunk of the tree. There are occasions, however, when site conditions are so restricted that not even this minimum protection distance is possible. In such cases the best solution is to protect the trunk by wrapping around it two or three layers of chestnut palings to a height of approximately 1·52 m (Fig.7). Where there is a risk that equipment or buildings may foul branches of trees the designer should consult with the contractor to decide the minimum amount of tree surgery needed to eliminate the obstruction without detracting from the tree's appearance. In such cases the advice of an arborist should be sought before starting operations on site.

Penalty for damage to trees

The replacement of mature trees can be a very costly operation—in some instances they are irreplaceable. It is now common practice to insert a penalty clause in the bills of quantities (or specification) to discourage the contractor from causing damage to any tree that is to be

Fig. 7　Temporary protection of tree trunks

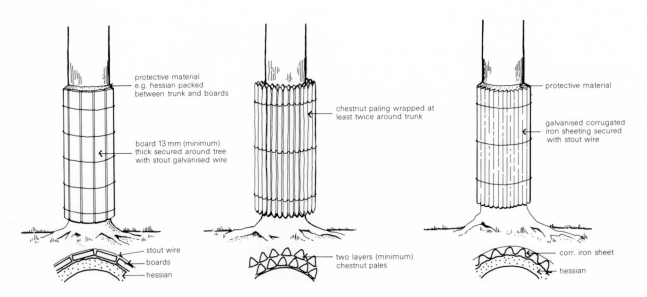

protective material e.g. hessian packed between trunk and boards

board 13 mm (minimum) thick secured around tree with stout galvanised wire

stout wire
boards
hessian

chestnut paling wrapped at least twice around trunk

two layers (minimum) chestnut pales

protective material

galvanised corrugated iron sheeting secured with stout wire

corr. iron sheet
hessian

retained. The amount of the penalty depends upon both the amenity value of the trees and the problematical cost of replacement. A fine old oak is beyond monetary value, but its loss could considerably affect the amenity of the area and to the client may be worth far more than, say, £1000. On the other hand, a young mountain ash may be replaced for one-tenth of that amount.

It is advisable to discuss with the client beforehand the amount of the penalty he wishes to impose.

Demolition of buildings

Walls may be demolished to a level of 150 mm below general ground line if the area is to be hard landscaped at the existing level, otherwise the foundations should be grubbed up to a depth of 450 mm below ground level. If trees or shrubs are located in close proximity, care must be taken to prevent any damage.

Existing services to the demolished building must be sealed off and left in a safe condition. Drains and manholes to be retained must be kept free from dirt, rubble and other foreign matter. Old gulleys should be grubbed up, manholes broken up, voids filled in with clean hardcore and old drains stopped off with cement at both ends. Reference should be made to CP 94:1971.

Materials to be retained

Any materials which the designer wishes to retain for re-use on the site should be recorded in a schedule and any items to be numbered should be clearly indicated. If demolished brickwork is to be used for hardcore fill, this should also be stated.

Clearing the site

Site-clearing operations may include the demolition of buildings, getting out old foundations, clearing away boulders, stripping turf, breaking up roadways, grubbing out drains and gulleys, cutting away undergrowth, taking down saplings and getting out hedges, etc. Whatever work is involved, the operations the contractor is required to carry out and his responsibilities to the client should be clearly stated. The area of site clearance should be shown on a site plan and any buildings to be demolished clearly indicated.

Clearing often involves the removal of vegetation of one kind or another. Areas to be excavated, filled or graded often must be cleared first. All the cleared vegetation is burned at the same time as it is piled. Precautions must be taken to see that no bonfires are lighted near any trees or anything likely to be damaged or adversely affected.

Burning off areas of vegetation

Instead of clearing out herbage and vegetation and burning it as it is piled, it may be a simpler task to burn off these areas. Precautions must be taken to ensure that all burning is kept under strict watch and effective measures available should the fired areas get out of control. Safeguards must also be taken when storing inflammable material for use in the burning-off process.

Turf stripping

Turf on the site may be required for immediate re-use elsewhere, but if it is not possible for it to be relaid within a few days of being stripped the contractor should be permitted to dispose of it, making an allowance for this in his tender.

Removal of old tree stumps

The size and height of a tree stump usually determines the method of its removal and it can either be dug out (by hand or machinery), pushed or pulled out, blasted out or burned (a somewhat slow method).

(a) *Digging out.* Hand digging is a very tedious job because much of the soil between the roots must be dug with a trowel or small tool, and roots severed as work proceeds. Generally, mechanical equipment, such as a bulldozer or scraper, is best used for this work.

(b) *Pushing or pulling out.* Where the length of the trunk is sufficient to use the blade of a dozer, the stump may be pushed out. Another method of taking out stumps is to pull them by means of a chain, cable or rope around the trunk attached to a machine or winch. The chain or cable is generally a choker type which tightens its grip as the pull increases. Line pulling is preferred when the ground is too soft or too rough to allow machinery to get at a stump directly.

(c) *Blasting out.* As mentioned previously, a permit must be obtained from the local Superintendent of Police; it is advisable to employ specialists to carry out the work. The Ministry of Agriculture Bulletin *Tree, Bush and Stump Clearance* describes the use of explosives.

(d) *Burning.* Stumps which are partially rotted may be difficult to pull because of their tendency to fall apart; one method of dealing with this is to burn them. This, however, may take time to get under way, especially if there is still a certain amount of sap present. It may be easier partially to dig out and then burn the stump.

Whichever method is adopted, all roots exceeding 50 mm in diameter should be taken out and the area of excavation backfilled with soil (or hardcore as the case may be) and consolidated to the original ground level.

Grubbing up and clearing hedges, bushes and saplings
Bulldozers and bush grubbers are probably the best machines to use. Where a hedge is planted on a bank the bulldozer is the better machine because in one operation it can push out the plants and level the ground.

The bush grubber is of similar construction to the bulldozer but has a spade-like tool with large serrated teeth in place of the shovel, which enables it to dig into the soil under a hedge (or bush) and then lift and push it out of the ground. It is ideal for grubbing up hedges planted on flat ground; a bulldozer used in this sort of situation has to shift a lot of unnecessary soil before being able to move the hedge.

If any stone is incorporated this should be taken out by hand prior to tackling disposal of the hedge. After the plants are grubbed up the site should be cleaned up and all rubbish burned and carted away. Extra care must be taken to remove all traces of any poisonous plants such as yew, laurel, box, cypress, rhododendron, etc., especially where there is livestock in the vicinity.

Clearing lakes and streams

The operation of clearing may comprise anything from dredging and disposal of silt from a lake to the clearing and disposal of a few weeds and rubbish from a small ornamental pond. Most lakes are natural outfalls for water-gathering grounds and if they become silted up so that they do not function properly the result may be considerably detrimental to the natural drainage of the area. Where trees and vegetation are growing close to or on the banks of a lake or stream it may be advisable to consider the need for thinning and removal of some of them to allow more light to penetrate.

Silting is a common problem, producing a soft black organic mud deposit which dirties the water and makes it shallower. Removal of the silt by machinery usually necessitates draining or pumping out the water, to avoid distributing disturbed mud throughout the lake, and then allowing the silt to dry out before proceeding with the work. This drying out (hardening process) can be assisted by hand-ditching into the subsoil—a somewhat sloppy and discouraging job initially because of the flow-back of mud into the ditch. The first ditching, therefore, should be very shallow and the depth then increased as the area drains.

It is general practice to take off more than just the mud from the bottom : about 150 mm of native soil is dug out as well, giving an opportunity for the pond to be deepened. The mud itself is of little agricultural value when freshly dug, but after curing for a year or so it makes excellent top soil. Mixing with a sandy soil speeds up the process of curing and lime added in the right quantity should correct the acidity of the soil.

The use of a hydraulic dredge is seldom practical because of the cost of transport as well as the need for adequate water inflow and suitable disposal areas. If the lake is narrow and sufficiently accessible, so that all parts of it can be reached by a dragline stationed on the banks, it may not be necessary to wait until the mud has dried out. The chief problems encountered in using a dragline are access and the positions of trees—especially where these are sited on banks and may interfere with the boom.

The alternative method is to use dozers, after allowing the mud to dry out. This probably necessitates forming a ramp to enable the dozer to climb with a load, since the average lakeside edge is normally too steep for this type of equipment to negotiate it.

Quite often the biggest problem encountered in dredging is the disposal of the mud. If it is possible either to deposit this on the banks or to spread it on adjoining land, the cost of the operation can be considerably reduced by avoiding transporting the dredged material to another site.

Where the flow of water in a stream is impeded, the cause is usually deposited rubbish or excessive growth of vegetation. In some cases it may be necessary temporarily to divert the stream while clearing operations are carried out, but the legal aspects of such action must be considered. If diversion is impossible, clearing should be carried out in sections, starting at the upstream end and moving downstream.

Erosion of banks is a common defect ; clearing operations afford the opportunity to counter this by repairing banks with some of the excavated material.

Two Ground Contouring and Soil Preparation

SOILS AND THEIR INFLUENCE ON PLANTS

The principal soils

Climate is a major factor in determining soil types and the kind of vegetation they support. The various types of soil characteristic of certain climatic conditions have been classified into groups, termed 'zonal soils'.* These groups occur in belts throughout the world, but are not uniform or constant. Within each zone are found divergencies, due to the presence of certain chemical constituents (water and salts of various kinds), which modify the characteristics of the zonal soil. Soils dominated by such conditions often occur in more than one zonal region, overlapping at the boundaries separating one zone from another, and are known as 'intrazonal soils'. There are also geologically young soils which, because of their undeveloped materials, do not possess the typical characteristics of the mature zonal and intrazonal soils; they are known as 'azonal (skeleton) soils'.

*Controversy exists among pedologists regarding soil classification (which is a complicated subject beyond the scope of this book) ; that established by the Russian School has been largely superseded, but is adopted here purely for the purpose of giving a simple explanation of the occurrence of soil classes.

Although this particular classification is based upon climatic influences, it must be remembered that other factors, such as altitude, geological material, drainage and vegetation, as well as the length of time during which pedogenic processes have been at work, all have an important bearing upon soil properties.

The principal soils occurring in Britain are described below:

1. *Zonal soils*

Soils of the humid climatic group include Podzols and the Brown Podzolic soils.

Podzols. Compounds of aluminium and iron are leached from the upper soil horizons and accumulate at a lower level—a process referred to as 'podzolisation'—causing the soil to have a greyish tinge at the surface and an ash-grey horizon not far below it.

Podzols are generally produced on sandy geological formations, such as those of the Cheshire Plain and the Kent and Surrey heaths.

Brown podzolic soils. These soils are characteristic of the cooler and wetter climate of the northern and western parts of Britain. The precipitation/evaporation (P/E) ratio is markedly higher than that of the Brown Earth (see below) climate, with the result that the downward movement of water is much stronger than the upward and therefore leaching of the upper horizons takes place but has not formed the ash-grey horizon characteristic of typical podzols (Fig.8b). Some of the best-developed podzols are found on the Tertiary and post-Tertiary sands and gravels

Fig. 8   Soil in its undisturbed state

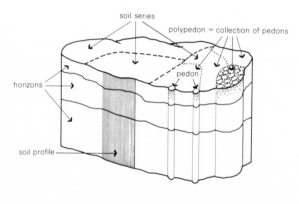

a. Diagrammatic explanation of soil terminology

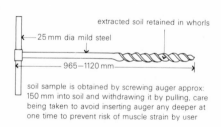

soil sample is obtained by screwing auger approx. 150 mm into soil and withdrawing it by pulling, care being taken to avoid inserting auger any deeper at one time to prevent risk of muscle strain by user

c. Hand-operated soil auger

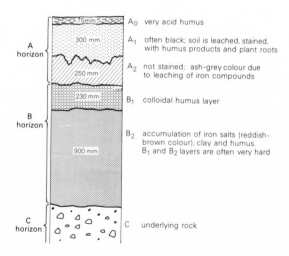

b. Soil profile showing horizons in a typical podzol

of southern England, such as the Reading Beds and Bagshot Sands.

In general, podzols do not provide conditions favourable to the growth of broadleaved trees because of the impoverished soil surface, but pine and birch (which ecologically belong to the northern coniferous type of forest) establish themselves, also spruce where the soil is not too shallow. Apart from heath and moor plants the majority of shrubs and herbaceous plants are unable to tolerate the high acidity of these soils. It is due to such acidity that podzols do not make good growing soils, although their acidity may be corrected by heavy applications of lime, after which they approximate to the Brown Earth type. If such soils are left derelict or unregulated they rapidly revert to podzols.

Some soils, classed between podzols and Brown Earths, arise by partial podzolisation of a Brown Earth soil (referred to as Degraded Brown Earth). Earthworms are rarely present in podzols.

2. Intrazonal soils
Soils of the groups whose formation is due to modifying substances include:

(a) Soils formed under conditions of excessive water.

Meadow soils (riverside soils). The moisture content of these soils varies with the fluctuations of the water-table level, depending upon the time of year. During wet periods the surface soil is often flooded and, consequently, during such periods detrital material is carried down in suspension by river waters.

In the dry season of the year the surface soil, which is often a dark colour due to the accumulation of organic material, may be quite dry but the lower horizons are usually greyish in colour with rust and blue-coloured streaks typical of a gleyed soil, indicating deficient drainage.

These soils support grassland, often used as pasture, occupying flat ground which coincides with the alluvium of river valleys. They are fertile soils that are neither acid nor deficient in oxygen, due to the constant movement of water. Poor drainage and a fluctuating water-table lead to impeded leaching and the development of a gley horizon. Where this type of soil is thoroughly drained, so that leaching takes place, it tends to convert to a Brown Earth type.

Bog soils (peats). There are two types: fen and acid peats. Both produce rich organic soils and generally possess well-defined profiles.

(i) Fen peat (alkaline) is rich in nutritive (basic) salts, i.e. 'eutrophic', and is a pure organic soil found in lake basins and the upper parts of old estuaries fed by waters rich in bases. The fenlands of East Anglia, the Norfolk Broads and parts of Somerset are examples of this type of soil.

In humid or sub-humid climates the accumulation and breakdown of plant debris in marshy or swamp areas is prevented from becoming acid by the alkaline mineral substances, originating from rocks, dissolved in natural drainage water. The extremely moist conditions result in the exclusion of air from the soil and, with the absence of oxygen, the complete disintegration of the peat is prevented.

Very little detritus is brought into the decaying vegetation by streams and the accumulation of plant debris may, eventually, result in raising the surface level of the peat above that of the alkaline water. In such conditions the exposed peat may break down to produce an acid peat which possesses different properties.

'Half bog soil' is the description given to peat soil having a grey, waterlogged mineral accumulation of clay, sand or gravel underlying the surface horizon.

(ii) Acid peat is poor in nutritive salts ('oligotrophic') and is formed in extremely wet conditions. Where precipitation greatly exceeds evaporation the soil type is called 'blanket bog peat' and in a less wet climate a similar type of acid peat may develop in a fen basin above the level of the neutral or alkaline waters; it is then known as 'raised bog peat'.

Blanket bog soils are found in West Scotland and large parts of the Scottish Highlands, and on elevated plateaux such as Dartmoor and the Pennines. Raised bog soils (built on ancient fen) are found in the Central Irish Plain and in parts of Scotland. Many parts of the West of England and Wales were originally raised bogs before drainage destroyed this character.

Acid peats occur in regions of high rainfall or mist where total precipitation of moisture exceeds evaporation and alkaline drainage waters are absent as acid peat develops. Where such peat overlies well-drained non-calcareous rock the mineral material often shows signs of podzolisation.

Pseudoglei soils (surface-water-glei). In soils overlying impermeable rocks, such as the heavy boulder clays and clays of the solid formations (e.g. Weald Clay and Oxford Clay), there is no true water-table, resulting in seasonal waterlogging. The thin, heavy-textured surface horizon is a dark greyish-brown overlying a heavy lighter-coloured horizon; below this a more heavily mottled horizon, rich in concretions of oxides of iron, reaches down into the clay rock. These soils are widely distributed in Britain.

(b) Soils based on the presence of calcareous substances.

Brown Forest soils (*Brown Earths*). These occur on loams or clays under deciduous forests in temperate, humid climates and are often alkaline in reaction due to the calcium compounds present in the soil from decaying leaves. The surface layer is a slightly acid, dark-brown horizon, rich in humus, which overlies a light-coloured leached horizon showing little, if any, signs of podzolisation since there is hardly any removal of compounds of iron and aluminium from the upper horizons to the lower ones in the profile. Earthworms usually abound in Brown Earths.

Much of the good agricultural land in Britain is of the Brown Forest soil; it occurs chiefly in lowland areas and may support deciduous woodland.

Rendzina. This type of soil is developed from calcareous materials (especially limestones), traces of which are to be found in the surface horizon—a black, brown, yellowish-brown or grey friable loam—overlying the limestone rocks. These soils occur most typically on fairly steep slopes. On steep northern grassland chalk slopes in permanently moist conditions the soil is fairly deep and extremely rich in humus, which shrinks into a tough cohesive mass. At the other extreme the soils may be shallow and greyish-white, derived from chalk or other soft limestones, supporting beechwoods in the south and ashwoods in the north and west of the country, but mainly grassland. Of the intermediate soils between these two extreme conditions, the most common have a reddish-brown, loamy layer between surface humus and underlying chalk.

3. *Azonal soils*
Geologically young soils may be classified into:

(a) *Alluvial soils.* These are sands, silts and clays (often mixed together), accompanied by gravel and a certain amount of organic material; they usually show signs of gleisation and often support grassland.

Many soils formed in alluvium have well-developed profiles and may be classified under the soils described above.

(b) *Dry sands.* Soils lying immediately behind the coastline are subject to slow podzolisation which may vary according to climatic and other factors. Examples of these soils are found in many parts of England and Wales, e.g. Lancashire, Kent and Caernarvonshire.

Soil acidity

The chemical reaction of a soil may range from extreme acid to very strong alkaline, the intensity of which may be described in terms of the pH scale* as follows:

Below 4·5	Extremely acid
4·5–5·0	Very strongly acid
5·1–5·5	Strongly acid
5·6–6·0	Medium acid
6·1–6·5	Slightly acid
6·6–7·3	Neutral
7·4–8·0	Mildly alkaline
8·1–9·0	Strongly alkaline
9·1 and above	Very strongly alkaline

Soils overlying areas of well-drained sandstone are generally acid in reaction; alkaline soils are found in limestone districts. Each type of soil reaction is reflected in the plant community which it supports. Although many plants are tolerant of a variety of conditions the majority tend to prefer soils having a slightly acid–neutral reaction which allows them readily to obtain nutrients from the soil. Hardly any plant is capable of thriving in a soil whose reaction is pH 3·5 (even bacteria cannot work in such conditions) and no plants are able to grow in soils of pH 9·0.

Soils of horticultural value

Soil requirements of plants differ; it is important, therefore, that the type of soil in which they are intended to grow is borne in mind when selecting plant material.

Light (*or very light*) *sandy loams.* In areas where the rainfall exceeds 760 mm a year the sandy loams are able to support a wide range of plants, but the extreme types (podzols) are only suitable for heath-type plants, e.g. gorse, ling, etc. Drainage of these soils is good, allowing high-class swards to be produced and making them ideal for the construction of golf-courses.

Medium loams. These are the best kinds of soil because they have a nice balance of particles with good drainage.

*p=potential; H=hydrogen; pH (potential of hydrogen ions) is the chemical term used to indicate the degree of acidity or alkalinity.

They are very adaptable and capable of supporting a wide range of plants.

Heavy loams. Although useful, these soils are not as good as the medium loams and require more careful pre-planting preparation.

Clay. This makes for a heavy soil and drainage is usually imperfect. Large open spaces, such as parks, are often planned on this type of soil. With satisfactory drainage, clay soils are able to support a wide range of shrubs (roses do well), herbaceous plants and bulbs.

Calcareous soils. These are soils derived from geological material such as limestone and chalk. Those found on excessively drained chalk are poor and difficult; better soils are found overlying chalk having glacial drift deposits. Lime-loving plants, such as iris, clematis, dianthus, etc., thrive under these conditions.

Peat soils. Associated with very bad drainage, the character of these soils differs according to their location. The peat occurring at high altitudes is strongly acid but that of the lowlands is much less so, providing scope for the introduction of bog plants. Willows and poplars also thrive in lowland situations. Where there is free drainage, rhododendrons, azaleas and plants of the *Ericacae* family may be planted.

Soil and plant growth

A plant's life cycle takes place within the soil; from the sowing of the seed until maturity the plant relies upon the soil for support and food. Initially the soil is a resting place for the sown seed, providing water, air and a suitable temperature to encourage germination.

In the early stages of germination, food stored in the seed is transferred to the growing parts and, as the germination stage reaches its climax, root hairs develop in the radicle and chlorophyll starts to develop in the plumule as it emerges above the ground's surface. This development enables the plant to take up nutrients from the soil and to assimilate carbon dioxide from the atmosphere (Fig.9). In the development of the plant, soil constituents play a major role and have a controlling influence on the chemical, physical and biological factors which relate to plant growth. Defects or deficiencies may result in infertility and plant failure.

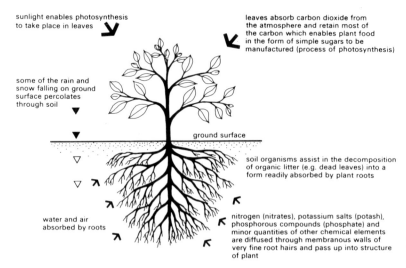

Fig. 9   Role played by soil in plant nutrition

The importance of soil fertility

Soil fertility may be defined as the capacity of any soil to produce and support healthy plants. It is dependent upon a number of properties which may be grouped under three broad headings: pedological, edaphic and biotic factors.

1. Pedological factors
Constituents of the soil and their proportions within it depend upon the nature of the parent material and the processes to which it has been subjected.

Origin and development of soil. The majority of soils are mineral in character, derived from solid geological deposits, and are the source of nutrients for plant life. Although rich in plant foods, some minerals are not always in a form available to plants. Quartz, one of the most important minerals occurring in the form of sand, is valuable in reducing cohesion, so promoting free working of the soil.

Climate plays a large part in determining the type and development of the soil in a particular region and is reflected in the Russian classification of soils.

Character and texture. Most soils occur in distinct layers (horizons) whose arrangement provides a record of the properties and capabilities of each type (Fig.8a). The soil colour reflects its chemical or mineral composition. The latter plays an important part in determining soil texture—a definite and measurable property. Mineral particles are derived from the weathering and disintegration of rock, caused by action of the elements. A soil is classified, according to the size and proportion of mineral particles present, as sand, silt or clay.

2. *Edaphic factors*

Various properties having a positive bearing on plant growth are related to the nature of the soil, the amount of air and water contained therein and the presence of essential minerals. These are referred to as 'edaphological' properties.

The roots and underground stems of plants are supported and protected by the soil and supplied with food from it (Fig.9). Of the nutrient elements necessary for healthy plant growth, the carbon and part of the oxygen are derived from the atmosphere by the aerial tissues of the plant; the remainder are mostly absorbed (by root cells) from the soil in the form of mineral salts in solution (in which soil organisms play an important part in rendering many of the natural soil minerals soluble).

Mineral nutrients are essential for plant growth and are divided into major and minor (trace) elements ;* these two terms do not refer to the relative importance of each but to the quantities in which they are required by plants.

Major elements. The major plant nutrients are :

(a) Nitrogen. The quantity available to plants is dependent upon the activities of soil organisms but is greater in those rich in organic matter. Excessive nitrogen depresses the uptake of the other two major elements, phosphorus and potassium. Nitrogen starvation results in yellowing of foliage and stunted growth. Humus helps to maintain adequate growth conditions and permits the development and maintenance of a large microbiological population which is responsible for providing the nitrogen so essential to fertility.

(b) Phosphorus. Essential for the growth and development of plants; its availability is also dependent upon the activities of soil organisms. Deficiency or absence of this element may prevent the uptake of other nutrients by plants.

(c) Potassium. Growing plants require relatively large quantities of potassium which assists in plant metabolic processes. Excess potash reduces the uptake of magnesium but renders iron more available.

*Also referred to as macro- and micronutrients.

Minor elements. In addition to the major plant nutrients, other elements are essential to the healthy development of plants :

(a) Calcium. More important as a soil conditioner than a nutrient, it occurs more particularly in soils derived from chalk or limestone. It is useful in rectifying soil acidity but is rapidly leached from light soils. Malformation of the growing parts of plants may result from calcium deficiency.

(b) Magnesium. More readily available when there is excess nitrogen in the soil, but excess potash reduces its uptake. It is easily leached, especially from lighter soils. A deficiency may cause early defoliation.

(c) Iron. As soil acidity increases, more iron is rendered available to plants. Calcareous soils are deficient in iron. The iron content is reflected in reds and rich brown colours of soil. It may be rendered inactive by an excess of manganese, resulting in yellowing of foliage (iron-chlorosis).

(d) Sulphur. An important constituent of the soil solution present as sulphate. It is a major ancillary element in the common inorganic fertilisers, e.g. ammonium sulphate. Stunted growth and yellowing result from sulphur deficiency.

(e) Manganese. The most abundant of the trace elements, available under acid conditions but in strongly acid soils may reach toxic concentration. Peats, rich organic soils and those with a high water-table are often deficient in manganese. The activity of manganese and iron is inter-related, any deficiency producing similar effects.

(f) Boron. The extractable boron in soils ranges from one to one hundred parts per million. Its availability depends, to a large extent, upon the pH value of the soil, being low in soils originating from sandstone but high in those derived from shales and alluvium. Nitrogen fixation by bacteria in legumes is dependent upon both boron and molybdenum.

(g) Molybdenum. Present in minute quantities in many soils. The amount required by plants is very small and its uptake is influenced by soil reaction, its availability decreasing markedly as acidity of the soil increases. Maximum uptake of this nutrient by plants appears to take place between pH7 and pH8.

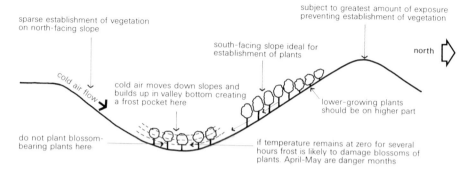

sparse establishment of vegetation
on north-facing slope

subject to greatest amount of exposure
preventing establishment of vegetation

south-facing slope ideal for
establishment of plants

north

cold air flow

cold air moves down slopes and
builds up in valley bottom creating
a frost pocket here

lower-growing plants
should be on higher part

do not plant blossom-
bearing plants here

if temperature remains at zero for several
hours frost is likely to damage blossoms of
plants. April-May are danger months

a. Effect of slope and exposure on plant establishment

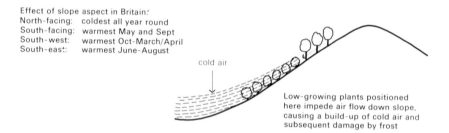

Effect of slope aspect in Britain:
North-facing: coldest all year round
South-facing: warmest May and Sept
South-west: warmest Oct-March/April
South-east: warmest June-August

cold air

Low-growing plants positioned
here impede air flow down slope,
causing a build-up of cold air and
subsequent damage by frost

Fig. 10   Slopes and exposure

b. Effect of wrong siting of plants

(h) Cobalt and selenium. Although not essential for plant growth, these play an important role in animal nutrition. Herbage grazed by sheep should have a cobalt content of not less than 0·08 parts per million of dry matter to prevent pine disease in the animals. Selenium deficiency may cause muscular dystrophy.

(i) Zinc and copper. Nutritional deficiencies of these elements occur mainly in peat soils, resulting in weak growth and rapid wilting of plants ; excess zinc or copper in the soil lowers the availability of iron.

3. *Biotic factors*
Of all the influences exerted on the soil by living creatures and plant life the major role is played by man, whose many and varied activities fall into three main groups :

(a) *Cultivation*. The process of ploughing, wherein the upper layer of the soil is turned over, ensures that the surface organic matter is buried and its products distributed within the soil. The addition of fertilisers in the right proportions assist in producing a greater crop yield from the

soil. Soil acidity may be reduced by incorporating lime.

(b) *Drainage*. Waterlogged soils support few plants and create drainage problems. Problems of drainage may be solved either by reduction of the water-table with the installation of a land drainage system or by the incorporation of porous material to improve soil texture.

(c) *Alteration of microclimate*. Soil is heated primarily by radiation from the sun, the amount falling on a particular area varying according to the physical aspects of the site and atmospheric conditions (Fig.10). The planting of shelterbelts has a marked effect on soil temperature which is reflected in the soil fertility (Fig.11).

Soil indicators

Surface vegetation may indicate type of soil and the plant species that are likely to do well :

Fertile soils   Nettle, rosebay willow-herb, foxglove,
                       bramble, bracken and bluebell

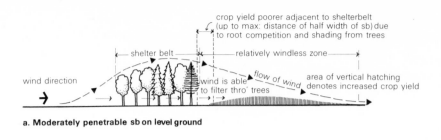

crop yield poorer adjacent to shelterbelt
(up to max: distance of half width of sb) due
to root competition and shading from trees

← shelter belt →   ← relatively windless zone →

wind direction

wind is able
to filter thro' trees

flow of wind

area of vertical hatching
denotes increased crop yield

a. Moderately penetrable sb on level ground

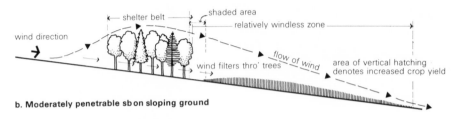

← shelter belt →   shaded area

← relatively windless zone →

wind direction

wind filters thro' trees

flow of wind

area of vertical hatching
denotes increased crop yield

b. Moderately penetrable sb on sloping ground

← shelter belt →

density of planting prevents
wind filtration

wind direction

low pressure in this area, due to lack of wind
penetration of sb, results in suction effect
causing intense turbulence on leeward side

flow of wind

c. Dense shelterbelt

Fig. 11   Influence of shelter belts
on microclimate

Poor soils	Ling, bell heather, cross-leaved heather, bilberry and matt grass
Heavy clays	Ferns and horsetails
Wet soils	Iris, kingcup, rushes, sedges and cotton grass
Chalk	Yew, wayfaring tree, juniper, spindle, dog's mercury, rock rose, sanicle, wild thyme, wild strawberry, old man's beard and wild clematis

The presence of any one of these plants must not be taken as conclusive evidence, since other factors are relevant.

TREATMENT OF DERELICT LAND

Types of dereliction and their effect upon the landscape

Derelict land may be defined as land which, because of the industrial activity, excavation, extraction, deposition of toxic or unusable material or other detrimental activity undertaken therein, is incapable of being put to beneficial use without remedial work first being implemented. Land which has been neglected or become useless because of the processes of nature, e.g. swamps, does not fall under the definition of derelict land. Nevertheless, some of the processes of reinstatement are applicable to such land.

Dereliction occurs in three distinct forms: spoilheaps and mounds, pits and excavations and abandoned industrial sites.

Spoilheaps and mounds

This type of dereliction results from any of the extraction or manufacturing industries which produce (or have produced in the past) large volumes of waste materials that cannot be disposed of other than by depositing them in spoilheaps. The main industries responsible are coal-mining, stone-quarrying, clay-working, iron and steel and chemical manufacturing, which produce vast quantities of unusable waste. The shape of the resultant spoilheaps depends largely on the equipment used for tipping and may be in the form of a high conical tip, occupying a comparatively small area of land, a high ridge hogsback-shaped tip, or a fairly low flat-topped spoilheap occupying a considerable area of land. Open-cast mining waste in the past was often in the shape of hill and dale formations.

Pits and excavations

In contrast to spoilheaps, the problem here is not one of

Plate 1
Gravel workings at
Dorchester-on-Thames
above in production
below after reclamation
(SAGA Award, 1970).
*Photo: J. W. Thomas,
ARPS, Oxford.*

disposal but of finding suitable material from a convenient source with which to fill the hole. The winning of minerals may result in deep pits, such as marlholes, or comparatively shallow excavations like those of many gravel pits. Surface depressions, referred to as subsidence, may also occur where underground mining has taken place. Those filled with water are known as 'flashes'. Often dereliction resulting from excavation is spread over a wide area and, although not always considered as unsightly as that caused by the tipping of waste, results in land lying idle that has a potential use value.

Excavations may be either dry or waterlogged; where carried out below the water-table, they are flooded. Quarrying may be at or below ground level or cut into a hillside.

Abandoned industrial sites
Dereliction of this nature stems largely from the results of entrepreneurial activity during the early days of the Industrial Revolution and in many cases is linked with exhausted mineral winning. Often these sites are quite small and may either be scattered over a wide area or form part of a pattern, such as that found in Coalbrookdale. In many respects these abandoned sites form one of the worst kinds of eyesore; although quite a number were already lying disused before the turn of this century some still remain, serving as a grim reminder of the ugliness that heralded the industrial dawn of this country's prosperity. Rusting mechanical equipment and plant, buildings fallen into ruin, tall chimneys, railway sidings, disused canals and a heap of industrial junk make up the squalid picture of industrial dereliction.

Potential uses of derelict land

The nature of the dereliction dictates the use to which the land can be put and each case must be given careful individual consideration before any remedial action can be taken. Inevitably the economics of a scheme dictate whether the benefits accruing from the removal of a spoil-heap justify carrying out such work ; it may be necessary to consider an alternative approach whereby the spoilheap, as such, remains but is given a 'face-lift'.

Commercial

Although research shows that some waste materials have a potential use, most of them have little, if any, commercial value. Unwanted wastes resulting from mining and other industries have the added disadvantage of being incapable, in their raw state, of supporting plant life, thereby stagnating large areas of land.

Colliery waste-tips that have thoroughly burnt through are quarried for use in road and footway construction and the fused red ash is crushed and screened to produce a suitable surfacing material for paths and athletic tracks. Unburnt shale that is generally free from stone is used for brickmaking. Much of the waste from the heavy chemical industries is sterile and cannot support any plant life.

Recreational and amenity

The uses to which derelict land, resulting from the carrying out of excavations, may be put depend upon whether these are dry or flooded. Shallow, extensive excavations may be graded out to form a landscape feature ; where they are deeper, the problem of filler material arises.

Disused stone quarries, particularly those near towns, present all sorts of exciting opportunities for projects such as sports stadia, ampitheatres, adventure playgrounds, etc., while rural quarries, especially those near the coast, may be successfully landscaped to provide caravan sites.* Flooded excavations afford excellent facilities for water recreation ; one of the most successful schemes is that at Dorchester, Oxfordshire, where an old gravel-pit was re-claimed to provide a sailing area complete with all the necessary sailing facilities and a shingle beach.

Spoilheaps that cannot economically be removed but are capable of supporting a certain amount of plant life may be regraded to a moderate extent and, with grass sown and some tree-planting, will ultimately provide an amenity area which blends into the existing landscape. High spoilheaps may be graded and equipped with artificial snow and a ski-lift to form a ski slope ; in fact, a whole area could be converted into a sports and recreational centre.

*Planning of caravan sites is controlled by the Caravan and Control of Development Act, 1960.

Implementation of a reclamation scheme

Land reclamation, like any other development of land, requires a considerable amount of planning and discussion before any physical work is undertaken.

Reconnaissance of the site should give a rough idea of the extent of the area involved and also determine the amount and sequence of survey work and investigation required. At this stage trial holes should be made and samples of material obtained at varying depths. Subsequent tests are then made on these materials to determine their structure, composition and potential commercial or industrial value, if any. CP 2001 : 1957, includes sections dealing with geology, the definitions of soils and rocks and methods of obtaining and testing samples.

The preliminary site investigation and the broader aspects of design policy should reveal many of the problems that are likely to be encountered. After the initial assessment it should be possible to draw up an outline scheme (or alternative schemes) for reclamation proposals and to judge them according to their merits in the light of the problems previously revealed. One of the major questions to be considered is whether the proposed scheme is capable of being implemented as one operation or whether it is necessary to carry out a phased reclamation programme. Where a number of problems remain unsolved (or only partially solved) it may be advisable to carry out a pilot scheme before embarking upon a major project.

Under the Local Employment Act, 1970, local authorities are able to obtain government grants towards the cost of the acquisition and reclamation of derelict land where such an undertaking will assist the development of local industry. They are empowered also to clear derelict land and to plant trees or carry out remedial works under the National Parks and Access to the Countryside Act, 1949, and the Local Authorities (Land) Act, 1963.

The outline plan provides a basis on which policy decisions are taken, but before the proposals can be put into effect it is necessary (as in all other landscaping schemes) to prepare a series of detailed drawings and documents showing exactly what work is to be undertaken. This involves a physical survey recording levels, boundaries or demarcation lines and the location of any public utility services. Old mine shafts must be plotted (prior to 1872 many of these were not recorded) which may necessitate sinking a regular pattern of boreholes. In flooded excavations soundings should be taken to ascertain depth of water and type of underlying strata.

Implementation of the scheme depends upon the nature of the dereliction and the work involved. Many of the initial operations require the use of plant and equipment to carry out adjustments to the site contours. The quantity and nature of the material to be moved is likely to dictate the types of machine that should be used, which may include excavators, dozers, scrapers, face-shovels and draglines. Where hard ground needs to be broken up prior to the use of earthmoving equipment, ripping tines are employed; on filled ground, consolidation is carried out with the help of sheepsfoot rollers.

Sources of material for filling dry excavations often present a problem. If the site is within reasonable distance of a town, controlled tipping of town refuse may be undertaken. This involves depositing refuse in layers of not more than 900 mm, each layer being covered with a minimum of 230 mm of soil and consolidated before the next layer is tipped. The final layer of soil should be not less than 300 mm thick and may include a quantity of compost.

Flooded excavations range from deep pits with almost vertical sides to comparatively shallow depressions or lagoons within or around which are dotted numerous islands or hummocks of overburden. Underground water supplies must be protected and, as a safeguard, no filling material likely to contain toxic substances or organic matter must be used. Pulverised ash, clinker or waste from industrial processes may prove suitable filling material and, wherever water is present, should be used for this purpose to a height of at least 600 mm above water level. Above this height controlled tipping, as described above, may be carried out, finishing with a final layer of topsoil.

Some excavations, e.g. those to be used ultimately for water recreation, may be filled only up to a certain level and the sides of the excavated area then graded to form a shallow beach. Generally, it is desirable that the depth of water should not exceed 2·43 m. If subsidence is present (i.e. where there are flashes) filling may result in flooding elsewhere. Where drainage requirements may involve linking up with a natural watercourse, the appropriate River Authorities should be consulted.

Establishment of a growing medium

Once regrading of the derelict land has been completed, some form of vegetation needs to be established so that the site may eventually marry in with the surrounding area. Several factors affect the establishment of vegetation on derelict land: aspect, height and slope of a spoilheap determine the intensity of exposure to the elements. This is reflected in the moisture content of the surface, dictating the type of vegetation that is able to establish itself there. The least amount of exposure is found in the lower, sheltered hollows where pioneer vegetation more readily establishes itself, but the conical tip of a spoilheap (subject to the greatest amount of exposure) remains devoid of any type of vegetation. This is also true of the northerly faces of a spoilheap. Where there are steep slopes, gulley erosion results in surface movement; on all straight or convex slopes, slipping of surface material is bound to occur until a state of equilibrium is reached—a much slower process where there are heavy clays, shales or materials having slight cementation properties. Slopes need to be reasonably stabilised before preparations for the establishment of pioneer vegetation are implemented (Table 11, page 33).

Plants require a certain amount of food if they are to thrive and the source of their food is within the soil in which they grow. To support plant life, therefore, a spoilheap must not only provide a stable surface wherein the roots of plants can take hold, but also contain a sufficient quantity of nutrients to maintain the vegetation. Many spoilheaps are located in areas of high atmospheric pollution—a major obstacle to the establishment of plant life.

Where the soil is sterile or of an unpromising nature it is necessary to promote a certain degree of fertility. In extreme cases of high toxicity it may be necessary to dig out the soil and replace it with innocuous material. Soils of high acidity may be neutralised by liberal applications of lime, depending upon the pH value of the in-situ material.

Methods of promoting soil fertility

Because of the scarcity of good quality topsoil and the cost of transporting it to the site it is often worth considering the possibility of restoring fertility to the soil in-situ. The prevailing conditions determine the treatment required; from tests carried out during the survey of the site some idea should be obtained of its level of fertility and what further treatment is necessary in order to establish vegetation. The object of improving the in-situ material is to build up a layer of at least 50–80 mm of topsoil, possessing all the attributes necessary to promote root development, by applying a heavy dressing of organic material and ploughing or disc-harrowing it into the surface. The organic matter provides plants with valuable nutrients gradually over a long period, helps to improve the water-holding capacity of soils and promotes beneficial bacterial activity. Inorganic fertilisers supply certain plant foods in concentrated form (see below, 'Surface grading and cultivating').

Where steep slopes are to remain, the use of soil-conditioning techniques should be considered. Although more expensive than traditional methods of increasing fertility, the extra cost may be justified in places where it would not otherwise be possible to establish vegetation. The technique involves using a machine capable of drilling the soil conditioner (poly-electrolyte resin), mixed with seeds and fertilisers, into the slopes—the first stage in establishing pioneer vegetation.

Treatment of reclaimed flooded excavations
The water in abandoned mineral workings is usually sterile, tending to be acid, which makes it an unsuitable medium for the promotion of aquatic life. The excessive depth of some excavations prevents penetration of sunlight (a promoter of plant growth) but in the shallower parts sunlight is able to penetrate once the suspended matter has settled at the bottom.

Before plant life can be established in the deeper parts, some remedial treatment is necessary. This consists of dosing the water with lime (calcium carbonate), evenly distributed throughout, according to the acidity of the water. The lower the pH value the greater the quantity of lime required, as may be seen from Table 3. A pH value of 7 or 8 is required for the promotion of fish life.

Table 3
Lime dosage for rectifying acid waters

pH value	Lime requirement (kg/m^2)
6·5	0·087
6·0	0·100
5·5	0·187
5·0	0·300

The initial lime application is usually sufficient to set in motion the organic cycle which ultimately creates the right conditions wherein hardy aquatics are able to establish themselves. Fertilisers may be applied later, starting first of all at the shallower edges and then gradually working inwards towards the centre. Quicker results are achieved by implementing a planting scheme in the early stages with the object of creating competition for some of the weeds which tend to infest the water. In addition, planting at the water's edge adds to the maturity of the scene and helps to soften the outline.

Pioneer vegetation on reclaimed land

Plant selection must be made according to the nature of the soil or in-situ material and site conditions. In many cases the soil acidity is high and before pioneer vegetation can be established it is necessary to provide liberal applications of lime in order to reduce or neutralise the acidity.

Grasses and other hardy plants
Often grass is selected as pioneer vegetation because it is quick to establish itself and produces a fresh green carpet fairly rapidly. Seed may be sown, using the hydraulic seeding technique whereby the seed is mixed with fertilisers and water and pressure-sprayed onto the surface, followed by the application of a mulching layer consisting of chopped straw and bitumen emulsion which is sprayed onto the seeded surface to protect the seed during its initial growth period. Often these two applications are

Table 4
Grasses suitable for establishing vegetation on difficult sites

Botanical name	Common name	Remarks
Agropyron repens	Couch grass or creeping twitch	Tenacious weed which spreads by creeping rhizomes. Useful for holding soil on loose slopes.
Avena fatua and A. ludoviciana	Wild oat	Useful for quick development of cover on poor soils.
Cynosurus cristatus	Crested dogstail	A deep rooting, drought-resistant grass able to withstand cold. Useful for poor soils.
Holcus lanatus	Yorkshire fog	Coarse, tufted grass which grows on a wide range of soils.
Holcus mollis	Creeping soft grass	Creeps by surface runners ; is particularly useful on sandy, light soils, especially in shady situations.
Phleum bertolinii	Lesser catstail	A smaller species than *P. pratense*; it tillers more freely and can withstand greater defoliation.
Phleum pratense	Timothy or catstail	Tufted, shallow-rooted grass with tall habit of growth if allowed to develop. Cold-resistant and very hardy. Succeeds best on heavy, clay type soils.
Poa annua	Annual meadowgrass	Resistant to waterlogging but not drought-resistant ; useful for rapid cover and is best sown as a mixture with *P. trivialis*.
Poa trivialis	Rough meadowgrass	Tufted grass which grows by means of slightly creeping underground stems. Does best on moist, heavy soils and is useful for shady situations.

carried out simultaneously. The technique is particularly useful on steep slopes where the soil is poor.

The grasses listed in Table 4 are the coarse-leaved varieties with tough constitutions, able to withstand adverse growing conditions. Table 5 includes both herbaceous and shrubby plants, many of them furnished with drought-resistant foliage or rapidly extending rootstocks.

Table 5
Herbaceous and shrubby plants suitable for establishing vegetation on difficult sites

Botanical name	Common name	Remarks
Achillea millefolium	Yarrow or milfoil	A drought-resistant weed spreading by means of underground stems. Useful for poor sandy soils and for retaining soil on slopes.
Convolvulus arvensis	Field or lesser bindweed	Vigorous weed with extensive creeping rootstock.
Epilobium angustifolium	Rosebay willow-herb	Readily establishes itself on waste land, particularly on light soils and under moist conditions.
Geranium molle	Soft cranesbill	Annual with a tough, matted rootstock. Does best on light, dry soils.
Lupinus polyphyllus	Lupin	Very useful for building up fertility of poor sandy soils by increasing the nitrogen content.
Ononis spinosa	Prickly restharrow or cammock	Spiny, low-growing shrub. Tough spreading rootstock : useful for binding loose soil.
Plantago lanceolata	Ribwort plantain	A weed that occurs on most non-acid soils. Drought-resistant ; provides useful bottom growth.
Ranunculus ficaria	Lesser celandine	A weed capable of rapid reproduction by means of a large number of tubers. Thrives in moist shady situations.
Sagina procumbens	Common pearlwort	Small tufted weed forming dense patches by means of aggressive stolons.
Sarothamnus scoparius	Broom	A leguminous flowering shrub which thrives on poor soils ; drought-resistant. Quicker developer than gorse.
Sinapis arvensis	Charlock	An annual belonging to the cabbage family. Prefers light dry soils.
Ulex europaeus	Furze or gorse	A slow-developing shrub which provides good cover when established. Thrives in poor, dry, slightly acid soils.

Table 6
Deciduous trees suitable for planting on derelict land

Botanical name	Common name	Remarks
Acer pseudoplatanus	Sycamore	Strong-rooted tree of rapid growth ; withstands exposure. Readily reproduced. May occasionally suffer from die-back.
Alnus glutinosa	Alder	Excellent nurse species, quickly provides shade and shelter. Dislikes highly acid and peaty soils. Under poor conditions may be in the form of a large bush. Prefers a damp situation.
Alnus incana	Grey alder	Spreads by root suckers. Tolerates much drier sites than A. glutinosa.
Betula pendula	Silver birch	Very hardy ; thrives at high altitudes, penetrating furthest north. Tolerates smoke but can be difficult to establish on unburnt shale. Shallow-rooted, prefers a well-drained, slightly acid soil.
Corylus avellana	Hazel	Quick-growing, useful as a nurse species. Grows almost anywhere (except in good soil) but is generally found growing in the form of a shrub.
Crataegus monogyna	Hawthorn	Slow-growing but very hardy, tolerating exposed situations.
Populus alba	White poplar	Excellent tree for checking erosion, able to grow in loose soil.
Populus trichocarpa	Black cottonwood	Most valuable poplar for planting on poorish sites.
Prunus avium	Gean	Fast-growing, thrives in most soils but prefers well-drained alkaline soils.
Robina pseudoacacia	False acacia	Hardy, fast-growing tree, smoke-tolerant but shallow-rooted and not suitable for exposed positions.
Salix caprea	Sallow	⎫ ⎧Graceful, rapid-growing
S. cinerea	Grey sallow	⎬ trees useful for
S. viminalis	Osier	⎭ ⎩damp situations.
Sambucus nigra	Elder	Early rapid growth providing shelter or screening. Prefers moist conditions.
Sorbus aucuparia	Mountain ash	Useful nurse species. Hardy, tolerates high altitudes.

Table 7
Conifers suitable for planting on derelict land

Botanical name	Common name	Remarks
Larix decidua	European or common larch	Withstands prolonged cold conditions. Good pioneer on raw subsoil material provided it is not too heavy and compacted.
Larix eurolepis	Dunkeld larch	Hybrid between *L. decidua* and *L. kaempferi*. Excels both, being more hardy and tolerant of difficult soil conditions. Faster growing.
Larix kaempferi	Japanese larch	Tolerates a wider range of conditions than *L. decidua*, including less soil fertility and greater exposure. Vigorous grower in early stages of life. Thrives on hillsides in high rainfall areas.
Picea omorika	Serbian spruce	Withstands atmospheric pollution better than most conifers.
Picea sitchensis	Sitka spruce	Fast-growing. Withstands exposure at high altitudes. Surface root system. Thrives in wet cold soils but dislikes warm dry conditions.
Pinus contorta	Beach pine	Small tree that grows well in chalk-free light stony soils. Provides shelter in exposed situations.
Pinus contorta latifolia	Lodgepole pine	Excellent pioneer tree, fast-growing. Withstands severe exposure, high rainfall and infertile peaty soils.
Pinus mugo	Mountain pine	Slow-growing but very hardy. Thrives on poorer soils. Transplants well and is suitable for planting on slopes.
Pinus nigra	Austrian pine	Probably the most resistant conifer to atmospheric pollution. Thrives in almost pure sand and is useful for fixing sand dunes.
Pinus sylvestris	Scots pine	Wind-firm tree with deep tap root. Thrives in poor stony soils but unsuitable for chalk.
Tsuga heterophylla	Western hemlock	Quick-growing, easily established tree. Tolerates poor soil conditions but dislikes damp, acid soils or shallow dry chalk. Often planted with *Picea sitchensis*. Shade-tolerant.

Table 8
Aquatic and marginal plants suitable for pioneer planting

Botanical name	Common name	Remarks
Callitriche spp.	Starworts	Useful for planting in water up to 1 m deep.
Caltha palustris	Marsh marigold	Useful for giving a touch of colour to pond edges. Golden flowers and large glossy leaves.
Carex paniculata	Great panicled sedge	Hardy marginal plant forming large tussocks. Mass of strong roots useful for consolidating loose soil.
Catabrosa aquatica	Water whorl grass	Perennial grass ; useful for growing in shallow water and on wet banks. Water fowl like the young leaves.
Hippuris vulgaris	Mare's-tail	Good aerator that grows in water up to 2·45 m deep.
Iris pseudacorus	Yellow flag	Attractive marginal plant with a 600 mm stem and bright yellow flowers. Horizontal creeping root stock.
Lythrum salicaria	Purple loosestrife	Marginal plant with creeping root stock from which rise stems bearing spikes of purple flowers.
Mentha aquatica	Water or fish mint	Marginal plant with creeping root stock.
Nuphar luteum	Yellow water-lily	Creeping root stock ; heart-shaped floating leaves and yellow flowers.
Potamogeton crispus	Curled pondweed	Grows in water up to 900 mm deep.
Ranunculus aquatilis	Water crowfoot	Excellent for ponds and shallow waters.
Sagittaria spp.	Arrowhead	Good oxygenators ; grow in shallow and medium depths and provide food and shelter for fish.
Scirpus spp.	Club rush	Useful marginal plants.

Trees

A number of trees possess pioneer qualities which enable them to be planted on derelict land, provided the soil has not been poisoned by industrial wastes and the concentration of atmospheric pollution is not too severe.

Tree-planting is a long-term solution to the problem of establishing vegetation and it is most important to decide whether the trees are to be grown for their amenity value or their commercial potential, since this dictates both selection and planting distances.

On exposed sites subject to severe conditions the stock selected should be hardy and fast-growing and, where necessary, a fairly high proportion of nurse species included to protect the less robust. The deciduous trees listed in Table 6 are those capable of surviving in fairly severe conditions. On more favourable sites where amenity planting is proposed the following trees may be introduced:

Ash (*Fraxinus excelsior*)
Beech (*Fagus sylvatica*)
Hornbeam (*Carpinus betulus*)
Laburnum (*Laburnum anagyroides*)
Lime (*Tilia europaea* and *T. platyphyllos*)
Oak (*Quercus robur* and *Q. rubra*)

A selection of hardy conifers is shown in Table 7; in reclamation site planting, the spruces and firs are the less-used conifers.

Aquatic life for reclaimed waters

Aquatic and marginal plants

Table 8 contains a list of aquatics and marginal plants suitable for use as pioneer planting. Some plants that are able to establish themselves fairly quickly may be useful in the larger expanses of water but care must be taken to see that they do not create maintenance problems. In a small pool they are liable soon to choke the water and require clearing at fairly frequent intervals. Such plants include fairy moss (*Azolla caroliniana*), Canadian pondweed (*Elodea canadensis*) and hornwort (*Ceratophyllum demersum*). A floating plant that remains on the surface for most of the year is also likely to be troublesome if not kept in check.

Animal and insect life

As plant life becomes established the water should be stocked with those creatures upon which fish normally feed so that a good supply of food is built up before fish are introduced. Water fleas, snails of various sorts, willow flies, water beetles, black gnats, crayfish and minnows are all food for fish.

The type of fish selected depends upon the extent of the water into which they are to be introduced. It is generally not advisable to develop coarse fisheries in water whose surface area is less than 12 hectares. The conditions into which they are introduced should be similar to those of the source from which they are obtained. Fish selected for waters to be used by angling clubs should include bream, roach and tench. In deeper water perch may also be included. Rudd and gudgeon are extremely useful because they seem to thrive almost anywhere.

EARTHMOVING AND EXCAVATING OPERATIONS

Site investigation and preparatory work

Before beginning earthworks it is necessary to determine certain factors which affect soil-moving operations on site. The purpose of such investigations is to ascertain:

existing ground levels
depth and nature of the topsoil
nature of the subsoil
location of watercourses, ground water and the
    water-table level
presence of services, underground workings,
    overhead wires, pylons or other artefacts
type and location of any trees and hedges
location of buildings, fences, etc.

In addition it may be necessary to locate access points on the boundary of the site to determine which one is the most suitable for bringing in machinery or carting away spoil from the site. Reference should be made to CP 2001:1957, which deals with the civil engineering aspects of site investigation, and BS 4428:1969. The nature of the investigations is determined by the extent of the site and the ground-modelling proposed; larger sites may need an aerial survey. In all cases the survey should extend beyond the site perimeter and, where relevant, geological maps of the area should be consulted.

Ground levels should be recorded and plotted on a grid covering the whole site, the grid spacings ranging from 6 to 30 m, depending upon site conditions. From this, contour lines are interpolated at 0·5–1 m intervals so that the extent of cut and fill operations may be calculated.

Investigation of the nature of the ground and strata

involves taking test bores or digging pits in order to examine the soil profile which shows the composition and depth of the various layers (Fig.8) ; obstacles such as rock, silt or running sand are also revealed. The presence of ground water or a high water-table must be recorded since drainage may be required. Buildings, trees, hedges, pylons and any other artefacts should be accurately located if any of them are to be retained. The site survey should also record the position of all watercourses and their depths at both high and low water level. Where the nature of the proposed works warrants mechanical analysis of the soil, this should be carried out in accordance with the recommendations set out in BS 1377:1967.

Physical properties of soil

Soils exhibit certain peculiarities in their physical properties and are essentially mixtures of varying-sized mineral particles closely associated with clay and colloidal organic matter.

Texture (Fig.12)

In soils comprising smaller particles there is a greater frictional resistance to the removal of excess water caused by under-drainage. Soils having a greater proportion of

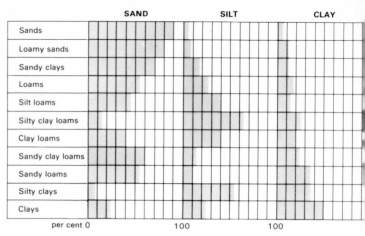

Fig. 12 Textural classification of soil

larger-sized particles are more readily drained. Classification of soils according to particle size is, basically, as follows :

2 mm and over	Gravel
2–0·006 mm	Sand
0·006–0·002 mm	Silt
Under 0·002 mm	Clay

Texture of a soil may be determined by handling it (Table 9).

Table 9
Method of determining soil type in the field by handling

Impression given by moist (not wet) soil moulded in the hand and felt between the fingers	Properties	Analysis
Gritty : sand predominates	Does not dirty fingers	SAND : coarse to very fine, depending on particle size
	Dirties fingers. Cannot be moulded into cohesive ball	SAND : loamy coarse (large grains) to loamy very fine (grains only just visible to naked eye)
	Dirties fingers. Can be moulded into cohesive ball	LOAM : coarse sandy (large grains) to very fine sand (grains only just visible to naked eye)
Sticky : clay predominates (can be polished by pressing between finger and thumb)	Resistance to moulding overcome without difficulty	{ SANDY CLAY LOAM if gritty / SILTY CLAY LOAM if silky
	Resistance to moulding overcome with difficulty	CLAY LOAM
	Resistance to moulding overcome with extreme difficulty	{ SANDY CLAY if gritty / SILTY CLAY if silky / CLAY if neither gritty nor silky
Silky : silt predominates (cannot be polished between finger and thumb)	Silky feeling only just recognisable } Little resistance to deformation }	SILT LOAM
	Silky feeling obvious } Considerable resistance to deformation }	SILT
None of the above (grittiness, stickiness and silkiness neutralise one another)		LOAM

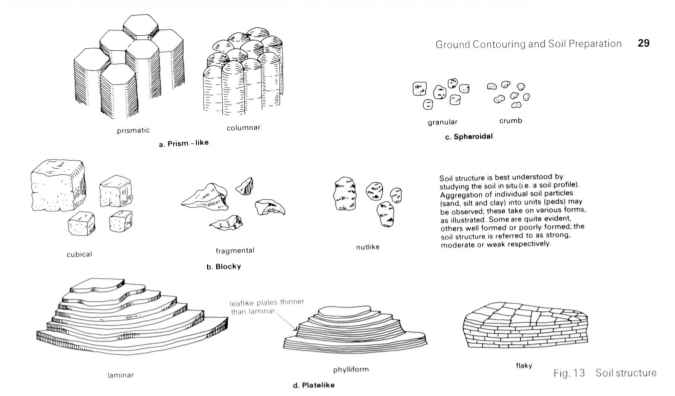

prismatic   columnar

a. Prism - like

granular   crumb

c. Spheroidal

cubical   fragmental   nutlike

b. Blocky

Soil structure is best understood by studying the soil in situ (i.e. a soil profile). Aggregation of individual soil particles (sand, silt and clay) into units (peds) may be observed; these take on various forms, as illustrated. Some are quite evident, others well formed or poorly formed; the soil structure is referred to as strong, moderate or weak respectively.

laminar   leaflike plates thinner than laminar   phylliform   flaky

Fig. 13   Soil structure

d. Platelike

Structure

Soil must be examined in its undisturbed state in order to ascertain its structure, determined according to its classification into structural groups or units (peds) (Fig.8a). There are four main types (Fig.13) :

Prism-like   Prismatic or columnar
Blocky   Cubical, fragmental or nut-like
Spheroidal   Granular or crumb
Plate-like   Laminar or flaky

Character of colloidal content

Most soils contain a proportion of finely divided jelly-like material (colloids). It is abundant in clays, often limiting or destroying their permeability, causing a serious drainage handicap. One of the most characteristic properties of colloids is their ability to absorb dissolved substances from solution, due to reactions essentially chemical and ionic in character. In any appreciable volume of soil they aggregate an enormous surface area, having great absorptive capacity, and swell enormously when wet but shrink and crack when dry.

Moisture content and density

The density of soil (weight per unit volume) is dependent upon the specific gravity of soil particles, the ratio of voids to solids and whether or not the voids are completely filled with water. Moisture content and density of the soil are related and interdependent and may be adjusted to give maximum soil strength. Relative stability, or the load-carrying capacity of a soil, increases as the voids ratio decreases. The density to which a soil is capable of being compacted is determined by using various moisture contents and forces of compaction. High maximum density ranges from 2000–2320 kg/m^3; low, from 1360–1600 kg/m^3. Low optimum moisture coincides with high maximum density and is about 8 per cent, while high optimum moisture coincides with low maximum density and is in the region of 20 per cent.

Nature of the ground

Some soils are more difficult to excavate or handle than others. Their resistance depends upon hardness, weight, cohesion, adhesion and friction. Although there is no clear-cut distinction between soil and rock the excavation techniques adopted depend upon the nature of the material, which may be classified into three principal groups :

Rock   Resists penetration and
                  requires drilling or blasting to
                  facilitate its removal

Compact and hard   May be dug by heavy machinery
or loosened by rippers prior
to digging

Soft or fine loose   Readily dug

Materials containing hard lumps may be penetrated but the force involved results in increased friction (absorption of energy expended). Moisture content and soil particle size are other factors that affect earthmoving operations. In wet, sticky soils excavation may be hampered by the material adhering to the digging implement. Firm materials without bedding or cleavage planes (i.e. planes of weakness) are often difficult to dig because of their strong and uniform cohesion. The weight of a soil limits the amount which may be got out and transported at each dig cycle; soil is heavier when wet (Table 10).

Table 10
Weights of materials

Material	Weight (kg/m^3)
Topsoil	1440
Earth : vegetable	1120
Earth : moist compact	1600
Clay : stiff	1920
Loam	1280
Peat : dry	800
Peat : wet	960
Sand : dry, fine	1280
Sand : dry, coarse	1600
Sand : wet, fine	1520
Sand : wet, coarse	1920
Sand and gravel : mixed	1760
Gravel	1920
Shingle : 19 mm > 6 mm	1620
Chalk : solid	2160
Chalk : in lumps	1200
Sandstone	2320
Limestone : lias	2480
Quartz	2640
Granite	2720
Slate	2800
Shale	2600
Flint rubble	2370
Concrete (1 : 6)	2080
Brick : broken	1790
Masonry rubble	2240
York stone paving	2500

Soils are an aggregation of particles separated by numerous voids filled with either air or water and forming comparatively soft, loose layers in the ground strata. The layers of soil which lie between the topsoil and rock are loosely referred to as subsoil and vary in physical and chemical character. They may be broadly classified into gravel, sand, silt or clay according to the size of the solid particles (see above). Rocks consist of strongly cemented substances which occur as laminated or massively bedded strata with varying degrees of hardness. Technically the term 'rock' is applied to any bulk material which forms part of the earth's crust, but in excavation work it is used to describe those materials which are hard and cannot be as readily dug as soils.

Sands and gravels
These are the principal non-cohesive soils whose structural properties depend upon the density of packing. Deposits often contain silt, clay or organic matter and are very permeable. In some cases the individual particles may consist of relatively soft material, e.g. chalk, and be of varying sizes.

Care is generally necessary in their excavation to prevent internal erosion of the ground which could result in damage to any nearby structures. These soils are held together by weight and friction between the individual particles; when subjected to external forces, such as the action of excavating machinery, they are liable to fairly rapid movement.

Silts
The very fine grains, too small to be classified as sand, washed down by rivers accumulate to form silt. Closely compacted grains are hard, in the form of siltstone in thin layers which may be readily split. Silts containing organic material are very soft and retain water; they are subject to heave in excavations. The properties of silts lie intermediate between those of sands and clays.

Clays
Pure clays are seldom encountered and most natural clay deposits contain up to 70 per cent sand or silt. All of them are cohesive and relatively impermeable, the extent of these properties depending upon their solid : void ratio. Some are soft and easily moulded in the fingers; others, such as the stiff-to-hard boulder clays, require a pick to assist their removal. All clays soften and swell when in contact with water, but in dry weather shrinkage occurs causing surface cracks and fissures to develop. Soil movement is particularly noticeable in the stiff, fissured heavy clays. Shrinkage of clay soils may increase where trees are growing nearby; if these are cut down, swelling of the soil may result from the excess moisture. Clays are best dug when dry, and should immediately be removed from the

excavation area. Well-wetted clays churned up by the action of excavating machinery make for very messy working and often hinder other work on the site.

Clay is also found in combination with other rocks:

(a) *Marls*. These limey clays, containing varying proportions of calcium carbonate, are classified as soft rocks. Patches of marl are found in chalk formations. Keuper marl, which occurs in the north-western part of the Midlands, is strong in its unweathered state and often highly fissured but, like other marls, is readily softened when in contact with water. Marl is much used as a top-dressing on light, gravelly or sandy soils or peat and for sports pitches as it helps to bind the soil surface together and prevent its disintegration under heavy wear.

(b) *Loams*. Mixtures of clay, sand and humus are termed 'loams' and are excellent growing media. Loams are described by reference to their proportions of sand and clay: e.g. a heavy loam contains a high proportion of clay; a light loam is one having a considerable amount of sand in it.

(c) *Mudstones and shales*. These are the toughest types of clay. Fine grains of clay welded into solid unlayered rock are called mudstone. Thin layers of this material are termed 'shale'. Uncemented types are liable to deteriorate when in contact with water. Soft mudstones and soft shales are classified as materials intermediate between hard, cohesive soils and rock. Layers of clay or shale often separate thinly bedded limestones and sandstones.

(d) *Sandstone*. A bedded sedimentary rock, made up of sand grains welded together in parallel layers; the cementitious material may consist of clay, ironstone, limestone or silica, the latter producing a very hard rock (quartzite). The individual sand grains differ; some are fairly smooth, others angular. The latter are termed 'grit', e.g. Millstone Grit, whose texture is similar to that of Mountain Limestone (associated with coal measures). In some places the sandstones are divided into large rectangular blocks, created by faults running perpendicular to the horizontal layers. This type of stone (freestone) provides valuable building material.

(e) *Limestones*. Although resembling chalk in composition, limestones are harder and vary greatly in colour and degree of hardness. Some are soft enough to be sawn, others are so hard that they need to be hewn. Limestones also vary in structure, consisting of parallel beds some of which may be traversed by vertical faults forming free-stones. In both limestone and chalk strata there may occur vertical swallow-holes, pot-holes and horizontal caverns. Tufa is a calcareous crust which is often found surrounding springs in the limestone.

(f) *Chalk*. One of the softer and more readily excavated rocks, chalk is a form of calcite, a mineral consisting of calcium carbonate. It may be cut with a knife, but when broken shatters into shapeless lumps and powders quite easily. Deposits form a mass of parallel layers but, like soft limestones, chalk deteriorates when exposed to water or frost. It is particularly susceptible to solution by ground water containing carbon dioxide.

(g) *Conglomerates*. Mechanically-formed sedimentary rocks comprising an accumulation of debris (resulting from the destruction of pre-existing rocks and their transportation by wind, water or ice) vary in their degree of hardness. Large grains of sand grade into pebbles and the pebbles are welded by natural cement, which may be of sand, clay, limestone or ironstone, into rock (termed 'puddingstone' or conglomerate) which is often so dense that it needs to be treated in a similar manner to homogeneous rock. In some cases the pebbles are loosely packed like a shingle bed and are readily excavated.

Where angular rock fragments are cemented together the rock is referred to as a 'breccia'. The sizes of aggregate in both types vary greatly and may consist of any type of rock in either parallel layers or haphazard deposits.

(h) *Peat and organic soils*. Soils which consist of a high proportion of vegetable matter mixed with varying amounts of sand, silt or clay occur in deposits up to several metres thick and are also found as layers in alluvial material. Peat has a tendency to retain water and swell, but shrinks considerably when it dries out.

(i) *Topsoil*. The top layer of soil is very valuable since it contains organic material which forms the growing medium for vegetation, and nutrients necessary for plant growth. It is readily distinguishable from the lighter-coloured subsoil in the layers beneath. Before excavation, topsoil must be stripped and stockpiled on site ready for re-use later. The importing of topsoil from a source outside the site is usually a costly operation and its availability and quality cannot always be guaranteed. Care must be taken to ensure that no subsoil is mixed with the topsoil thereby ruining the latter's quality. Generally, spoilheaps should not exceed 1·82 m in height, otherwise the quality of the topsoil at the bottom is likely to deteriorate over a period and may take on the properties of subsoil. The surface of the spoilheap should be sprayed with a weedkiller during the growing season to prevent any weeds from seeding.

Earthmoving machinery

Excavation plant runs on either caterpillar tracks or rubber tyres. Shovels are the basic tools for digging and dumping and many have interchangeable bucket equipment. They are more economical in operation than dozers.

Faceshovel
Used for excavating clay, chalk and loosened rock, the faceshovel operates at its own level. It has an open-type bucket or dipper, which is filled by driving it into the material being excavated. Operating capacity ranges between 0·4 m³ and 3·8 m³ with a working radius of 6·4–11·6 m and a lift of 5–8 m.

Backshovel or dragshovel
Similar to the faceshovel except that the working stroke is towards the machine; it is capable of excavating at a level below that of the machine's tracks. The back-acting shovel is more precise in operation but of lesser output. It is ideal for use in confined spaces.

Trencher or ditcher
An alternative to the backshovel, this machine is capable of excavating narrow, vertical-sided trenches, ranging from 0·15 to 1·52 m wide and 0·75–4·20 m deep.

Skimmer
Although similar to the faceshovel, the skimmer has more restricted movement and a lower output but is able to produce an accurate finished level. It is suitable for shallow digging.

Dragline
The excavating bucket is filled by dragging it towards the machine. It has a capacity of 0·4–3·8 m³ operating at a radius of 14·6–26 m and a lift of 11–17 m high. The dragline is able to excavate at a level below that of the machine tracks and is particularly adaptable for excavating in soft materials and swampy sites, but its earth-modelling uses are limited.

Bulldozer
The front of this machine is fitted with a rectangular steel blade, usually 1·37 m wide by 0·61 m high, which may be raised or lowered. It is used to push earth or broken rock, but its capacity for operating over large distances is limited.

Angledozer
A refinement of the bulldozer, operating on the same principle and having a blade 2·74–3·90 m wide by 0·71–1·07 m high. Its function is to push the earth aside, to the left or right, rather than ahead.

Sideboom dozer
The cantilevered blade that operates from the side of this machine is adjustable in the vertical plane and is used principally for trimming slopes to an even batter.

Grader
Final grading operations are carried out by a steel blade attachment of curved section 3–4·3 m wide, which may be rotated in horizontal or vertical positions. It is suitable for excavating shallow cuts but cannot operate on very wet sites.

Rippers and scarifiers
Hard compacted ground may be broken up by these machines which consist of steel teeth or tines (three, four or five in number), mounted on a frame. Their cutting depth ranges between 400 mm and 600 mm.

Excavation and fill

Changes in volume
When soil or rock is dug out of virgin ground the excavation process disturbs the strata. The soil is broken up into smaller units or agglomerations of particles which, separated by voids, result in an increase in bulk when the material is used as fill (or carted away from the site). These voids disappear when the soil is subjected to compaction, causing it to shrink in bulk. The difference between the quantity as dug in the solid and that deposited as fill (or carted away) may vary–in the case of rock, by up to 100 per cent. Economically, cut and fill should balance, allowing approximately 25 per cent more cut than fill to cater for the effects of compaction.

Changes occur in the volume of clay during the wet and dry seasons. Shrinkage may be increased by the presence of trees and other vegetation, depending upon their sizes and species; this may affect the soil to a depth of 5 m.

Fine-grained soils (silts, fine sands, chalk and some clays) expand when frozen, particularly where ground water level is near to the surface, causing frost heave. The effects of frost are not generally of significance below 460 mm of the surface but in periods of severe frost they may extend down to 900 mm.

Dewatering
Wherever possible, excavation operations should be avoided below the water-table level. It is important that all excavations are kept free from water and, where necessary, temporary provision must be made to channel any ground water away by means of ditches, drains or watercourses. If this is not feasible it may have to be pumped, but precautions must be taken to avoid continuous pumping in case this lowers the water-table to such an extent that foundations on adjoining sites are adversely affected. Where existing watercourses have to be diverted the original channels should be cleared of all soft deposits and filled in with suitable material.

Excavating rock
Rock which is too hard for earthmoving machinery to dig and shovel requires blasting. This involves the use of explosives to loosen the bulk rock from its natural position, reducing any oversize rocks to manageable pieces, by either blasting or splitting with hammers, so that they are small enough to fit into the excavating shovel bucket. Adequate precautions must be taken to avoid any damage or injury when blasting, heavy blasting mats being used, where necessary, to prevent dispersal of material. The removal of numerous individual boulders, using chains and lifting tackle, is an expensive operation which is only justified in quarrying building material. Mineral rights within the site strata normally belong to the owner and the contractor must seek permission before exploiting any minerals. In cuttings where the strata reveal alternating layers of hard and soft materials it may be necessary to excavate the softer layers and replace them with concrete in order to prevent the risk of uneven weathering.

Treatment of slopes
The sides of excavations (unless of reinforced soils or hard, stable rock) should be sloped back to their natural angle of repose (Table 11); where site conditions do not permit this, some form of support must be provided to prevent collapse. The angle of slope should be considered in relation to

the maintenance operations required, particularly where grass will have to be mown. The maximum gradient for mowing is 1:3; for hand maintenance (usually confined to small areas) the gradient must not exceed 1:1. Planted banks should not exceed 1:2 but those requiring no maintenance may be as steep as 1:1. If slopes steeper than 1:1 are to be topsoiled, provision must be made for the soil to be retained in position by means of frames, wire mesh or plastic netting. In all cases drainage should be provided at

Table 11
Natural slopes of different types of soil

Type of soil	Angle of repose	Base of slope:height
Earth : very wet	18°	3:1
Sand : very wet	22°	2·5:1
Clay : damp and plastic	27°	2:1
Alluvial soil : dry	27°	2:1
Vegetable earth : dry and loose	29°	1·75:1
Sand : fine and dry	33°	1·5:1
Gravel : with sand	38°	1·25:1
Shingle : loose	39°	1·25:1
Clay : dry	39°	1·25:1
Clay : well drained	45°	1:1
Gravel : compact	45°	1:1
Peat : firm	45°	1:1
Earth : compact	50°	0·75:1

Note: Well-drained earth is able to stand permanently in embankments of approximately 1·5 horizontal to 1·0 vertical or, say, 33°, and should be flatter towards the bottom of the slope (imperfectly 2:1).

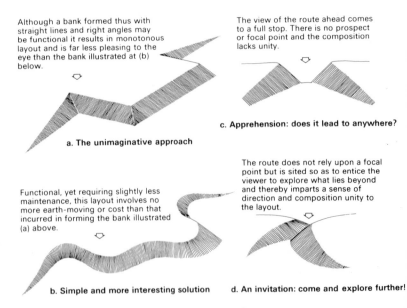

Although a bank formed thus with straight lines and right angles may be functional it results in monotonous layout and is far less pleasing to the eye than the bank illustrated at (b) below.

a. The unimaginative approach

The view of the route ahead comes to a full stop. There is no prospect or focal point and the composition lacks unity.

c. Apprehension: does it lead to anywhere?

Functional, yet requiring slightly less maintenance, this layout involves no more earth-moving or cost than that incurred in forming the bank illustrated (a) above.

b. Simple and more interesting solution

The route does not rely upon a focal point but is sited so as to entice the viewer to explore what lies beyond and thereby imparts a sense of direction and composition unity to the layout.

d. An invitation: come and explore further!

Fig. 14 Ways of dealing with embankments

both the top and bottom of the bank so that the soil is affected only by the moisture falling onto its face.

Forming embankments

Material deposited to form embankments should be built up evenly over the whole area with a sufficient camber to permit drainage from its surface (Fig.14). Each layer should not exceed 250 mm in depth and should be well compacted with suitable machinery until the required level is achieved. Deposits of rock or hardcore, in layers of 450 mm, are best compacted with a 15 tonne crawler tractor. Materials of different characters should be deposited and compacted separately. Sands and granular soils respond to compaction by pneumatic-type roller or vibratory roller; on cohesive soils a sheepsfoot roller is often used.

Soil movements

Resistance to movement depends upon the cohesion and friction of the soil particles. An increase in the water content causes loss of cohesion of a soil. Friction is reduced by the weight of overlying material and is related to the angle of slope.

Plate 2
Existing trees retained in a development where ground levels have been altered: Marquess Road residential development, Islington, London.
Photo: Henk Snoek, London.

Applied loads are not the only cause of soil movement. Surface subsidence often occurs in mining areas and may be due to collapse of the roofs of workings. Swallow holes, i.e. cavities eroded by the action of water, occur in chalk or limestone districts, causing collapse of the soil surface.

Soil movement is particularly noticeable in cohesive soils, such as silts and clays, and is the result of a change in the amount of water in the soil voids. These soils swell when wet and shrink when dried. Where the water-table is high, frost heave may occur in the surface layers causing displacement of newly planted vegetation; silts, sandy clays and chalk are the most susceptible soils. Plant roots are sometimes responsible for soil movement; those of large trees may affect the soil for a depth of up to 5 m during periods of low rainfall.

Slides are liable to occur on earth embankments of non-cohesive soils, such as sands and gravels, where the slope is greater than the natural angle of repose of the material. Rock slides sometimes occur where rock debris has accumulated. In clay formations the soil is liable to creep

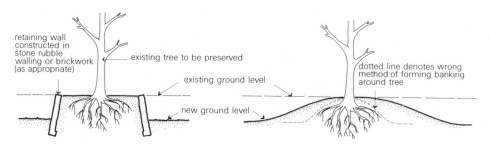

a. Lowering existing ground level in vicinity of tree

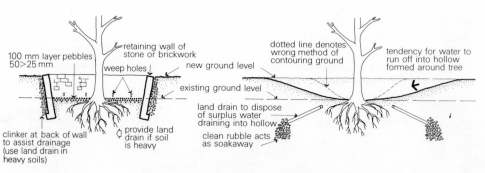

Fig. 15   Preserving trees where ground levels are altered

b. Raising existing ground level in vicinity of tree

slowly down a slope steeper than 1:10; embankments formed in this type of soil should be fairly low and the slope shallow.

Cohesive soils suffer a lack of cohesion when subjected to increased moisture. On cuttings and embankments where there is lack of drainage, softening of the soil at the bottom of a slope may be accompanied by shrinkage and cracking at the top, allowing further penetration of water through its surface. This results in a deep-seated softening of the soil which ultimately causes rotational shear slip and collapse of the slope itself.

Earthmoving in the vicinity of trees

Precautions must be taken to protect trees retained on the site. Within the perimeter of the spread of tree branches the ground level must be preserved and no deposit or removal of the soil in that area permitted. It is also important that any ground-modelling which involves changes of level in the vicinity of trees does not result in their lying in a basin and thereby being subjected to waterlogging (Fig.15).

Where trenches are dug close to trees, care must be taken, using hand digging and tunnelling, so that roots are not severed. Roots must not be left exposed for long periods, when they are liable to dry out; this can cause irreparable damage to the trees.

SURFACE GRADING AND CULTIVATING

Surface grading

After completion of major grading, final shaping of the ground formation is required to create running contours and involves minor adjustment of levels within the depth of the topsoil. Sometimes it is possible to adjust small surface irregularities during the cultivation process. Surface grading is carried out by a blade grader or, in small areas, by hand using a levelling board or rake to produce an even surface.

Where topsoil has been stripped to permit grading to be carried out it must be replaced, spread and levelled to the required depth (minimum 150 mm) and cultivated to bring it to a suitable tilth for blade grading. It is important that efficient supervision is given to all grading and topsoiling operations; work continued when the soil is wet can cause over-compaction of the ground, resulting in damage to the soil structure and sub-surface drainage.

When dealing with embankments the aim should be to create a natural-looking feature. This may be achieved by rounding off the top of the slope and slightly flattening the bottom. A gently curving bank, on plan, produces a more interesting effect than one that is perfectly straight (Fig.14).

Cultivation

Cultivation involves ploughing or digging the soil, the object being to destroy any weeds growing within it and to break up the surface layer to enable air to penetrate and so assist in the natural processes whereby plant food within the soil is liberated.

Surface cultivation

Ground which is intended to be soft-landscaped requires cultivating, the extent of the cultivation depending upon the nature of the soil and surface conditions. Virgin soil supporting scrub, rough grass and other vegetation may require a certain amount of clearing or burning off before the ground is ploughed to the full depth of the topsoil and the vegetation (or its remains) buried beneath the surface layer of soil. Land previously cultivated and containing weeds and other herbage should be turned over by a disc plough. In both cases the soil is then further broken down using a disc harrow. A rotary tiller may be used on those areas which are too small to accommodate a plough; confined plots should be dug by hand. Large tufts of grass and any roots exceeding 38 mm diameter should be raked out and burned. On hard, compacted ground it may be necessary to employ rippers, but to avoid root damage these must not be operated within the branch spread of trees; similarly, the use of a plough within such areas must be avoided. When working in close proximity to manholes, ducts, etc., care must be taken to see that no soil is deposited or washed onto any removable covers.

Subsoil cultivation

Ground crossed by vehicle tracks is often compacted and so hard that it becomes impermeable. Soil with impeded drainage may also require subsoil cultivation. Deep ploughing should be carried out using either a subsoil plough or a mole plough fitted with a subsoiling attachment. This latter method of ploughing is not the same as mole ploughing; the object is not to form drainage channels but to break up the subsoil without churning it up into the topsoil.

Subsoil cultivation may be carried out before or after

topsoiling but usually it is best done after the replacement of topsoil because of the risk of ground compaction by tracking vehicles depositing and spreading the soil.

Where space does not permit the operation of machinery, deep cultivation may have to be done by hand. The soil must be dug to a depth of at least two spits (i.e. 500 mm, twice the depth of the blade of a spade which is approximately 250 mm).

Soil improvement

The process of cultivation provides an opportunity to improve the texture of the soil and to adjust its pH value or rectify any plant nutrient imbalance. Organic matter and fertilisers may be incorporated according to the deficiency of the soil.

1. Organic matter
Decaying animal or vegetable matter forms the basis of organic material, which is gradually broken down by the activities of soil bacteria and provides a source of plant nutrients. It is of particular value on sandy and silty soils since successful plant growth on these depends largely upon the presence of sufficient quantities of organic matter to assist in retaining the minerals that are readily leached; it also improves the soil tilth.

Sources of bulky organic matter include:

Rotted farm manure	Initially a source of potash, it contains nitrogen and phosphates
Poultry manure	Very rich in nitrogen and also has quantities of phosphates
Peat	Has a high water-holding capacity but contains very little plant nutrient
Leaf mould	A valuable source of organic matter but unsuitable for use on soils where lime-hating plants are growing because of the calcium carbonate which is present in the leaf mould

2. Fertilisers
Plant nutrients are obtained from the soil, whose pH value has a bearing upon their availability; deficiencies often occur above pH 7·5. Fertilisers are incorporated into the soil to supplement these deficiencies.

A mixture which contains the three basic elements, nitrogen (N), phosphorus (P_2O_5) and potassium (K_2O), is referred to as a 'complete' fertiliser; two of the nutrients constitute a 'compound' fertiliser and that which supplies only one food is a 'single' fertiliser. The amount of nutrient contained is always expressed as a percentage of the total weight.

(a) *Nitrogenous fertilisers*. Applications of nitrogen must be balanced by the addition of phosphate and potash, since the additional growth which is stimulated as a result of the extra nitrogen puts more demand upon the phosphate and potash within the soil. The nitrogen assists plants in making lush growth and a good coloured foliage; deficiency of this nutrient results in stunted plant growth and a lack of green colour in the foliage.

(i) *Organic*. These slow-acting nutrients are animal protein and are more expensive than the quick-acting fertilisers derived from inorganic sources.

Shoddy	5–12% N
Hoof and horn	13% N: the finer the grist the higher the nitrogen available
Dried blood	12–14% N: unlike the other organic nitrogenous fertilisers, this is quick-acting.

(ii) *Inorganic*. Quick-acting fertilisers.

Nitrate of soda	16% N: slightly quicker-acting than sulphate of ammonia. Its effect is diminished by watering which causes the nutrient to be washed out. Should not be used on heavy soils.
Nitrate of lime	13–15·5% N: useful as a top-dressing on dry soils.
Sulphate of ammonia	21% N: slightly slower-acting than other nitrogenous fertilisers, useful on chalk or lime-rich soils. An overdose may scorch leaves and stems.
Ammonium nitrate	33–35% N: most concentrated and rapid of the inorganic nitrogenous fertilisers. Has explosive properties.

(b) *Phosphatic fertilisers*. The availability of phosphates is largely dependent upon the pH value of the soil and is highest in soils with pH 6·0–6·5. Those with pH 5·0 or below should be given an application of lime prior to incorporating a phosphatic fertiliser. Unless it is mixed with the soil during the cultivation process, the applied phosphate remains on or near the surface, especially on heavy soils, so that only the fertiliser in close proximity to the plant roots is absorbed. The development of growing plants, particularly seedings, relies upon the availability of phosphates.

(i) *Organic*. These are slow-acting fertilisers derived from animal waste.

Bonemeal	16–22% P_2O_5 and 4% N : useful as a long-term nutrient.
Steamed bone flour	25–30% P_2O_5 and 1% N : this bonemeal variant has the gelatine and fat content removed.

(ii) *Inorganic*.

Superphosphate	18–19% P_2O_5 : a quick-acting single fertiliser which contains a fair proportion of gypsum.
Triple superphosphate	46% P_2O_5 : although identical in appearance with the 'single' superphosphate it contains no gypsum. Both fertilisers are rapid in action and their effects long-lasting.
Basic slag	10–18% P_2O_5 : in addition to the phosphoric acid it contains certain calcium compounds which provide an ideal slow-acting fertiliser for acid soils that are lime-deficient.

(c) *Potassic fertilisers*. Potassium plays an important role in the uptake of water by plants, and in the process of photosynthesis and the production of carbohydrate within them. Heavy soils generally contain sufficient quantities of potassium but very little is retained in light sandy soils due to leaching. Less potassium is available in lime-rich soils.

(i) *Organic*.

Wood ash	5–15% K_2O : the potassium is in the form of carbonate of potash ; calcium and other nutrients may also be present. As this is a soluble chemical it is quickly leached when exposed to rain.

(ii) *Inorganic*. There are two major sources of this potassic fertiliser :

Sulphate of potash	48% K_2O and 12–14% N : the most widely used potassic fertiliser for horticultural purposes, but more expensive than muriate of potash. Quick-acting and water-soluble but not washed out by rain.
Potassium nitrate	45% K_2O, 13% N : better known as saltpetre. Although a useful food for special purposes, e.g. liquid feed for glasshouse plants, it is too expensive for widespread use as a fertiliser.
Muriate of potash	60% K_2O : because of its chlorine content this fertiliser is not as safe to use as sulphate of potash. Used in mixtures.

3. *Lime*

Three forms of lime are applicable to horticultural work :
(a) *Calcium oxide*. Known as quicklime or burnt lime, this is the most concentrated and may be either in lump or powdered form. It is caustic in action and must only be used on vacant ground. When exposed to air it quickly absorbs moisture, when its form becomes that of slaked lime.
(b) *Calcium hydroxide*. Known as slaked or hydrated lime, its effect upon the soil is the same as that of quicklime except that its action is not as caustic.
(c) *Calcium carbonate*. A form of lime which occurs naturally in limestone and chalk. It is slower in action than the other two limes although the rate increases the more finely it is ground.

Lime is occasionally required to rectify a calcium deficiency in the soil but its usual application is to reduce soil acidity. It should be applied as a top-dressing and not mixed with animal manure, which is best well dug in some weeks earlier. Mixing with the manure would cause a reaction resulting in the liberation of ammonia gas and a consequent high loss of nitrogen. Over-liming should be avoided.

Rates of application for manures and fertilisers

The food requirements for plants differ greatly and it is impracticable to deal with each plant according to its individual needs except under special circumstances. A

Table 12
Rates of application for manures and fertilisers

Type	Rate of application	When to apply
Nitrogenous		
Shoddy	272 g/m²	Autumn ; winter
Hoof and horn	68 g/m²	Autumn ; winter
Dried blood	68 g/m²	Spring ; early summer
Guano	68–102 g/m²	Growing season
Fish wastes	As manufacturer's instructions	As manufacturer's instructions
Nitrate of soda	17–34 g/m²	Summer
Nitrate of lime	17–34 g/m²	Spring ; early summer
Sulphate of ammonia	17–34 g/m²	Spring ; early summer
Nitro chalk	34 g/m²	Spring ; early summer
Calcium cyanamide	17–34 g/m²	Winter ; early spring
Phosphatic		
Bonemeal	136–204 g/m²	Autumn ; winter
Steamed bone flour	68–136 g/m²	Autumn ; winter
Superphosphate	34–68 g/m²	Spring ; early summer
Triple superphosphate	17–34 g/m²	Spring ; early summer
Basic slag	136–272 g/m²	Autumn ; winter
Rock phosphate	102–136 g/m²	Autumn ; winter
Potassic		
Wood ash	204–272 g/m²	Spring ; summer
Sulphate of potash	17–34 g/m²	Any time of year
Nitrate of potash	17 g/m²	Growing season
Muriate of potash	17–34 g/m²	Autumn ; winter
Kainit	68–102 g/m²	Autumn ; winter
Lime (applied every 3 years)		
Hydrated	272–544 g/m²	Any time of year
Quicklime	406–544 g/m²	Autumn ; winter
Ground limestone	0·54–1·08 kg/m²	Autumn ; winter
Bulky organic		
Farmyard manure	4–6 kg/m²	Autumn ; winter
Poultry manure (dried)	204–340 g/m²	Growing season
Horse manure (composted)	4–6 kg/m²	Autumn ; winter
Leaf mould	3–4 kg/m²	Autumn ; winter
Peat	3–4 kg/m²	Autumn ; winter
Compost	6–8 kg/m²	Autumn ; spring

properly balanced application of nutrients which caters for the average needs is therefore adopted. The best results are generally obtained by combining bulky organic matter and concentrated chemical fertilisers so that soil texture is improved and plant nutrients supplied simultaneously. Generally, the bulky manures should be incorporated into the soil during the winter months and the chemical fertilisers applied as a top-dressing later.

For general horticultural purposes farmyard manure, garden compost, shoddy and compound fertilisers are used.

The rates of application must be adjusted to suit particular needs ; Table 12 gives an indication of the quantities required on normal soils.

Three # Structures in the Landscape

STRUCTURES FOR RETAINING EARTH

A retaining structure may be permanent or temporary, constructed either in-situ or of fabricated units assembled on site. The design of all but the simplest, low retaining wall should be entrusted to a qualified engineer.

Retaining walls
In excavated ground where the sides are not battered to form a stable slope, some kind of support is required to retain the earth (Fig.16). It may be either a mass (relying on weight and gravity for stability) or a cantilevered wall (whose stability is increased by the weight of backfill upon the cantilevered toe of the wall).

Another form of retaining wall is the crib structure, which is basically an interlocking framework within which soil is retained. It performs a similar function to that of the mass retaining wall and is particularly useful where deposited soil is to be retained. The erection of the framework should allow for a 1 : 6–1 : 8 batter. Planting may be introduced to provide a cover to the face of the crib and to help to bind the soil.

A mass retaining wall may be constructed of any of the following materials and should meet the requirements of the relevant Code of Practice or British Standard :

Concrete	CP 111 : Part 2 : 1970 and CP 123.101 : 1951
Reinforced and prestressed concrete	CP 2007 : Part 2 : 1970
Stonework	CP 121.201 : 1951
Clay bricks	CP 121 : Part 1 : 1973
Concrete bricks	BS 1180 : 1972

The cantilever type of wall is constructed of either re-inforced or prestressed concrete. Timber, steel or precast concrete is used in the crib structure.

Dispersal of ground water is of the utmost importance in maintaining stability of a retaining wall. Weepholes should be provided in the wall at regular intervals (usually 900 mm) and a filter of hardcore or clinker placed at the back of it to ensure free drainage. Provision must also be made for the dispersal of water from the front of the wall to prevent seepage.

Piling
Recommendations for pile design are laid down in CP 2004 : 1972 ; reference should also be made to BRE Digests (2nd series) Nos. 63, 67 and 95. Piles may be driven or bored and must extend beyond the depth of the excavation to allow for stability.

Sheet piling comprises interlocking steel sections driven into the ground. Bored piles are tubes of steel or concrete set in bored holes and acting as a retaining structure. In many cases a diaphragm wall is used instead.

Diaphragm walling
This is basically a concrete wall constructed in a deep trench so that it acts as a cut-off or retaining wall.

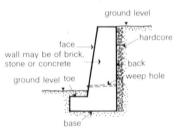

Retaining wall must be capable of withstanding lateral pressure imposed by retained material at back of wall. This pressure varies according to type of soil and groundwater conditions; presence of groundwater increases pressure on back of wall.
It is most important that drainage is provided at back of wall by incorporating weep holes at intervals at base of wall and laying clinker or hardcore immediately at back of wall to act as filter material.

a. Mass wall

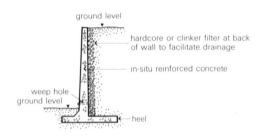

hardcore or clinker filter at back of wall to facilitate drainage

in-situ reinforced concrete

heel

b. Cantilever wall

Diaphragm wall acts as a cut-off and basically serves same purpose as sheet sheet piling but is constructed in-situ of reinforced concrete. It is very useful when working in confined spaces–e.g. in built-up areas. Excavated spoil from trench is replaced with bentonite mud (a kind of clay which possesses high expanding properties).

size and position of block dependent upon type of soil
c. Diaphragm wall

plants may be incorporated between beams and set towards top of crib wall so that they cascade over face

tie beams

slope of embankment

Concrete, steel or timber beams are laid to form a crib framework which by the nature of its construction is capable of resisting overturning and serves the same function as a mass wall. This type of retaining structure is useful in situations where earth is to be tipped to form an embankment but it should not be used in the close vicinity of buildings or in situations where the ground is unstable and liable to slip. The crib wall should be constructed with a batter of not less than 1:8 nor greater than 1:6.

ground level
d. Crib wall

Fig. 16 Structures for retaining earth

Cofferdam
To eliminate the need for dewatering, a temporary retaining structure is driven into the ground below the level of the water-table. It consists of a double row of interlocking piles filled with granular material to give it stability. Reference should be made to CP 2004 :1972.

Shoring
Temporary support is often necessary to prevent the sides of an excavation from collapsing. In shallow excavations boards, supported by either struts or raking shores, are used, depending upon the nature of the ground and depth of excavation.

DAMS, WEIRS AND BRIDGES

These three structures are involved in the retention of water and access across it. The design and constructional requirements of all but the simplest calls for the services of a qualified engineer.

Dams (see also page 93)

Earth, concrete, masonry or a combination of the last two may be used to construct a dam, but whatever material is employed the structure must be stable so that it does not fracture, slump or leak.

(a) *Earth*
This form of construction is unsuitable for a confined space since the width of the base needs to be at least 2 m for a structure two-thirds that height. The slope of the downstream and upstream faces should not exceed 1 : 2 and 1 : 3 respectively (Fig.17).

Fig. 17   Basic principle of earth dam construction

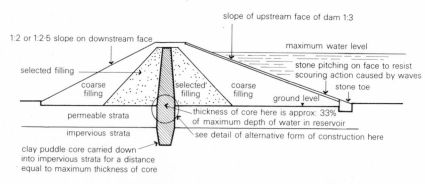

a. Cross-section through dam

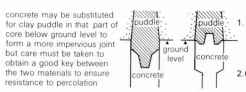

concrete may be substituted for clay puddle in that part of core below ground level to form a more impervious joint but care must be taken to obtain a good key between the two materials to ensure resistance to percolation

b. Detail of core construction

Formation of embankment on both sides of puddled clay wall in centre of dam consists of two classes of material:
1. Inner part: specially selected material of a predominantly clayey character which is placed on upstream side to prevent water penetrating clay puddle and on downstream side to prevent puddle from drying out.
2. Outer part: coarser material, thoroughly compacted to prevent undue settlement later.

Although clayey soils are best for sealing off water they are inclined to slump when saturated. The use of bentonite, a volcanic clay which has high expanding and gelling properties, seals the soil against water seepage.

(b) *Concrete*

Slow-setting and slow-hardening cement must be used for this type of structure to avoid the risk of cracking which is likely to occur with the use of rapid-hardening cement. The mix should be fairly rich, incorporating carefully graded aggregate. In larger structures a considerable portion of the dam interior comprises large irregular stone blocks (plums) which help to increase the weight of the structure, giving it stability and a resistance to shear. They also reduce the quantity of cement required and assist in binding together successive layers of concrete. Care must be taken to see that the concrete is well punned to avoid leaving any air pockets.

(c) *Masonry*

Local stone, if readily available, may be used in lieu of, or in conjunction with, concrete. The width of the base of the dam (whether of stone or concrete) should be 600–900 mm for every 900 mm of height.

Fig. 18   Simple types of weir

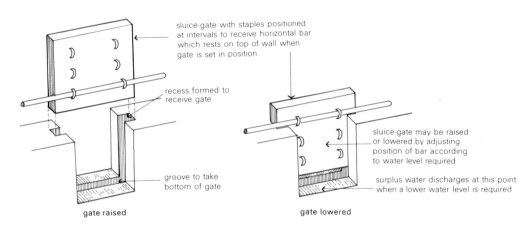

sluice-gate with staples positioned at intervals to receive horizontal bar which rests on top of wall when gate is set in position.

recess formed to receive gate

groove to take bottom of gate

gate raised

sluice-gate may be raised or lowered by adjusting position of bar according to water level required

surplus water discharges at this point when a lower water level is required

gate lowered

a. Weir controlled by solid sluice gate

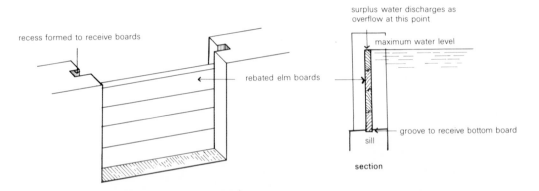

recess formed to receive boards

rebated elm boards

surplus water discharges as overflow at this point

maximum water level

groove to receive bottom board

sill

section

b. Weir controlled by removable timber board

Fig. 19 Examples of
traditional types of
simple footbridge

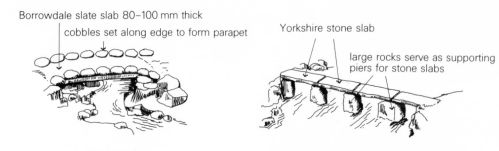

Borrowdale slate slab 80–100 mm thick
cobbles set along edge to form parapet

Yorkshire stone slab
large rocks serve as supporting
piers for stone slabs

a. Cumberland bridge

b. Clapper bridge in a Yorkshire dale

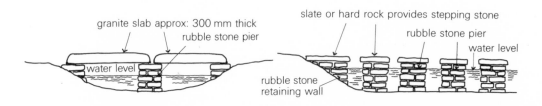

granite slab approx: 300 mm thick
rubble stone pier
water level

slate or hard rock provides stepping stone
rubble stone pier
water level
rubble stone
retaining wall

c. Basic type clapper bridge, Dartmoor

d. Stepping stones based on clapper bridge

Weirs (Fig.18)

The level of water may be controlled by the installation of a weir and any surplus channelled into an outfall so that overflow water is controlled and prevented from flooding the adjoining area.

A weir should be of simple design and may be constructed of concrete, brickwork, stonework or a combination of any of these materials. Timber boards set horizontally in recessed channels are sometimes incorporated as the controlling device to maintain the water level at the required height. Another method of regulating the water is to place an outlet pipe adjacent to the weir, with the invert level 150 mm above that of the bottom of the pool. Control is effected by means of a screwdown gate-valve fixed to the pipe on the other side of the weir.

Bridges (Fig.19)

A bridge is a means of gaining access across water or any similar obstacle. The scale of the structure should be in keeping with the layout of the area and its design simple but functional. It is advisable that the services of a qualified engineer should be enlisted for the design of all bridges, other than those of the simplest nature, such as footbridges. BS 153:3B and 4:1972 deals with the design and construction of simply supported steel girder bridges of spans up to 100 m.

Examples of traditional types are the little stone bridges of Cumberland (Cumbria) and the south-west of England. These are a kind of clapper bridge, originated on Dartmoor where the granite rock is very hard, constructed of 3·0–3·5 m long slabs 600 mm wide and 300 mm thick. Two or three of these slabs form the bridge. The Cumberland bridge consists of Borrowdale slate, usually up to 2·75 m long by roughly 460 mm wide and 80–100 mm thick, laid on top of walling formed of rockstones or the flatter cobbles. A row of cobbles is often set along the edges of the slate to form a small parapet.

Where large blocks of stone are not readily available, a design similar to that of the clapper bridge may be achieved using slabs of reinforced concrete. In wooded areas a series of logs may be lashed together to provide a kind of makeshift pioneer type of bridge.

Stepping stones, of course, are a simple type of bridge but need not necessarily be of stone. Bricks or timber may be used provided they are firm and adequately set in position.

Plate 3
Stepping stones : *Pflanzen und Blumen* display at Hamburg.
Photo: S. W. Newbury.

WALLING

The function of a wall is to serve as a barrier, enclosure, screen or retaining structure. It may be built of a variety of materials (stone, brick, concrete, etc.) but these and the type of construction must be chosen to harmonise with their surroundings and should take into account local traditions and craftsmanship. In all cases it is essential that the wall is laid on an adequate foundation (set below the level at which frost occurs) on firm stable ground. The height : width ratio of the wall must be sufficient to maintain the structure in equilibrium.

Stone walling

Almost any kind of stone may be used for wall construction: granite, limestone, sandstone or slate. Care must be taken to avoid close association of limestone and sandstone since the latter is likely to decay if calcium sulphate from the limestone is washed onto it. BRE Digest No.177 explains the causes of decay of stone and gives recommendations for its preservation.

The two main kinds of stone walling are ashlar and rubble, the latter comprising three principal groups :

Random rubble	Uncut stone (coursed and uncoursed).
Squared rubble	Roughly dressed stone (regular-coursed, irregular-coursed and uncoursed).
Miscellaneous	Rubble walling of traditional materials and construction appertaining to a particular locality.

Compound walls comprise a combination of rubble stone (or brickwork) and dressed stone.

Ashlar

Walls built of carefully dressed stone, accurately bedded with fine joints, are termed 'ashlar' (Fig.20). Because of the nature of their construction, finish and the materials used, such work calls for the employment of skilled masons and consequently is generally the most expensive type of walling.

The sizes of the individual blocks must be in scale with the overall size of the wall and the length of each one

Plate 4
Functional use of traditional materials : Durham City.
Random rubble and brickwork provide the walled enclosure to these ancient perrons constructed of stone cobbles and setts. *Photo: Sam Lambert, London.*

should be not less than twice nor more than three times its height, so that adequate bond of the stonework is obtained. All ashlar work should be in accordance with the recommendations set out in CP 121.201:1951 and may be laid in diminishing courses, alternate thick and thin courses or random-coursed (an inferior form of ashlar).

In hammer-dressed ashlar, only the beds and joints are roughly dressed ; this is the roughest form of ashlar and may be said to lie between ashlar proper and rubble work. Ashlar quoins are sometimes used in conjunction with squared coursed rubble or uncoursed random rubble. The bed of the ashlar stone should be clearly marked to assist erection by the mason.

Compound walls consist of an ashlar face with a backing of either stone rubble walling or (more often) brickwork, the facing bonded into the backing to give stability. Where the stone is in contact with brickwork its surface should be coated with bitumen to prevent any soluble salts contained in the brickwork from coming into contact with and damaging the stone facing.

Fig. 20   Ashlar walling

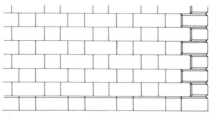

a. Coursed

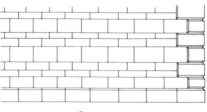

b. Random

Ashlar is a class of masonry formed with blocks of accurately dressed stone finely bedded with joints seldom more than 5mm thick. It may be built as as illustrated or with the same face arrangement as rubble work.

Coursed ashlar is the best quality work with all the stones of the same height built to regular courses. An inferior form is random ashlar comprising stones of varying sizes built to irregular courses.

Hammer dressed ashlar is much used in civil engineering structures and constructed with roughly dressed stones whose bedding and jointing is not of the same fineness as that of coursed ashlar. It may be said to rank between ashlar proper and rubble walling.

The length of stone used in ashlar work generally is 2–3 times its height and may be up to 5 times where there is no risk of fracture due to settlement.

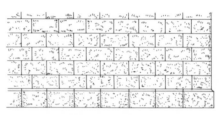

c. Hammer dressed

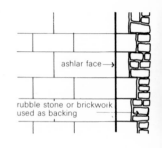

ashlar face→

rubble stone or brickwork used as backing

d. Compound wall

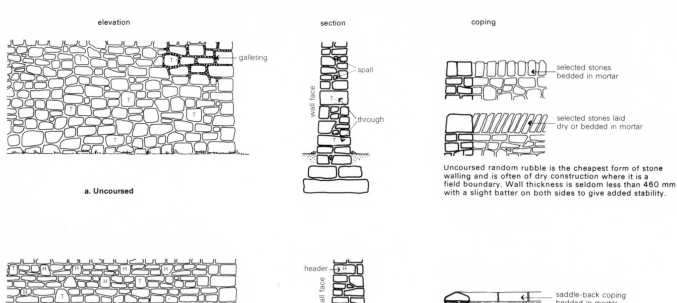

elevation

section

coping

— galleting

a. Uncoursed

wall face

spall

through

selected stones
bedded in mortar

selected stones laid
dry or bedded in mortar

Uncoursed random rubble is the cheapest form of stone
walling and is often of dry construction where it is a
field boundary. Wall thickness is seldom less than 460 mm
with a slight batter on both sides to give added stability.

header

wall face

through

header

saddle-back coping
bedded in mortar

Coursed random rubble is of stronger and rather neater
construction than uncoursed. Stones are roughly squared
up by knocking off projections with a hammer and built
in courses 300–460 mm deep, according to size of stones.
Through stones (throughs) extend the full width of the
wall and are spaced at approx: one metre intervals.
Headers (also known as bonders) extend beyond the
centre of the wall and are set at approx: half metre.
These and throughs ensure sound transverse bond.

b. Laid to courses

Fig. 21   Random rubble walling

Random rubble walling
The blocks of stone used for this kind of walling come in
all shapes and sizes and are picked more or less at random
from the mass. No labour or cutting is done, apart from
snapping off inconvenient corners with a walling hammer.
The stones are placed so that there is an adequate distribution of pressure over a maximum area and no long continuous vertical joints. Transverse bond is achieved by
the use of 'headers' (bonders) and 'throughs' which
constitute at least one-quarter of the wall face; to every
square metre there are two headers and one through.
Construction of the wall may be either uncoursed or
coursed but should be in accordance with the recommendations set out in CP 121.202 : 1951.

(i) *Uncoursed* (Fig.21a). The use of an assortment of
shapes and sizes of stone produces a considerably varied
face appearance. Larger stones are bedded flat and packed
up with small pieces of stone (spalls); joints are well filled
and flushed with mortar. Sometimes face joints have small

pieces of stone driven into the mortar; this is known as
'galleting'.

(ii) *Coursed* (Fig.21b). A similar type of construction is
used but the stones are more carefully selected so that
they are roughly levelled up to form courses. These may be
300–460 mm thick, coinciding generally with the varying
heights of the corner stones (quoins).

Random rubble walling is sometimes constructed with
soil joints in lieu of mortar which allows alpines to be
planted in the wall.

Squared rubble walling
The stone used for this type of walling is obtained from
either thin beds in the quarry or the thicker beds of laminated stone which are readily split. Very little labour is
required to form a comparatively straight bed and side
joints. The three forms of construction are described below,
each having variations according to local traditions.

elevation   section

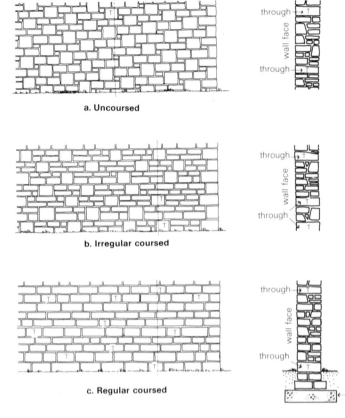

a. Uncoursed

b. Irregular coursed

c. Regular coursed

Stones of varying sizes (actual dimensions depend upon source of material) are not laid to courses but arranged in an irregular pattern which can be quite attractive if the number of stone sizes is restricted to four or five. The use of small stones (snecks or checks) eliminates the disadvantage of long continuous vertical joints on the wall face and is the reason why this type of walling is often referred to as 'square-snecked rubble'.

The walling illustrated here is a typical example of this form which is also known as 'coursed header work'. Its construction is similar to that of coursed random rubble. Like other kinds of squared rubble walling it consists of roughly squared stones with reasonably straight joints and beds. The face may be hammer-dressed or straight cut. Variations of pattern occur in the different stone-building districts.

In this type of walling the height of the courses varies but that of the individual stones in each course is the same. Generally the thinner beds of stone used here give a more pleasing appearance than the thicker beds whose proportions are more akin to 'block-in-course' work which is closely associated with civil engineering construction (e.g. retaining walls and sea-defence structures).

concrete foundation   Fig. 22   Squared rubble walling

(i) *Squared uncoursed* (Fig.22a). Often termed 'square-snecked rubble' because of the small stones (snecks) which are used in its construction. These are used to fill rebates formed by adjoining stones so that continuous vertical joints are avoided. Sizes should not be less than 76×76 mm. The snecks, stretchers (levellers) and risers (jumpers) are incorporated in the proportions of 1 : 2 : 3. Generally the height of risers should not exceed 250 mm and that of stretchers not more than two-thirds the height of the adjoining riser.

(ii) *Squared irregular-coursed* (Fig.22b). Stones similar in size to those described above are built to courses of varying depths (300–900 mm) but no snecks are required. In some cases each course may consist of quoins, 'bonders' and 'throughs' of the same height with smaller stones set in between them, up to the height of the larger stones, to complete the course. This arrangement is referred to as 'coursed header work'.

(iii) *Regular coursed* (Fig.22c). The stones in any particular course are all of the same height but course heights may vary. Sometimes smaller stones (pinnings) are set in the courses to produce a chequered effect. 'Block-in-course' consists of large square blocks of hammer-dressed or pitch-faced stone laid in deep courses and is used in civil engineering structures such as retaining or sea walls.

Miscellaneous types of rubble walling
Many variations of rubble walling are to be found in a number of localities and the materials and methods employed are traditionally associated with those areas. Three of the well-known variations are described below :

(a) *Polygonal.* Commonly found in the southern counties of England and often referred to as 'Kentish rag' due to the limestone quarried in Kent which is used fairly extensively for this type of work. There is no pronounced stratification

elevation   section

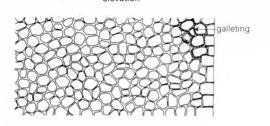

→ galleting

Stones of stratified limestone are roughly dressed,
the face being hammer-pitched (also known as quarry-
pitched or rustic-faced) so that it is an irregular
polygonal shape, and laid in such a manner that the
wall face represents a honeycomb arrangement
with joints in no defined pattern but running in all
directions, and stones approximately fitted together.
Although most walls constructed in this manner have
a brick backing, stone may also be used.

← stone backing

a. Rough picked

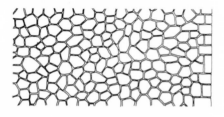

This type of walling is constructed in a similar
manner to that of 'rough picked' but the face edges
are more carefully dressed so that the stones bed
reasonably accurately together to form the irregular
pattern illustrated. Because of its close association
with the use of a limestone which occurs in Kent
this form of walling is commonly known as Kentish Rag.
In the West Midlands a similar type of walling is
to be found constructed with a local sandstone and
referred to as Rowley Rag.

← brick backing

b. Close picked

Fig. 23   Polygonal walling

Elevation   Section

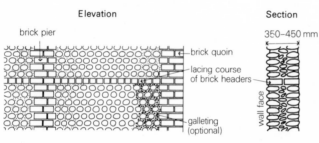

brick pier

350–450 mm

→ brick quoin

→ lacing course
of brick headers

→ galleting
(optional)

wall face

Stones of similar size varying in colour from
greyish blue to white (depending upon their
source) are laid as headers with mortar joints
on the wall face well raked back or, alternatively,
the mortar is finished flush and small stones
inserted in the joints (galleted) to wedge up the
stones (i.e. flints or cobbles). The two sides of the
wall are of similar appearance, with a hearting of
smaller stones tightly packed between the headers.
A lacing course of brick or stone headers is provided
where the wall height exceeds 900 mm and piers are
incorporated at approx: 1·5 m intervals.

a. Undressed

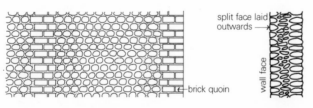

split face laid
outwards →

wall face

→ brick quoin

The stones are snapped across transversely
(polled) to reveal a shiny black or dark grey surface
which is laid so that it faces outwards. The length
of each polled flint should not generally be less
than 100 mm in order to ensure that it is well bonded
into the body of the wall. The inner face comprises
undressed flints flushed up with mortar and of
similar construction to that described above.
Sometimes galleting is incorporated and lacing
courses may be included if necessary. Quoins
and piers are generally in brickwork.

b. Polled

lacing course

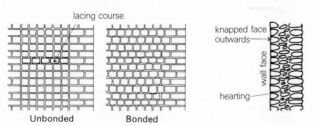

knapped face
outwards →

wall face

hearting →

Unbonded   Bonded

Larger stones are employed in this type of wall facing
so that the split face of each flint when dressed
(knapped) is approximately 100×100 mm. Construction
is similar to that of polled facing but mortar joints
are thinner. Where knapped facing is intended to
provide a decorative wall face the flints are laid
with continuous vertical joints between brick piers.
Lacing courses are included.

c. Knapped

Fig. 24   Flint walling

in the stone, which is bedded with face joints running irregularly in various directions. Two classes of work are used :

(i) *Rough picked* (Fig.23a). The stones are roughly shaped so that they fit together only approximately ; a hammer-pitched surface is used.

(ii) *Close picked* (Fig.23b). The face edges of the stones are more carefully formed to allow them to fit more compactly together. The face finish may be either hammer-pitched or hammer-dressed.

(b) *Flint.* Generally associated with chalk or limestone areas where gravel beds occur, providing the raw material. In some coastal districts flints or cobbles (popples) are to be found on the beach. This type of walling, traditionally found in East Anglia and the southern counties, occurs in three forms :

(i) *Undressed* (Fig.24a). The flints are used in their natural state (76–150 mm thick and 150–300 mm long), laid as headers, with mortar joints well raked back, and may be built either to courses or uncoursed. Usually a course of through stones (long thin stones, tiles or bricks) is introduced at 900–1800 mm intervals to provide 'lacing courses' which serve to strengthen the structure. Additional stability may be achieved by constructing brick piers at 1·5 m intervals.

(ii) *Polled facing* (Fig.24b). Flints are snapped (polled) transversely across the centre and laid with the split face showing outwards in courses ; undressed flints are used for backing. Lacing courses of bricks may be incorporated, depending upon the height of the wall. Thin flakes of flint are sometimes used to gallet the mortar joints.

(iii) *Knapped flint facing* (Fig.24c). This is the best type of flint walling and is often referred to as 'gauged' or 'squared flint'. Similar to polled facing, this method uses larger-sized cobbles which are snapped across the centre with the split surfaces dressed (knapped) roughly 100 mm square and laid in courses.

(c) *Lake District masonry.* Parts of Cumbria are associated with local quarried slate walling. The slate blocks vary

Fig. 25   Lake District masonry

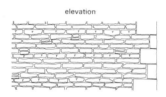

elevation   section

a. Rough-faced random

Blocks of slate are broken into irregular shapes, roughly dressed in situ to the required size and laid so that they fit fairly close together, small pieces of stone (spalls) being used to pack up the face stones where necessary. Mortar is used for partial bedding, set back 50–76 mm from the face so that the weight of the stone causes the mortar to be squeezed out to some 130 mm across, giving a thin bed joint. Through stones are incorporated at 600–900 mm intervals to form a continuous more or less horizontal joint and tilted downwards towards the outer wall face. These provide what is referred to as the watershot and as the work proceeds all the other stones are tilted in a similar manner.

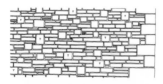

b. Best-faced random

'Blue' slate (olive green in colour) is a very durable material and is employed for this method of walling which has a similar arrangement on face to that of square snecked rubble. Although in principle construction follows that described above, the through stones in this case are staggered–usually two to every square metre of wall face. The face of each stone is squared with the hammer and is naturally smooth (self-faced).

from quite small pieces to approximately 600 × 900 mm, and are broken to size and dressed as required by the waller as the work proceeds. Much skill is required in the construction of this unique type of walling, which incorporates through stones tilted downwards towards the outer face, known as 'watershot'. The wall itself comprises an inner and outer face (the face stones being given a similar watershot) with a core of smaller stones (hearting) laid dry. This method of construction is most effective in resisting dampness and occurs in two forms:

(i) *Rough faced random* (Fig.25a). The stones are of various shapes, roughly dressed and closely set together using small pieces (spalls) to pack up the larger stones. Hammer-dressed limestone is used for quoins and jambs and the stones coursed up to the level of the watershot to form a more or less horizontal continuous joint at approximately 600 mm intervals.

(ii) *Best random faced* (Fig.25b). Similar in appearance to square-snecked rubble, consisting of self-faced stones (normally smooth) laid uncoursed with through stones staggered at the rate of two to each square metre of wall face.

Mortars for masonry

Mortar used for jointing masonry varies according to the nature of the stone and construction. Portland cement is used, generally, as the cementing agent in situations where strength and frost resistance are of prime importance. Where workability is the main criterion the use of lime in lieu of or in combination with cement is recommended. Ideally, the mortar used in masonry should be slightly weaker than the stone which it is bonding together, so that where any settlement takes place the risk of fracture is confined to the joints and not the stone itself.

Guidance on the use of mortar mixes for stonework is given in Table 13.

Brick walling

Brickwork should be in accordance with CP 121 : Part 1 : 1973. BRE Digests Nos.164 and 165 deal with the selection of clay bricks and the behaviour of brickwork in differing conditions of exposure.

Three types of brick are suitable for external work and all of them should comply with BS 3921 : 1974.

Table 13
Mortar mixes for masonry

Situation	Cement	Lime putty	Crushed stone	Remarks
Free-standing walls exposed to severe weather conditions	1	1	5–6	Normal construction in ashlar work
Free-standing walls in normal conditions of exposure to weather	1	2	8–9	Normal construction in ashlar work and rubble walling
Rubble walling	1	1	6	Normal situation not too exposed
Construction of stone walls below DPC	1	0·25	3	Dense strong mortar
Granite walling (i)	1	0·25	3	Inclusion of lime to produce workability is optional
(ii)	1	–	2	
Sandstone : ashlar	1	1	4	Lime is optional and may be less than that stated
Portland stone : ashlar	1	2·5	3·5	Neat cement should not be used for grouting as it stains face of block
Sandstone : general facing and rubble walling	1	–	3	Strength of work depends largely upon that of mortar
Limestone : general facing work	1	3	10–12	Mortar for pointing may be slightly stronger
Faced work generally (i)	1	3	10–12	Depending upon permeability of stone
(ii)	1	4	16	
(iii)	2	5	7	

Commons. These have no claim to attractive appearance and are manufactured for general purposes under three classifications. The 'special quality' is the most durable and may be used in the construction of retaining walls and other structures in exposed positions.

Facings. Where appearance is of prime importance, facing bricks are specified. These may be either self-coloured or surface-coloured (using specially stained sand which becomes colour-fast when the brick is fired in the kiln). There is a risk that chipping of the latter type of brick is likely to reveal the different body core and extra care in handling is necessary to avoid this.

Engineering. Hard impervious bricks of high compressive strength are manufactured in two grades :

Class A	average 689 50 kN/m^2
Class B	average 482 65 kN/m^2

'Special' bricks are also produced whose range of shapes is almost unlimited. Although calcium silicate (sand-lime and flint-lime) bricks may also be used for external work their selection requires careful consideration since uniformity of colour and texture makes for a somewhat harsh appearance which may be unharmonious with some aspects of landscape work. Reference should be made to BS 187 : Part 2 : 1970, which gives guidance on the choice of brick and the appropriate grade of mortar for the six classes produced. BRE Digest No.157 also gives guidance on calcium silicate brickwork. One advantage of this type of brick is the absence of efflorescence (salting or whitish deposits which sometimes appear on the face of new clay brickwork, due to the crystallisation of soluble salts, e.g. calcium sulphate, as moisture dries out).

Table 14
Bonds employed in brickwork

Type of bond	Construction	Remarks
English (Old English)	One course headers, one course stretchers (alternately)	In walls that are 1, 2, 3, etc., bricks thick, the elevation is the same on both wall faces. In walls having an odd half brick dimension, the front elevation differs from the back.
Double Flemish	Header + stretcher alternately in same course	Weaker than English bond, due to the large number of bats and stretchers used, but considered to look better on face. Economical because it allows the use of a large proportion of bats.
Single Flemish	Header + stretcher alternately in same course (as in Double Flemish) and English bond as backing	Generally specified where more expensive bricks are selected for facing. This bond can only be used for walls 1½ bricks thick or more.
Stretching	All bricks laid as stretchers	Used for walls of ½-brick thickness, e.g. cavity, and in half-timbered work.
Heading	All bricks show as headers on face of wall	Used mainly for footings and rounding curves.
English garden wall	One course headers, three or five courses stretchers	Economical construction. This bond is used where walls one brick thick are to be rendered.
Garden or boundary wall	Three stretchers to one header laid in same course alternately	Used for walls one brick thick that are seen from both sides.
Flemish garden wall	Three or five stretchers to one header in each course	Known as 'Sussex bond' and 'Scotch bond'.
Monk	One header and two stretchers in each course	Variation of Flemish garden wall bond : header falls centrally over joint between a pair of stretchers.
English cross	Alternate courses of headers and stretchers	Similar to English bond, but each alternate stretching course has a header placed next to the quoin stretcher.
Rat-trap	Bricks laid on edge to give face appearance of Flemish bond	Brick-on-edge construction leaves a cavity between courses. Cheap and economical.
Silverlocks	Alternate courses of headers and stretchers laid on edge—resembing English bond	Stronger than rat-trap bond but not so economical.

Plate 5
Traditional use of
brick : Marquess
Road residential
development,
Islington, London.
The use of brick
pavers provides a
psychological
demarcation of
floorscape functions
and marries in with
the adjacent brick
walls.
*Photo: Henk Snoek,
London.*

Bond

Arrangement of bricks within a wall is referred to as 'bond' and is identified by the external face. The merits of the various types of bond are assessed on appearance and ease of construction, rather than their effective strength, but the purpose of the bond is to assist in spreading the stresses transmitted from point loads imposed upon the wall. The various bonds employed are described in Table 14.

Reinforcement

In some instances introduction of steel reinforcement (in the form of rods, flats, woven wire or expanded metal) may be necessary to counteract tensile and sheer stresses which may occur in addition to compressive stress. No lime should be incorporated into the mortar mix since it may have an injurious effect upon the metal.

Mortar for brickwork

The mix specified depends upon the strength of brickwork required and its situation. For most external work subject to normal exposure the following mortars are suitable for use with clay or sand-lime (Class A) bricks:

    1:1:8–9   cement:lime:sand
    1:1:5–6   cement:lime:sand
    1:3   hydraulic cement:lime

Lime (to BS 890:1972) is used to improve the working qualities of the mortar and helps to prevent shrinkage and cracks when drying out. Hydraulic lime possesses the ability to harden under water or in damp conditions.

Brickwork which is liable to saturation with water and subject to severe exposure and freezing temperatures should be constructed with one of the following mortars:

    1:1:5–6   cement:lime:sand
    1:5–6   cement:sand (and a plasticiser added)

These mixes are suitable for use with Class A or B clay engineering (BS 3921:1974) or sand-lime bricks. Where high strength is required a 1:3 cement:sand mix may be used with clay bricks but not in conjunction with calcium silicate bricks.

Unless the site is wet or there are other controlling factors present the following mortar mixes may be used with clay bricks or sand-lime bricks Class A for work below ground or DPC level:

    Clay bricks   1:5–6   cement:sand
                   1:3   cement:sand
    Sand-lime   1:1:5–6 cement:lime:sand
    bricks

Reference should be made to BRS Digest (2nd Series) No.58 and to the following British Standards:

BS 187:Part 2:1970	Table 5 contains mortar mixes recommended for use with various types of calcium silicate bricks. Mortar mixes are shown in Table 6.
BS 4721:1971	Ready-mixed lime:sand for mortar. Pigments should comply with BS 1014:1961.
BS 1200:1955	Sands recommended for plain and reinforced brickwork, block walling and masonry.

BS 890:1972	Building limes; classifications given for:
	    Hydrated lime (powder)
	    –4 classes
	    Quicklime–3 classes
	    Lime putty–4 classes

BS 3148:1959	Water for making concrete.
BS 4551:1970	Methods for sampling and testing mortars.

Pointing

Joints on the face of brickwork may be finished in a variety of ways, the object being to compress the mortar in the joint between the bricks on the face in order to eliminate any pore spaces along which water may travel. This process is known as 'pointing', but where the finish to the joints is carried out simultaneously with bricklaying operations it is referred to as 'jointing'.

Concrete walling

Concrete walling is of two kinds: in-situ mass concrete and precast concrete blocks or units.

(i) *In-situ*. Mass concrete walling cast in-situ is generally employed for retaining walls and similar structures whose dimensions and function call for this type of construction, which involves the use of formwork and shuttering.

(ii) *Precast*. Concrete blocks are manufactured in a variety of shapes and finishes; they should conform to the requirements set out in BS 2028, 1364:1968.

Plain blocks have little aesthetic appeal for outdoor use

and are best rendered on their exposed face. Alternatively, the face of the blocks may incorporate stone dust, giving the impression of stonework, or exposed natural aggregate. Decorative surface finishes of a wide variety may be applied to the blocks or a low relief pattern incorporated into the mould during the casting process.

In addition to these precast solid blocks of concrete there is also available a range of pierced blocks whose individual shapes and arrangement within the wall create a pattern. Such walls generally serve an aesthetic rather than a structural need.

In all concrete structures, including walling, there are three essential constituents: cement, aggregate and water. The proportions used depend upon the strength of concrete required, its function and location. Steel reinforcement may also be incorporated to give additional strength.

Types of cement
Several kinds of cement are produced, each with different qualities and uses and complying with the respective British Standard.

Portland (BS 12 : Part 2 : 1971). The most commonly used cement and available as either 'normal' or 'rapid-hardening'.

White and coloured Portland. The properties of these cements are the same as those of ordinary Portland. In order to balance any loss of strength, due to the addition of pigments (complying with BS 1014 : 1961), the cement content of the mix should be increased by approximately 10 per cent. The problems likely to arise from the risk of efflorescence occurring should be borne in mind where a black pigment is selected.

Portland-blastfurnace (BS 146 : Part 2 : 1973). A mixture of ordinary cement and finely powdered blastfurnace slag produces a slow-hardening cement which is of particular value for use in constructional work in sea-water. A rich mix (1 : 1·5 : 3) is recommended to obtain maximum density and must be properly matured before exposure since the concrete must be capable of resisting the action of sea-water and erosion and attrition by waves, sand and shingle.

High alumina (BS 915 : Part 2 : 1972). This rapid-hardening cement has a high resistance to the action of sea-water and is also valuable for its resistance to sulphates, which is greater than that of sulphate-resisting cement. A rich mix (1 : 1·5 : 3) is recommended in order to obtain maximum density. High alumina cement must be stored in a separate place because if it becomes mixed with Portland cement a flash set takes place.

Low-heat Portland (BS 1370 : Part 2 : 1974). The heat generated by this cement during the hardening process is less than that of normal Portland. It is used in the construction of large concrete mass structures, such as dams and retaining walls, to prevent structural cracks (due to expansion and contraction during the setting and hardening processes).

Aggregate
Materials classed as aggregate range from 'fine' to 'coarse' and may consist of sand, gravel or crushed stone. They must be clean, free from injurious chemicals and organic matter and should comply with BS 882 : Part 2 : 1973. Their grading is governed by the degree of workability required and the nature of the work to be executed. Aggregate used for concrete may be one of the following:

Coarsely graded. Contains a high proportion of large particles retained on a 5 mm BS test sieve.

Finely graded. The majority of the particles are small, passing a 5 mm BS test sieve.

All-in. Composed of a mixture of coarse and fine particles. Coarse and fine aggregate should be batched separately before being mixed together. This type of aggregate is seldom used for reinforced concrete work because the grading may vary considerably.

Methods used for sampling and testing aggregate should be in accordance with BS 812 : 1967.

Water
Although water may be perfectly fit for drinking purposes it may contain impurities harmful to cement. Tests should be made, therefore, in accordance with BS 3148 : 1959 to ensure that the water is suitable for concrete mixing.

Reinforcement
Steel reinforcement in concrete provides tensile and shear strength. It must be rigidly fixed and correctly positioned so that it is capable of counteracting the various stresses imposed upon the structure. An adequate cover of con-

crete must surround the reinforcement; minimum standards are laid down in CP 114 : Part 2 : 1969 and CP 116 : Part 2 : 1969.

Concreting operations involve mixing and placing the wet material; where reinforcement is included this is positioned prior to placing the concrete. In its wet state concrete takes on no particular form and must therefore be moulded to the required shape with the assistance of formwork and shuttering (complying with the recommendations in CP 114 : Part 2). This needs to be of sufficient strength and rigidity to carry working and incidental loads and capable of supporting the weight of the wet concrete. Mixing may be either in-situ (by machine) or at a central mixing plant from which the concrete is delivered to site in mobile revolving containers. Ready-mixed concrete should comply with the requirements in

Plate 6
Composite walling : reinforced concrete faced with bonded broken paving flags. Perimeter wall to the Arena at the Midlands Arts Centre for Young People, Cannon Hill, Birmingham. The project was constructed by young volunteers at International Work Camps held there during several summers.
Photo: Henry Southwell Eades, Birmingham.

BS 1926:1962. Test cubes should be taken during the mixing and placing of the concrete in accordance with BS 1881 : Part 1 : 1970.

During cold weather calcium chloride may be added to the mix (in the proportion of 2·5 per cent of the total weight of the concrete) to prevent frost action. This salt increases the early rate of hardening of the concrete at normal temperatures but during cold weather assists in minimising the delay caused by low temperatures.

If pigments are to be incorporated in the mix they should comply with BS 1014:1961 and must be thoroughly mixed with the cement prior to the addition of the aggregate. The amount of pigment used should not exceed 5 per cent of the weight of the cement.

Walling foundations

A wall must be constructed upon stable and adequate foundations (footings) so that any risk of structural movement is eliminated. The bearing capacity of soils varies and may fluctuate considerably in those with a high moisture content, such as clays. It is not possible, therefore, to lay down precise rules as to dimensions of foundations to be adopted for various types of walling. The depth below ground to which the foundations are taken is dependent upon the level at which frost or movement of ground moisture occurs. In most cases a depth of 450–600 mm below the surface is usually sufficient to meet general needs. Unless there are difficult site conditions a concrete mix of 1 : 2 : 4–6 is adopted for normal wall foundation work.

FENCING

A fence serves a similar purpose to that of a wall but need not necessarily take the form of a solid barrier. The composition and structure of urban and rural environments differ in many ways; it is important therefore that the design of a fence and the materials used in its construction should be in harmony with the surroundings in which the structure is located. Although functional needs are likely to dictate the nature of the fence selected, the economics of installation and maintenance costs inevitably play a major role in determining its quality and durability.

Some types of fencing are fabricated, others constructed in-situ, but all should be erected by skilled workmen in an efficient manner. Strict attention must be paid to the siting of a fence which is set along the line of demarcation between two properties to ensure that no encroachment is made on either side. It is usual practice with boundary fences to fix the best side (fair face) showing outwards from the site and the posts visible from within it. On sloping ground the fencing should follow the contours.

Timber, metal and concrete provide the materials for the three main groups of fencing described below; there are also a few special types of structure which, for convenience, are grouped here under the heading of 'Miscellaneous'. British Standard references are given where applicable.

Timber fencing

The principal woods used for the construction of timber fencing are oak (English and European), larch, western red cedar and sweet chestnut. The use of other kinds depends to some extent upon their availability and suitability for such work and may include spruce, Douglas fir, Scots pine, ash, elm, beech, hornbeam, lime, etc. Care should be taken to see that the same species is used throughout the construction of a fence so that differences of shrinkage do not occur. In all cases the bark must be stripped off to prevent premature decay of the wood. Most of the timber used for fencing requires some form of protective treatment (see below). It is particularly important that the ends of timber posts set in the ground should be given preservative treatment. In some fencing (e.g. close-boarded), concrete posts may be used in lieu of timber but the size of hole (on plan) for both types should be as small as possible and of adequate depth.

Close-boarded fences: BS 1722 : Part 5 : 1972 (Fig.26a)
Although prefabricated panels are obtainable in stock sizes this type of fence is generally constructed in-situ. Recommendations for oak pale fencing are also included in BS 1722 : Part 5 which specifies dimensions for the various components and the suggested uses for the various heights of fence.

Components include the following (those items marked with an asterisk are optional) :

Posts. Timber or reinforced concrete, mortised to receive rails, spaced not more than 2·74 m apart.

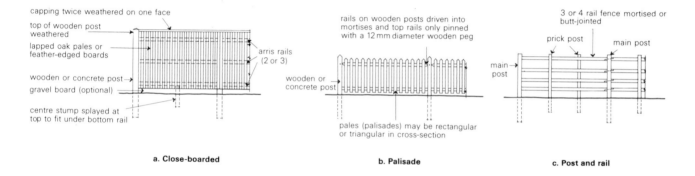

a. Close-boarded
b. Palisade
c. Post and rail

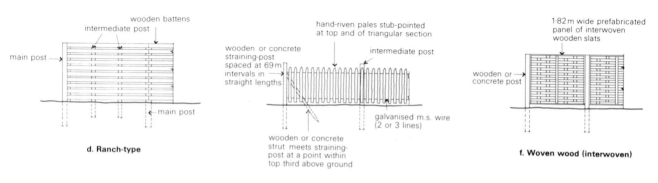

d. Ranch-type
e. Cleft-chestnut pale
f. Woven wood (interwoven)

Fig. 26   Various types of timber fencing

Arris rails. Two or three (depending upon height), triangular (sometimes rectangular) section.

Pales or boards. Feather-edged boards, 100 mm wide, are lapped 38 mm and secured to the arris rails (and counter-rail, if any). Pales are of oak, 90 mm wide and lapped 19 mm.

*Gravel boards. Timber or reinforced concrete secured each end to either wooden or angle cleats (as applicable).

*Capping. Twice-weathered on one face and secured to a counter-rail onto which boards or pales are also nailed.

*Barbed wire (to BS 4102:1971). Used in conjunction with 1·82 m high fences. One, two or three lines are supported on an extension arm bolted onto each post. A single line may be secured direct onto the tops of posts.

Palisade fences: BS 1722:Part 6:1972 (Fig.26b)
The construction and function of this type of fencing is similar to that of the close-boarded but the pales are more widely spaced. These may be either rectangular or triangular in section and the tops pointed, cut either square or to a sweep, as desired. Triangular palisades must be weathered. Gravel boards and capping are not included in the design.

Post and rail fences: BS 1722:Part 7:1972 (Fig.26c)
An agricultural type of fence, of which there are two versions: mortised and nailed. In the former type the rails are fitted into mortised posts and also nailed to prick posts. The rails in nailed fences are butt-jointed on the centre of each post. Heights are the same for both types of fence.

Posts. Main posts may be either sawn or half-round, spaced at intervals of 1·82 m for nailed fences and 2·89 m for the mortised type.

Prick posts are used in mortised fences only, positioned one to each bay. They may be either sawn or cleft, tapered if desired, and pointed to facilitate driving into the ground.

Rails. These are rectangular sawn, half-round or cleft.

A cheaper version of this type of fencing is sometimes adopted for paddock enclosures. Round or half-round posts are used with two rows of half-round rails secured to them.

Ranch-type fences (Fig.26d)
Materials and construction for this type of fence, which has many variations, should generally follow the recommendations for timber fences in BS 1722. Horizontal boards spaced at regular intervals are secured to posts set not more than 2·74 m apart. Heights of fences are usually 1·37–1·82 m.

Cleft-chestnut pale: BS 1722 : Part 4 : 1972 (Fig.26e)
This simple rural type of fence is sometimes adopted for housing layouts and other urban locations. The level of the top of the fence follows that of the contours.

Posts. These consist of three different types and may be of sweet chestnut or reinforced concrete.

(i) *Straining posts* are fixed at every corner and change in direction and at each end of the fence. On straight runs the posts are set at intervals not exceeding 68 m or less than 45 m. The cross-section of each concrete post must be the same throughout its length. Natural round (not cleft) wooden posts may be pointed at the thicker end for driving into the ground.

(ii) *Intermediate posts* are spaced at intervals of not more than 2·28 m (wooden) or 2·74 m (concrete).

(iii) *Struts* are fitted to the straining posts in the direction of the line of fencing secured to them.

Pales. These should be hand-riven from reasonably straight lengths of sweet chestnut, held in position with two or three lines of mild steel wire (to BS 4102 : 1971).

Wire. Each line of wiring consists of four wires twisted together between the pales and secured to the posts. Line, stirrup and barbed wires should be in accordance with the requirements set out in BS 4102 : 1971.

A similar type of fence (chestnut spile) is constructed with cleft spiles which are driven direct into the ground, spaced so that there are six spiles to each metre length. The spiles are connected by either one or two lines of galvanised wire twisted around each spile alternately clockwise and anticlockwise. Although this is a stronger form of construction than that of cleft-chestnut pale fencing the durability of both types depends to a certain extent upon the quality and gauge of the wire employed.

Woven wood (interwoven) fences: BS 1722 : Part 11 : 1972 (Fig.26f)
The life-span of this fencing is dependent upon the quality of the materials used for the slats. Oak and cedar require very little regular maintenance and should give a reasonable length of service, but those of softwood tend to become brittle unless given regular preservative treatment.

The slats are interwoven and fabricated into framed panels which are secured to posts.

Posts. Rectangular reinforced concrete or timber (oak, larch, sweet chestnut, western red cedar or Scots pine) are set not more than 1·82 m apart.

Panels. Standard-size framed interwoven slats. Maximum size 1·82 × 1·82 m.

Trellis fences
Although this type of fencing is not covered by a British Standard specification the materials and workmanship used in its construction should be generally in accordance with the recommendations set out in BS 1722 : Part 11 : 1972. Standard-sized panels, up to 1·82 × 1·82 m, are fabricated with horizontal and vertical laths (not less than 25 × 19 mm) to form a mesh, consisting of squares approximately 114 × 114 mm, which is set within a frame in a similar manner to that employed for woven wood fences; the method of erection is also the same.

Metal fencing*

There are two basic forms of metal fencing, each requiring a different method of erection.

The first comprises line wires or wire mesh strained between each pair of supports. Strained wire, woven wire, chain-link and anti-intruder chain-link fall into this category.

*See also Lightning protection : metal fences, Chapter 5.

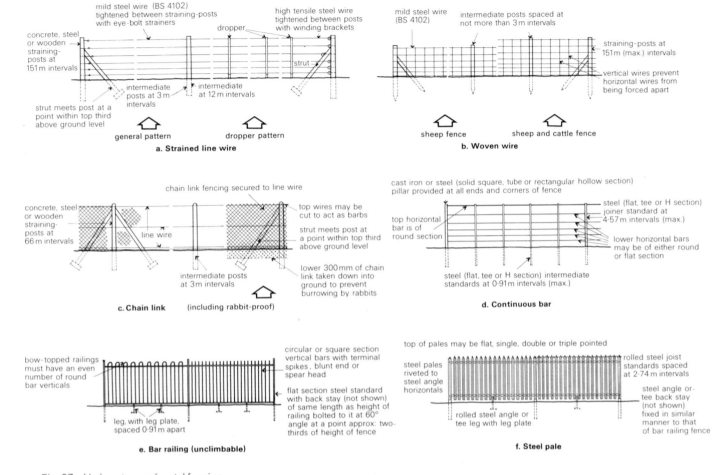

Fig. 27   Various types of metal fencing

The second is composed of steel bars (horizontal or vertical) or pales which are fabricated in panels and secured to metal supports. Examples are continuous bar, unclimbable fences (vertical bars) and steel palings. The metal employed in this group is either mild steel (BS 4360 : 1972) or wrought iron and requires the application of some form of protective treatment, preferably after erection.

Strained line wire fences: BS 1722 : Part 3 : 1973 (Fig.27a) There are several variations of this type of rural fence but the British Standard specifies four main classes, all very similar in their basic design :

(i) *General pattern*. Line wires supported on straining and intermediate posts which may be of concrete, steel or wood.

(ii) *Dropper pattern*. The intermediate posts are spaced further apart and droppers used between posts to correct the spacing of the wires (types of dropper vary, according to choice).

(iii) *Scottish pattern*. Of similar design to that of the general pattern, but wooden posts are used. In addition to straining and intermediate posts, stobs are employed as support for the strained wires.

(iv) *Scottish dropper*. This follows the Scottish pattern except that the stobs are spaced further apart and droppers are also provided.

The height of the fence ranges between 0·83–1·37 m and the number of wires (3–8) is related to the fence height. Line wire (to BS 4102:1971) may be either mild steel or high tensile (carbon) steel.

Posts. Straining posts in the general and dropper patterns are positioned at all ends, corners, changes in direction and level and also at intervals of not more than 151 m on straight lengths. In the Scottish types the spacing on the straight runs is reduced to 137 m.

Struts are fitted to all straining posts in the direction of the fencing secured to them.

Intermediate posts are positioned at maximum intervals of 3 m in the general pattern and 12 m in the dropper pattern.

Wooden stobs are employed in the Scottish versions of this type of fencing; spacing is at 2·75 m but in the Scottish dropper this is increased to 7·30 m intervals.

Droppers. These are used to permit wider spacing of the intermediate posts. Distances between two droppers or a dropper and a post should not exceed 3 m (1·82 m in the Scottish dropper).

Woven wire fences: BS 1722:Part 2:1973 (Fig.27b)
This agricultural fence, used for enclosing farm stock, ranges in height from 0·76 to 1·14 m. Vertical and horizontal wires form a rectangular mesh whose horizontal spacing diminishes in depth towards the bottom of the fence. Small animals are prevented, therefore, from getting through it. Wires of a heavier gauge (to BS 4102:1971) are used at the top and bottom of the fence to provide additional rigidity and strength.

Posts. Wood, concrete or steel may be specified. Straining posts are positioned at all ends, corners, changes in direction and level and on straight lengths, at intervals of not more than 151 m.

Intermediate posts are spaced no more than 3 m apart.

Chain-link fences: BS 1722:Part 1:1972 (Fig.27c)
A comparatively cheap form of fencing which provides a better barrier than that of line wires and is fairly simple and speedy to erect.

Posts. Steel, concrete or wood (specified in Appendix B of BS 1722:Part 1) may be employed.

Straining posts are erected at all ends, corners, changes in direction and level and at 69 m (maximum) intervals on straight lengths. Struts are similar to those used in strained wire fencing.

Intermediate posts are erected at not more than 3 m intervals.

Wire. Three galvanised or plastic-coated line wires are provided (except for the 0·91 m high fence), equally spaced apart and secured to each post. All wire must comply with BS 4102:1971.

Chain-link. The fencing is strained between each pair of straining posts and secured thereto. In addition, it is fastened at short intervals to each line wire. Where there is risk of corrosion aluminium wire may be used (but not for line wires), otherwise the chain-link should be either galvanised (to BS 443:1969) or plastic-coated.

Hexagonal mesh wire is similar in manufacture to chain-link but does not compare in strength or durability. It is sometimes used as a cheap substitute for chain-link in the erection of tennis court fencing.

Rabbit-proof fences (Fig.27c)
Although the materials employed are the same as those described above, the design of the fence is slightly different. A trench 230 mm wide and at least 150 mm deep is excavated in which not less than 150 mm of the bottom of the chain-link is buried so that rabbits are prevented from burrowing under the fence. Erection is similar to that of ordinary chain-link fencing, but a straining wire is positioned above the top level of fencing which is secured to it with tying wire. This prevents sagging of the chain-link and so discourages the rabbits from jumping or climbing over slack fencing.

Anti-intruder chain-link: BS 1722:Part 10:1972
The design and erection of this type of fence is similar in principle to that of ordinary chain-link but it is much more robust in construction and approximately 2·4 m in height, with additional security provided by the use of extension arms and barbed wire.

Posts. Concrete or steel posts are specified. Straining posts are provided at all ends, corners and changes in direction or level and positioned so that, as far as possible, no angle of less than 130° is formed. Posts are also provided at intervals of not more than 66 m on straight lengths of fencing. Struts are fixed to all straining posts in the direction of the line of fencing. Intermediate posts are erected at intervals of 3 m (maximum).

Wire. Four line wires are spaced equally (the top wire being doubled) and secured to each post.

Chain-link. Heavy-grade galvanised or plastic-coated wire with a mesh size of 50 mm is strained between and secured to each pair of straining posts. One top line of wire is threaded through the adjacent row of meshes and the fencing is also secured at short intervals to the line wires.

The bottom 300 mm of the fencing may be buried vertically in the ground or 'hair-pin' staples threaded through the bottom row of mesh at short intervals and grouted 150 mm in a hard formation. Alternatively, a continuous concrete sill may be constructed level with the ground surface and 25 mm below the bottom of the fencing and 'hair-pin' staples provided as already described.

Continuous bar: BS 1722 : Part 8 : 1966 (Fig.27d)
This simple type of fence, ranging in height from 1·06 m to 1·37 m, is much used in rural areas and may be constructed of mild steel (BS 4360 : 1972), wrought iron or cast iron (BS 1452 : 1961). The fencing is fabricated in lengths of 4·57 m, employing vertical standards and metal bars or rods. Hurdles, for use as temporary enclosures, are manufactured of similar design, generally in 1·82 m bays.

Pillars. These are set at each end of the fence and at all changes in direction. If manufactured of mild steel the section may be solid square (BS 4 : Part 1 : 1972), hollow (BS 4 : Part 2 : 1969) or tubular (BS 1775 : 1964).

Standards. The choice may be made from three types of metal section : flat, T or H ; these are spaced at 900 mm centres and driven into the ground not less than 450 mm (or 300 mm if a flat metal section with pronged feet is specified). T or H sections may require wing plates, depending upon the fence height. A flat section should be provided with transverse bars.

Joiner standards are necessary at intervals of not more than 4·57 m.

Bars. The top is always of round cross-section but the lower bars may be either round or flat, their spacing being dependent upon the fence height. Round bars are fitted into ferrules or sockets where they meet joiner standards and connected to intermediate standards by means of grub screws or rivets. Steel wedges are used to secure flat bars, except at joiner standards where overlapping should be employed.

Bar railing (unclimbable) fences (Fig.27e)
The purpose of this robust type of fence, whose height ranges from 1·21 to 2·13 m, is to deter intruders. Mild steel (BS 4360 : 1972) or wrought iron is used in its fabrication. BS 1722 : Part 9 : 1963 deals with this type of fencing.

Standards. These may be of flat, square or round section and spaced at intervals of not more than 2·75 m, driven into the ground to a depth of 530–600 mm (according to the height of the fence). If the standards are set in concrete they should be fitted with 200–250 mm square footplates.

Stays. The length of each stay should be the same as that of the railing, fixed at an angle of 60° to the horizontal and bolted into each standard at a point approximately two-thirds above ground level. The cross-sectional area of the stay, if flat, must be equal to that of the vertical railing.

Legs. Spacing of legs should be at 900 mm intervals and 900 mm from each standard, securely fixed to the lower horizontal member. Leg (or keeper) plates must also be provided.

Horizontals. The sizes of horizontal members must correspond with the sectional area of the vertical members in order to accommodate them.

Railings. The vertical bars forming the railings may be of either round or square section, the latter being set square or with the angle to view, as desired. The tops of the bars are normally pointed or blunt-ended ; alternatively, round bars may be bow-topped, in which case it is necessary to have an even number of verticals. Spacing of the bars depends upon the type of section employed and the number set in a panel.

Steel pale fencing (Fig.27f)
Predominantly employed as a security barrier for industrial and similar establishments, this type of fence is usually 1·52–2·44 m in height. Although there are a number of variations in its design none of them is covered by the requirements of a British Standard Specification.

Standards. Rolled steel joists, provided with a base plate, are set in concrete at intervals, depending upon the design and height of fencing.

Horizontals. Two rolled steel angles are riveted or welded to the standards, positioned so that the steel pales project 230–380 mm above the level of the top horizontal and 150–230 mm below that of the bottom one.

Pales. The section of the pales varies according to the design and manufacture of the fence; they may be corrugated, half-round or an angle, with flat or split tops. Each pale is riveted to the two horizontals; the number of pales to each panel is usually 17–23, according to the design adopted.

Decorative wrought iron fencing

There are numerous designs on the market purporting to be manufactured from wrought iron but, in fact, of cast iron (grey iron) which, being brittle, tends to break easily. Genuine wrought iron (malleable iron), although similar in appearance, weight and feel to cast iron, is made from the harder varieties of pig iron by extracting the carbon and other unwanted elements; generally, there is less than 0·15 per cent of carbon present in good quality wrought iron.

Since wrought iron oxidises fairly rapidly if exposed to a damp atmosphere it is usually japanned (see below) while hot. Where such treatment cannot be carried out, the metal should be given a protective coating prior to fixing and then a finishing coat applied immediately after erection in position.

Concrete fencing

The big advantage of concrete fencing is that it has a long life and requires no maintenance. Unfortunately its lack of weathering qualities prevents it from blending into its surroundings; its siting, therefore, must be chosen with care. Two types of concrete fence are manufactured: post-and-panel and palisading (an imitation of the timber version). Concrete posts are used in many other forms of fencing.

Fig. 28   Miscellaneous types of fencing

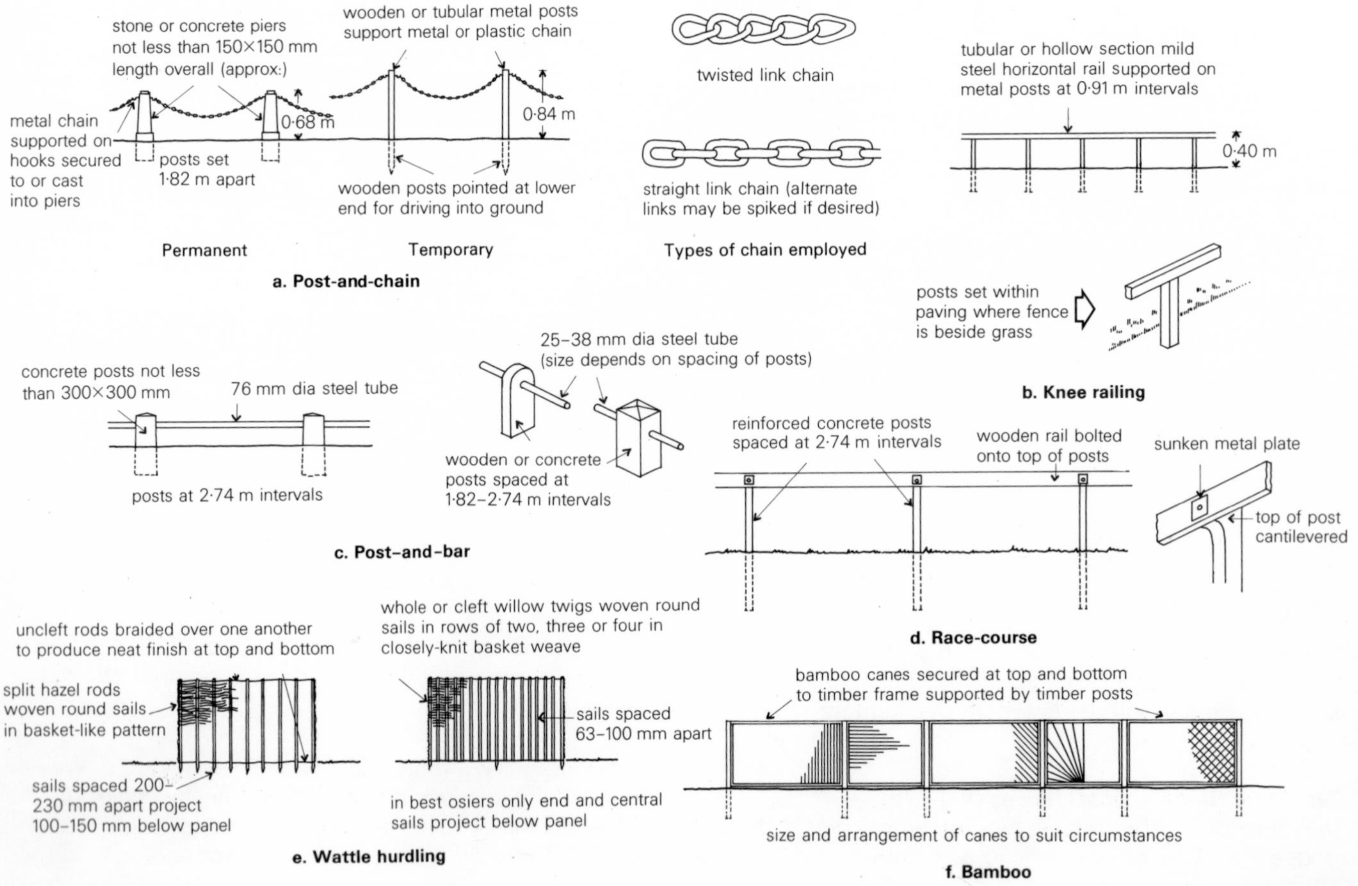

stone or concrete piers not less than 150×150 mm length overall (approx.)

wooden or tubular metal posts support metal or plastic chain

metal chain supported on hooks secured to or cast into piers

0·68 m

posts set 1·82 m apart

0·84 m

wooden posts pointed at lower end for driving into ground

Permanent   Temporary

a. Post-and-chain

twisted link chain

straight link chain (alternate links may be spiked if desired)

Types of chain employed

tubular or hollow section mild steel horizontal rail supported on metal posts at 0·91 m intervals

0·40 m

posts set within paving where fence is beside grass

b. Knee railing

concrete posts not less than 300×300 mm

76 mm dia steel tube

posts at 2·74 m intervals

25–38 mm dia steel tube (size depends on spacing of posts)

wooden or concrete posts spaced at 1·82–2·74 m intervals

c. Post–and–bar

reinforced concrete posts spaced at 2·74 m intervals

wooden rail bolted onto top of posts

sunken metal plate

top of post cantilevered

d. Race-course

uncleft rods braided over one another to produce neat finish at top and bottom

split hazel rods woven round sails in basket-like pattern

sails spaced 200–230 mm apart project 100–150 mm below panel

whole or cleft willow twigs woven round sails in rows of two, three or four in closely-knit basket weave

sails spaced 63–100 mm apart

in best osiers only end and central sails project below panel

e. Wattle hurdling

bamboo canes secured at top and bottom to timber frame supported by timber posts

size and arrangement of canes to suit circumstances

f. Bamboo

Post-and-panel fences

The design is based on the slotted post-and-panel principle, providing a solid type of barrier more suited to the needs of an industrial estate than the rural environment. No British Standard exists for this type of fence but its components should meet the requirements laid down in the relevant British Standard for reinforced concrete work.

Posts. Intermediate posts should be not less than 125×125 mm, grooved on two opposite sides to receive concrete panels, set into the ground to a depth of 600–750 mm, according to their height, and surrounded with concrete. Spacing is at 1·82 m centres. Corner, end and gate posts should be slightly larger in sectional area.

Panels. To facilitate handling, the depth of each panel is usually not more than 300 mm. Thickness should be not less than 38 mm, each panel being reinforced with mild steel bars of 6 mm diameter. Vertical bars are spaced at 450 mm centres and at each end of the panel; a horizontal bar is provided at the top and bottom. The horizontal junction between two panels is usually in the form of a rebate or a tongue-and-groove joint. A butt joint pointed in mortar is not very satisfactory since the joints are difficult to conceal; it is better, therefore, to emphasise them. Although the panels should be bedded in the posts in mortar it is not necessary to bed the horizontal joint between each panel.

Coping. A reinforced concrete coping set on top of the panel fencing both provides a finish and acts as protection against rain running down the panels from the top. It also gives additional strength to the top panel against the pressure of ladders or other objects placed against the fence.

Palisading or picket fencing

The basic design of this fence is similar to that of timber palisading; its height seldom exceeds 900 mm. Prefabricated panels, usually 900 mm wide, are slotted into rebated posts or fixed by means of dowels.

Intermediate posts should be not less than 76×76 mm and corner and end posts 100×100 mm, set into the ground to a depth of 450 mm and 600 mm respectively.

Miscellaneous types of fencing

Special types of fence which do not readily fit into the previous categories are described below.

Post-and-chain fences (Fig.28a)

This type of fencing is, in reality, little more than a line of demarcation and rarely exceeds 900 mm in height. Concrete or natural stone posts, of fairly substantial cross-sectional area in relation to their height, are usually positioned at 1·82 m centres. Galvanised hooks or eyes are provided to which the chain is secured.

Knee railing (Fig.28b)

Serving a similar purpose to the post-and-chain, this fencing is often set at the edge of grass or planting beds on housing estates to discourage pedestrians from straying from a defined path. Its height rarely exceeds 460 mm. A tubular or square section m.s. horizontal bar is welded onto m.s. posts set in concrete at 900 mm intervals. If designed to protect turf, the railing should be set in the adjacent paving to facilitate easy mowing of the grass.

Post-and-bar fences (Fig.28c)

This French crash-type barrier consists of 300×300 mm concrete posts 460 mm high, to which is secured a 76 mm diameter steel tube set 380 mm above ground level. Less robust versions of this design are used as pedestrian barriers on housing estates.

The Road Research Laboratory has patented a design (No.1141012) for a crash barrier which comprises a tensioned corrugated beam secured to Z-section steel posts.

Race-course fences (Fig.28d)

This is similar in principle to the previous fence, comprising stout concrete posts, not less than 125×100 mm, spaced at 2·75 m intervals and set 300 mm into the ground, surrounded by not less than 75 mm of concrete to within 230 mm of ground level. Tops of posts are offset on the course (inner) side of the fence and a hole formed to accommodate cup-headed bolts. A stout timber rail is bolted and clamped to the inner side of each post top by means of a metal plate, set flush with the rail, and a lighter rail is secured by the same bolt on the outer side. All arrises must be rounded off to prevent injury to the horses' legs.

Wattle hurdling (Fig.28e)

Although not a robust type of fence, wattle hurdles provide a useful screen which allows the wind to filter through. Two types are produced: one is made from hazel, the other from willow rods. Both are made in panels 1·82 m long and in varying heights, up to 1·82 m.

Hazel hurdles. Uprights (sails) approximately 25 mm in diameter are spaced 200–230 mm apart and split hazel rods of similar diameter closely woven in and out of the sails to produce a neatly interwoven (wreathed) panel of the required height. The sails themselves should project 100–150 mm below the level of the panel. To give a neat appearance, the top and bottom of the panel are of uncleft rods which are braided (ethered) over one another.

Osier hurdles (*willow wattle*). Two variations of this particular hurdle are available: willow hurdle and what is generally referred to as 'best osier' hurdle; the difference lies mainly in their finish.

Whole or cleft willow twigs are used for willow hurdles and woven round the sails (slewed) in rows of two, three or four together, giving a closely knit, basket-like finish. The sails are more closely spaced than those in hazel hurdles, usually 63–100 mm apart. In the best osier hurdle only the end and central sails project beyond the bottom of the panel itself, giving a much neater appear-ance. Intermediate sails are formed by setting two willow rods vertically side by side.

Bamboo screens (Fig.28f)
Bamboo canes may be used either in their natural state or split vertically and secured together as in cleft chestnut fencing, using galvanised wire, or secured to fabricated timber frames by means of staples. The screens may be of any size compatible with that of the canes used. Generally this type of construction is more suited to the smaller screen.

Canes are graded into the following lengths:

Thin and medium	0·30–2·42 m
Stout and extra stout	0·30–3·00 m

If the canes are set in a fabricated panel the construction may be akin to that adopted for interwoven timber panels and erection is similar. Where the canes are to be fixed in-situ they should be secured to rails supported by posts, as in close-boarded fencing, the canes being used in lieu of pales.

Fig. 29 Gates

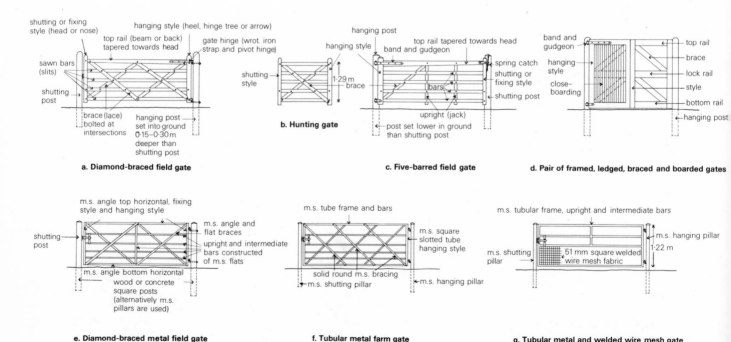

a. Diamond-braced field gate

b. Hunting gate

c. Five-barred field gate

d. Pair of framed, ledged, braced and boarded gates

e. Diamond-braced metal field gate

f. Tubular metal farm gate

g. Tubular metal and welded wire mesh gate

GATES AND THEIR ACCESSORIES

Where an enclosure is formed it is necessary to provide a means of access. The most commonly employed movable type of barrier is a gate, since it is simple in operation and requires very little maintenance. Sizes and designs vary; timber and metal are the principal materials employed in the construction. The choice should reflect the design and materials of the structural barrier within which the gate is set to ensure close harmony with its surroundings (Fig.29).

A gate must be light but sufficiently robust in construction to fulfil its function; it should hang well and close easily. Fastening devices for holding the gate open are important: the mechanism selected should be strong enough to bear not only the weight of the gate itself but also the wind force acting upon it (Fig.30c).

There are a number of variations on the design of a field gate; 3 m is the most economical width and 3·65 m is generally considered to be the maximum practical size for timber gates. Metal field gates up to 4·57 m wide, of either tubular or angle section, are sometimes specified where it is necessary to provide access for large agricultural machines. Recommendations for both timber and metal field gates are set out in BS 3470:1962; recommendations for domestic front entrance gates are contained in BS 4092: 1966.

Hanging a gate

A gate is hung between two pillars which may either form a structural part of the barrier within which the gate is set or be two free-standing independent units. The hanging pillars may be of any structurally sound material which is capable of supporting both the weight and action of the gate, the stress of which is transmitted via the hanging device by which the gate is secured.

Where timber posts are specified for hanging a field gate their cross-section should be not less than 175×175 mm, or 200 mm diameter where a circular post is used. Metal hanging pillars for the same purpose may be of either cast iron or mild steel, the cross-sectional sizes depending upon the dimensions and weight of the gate. Reference should be made to BS 3470:1962.

Ironmongery and accessories for gates

Basically, any single item of gate ironmongery serves one of the following functions:

(i)   A means of securing to allow movement to take place (e.g. hinge).
(ii) A facility providing the ability to actuate such movement (e.g. handle).
(iii) A restriction temporarily to prevent movement from taking place (e.g. bolt, lock).

Although the range of ironmongery for external use is somewhat limited compared with that available for internal applications, it is important that the quality and type of each item selected should be considered in relation to both capital outlay and maintenance costs. BS 1494:Part 2: 1967 (Section 2) and BS 1331:1954 (Schedule 1) contain recommendations for door and gate equipment.

Hinges (Fig.30a)
The type of hinge specified depends upon the size and weight of the gate it has to support. Recommendations for various types of hinge used in general building work are given in BS 1227:Part 1A:1967. Three types are most commonly in use:

Butt hinge. The most popular type of hinge in general use; its length exceeds its overall width. Sometimes a 'stop butt hinge' is used where it is necessary to limit the extent of opening. Only lightweight small gates should be fitted with butt hinges.

Tee hinge. So named because it takes the form of a letter T, this type is suitable mainly for ledged and braced doors and gates. Of the two versions available, the heavier is known as the 'weighty Scotch tee', and the lighter as the 'London tee'.

A variation of the tee hinge has both flaps alike and shaped like the tail of the tee; this is known as a 'strap hinge'. Cranked strap hinges are also manufactured.

Hook and band. Also known as a 'hook and rides' or 'coach house' hinge, this type is usually specified for the heavier type of gate. It consists of a bar or strap (screwed to the gate itself) with an eye which fits over a hinge pin carried by a hook. The latter may be built in, driven in or screwed onto the supporting pillar according to the nature of the material used in the construction.

In addition to these three forms there are other devices serving a similar function to that of the conventional hinge. These include:

Collinge gate hinge. Similar in principle to the hook and band, this consists of a strap (fixed to the gate) on the end

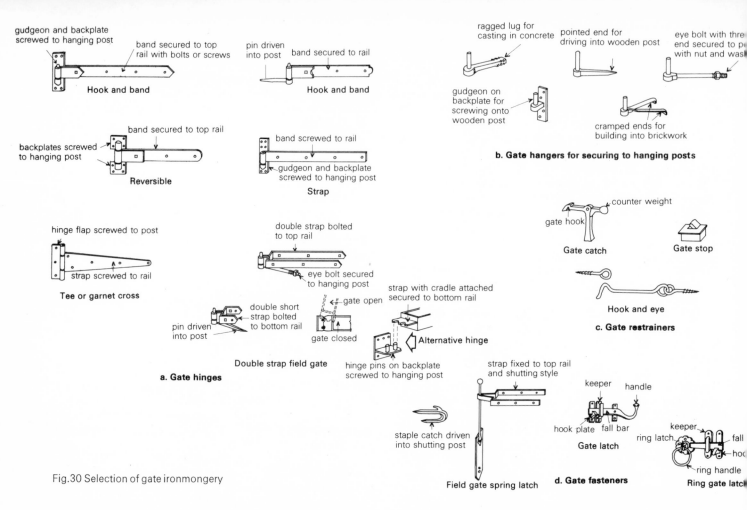

Fig.30 Selection of gate ironmongery

of which is a ball. The bracket (fixed to the post or pier) incorporates a cup that serves as a seating for the ball so that together they form a spherical joint. The particular advantage of this type of hinge is that it permits smooth action in operating the gate even where the fixing may not be perfectly true.

Field gate hinge. Also similar to the hook and band, except that the hinge member is usually made as a double strap so that it fits on both sides of the gate.

Self-closing hinge with cradle. Although not a hinge in the strict sense of the word, this device is sometimes fitted at the bottom of a gate instead of a conventional hinge. When the gate is pushed open the two pins cause it to tilt so that when no pressure is exerted on the gate (to open it) the action of gravity causes it to close.

Gate runner. Not a hinge but a roller mounted within a bracket which is fixed to the bottom of the gate. It acts as both a support and a guide for large heavy gates, running along a steel quadrant or semicircular track incorporated in the paved surface.

Handles

Many types of handle are produced, and even more variations. The three following are probably the most suitable types for use with gates.

Drop ring handle. Known also as a 'closing ring' handle. Where the ring handle is set flush with the face of a door or gate it is referred to as a 'flush ring' handle.

Latch handle. In general terms this description is applied to any knob or handle which operates a latch. More specifically it is used to describe a pull handle mounted on a back-plate with a thumb bit and lift-up lever which operates a latch bar.

Knob. Usually, though not necessarily, spherical in shape so that it is readily gripped for turning or pulling. It is usually attached to a spindle to enable it to operate the spring bolt in a latch or lock. Where the function of the knob is purely that of a door or gate pull (for the purpose of closing it) it is often of a larger size than that normally used and may be fixed to the centre of the door (or gate) and is then referred to as a 'centre door knob'.

Locks, latches and bolts

A lock may be described in general terms as a key-operated mechanism which contains a bolt that forms the fastening device. Two basic forms are available, according to the method of fixing:

Mortise   Set within a hole cut in the gate from the edge of the shutting stile.
Rim   Fixed to the face of the gate.

Technically, the term lock refers to a 'dead lock' in which the 'dead bolt' in the lock is moved in both the locking and unlocking directions by means of a key. The keyhole, which is necessary for any key-operated lock, is often embellished with an 'escutcheon' (a simple metal plate, larger than the keyhole itself, with the shape of the hole pierced in it).

The term 'latch' is used to describe a fastening mechanism which, although having a bolt (not necessarily a 'spring bolt') that is withdrawn by the action of turning or lifting a handle, is not operated by means of a key. A latch and a dead lock are often contained in the same case and a latch fixing may be either mortise or rim. Both locks and latches require striking-plates; these are metal plates (fixed to a jamb) provided with one or more bolt holes into which the spring bolt and (if provided) the dead bolt shoot.

'Bolt' is an abbreviation of the term 'door bolt' and is used to describe a variety of door fastenings containing a sliding part, called the 'shoot', which is set with a barrel casing that forms a guide; a socket or staple is provided to receive the end of the shoot. The section containing the bolt is fixed to the gate and the receiving socket to the jamb.

Handing of locks and fasteners

Gates may be hinged on the left or right hand and open inwards or outwards. The gate fittings must therefore be made to suit. Some locks and latches are double-hand reversible or otherwise adaptable. In the building industry locks and door furniture are specified as left- or right-handed, the lock being determined by the direction in which the bolt shoots, viewed from the inside face (or by the hand used to open the door from the inside).

This method of describing the handing of a door is not always satisfactory since there are situations where it may be impossible to adopt this kind of description, particularly in the case of gates. In this instance the clock method is adopted, the two faces of the gate being referred to as the 'leading face' and the 'trailing face'. The face on which the knuckles of the hinges are visible when the gate is shut is the leading face. A gate may open clockwise or anticlockwise; the specification should state that the lock is to be fixed on the leading face of the gate opening clockwise (or vice versa, as applicable).

STEPS, RAMPS AND PERRONS

Changes in level of pedestrian routes require a relatively easy means of negotiation; this may be achieved by incorporating steps, perrons or ramps. Although perrons and ramps provide a gentler ascent, they occupy more space than steps.

Steps

Pedestrians must be able easily to identify changes in level so that the presence of steps is unlikely to cause surprise and may be readily anticipated. For this reason the use of a single step is dangerous unless sited in an obviously familiar position (e.g. the kerb adjacent to a carriageway). Where the difference in level is such as to warrant the equivalent of only one step it is better to provide a short ramp or a flight of two or, preferably, three quite shallow steps.

The horizontal distance between the faces of two consecutive risers is referred to as the 'going' or 'run' of a step and the horizontal distance between the face of the bottom riser and that of the top riser is termed the 'going' of a flight, indicating the ease with which the steps may be negotiated. The inviting appearance of a shallow flight does not necessarily imply that it is comfortable to use. Ideally, external public staircases should be designed with tread widths of not less than 300 mm and risers 90–150 mm high. Long flights are to be discouraged and no more than twelve steps should form a single flight. Not everyone

Plate 7 (below)
Civic design : formal layout of steps and stepping stones,
King's Square redevelopment, Gloucester (Civic Trust
Award, 1972). *Photo: City Architect, Gloucester.*

Plate 8 (opposite)
Informal steps constructed of exposed aggregate slabs
(*Waschbeton*) : *Pflanzen und Blumen* display, Hamburg.
Note the contrast of foliage texture adjacent.
Photo: S. W. Newbury.

is able-bodied; generous provision should therefore be made for landings between flights, and handrails also included.

Any of the following materials or a combination of two or more may be used, the choice depending upon the character of the layout.

Stone

A hard durable stone having a non-slip surface should be used and may be in one of the forms described below:

Rectangular. This is the strongest form, consisting of solid rectangular blocks, the front bottom edge of one step rebated and supported on the top back edge of the one below.

Spandril. A rectangular block of stone is sawn so that it provides two spandril steps, triangular in cross-section, (except the ends where built into a wall). The underside (soffit) of the flight may be either flush, broken or moulded, with a splayed rebated joint formed between each step. The splay should be at least 50 mm for steps not exceeding 1·22 m in width and increased by 13 mm for every additional 300 mm in width.

Built-up. Relatively thin sawn slabs are employed with the treads often set on a concrete backing. Where the treads are supported only at each end and no backing is provided their minimum thickness should be 50 mm, increased by 13 mm for every additional 300 mm of unsupported length beyond 900 mm to prevent fractures. Sometimes brick is substituted for the stone risers.

Skeleton. Horizontal stone slabs built into a supporting wall serve as cantilevered treads.

Carved-out. In situations where the rugged nature of the terrain calls for such treatment, steps may be carved in-situ from solid natural rock, the exact nature of the design depending upon the mason's skill.

Reinforced concrete

The steps may be of almost any shape or size consistent with the design principles of reinforced concrete. Often it is used as a backing to other materials, such as stone or brick.

Steel

Steel is used as a supporting framework for other structures incorporating steps. Although relatively expensive, stainless steel is increasingly specified for outdoor use. Plastic-coated steel is another product that has opened up new fields of design.

Timber

Economical construction is readily achieved with the use of timber which, according to the choice of wood, may be for either temporary or permanent use. Tables 20–23 set out various kinds of wood suitable for outdoor situations and their uses.

Earth

By far the cheapest flight of steps may be constructed with the simplest of materials: earth and timber. Soil with a high gravel content or, alternatively, in-situ soil, with a small amount of aggregate mixed in it, is well compacted to form the treads which are retained in position by timber boards acting as risers. A layer of crushed stone or shingle may be rolled into the surface to give a neater finish.

Ramps

A ramp serves the same purpose as a flight of steps but allows the change in level to be negotiated at a more gentle pace. It is particularly required by persons in wheel-chairs or pushing prams. Ideally, wherever there is a need to construct steps provision for a ramp should also be made nearby.

The principal drawback is the amount of space required, since a gradient of 1:12 is necessary for easy negotiation by wheelchairs and prams (although deprecated, where space is limited a gradient of 1:10 is regarded as the absolute minimum). For short pedestrian ramps a gradient of 1:7 is acceptable. No ramp should be less than 1·05 m wide (preferably ≥1·22 m) or longer than 9 m (6 m is preferred). A ramp over 3·65 m long should be ≥1·35 m wide. In all cases a handrail should be provided.

Surfacing of the ramp should be given particular attention; it is most important that a non-slip finish is selected. Adequate drainage at the bottom of the ramp is essential to prevent ponding in wet weather.

Perrons

Where the difference in level is such as to require a long ramp, this may be planned either as a series of ramps with a flat landing between each or, preferably, in zig-zag form. If, however, the ascent by ramps is likely to prove too steep an incline it may be necessary to adopt a series of long ramped steps, referred to as 'perrons'. Each ramped section should be of gradient not less than 1 : 12 with steps not exceeding 115 mm in height for easy negotiation by those pushing prams. In some cases it may be necessary to introduce several steps between ramps. The nosings of steps should be readily apparent to avoid any possible risk of pedestrians accidentally missing their footing.

GLASSHOUSES AND FRAMES

Modern commercial production under glass calls for a variety of provisions and is a specialised field.

Glasshouses (Fig.31)

Basically, a glasshouse is a framed structure with glass infilling and may be constructed of metal or wood. Metal structures are fabricated in either mild steel or aluminium alloy; although ideal from a design angle, since it enables clear span trusses to be used, there is a risk of condensation problems arising due to the high conductivity of such metals. The most commonly specified timbers are red cedar or deal, the latter requiring some form of protective treatment. Glazing is usually with 680 g glass although a heavier weight (906 g) is sometimes used.

Glasshouse design varies, the principal types being ridge, parabolic and dutch-light; they may be either erected on a foundation at ground level or set on a dwarf wall (thus increasing the effective height of the glasshouse). Usually the dutch-light is built from ground level and is often employed as a temporary structure, so that a grower is able to cover a particular cultivated plot or growing crop for a limited period and then transfer the glasshouse to another plot for a similar purpose.

Commercial glasshouses are specified according to type and width, the length being adapted to suit the required conditions. The sizes shown in Tables 15 and 16 give some idea of the range available and the number of vents required according to the length.

Ventilation is a very important aspect of glasshouse culture and it is essential that adequate provision is made to ensure a healthy crop. Heating, ventilation and irrigation

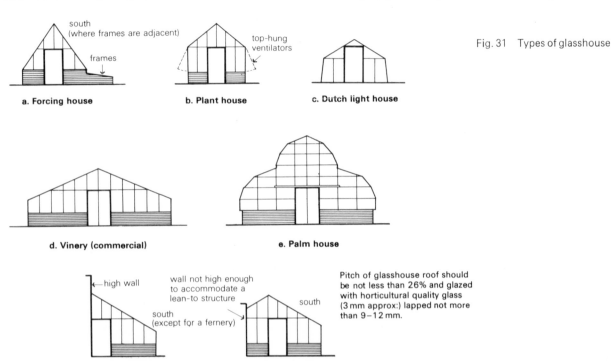

Fig. 31   Types of glasshouse

a. Forcing house

b. Plant house

c. Dutch light house

d. Vinery (commercial)

e. Palm house

f. Lean-to

g. Three-quarter span

Pitch of glasshouse roof should be not less than 26% and glazed with horticultural quality glass (3 mm approx:) lapped not more than 9–12 mm.

of glasshouses has been developed as a precision-controlled process and in commercial crop-growing is operated by remote control.

Table 15
Ridge-type glasshouse sizes

Width (m)	Length (m)	Roof vents (No.)
6·4	9·75	14
	15·85	24
	31·70	48
	41·14	64
	50·60	78
4·4	6·00	8
	9·14	12
	16·45	24
	24·38	36
	30·48	46
3·65	6·00	4
	15·24	12
	30·48	24
3·00	4·57	4
	7·62	6
	15·24	12
	22·86	18
	28·00	22

Table 16
Dutch-light sizes

Width (m)	Length (m)	Roof vents (No.)
3·58	3·35	2
	7·32	4
	9·75	6
	13·72	8
	15·24	9
	30·48	19

Frames

Timber and concrete are the two main materials used in the construction of frames. The difference in height between the back and front of a frame permits maximum use of solar radiation; the back height should be 500–700 mm and the front 180–380 mm lower so that the glass slopes down towards the front of the frame. Frame lights may be set on a sliding track or completely removable. Width of the frame is usually 1–1·5 m, the length being a multiple of approximately the same dimension.

ROCK GARDEN DESIGN AND CONSTRUCTION

Type of rock

Stone is used in the rock garden to represent a natural outcrop, the sedimentary rocks being those most suitable; limestone and sandstone are the principal rocks in this group. The igneous rocks, such as granite, and the metamorphic rocks (e.g. slate) are hard and unsympathetic to plant life and, therefore, not generally recommended for incorporation in rock garden construction.

Limestone
The principal limestones suitable include:

> Westmorland (waterworn)
> Cheddar (Mendip Hills)
> Derbyshire (waterworn)
> Cotswold
> Dorset (or Purbeck)
> Hornton

Limestones contain calcium carbonate which is subject to attack by the acids in areas of atmospheric pollution and therefore should not be employed in or near industrial localities. If ordinary limestone is used in association with magnesian limestone (such as that found east of the Pennines in parts of Yorkshire, Derbyshire and Nottinghamshire) decay of the former is likely to occur where it absorbs magnesium sulphate from the latter. The absorbed salts crystallise, producing an increase in volume where these crystals occur; the resulting pressure just behind the stone's surface causes it to disintegrate. Similarly, decay of sandstone may result if it is used in close association with limestone where calcium sulphate is washed from the limestone onto the sandstone surface.

Sandstone
Sandstones suitable for use in rock garden construction are to be found in the Bunter and Keuper series of the Triassic system, occurring in Warwickshire, Worcestershire, Shropshire, Staffordshire, Cheshire, Lancashire, Cumbria and Dumfriesshire. Invariably such stone is obtained from relatively small quarries producing material for local use. The stone is quarried in squarish or angular blocks, often with weathered faces, but only certain beds are suitable for garden use; the top tend to be too soft and those with ironstone running through them are too hard. Ideally, the rock should possess a certain degree of porosity (to suit plant life) but be impervious to weather.

Stone of this nature is generally found approximately 6 m below the surface.

Unlike other kinds of stone, sandstone does not outcrop but often occurs in the form of banks (Fig.32a). Heather, gorse and fir trees are typical of the plants found growing above it, their roots penetrating into the disintegrated layers. Sandstone is a rock which does not occur in a broken and weathered state (as other types of stone) but crumbles completely, remaining as a sandy layer on top of the harder beds beneath. It is important, therefore, that no soft stone is used in rock garden construction.

Basic design factors

The two most important considerations in rock garden design are those of aspect and the angle at which the site is viewed. Slope, drainage and soil type play an important role and must also be taken into account. A study of the microclimate is essential so that draughty and bleak locations are avoided. Most rock garden plants are sun-worshippers and, ideally, a site having a southern aspect should be sought. A south-east or south-west aspect is preferred to one that faces due south, which may be too hot for many plants. This does not mean that no other aspect is suitable, but east- and north-facing sites tend to restrict the choice of plant material.

The object of good rock garden design is not to simulate a whole mountain range in miniature but to present, as near as possible, a life-size outcrop—or series of outcrops—linked by irregular-shaped areas of stone chippings, alpine lawn, heathers or grass. The area of the site determines the scale of the design and the size of rocks used in its construction. A study of rock outcrops, banks or cliffs is likely to provide useful ideas for creating a main feature, while an examination of the natural grouping of smaller rocks should give some indication of how to lead up to it and round off the structure to present a unified and lifelike composition. A nucleus of big rocks, each weighing not less than 250–500 kg, should be specified and one or two specimens of over 500 kg selected for key positions. The remaining rocks should be of medium size, i.e. 150–200 kg; smaller sizes come freely enough with any load delivered.

Construction

The dimensions of the proposed site should be pegged out and levels adjusted before any preparatory work is done. On a flat site, pleasant undulations may be readily

Fig. 32 Basic construction of rock garden

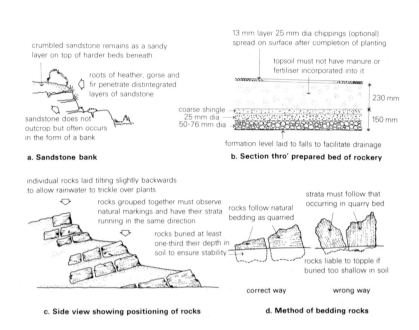

crumbled sandstone remains as a sandy layer on top of harder beds beneath

roots of heather, gorse and fir penetrate distintegrated layers of sandstone

sandstone does not outcrop but often occurs in the form of a bank

a. Sandstone bank

13 mm layer 25 mm dia chippings (optional) spread on surface after completion of planting

topsoil must not have manure or fertiliser incorporated into it

coarse shingle 25 mm dia 50-76 mm dia

230 mm

150 mm

formation level laid to falls to facilitate drainage

b. Section thro' prepared bed of rockery

individual rocks laid tilting slightly backwards to allow rainwater to trickle over plants

rocks grouped together must observe natural markings and have their strata running in the same direction

rocks buried at least one-third their depth in soil to ensure stability

c. Side view showing positioning of rocks

rocks follow natural bedding as quarried

strata must follow that occurring in quarry bed

rocks liable to topple if buried too shallow in soil

correct way   wrong way

d. Method of bedding rocks

achieved by excavating the soil approximately 300 mm to form valleys and paths, and depositing the material to form a carefully contoured mound, the slopes being in the region of 1 : 4 or 5.

Drainage of the soil is essential for alpine plants and must be efficient both on the surface (so that the plants are not surrounded by water) and underground. Soils, such as clay or heavy loam, where there is a risk of the ground holding stagnant water, must be adequately drained and provision made for the surplus water to discharge to an outfall or soakaway.

The site should be excavated to an average depth of 400 mm below surface level and a 150 mm layer of clean hardcore (broken bricks, stones or weathered clinker) spread over the area. The formation level must be provided with a slope to allow any water percolating through the soil to be discharged away from the site itself. All the excavated soil is then replaced on top of the hardcore and graded to finished levels (Fig.32b). Heavy soils should have sand or well-weathered ash mixed into them to open up the texture. No manure or fertiliser should be incorporated since alpine plants do not enjoy a rich soil.

All the rocks incorporated in the structure must be placed so that they look right and set firm so that they cannot be easily dislodged by anyone standing upon them. Generally, the bottom third or half (as applicable) should be buried in the soil to ensure stability (Fig.32d). In grouping rocks, natural markings should be observed and they should be laid so that their strata run in one direction. Ideally, each layer of rock should be of similar thickness, colour and character, individual rocks being positioned so that they tilt slightly backwards to allow rainwater to trickle from the rock over the plants (Fig.32c). This gives less risk of the soil being washed away, while the plants are provided with sufficient water. No small cavities around the rocks should remain unfilled since these provide an ideal home for rodents and undesirable kinds of insect.

The first rocks to be placed should be those commanding the most prominent position in the composition; this includes the largest ones. These 'keystones' set the pace for the whole design, the smaller rocks being built outwards away from them in various directions. The siting of the various sizes of rock is governed by the predetermined height of the finished construction and is related to the quantity of stone employed and the angle at which it merges into the background.

In a newly constructed rock garden the bare surfaces of freshly broken rock may appear harsh. To soften their appearance such rocks may be painted over with manure water or a mixture of milk and water; this encourages the growth of moss or lichens and thereby helps to give a mellowed appearance.

THE USE OF METAL AND TIMBER IN OUTDOOR STRUCTURES

Metal and timber are important constructional materials which play a significant role in the composition of many outdoor structures; their application is wide and varied.

Metals

Classification of metals falls into two main groups: ferrous and non-ferrous.

Ferrous metals
This first group comprises those metals derived from iron ore: cast iron, wrought iron, steel and alloy steels. The crude molten iron resulting from the processing of iron ore is graded according to its carbon content and used in the manufacture of the ferrous metals described below.

Cast iron. The graphite carbon content ranges from 3 to 4·5 per cent. Cast iron, as its description implies, is employed for castings. Grey iron contains the largest quantity of carbon, making it an easy metal to machine. Less carbon is present in mottled cast iron and only a very small quantity in white cast iron; both metals are harder and more brittle than grey iron. Castings of a general nature are manufactured from grey iron, mottled iron being used for the heavier castings.

Although similar to cast iron in appearance, weight and feel, malleable iron does not readily shatter or break in normal use and may be bent cold or welded without the risk of fracture. It is employed for making the more intricate types of casting which need to be machined to fairly fine limits, and for mass-produced items such as manhole covers, frames, gratings, etc.

Wrought iron. A malleable metal, softer than cast iron and easily forged or welded. Its tensile strength is less than that of mild steel which, nowadays, is often used as a substitute. Wrought iron is made from genuine puddled bar. The term 'wrought', as applied to metal, signifies that it has been subjected to one or more processes such as rolling or hammering (as opposed to being cast metal). Production of wrought iron in Britain is very limited.

In addition to its employment for decorative metalwork, wrought iron is still much used in chainmaking because of its ductility and the warning signs (bending and stretching) it reveals before breaking.

Both cast and wrought iron are subject to corrosion if left exposed to the atmosphere and require protective treatment.

Steel. The many kinds of steel produced are classified into two groups: mild (or medium) steel and hard steel; the former group, in its various forms, plays a major role in the construction industry and should conform to the requirements laid down in BS 4360:1972.

Steel is capable of being hardened and tempered but mild steel (whose carbon content is 0·2–0·5 per cent) cannot be tempered.

The addition of chromium or chromium and nickel to manufactured steel (not the iron ore) produces an alloy steel with corrosion-resistant properties. Different grades are produced; the proportions of chromium and nickel included vary according to the class of alloy desired.

Non-ferrous metals

Metals whose main constituents are not derived from iron ore include copper, copper alloys (brass, bronze), nickel, copper-nickel alloys, nickel-chromium alloy, aluminium, aluminium alloys, lead and zinc.

Copper. One of the earliest metals known to man; it is derived from copper pyrites and subjected to metallurgical processes. Copper is a very ductile and malleable material which may be pressed, beaten or spun into practically any shape. It hardens gradually when cold-worked but with annealing it may again be softened.

Because of its high conductivity copper is used by the electrical trades. Its application in the building industry is generally in sheet form. Where used externally it takes on a different appearance, the atmospheric conditions causing a protective green film (verdigris) to form. The slow process of this patina formation may, if desired, be speeded up by the application of a specially prepared solution to the copper surface.

Copper is extensively used as an alloying agent in the production of brasses, bronzes and copper alloys. The copper content of brass varies between 60 and 70 per cent. Small quantities of other elements, such as nickel, lead, tin, etc., may also be added, but the strength of brass is related to the percentage of its zinc content and is graded into three broad groups: alpha; alpha plus beta; beta

brasses. Alpha brasses (0–37 per cent) are ductile, possess a relatively high strength and may be cold-worked. The higher the zinc content, the paler the colour of the brass. The mechanical properties of the alpha plus beta brasses (37–46 per cent) are improved by the addition of small quantities of aluminium, tin, lead, nickel, iron or manganese; the last improves the tensile strength of the brass, which is sometimes wrongly referred to as 'manganese brass'. Beta brasses (46–50 per cent) have good corrosion resistance but are too brittle for use where tensile strength is required. Brasses are extensively used in the ironmongery trades and play an important role in lockmaking. The alpha beta brasses are employed in the manufacture of metal window sections and wood screws.

Bronze is an alloy of copper and tin to which may be added a percentage of lead, nickel, zinc or phosphorus to provide certain qualities in the resultant metal. Gunmetal has a percentage of zinc included in the alloy and is suitable for use in situations where there is a risk of corrosion by sea-water; it is valuable as a bronze for high-class sculpture, plaques, etc. Phosphor bronze, an extremely hard metal, is also ideal for marine situations and is employed in the production of masonry cramps and similar fixing-units.

Copper-nickel alloys contain varying percentages of nickel (a hard white metal which imparts a high strength to any metal with which it is alloyed) and possess a higher tensile strength than that of gunmetal. They also have excellent resistance to corrosion and may be readily worked and shaped to almost any form.

Nickel. Although unsuitable as a structural material, nickel becomes an easily worked metal if other metals, e.g. manganese, are added to it. Monel, the most important nickel-copper alloy (68 per cent nickel, 3 per cent iron and manganese), has a greater strength than the majority of ferrous alloys. Although highly resistant to many types of corrosion it is liable to be attacked by strong sulphuric or nitric acids. Iconel (76 per cent nickel, 15 per cent chromium and the rest mostly iron) is a non-magnetic metal of great strength, able to resist the detrimental effects of many acids and alkalis. Although unaffected by moving sea-water and salt spray, the metal is less resistant than monel to the action of static sea-water but is useful in sulphurous atmospheres. Nickel is used in electroplating processes.

Aluminium. The chief industrial source of aluminium is bauxite. To improve the strength of this soft metal small quantities of other elements are alloyed with it, producing certain characteristics according to the combination employed. Aluminium alloys may be divided into two principal groups: casting and wrought alloys. The uses to which these metals are put are many and various, ranging from roofing sheets, cladding, sectional frames for windows and doors to metal trims, ironmongery, decorative metalwork, etc.

Lead. The principal ores of lead are galena, anglesite and cerusite. The bluish-grey heavy metal, when freshly cut or in its molten state, reveals a bright metallic lustre that quickly oxidises when exposed to air. Its well-known colour is the result of a rapid-forming film (mainly lead carbonate) which acts as a protective covering to the metal. Although it has good corrosion-resistance, lead is subject to attack by certain organic acids, limes and cement; it is also subject to corrosive action by oak and certain other timbers. It is a very flexible material and readily adapted for use in ornamental leadwork; its ductility makes it an ideal material for expansion joints and damp-proof courses.

Lead may be alloyed with copper, nickel, tin, antimony (a very brittle white metal) and arsenic (an extremely brittle, steel-grey metal of brilliant lustre).

Zinc. Blende is the principal source of zinc, a durable and reasonably permanent metal. Although corrosion-resistant in marine atmospheres, it is unsuitable for use in heavily polluted inland locations and must not be placed directly in association with certain other metals, e.g. copper, unless their surface is protected because of the risk of electrochemical action taking place. Zinc, in sheet form, is often used as a substitute for lead or copper.

Protective finishes applied to ferrous metals
In addition to corrosion caused by chemicals within the atmosphere there are other forms, all of them electrolytic in character. The metals shown in Table 17, referred to as the 'electrochemical series', are positioned according to the degree of their corrosion-resistance. Those most susceptible to corrosion are placed at the top of the list; the metals possessing a high corrosion-resistance are at the lower end.

The danger of corrosion when two different metals are in close contact with each other is less in the case of those near together in the series than with metals appearing at opposite ends.

Although positioned high on the list, aluminium and its alloys soon form their own protective film after the initial stages of corrosion have taken place. In the process of anodising the metal is subjected to an electric current which results in a thicker, hard and abrasion-resistant surface.

Protective coatings applied to ferrous metals are described in Table 18. In all cases preparatory treatment of the base metal is necessary and may involve any of the following processes: sand- or shot-blasting, oxyacetylene burning, pickling or grinding. Reference should be made to CP 2008:1966 and BRE Digest (2nd Series) No.70.

Surface treatments applied principally to non-ferrous metals
Under normal conditions non-ferrous metals are subject to very little corrosion and surface treatments are usually employed for the purpose of improving their appearance. Metal coatings are deposited by means of electroplating (Table 19).

Another form of coating applied to both ferrous and non-ferrous metals is 'paint', a general description given to all types and grades of pigmented coating which, basically, may be classified into four groups: oil paints, water paints, chemically cured finishes and those consisting of a dissolved agent in a volatile solvent mixture drying by evaporation. Some of these coatings are applied in-situ, others in the factory fabricating the metal component. Reference should be made to BRE Digest (2nd Series) No.71 and to CP 231:1966 which describes the types of industrialised finish and technique and their particular uses.

Table 17
Electrochemical series

Corroded end (anodic)
Magnesium and magnesium alloys
Zinc, cadmium; galvanised iron or steel
Aluminium and aluminium alloys; chromium
Cast iron; wrought iron; mild steel
Stainless steel; chrome irons
Tin and lead-tin solders; lead
Brass (low copper content)
Nickel and nickel alloys (high content)
Copper; bronze; brass (high copper content); cupro-nickel
Precious metals
Protected end (cathodic)

Table 18
Protective finishes applied to ferrous metals

Finishing Process	BS	Description
Metalisation	2569 : Part 1 : 1964	Fine particles of molten metal, i.e. zinc, aluminium, cadmium, copper, stainless steel or lead, are sprayed onto the surface.
Hot dip galvanising	729 : 1971	Probably the most efficient type of coating for iron and steel. The articles to be coated are dipped in molten zinc. A widely accepted process for a range of builders' hardware of length $\leqslant 27$ m.
Sherardising	4921 : 1973	The items to be treated are heated and rotated in a drum containing zinc powder which impregnates their surface.
Zinc plating	1706 : 1960	Also known as 'electro-zinc' or 'electro-galvanising'. A cheaper method than that of cadmium plating but less resistant to attack by alkalis ; it produces a grey finish.
Cadmium plating	1706 : 1960	Another electroplating method. Although resistant to attack by alkalis the treated surface is easily affected by acids but under normal conditions affords fairly good protection to steel. For external use a heavier deposit is applied.
Japanning		A low-cost, attractive and relatively thick coating capable of concealing minor blemishes on the basic metal ; it is used on wrought ironwork, items of ironmongery and miscellaneous types of casting. Four kinds of finish are available : 1. Black bright japan (sometimes called varnish). 2. Brown varnish (an alternative to 1). 3. Semi-dull black (less bright than 1, but more so than 4). 4. Art black (a dull black finish).

Table 19
Metal coatings applied mainly to non-ferrous metals

Surface Coating	BS	Description
Brass plating		A finish used on zinc alloy metals (and also steel). An application of clear varnish is also sometimes given as an added protection and to preserve the colour of the plating.
Copper plating		Used to give a primary coat on non-ferrous metals to improve the adherence of nickel and chromium plating. Copper adheres to all metals and is also used as the basis for several antique bronze finishes.
Nickel plating	1224 : 1970	Employed as an undercoating on steel, brass and zinc-base diecastings where chromium is the finishing coat (to prevent corrosion between it and the base metal). Where nickel forms the finishing coat a copper undercoating is often used.
Chromium plating	1224 : 1970	A highly polished finish which may be used on any base metal except magnesium. Weathering qualities may be provided by applying an undercoat (copper or nickel on a ferrous metal base). Manufacturers use a colour-coding system : red indicates suitability for external use.
Real bronze metal antique known as 'real BMA' (to distinguish it from imitations)		A finish suitable only for bronze and gunmetal which is applied mainly to items of ironmongery. It is not suitable for very exposed situations. Imitations of this type of finish include brown bronze and Florentine bronze.

Table 20
Moderately durable hardwoods : 10–15 years average life

Trade name and colour	Botanical name	Density (kg/m³)	Moisture movement	Texture	Workability	Remarks
Kapur (yellow–brown/ red–brown)	*Dryobalanops spp.*	735	medium	medium	rather difficult	Sometimes called Mahoborn teak or Borneo camphorwood ; similar to gurjun but more resistant to decay and less liable to shrink and distort in use. Nails easily. Fittings should be non-ferrous metal. *Use* : Constructional work, bridge decking, etc.
Gurjun (red–brown) Apitong Keruing Yang	*Dipterocarpus spp.*	720	large	medium	medium	Liable to distort in use if not firmly held ; sometimes exudes resin. Discolours under clear varnish. *Use* : Constructional work, bridge decking, etc.
Sapele (red–brown)	*Entandrophragma cylindricum*	625–640	medium	fine– medium	good	Not a naturally stable wood ; requires careful seasoning. Often used cut on the true quarter to obtain the 'stripe' effect. *Use* : External joinery.
West African mahogany (light red/dark red)	*Khaya ivorensis* and *Khaya spp.*	560–705	small	medium	varies according to species and quality	A stable timber, moderately resistant to decay. Generally nails well. *Use* : External work generally.
Elm (grey/brown)	*Ulmus spp.*	560–625	medium	medium– coarse	medium	A relatively cheap timber. *Use* : Piles, heavy constructional work, weather boarding, etc.
Gedu nohor (red–brown) Edinam	*Entandrophragma angolense*	545	small	medium	medium	Similar to sapele and West African mahogany. Sometimes in short supply. *Use* : External work generally.

Timber

Wood employed for constructional purposes is referred to as 'timber' and is derived from various tree species which are classified commercially into hardwoods and softwoods, a classification established by long usage but not strictly accurate, so far as it relates to the degree of hardness of the woods concerned, since it refers to their botanical grouping. To avoid the risk of confusion the botanical name of the wood should be specified in addition to its commercial description ; such information is contained in BS 881, 589 : 1955.

Woods suitable for external use

Not all woods are suitable for use outdoors and most of those employed for such purpose need protective treat-ment. Careful selection must be made to ensure that the species chosen is the most suitable for the particular function or structure ; size, source of supply, durability, workability and moisture content must also be considered. Tables 20–22 give a selection of hardwoods suitable for external use, classified according to durability. Table 23 lists a choice of softwoods. Reference should also be made to CP 112 : Part 2 : 1971 which deals with the structural use of timber.

Moisture content and movement

The average tree when felled contains 25–40 per cent moisture and is immediately converted (i.e. sawn into various pieces) to ensure that shrinkage of the wood on drying out does not cause it to split. Being a hygroscopic substance, wood reacts to atmospheric change. If dried to

Table 21
Durable hardwoods : 15–20 years average life

Trade name and colour	Botanical name	Density (kg/m^3)	Moisture movement	Texture	Workability	Remarks
Utile (red–brown)	Entandrophragma utile	655–657	medium	medium	good	Available in very large sizes. Tiama is a similar timber but cheaper. Use : Constructional work where a stable, durable timber is required.
Idigbo (straw/yellow–brown)	Terminalia ivorensis	575	small	medium	medium	A good all-round, stable timber ; resistant to decay. Needs care in nailing to avoid splitting. Stains when in contact with ferrous metals in damp situations. Use : Timber buildings, fence and gate posts and where an inexpensive 'oak' finish is required.
Guarea (pink/red–brown)	Guarea cedrata and G. thompsonii	545–575	small	medium	good	Mahogany type of wood but not quite so stable ; liable to distort in use and sometimes exudes resin which may cause difficulty in finishing process. Nails well. Use : External work generally.
Sweet chestnut (straw/yellow–brown)	Castanea sativa	545	large	medium	medium	Sometimes used as an alternative to oak. Stains when in contact with ferrous metals in damp situations. Splits easily. Use : Fencing, gates, poles, beams, etc.
Agba (straw/light brown)	Gossweilerodendron balsamiferum	480–513	small	medium	good	A good all-round timber. Resistant to decay but gum exudation is sometimes troublesome. Nails satisfactorily. Use : Suitable for a wide range of uses including timber buildings, fence and gate posts.

the point where its moisture content will be maintained in equilibrium with its ultimate environment, it is unlikely to be distorted by shrinkage. A higher moisture content is permitted in timber used externally than in that for internal use : about 20–22 per cent for general carcassing timber and slightly less for that which is to be painted or varnished. Where humidity is high, it may be necessary to treat the timber with a preservative to counteract the risk of decay.

Defects in timber
Defects may develop during the growth of a tree or after it has been felled ; others may arise after the timber has been installed in its permanent position. Since wood is a natural material its quality inevitably varies. Certain minor characteristics (e.g. small tight knots) are permitted and reference should be made to BS 1186 : Part 1 : 1971 which specifies these and deals with the quality of timber.

Care in choosing the right kind of wood for a particular function will, to a large extent, control defects that arise after the installation of timber. Such defects may be grouped under the following four headings :

Mechanical wear. Often the destruction of timber is due to insufficient thought being given to the kind of wood, the manner in which it is sawn and its positioning so as to withstand the stresses and wear imposed upon it. This is

Table 22
Very durable hardwoods : 25+ years average life

Trade name and colour	Botanical name	Density (kg/m³)	Moisture movement	Texture	Workability	Remarks
Greenheart (olive green/brown)	Ocotea rodiaei	1040	small	fine	difficult	Twice as hard as English oak ; almost immune to fungal attack and highly resistant to marine borers. Use : Heavy constructional and marine work, dock gates, piers, etc.
Jarrah (dark red)	Eucalyptus marginata	801–850	medium	rather coarse	difficult	Has a tendency to shake in the heavier dimensions and to distort in use. Use : Heavy structural work, bridge decking, piles, marine work, etc.
Karri (pink/dark red)	Eucalyptus diversicolor	850	medium	medium	difficult	Similar to jarrah but slightly paler in colour and less durable. Use : Fencing, marine work and bridge decking.
European oak (yellow/brown)	Quercus spp.	720	small–medium	fine–medium	medium–difficult	Best European oak is from Yugoslavia (ex Austrian) but is more limited in size than that of the UK. Use : Gates, fencing and heavy constructional work.
Opepe (yellow/orange–brown)	Nauclea diderrichii	750	small	medium	fairly good	Should not be used for small sections : tends to split when nailed due to irregular grain. Use : Gate and fence posts ; outside work generally.

particularly applicable to decking where tangentially sawn timber is used.

Chemical decomposition. Wood brought into contact with certain chemicals, notably strong solutions of acid or alkali, may decompose. Some kinds of wood in the immediate vicinity of metals and sea-water may decompose and become quite soft under the action of acids or alkalis released by electrolysis of the salt. The galvanic action is caused by two dissimilar metals coming into contact with the moist, salt-laden timber. Acid dyes used on timber may have a similar effect ; continued exposure to sulphur dioxide gas may also bring about slow disintegration where the surface is unprotected.

Woods which stain when brought into contact with ferrous metals under damp conditions include afrormosia, chestnut, idigbo, kapur, oak and western red cedar. Those which exude a yellow dye when in contact with water, due to the reaction of tannin in the presence of iron salts, are afzelia, doussie and idigbo.

Insect attack. In timbers used externally the most troublesome organisms are the shipworm (Teredo) and gribble (Limnoria) ; these are marine borers whose activities cause damage to timbers in dockwork, jetties, fendering and river defence works, etc. No wood is immune from attack but jarrah, ekki and greenheart appear to offer the most satisfactory resistance.

Fungal attack. Conditions prevailing in such places as glasshouses are often favourable to the spread of fungi. Poriaxantha is a fungus commonly found in this type of environment ; once the timber becomes infected, decay is likely to spread quite rapidly.

Untreated timber in direct contact with the ground is liable to rot because of the permanently damp situation and infections which lie within the soil. Decay of the timber appears to be more rapid in light porous soils containing a high proportion of humus than in the heavy, badly-drained clay soils wherein the aeration is seldom sufficient for vigorous fungal growth. Timber posts set in chalky soils

TABLE 22—*continued*

Trade name and colour	Botanical name	Density (kg/m³)	Moisture movement	Texture	Workability	Remarks
Afzelia; Doussie (red–brown or yellow red–brown)	*Afzelia spp.*	705–817	small	coarse– medium	fairly difficult	A substitute for teak but harder and heavier; splits when nailed. Exudes a yellow dye when in contact with water. *Use*: External joinery and where outstanding strength, durability and good appearance are required.
Afrormosia (golden brown)	*Afrormosia elata*	689–705	small	medium– fine	fairly easy	A substitute for teak, which it resembles in appearance, but has a tendency to split when nailed. Liable to become discoloured in contact with water and will stain iron in damp conditions. *Use*: External joinery, where a superior stable timber construction is required.
Iroko; Mvule (yellowish dark brown)	*Chlorophora excelsa* and *C. regia*	655	small	medium	medium–difficult	Comparable to teak in durability but irregular grain may result in distortion. Hardwearing. *Use*: External joinery in damp situations.
Makore (pink/red–brown)	*Mimusops heckelii*	640	small	medium	fairly easy	Comparable to mahogany but stronger. Tendency to split when nailed. *Use*: In situations subjected to hard wear and in damp conditions.
Teak (yellow–brown)	*Tectona grandis*	640	small	medium	fairly easy	Very durable and exceptionally stable. Tendency to split when nailed. Has been known to discolour granite. *Use*: Garden furniture and high class joinery.

are likely to decay more rapidly than those in gravelly soils. Although timber embedded in peat undergoes certain changes it does not rot, as may be seen from the so-called 'bog-oak' relics of prehistoric forests submerged in old peat bogs for thousands of years.

Wood as a structural material
Although classed under the same trade heading, carpentry and joinery comprise two different classes of work. Carpentry embraces the framing together of timbers whose primary function is to withstand stresses imposed by external forces or to resist pressures exerted upon them. Such timbers may be of either a temporary or permanent nature; their finish is generally left rough from the saw (unwrought).

Joinery is distinguished from carpentry by the character of the work. The term is applied to wood which is dressed and brought to a high degree of finish, the labour entailed constituting a major factor in comparison with the quantity of material involved. Much of the work is executed at the bench in the joiner's shop and brought to the site for final assembling and fixing (usually in the latter stages of the work to prevent damage arising from other trades' activities).

BS 565:1972 contains a glossary of terms relating to timber and woodwork; BRE Digest No.156 gives guidance on specifying timber.

The sizes of structural members must always be calculated to take into account the maximum stresses likely to be imposed and the maximum pressures to be resisted, bearing in mind the practical constructional and assembly difficulties likely to be encountered in the course of the work. BS 4471:Part 1:1969 gives basic cross-sectional sizes of sawn softwood.

Joints play a vital role in any timber structure. Methods of connecting timbers depend upon the nature of the work and the type of wood employed but in the majority of cases the simpler the joint the better. Complicated joints are not only difficult to fit together but are liable to be affected by shrinkage of the timber. Timbers should be so arranged

Table 23
Softwoods suitable for external use

Trade name and colour	Botanical name	Average weight (kg/m³)	Moisture movement	Texture	Workability	Remarks
Pitch pine (light red)	Pinus palustris P. elliottii P. caribaea	655	medium	fine	fairly good	Very strong and durable but exudes resin which tends to affect workability. Obtainable in long lengths but wood is subject to heart shakes. Varnishes well; grain tends to show through paint. Use: Good class carpentry and external cladding.
Larch (red brown)	Larix decidua	590–592	medium	medium–coarse	fairly good	Most valuable home-grown softwood. Paints and stains satisfactorily. Use: Mainly for carpentry, heavy constructional work, fencing, gates, poles, etc.
Douglas fir (reddish-yellow/orange–brown)	Pseudotsuga menziesii	528–530	small	fine	good	Stains but does not paint well. Harder to nail than most softwoods. Non-ferrous fittings recommended. Use: Heavy constructional work and poles.
Baltic redwood (pink–brown/straw–brown) Red pine Red or yellow deal	Pinus sylvestris	530	medium	fine	good	Tough strong wood, moderately resinous; stains, paints and polishes well. Very durable when preserved but not quite as good as Douglas fir for first class work. Use: Carpentry and joinery, fencing, poles, etc.
Western white pine (pale straw/pink–brown)	Pinus monticola	450	small	fine	fairly good	Good dimensional stability; contains large knots. Use: Good class joinery work.
Western red cedar (light pink/red–brown)	Thuja plicata	368–385	small	medium–coarse	fairly difficult	Extremely stable under changes in moisture content and exceptionally resistant to decay, but stains when in contact with iron under moist conditions. Very durable but should not be used in situations where it is likely to be subjected to hard wear. Use: Ideal for most external uses; it needs no protective coating or preservative.

that their structural strength is weakened as little as possible by any joint in them, each abutting surface in the joint itself being placed perpendicular (or nearly so) to the pressure which it has to transmit. Where timber connectors are used they should comply with the requirements of BS 1579:1960. The usage and loadings of the various types of connector are dealt with in CP 112:Part 2:1971.

Depending upon the nature of the work, adhesives are sometimes used in timber construction. Synthetic resin adhesives are generally recommended and should comply with the requirements of BS 1204:Part 2:1965. Four classes of adhesive are specified but only the WBP class (i.e. weatherproof and boilproof) is recommended for external work. Guidance on choice of glues for wood is given in BRE Digest No.175. Synthetic resins giving high bond strength are usually based on urea formaldehyde and resorcinol formaldehyde; both are resistant to insect attack. Only certain types of phenolic resins (i.e. based on phenol formaldehyde) are classed as weatherproof. Care is needed in the selection of an adhesive for use with timber treated with a preservative, since there is a risk that the chemical content of the latter may affect the chemical reaction of the adhesive.

Preservation of timber

Most woods used out of doors require some form of preservative treatment to prolong their useful life. Wood preservatives are classified in BS 1282:1959 which gives particulars of three principal types:

Class A   Type TO–tar oil
Class B   Type OS–organic solvent
Class C   Type WB–water-borne

Preservative treatment should be in accordance with the recommendations laid down in CP 98 : 1964, all the necessary cutting and shaping of the timbers being executed prior to treatment. Four principal methods are employed: pressure impregnation; hot and cold open tank treatment; dipping and steeping; brushing and spraying. The types of preservative suitable for timbers in various situations, together with methods of application, are given in Table 24. Dipping is generally sufficient protection for timbers where there is little risk of decay. Any type of preservative may be used for brushing or spraying–the methods employed where deep penetration of the timber is considered unnecessary.

Care must be taken to ensure that no preservative is used which is likely to have a detrimental effect on other materials. The water-borne preservative mercuric chloride causes corrosion of any ferrous metal with which it comes into contact; the tar oil and organic solvent preservatives

Table 24
Timber preservatives suitable for various external situations

Function of timber to be treated	Pressure impregnation			Hot and cold tank			Steeping			Dipping or surface treatment		
Fencing posts and timbers in contact with ground	A1 A2	B3	C1 C2	A1 A2	B2 B3	C1 C2	A1 A2	B2 B3	C1 C2			
Heavy construction, e.g. bridges, jetty contruction, etc.	A1	B3	C1 C2 C3									
Fencing rails and boards, gates, weatherboarding and timber structures not in direct contact with ground (a) left unpainted	A1	B2	C1 C2 C3	A1 A2	B2 B3	C1 C2 C3	A1 A2	B1 B2 B3	C1 C2 C3	A1 A2	B1 B2 B3	
(b) to be painted after treatment			C1 C2 C3			C1 C2 C3		B1 B2 B3	C1 C2 C3 C4		B1 B2 B3	C1 C2 C3 C4
Timber in contact with fresh or sea water, e.g. marine piling, fendering, river defence timbers	A1		C1 C2									
Timber used for snow and duck boards	A1 A2	B3	C1 C2	A1 A2	B1 B2							
Timber used for horticultural purposes, e.g. glasshouses, staging and framing, etc.			C1 C2 C3		B2	C1 C2 C3		B2	C1 C2 C3		B2	C1 C2 C3

Method of application and type of preservation

Type A   *Tar oil type preservatives*
   A1   Coal tar creosote
   A2   Coal tar oil

Type B   *Organic solvent type preservatives*
   B1   Chlorinated naphthalenes, etc.
   B2   Copper naphthenate + zinc naphthenate
   B3   Pentachlorophenal and its derivatives

Type C   *Water-borne preservatives*
   C1   Copper/chrome
   C2   Copper/chrome/arsenic
   C3   Fluor/chrome/arsenate/dinitrophenol
   C4   Others: egiborates, copper sulphate, mercuric chloride, etc.

may adversely affect certain types of glue. Use of a urea resin glue should be checked with the manufacturer before pressure treatment is given. Although for durability purposes a resorcinol resin glue may not be necessary, its use is generally desirable where pressure treatment is specified. Normally, any type of glue may be employed in situations where the timber is to be either dipped or surface treated. Further advice should be sought from the British Wood Preserving Association where necessary.

CAR PARKING

The problem of parking cars off the street may be dealt with basically by any of the three following types of car park: surface, underground or multi-storey.

Surface car parks

This is the simplest and usually the cheapest form of car park and is the one which is often adopted. Since land is a fixed commodity which is in ever-increasing demand (and likely to remain so) it would seem ludicrous, particularly in urban areas, that parked cars should occupy valuable space which could be put to much better economic and aesthetic use.

Where the proposed life of a car park is comparatively short, the provision of a surface car park may be the most expedient solution. It is not necessary, however, for the area to be laid out as a sea of unbroken tarmac, particularly in rural or semi-rural areas. Surfaces other than non-porous pavements which are quite suitable for car parks include gravel, grass–concrete and stabilised grass.

Gravel. Unsealed or stabilised with bituminous emulsion (to BS 434 : 1973), sprayed at the rate of 1·5 litres/m², and blinded with coarse dry sand. After three to four days a second application is made at 1 litre/m², blinded with fine gravel (6 mm) and then rolled with a light roller (500 kg).

Grass–concrete. A combination of concrete units, soil and grass which, when the latter becomes established, is maintained as a grassed area in the normal way.

Stabilised grass. No concrete or other structural unit is involved but the grassed area is treated to give it a more durable surface. Newly-sown grass seed is spread with a 25–30 mm layer of sand which is sprayed with a water-based non-toxic bituminous solution at the rate of 0·75 litre/m². When the grass has grown through this layer, fine gravel is spread over it to a depth of 6–8 mm.

Underground car parks

Unfortunately economics almost invariably override aesthetics when surface versus underground car parking provision is being considered. The great advantage of an underground car park is its unobtrusive siting, leaving the ground surface free for other more pleasing development. With careful planning and foresight the existing landscaping of the proposed car park area may remain undisturbed.

Plate 9
Sunken car park planted with trees: shopping centre, Hartlepool, Co. Durham. Note the interesting surface texture of the ramp created by the pattern of brick pavers. There may be a tendency for this to retain rubbish and dirt. *Photo: G. Perkin, ARIBA.*

Close co-operation with the engineer is essential to ensure that engineering services (e.g. provision for ventilation of the underground car park) and artefacts are carefully sited so that they do not obtrude into the landscape.

Multi-storey car parks

This method is commonly adopted in city centres where land values and space are at a premium. In some cases the roofs of buildings in such areas are also used as car parks.

A compromise between underground and multi-storey car parking may be achieved where the fall of the ground is favourable (e.g. on a hillside) by adopting a split-level design, the varying levels of roofs being landscaped so that the structure blends in with its surroundings.

Layout of car parking bays

There are a number of ways in which the individual bays

may be arranged but all are based on one of the following design principles :

Parallel
At right angles
At angles ranging from 30° to 60°.

The pattern adopted is governed by the number of cars to be accommodated and the overall space allotted.

Bay lengths are usually 4·87–6·70 m with widths ranging from 2·36 m (minimum) to 2·59 m. In addition to the area of the actual bays, circulation space must be allowed. The aisle widths between rows of parking bays depend largely upon the angle of parking adopted ; the dimensions shown below are given as a rough guide.

Parallel parking	2·13 m minimum
30° angled parking	2·43–3·00 m
45° angled parking	2·74–3·65 m
60° angled parking	4·27–5·48 m
90° angled parking	6·09–7·31 m

Fig. 33   Suggestions for the treatment of surface car parks

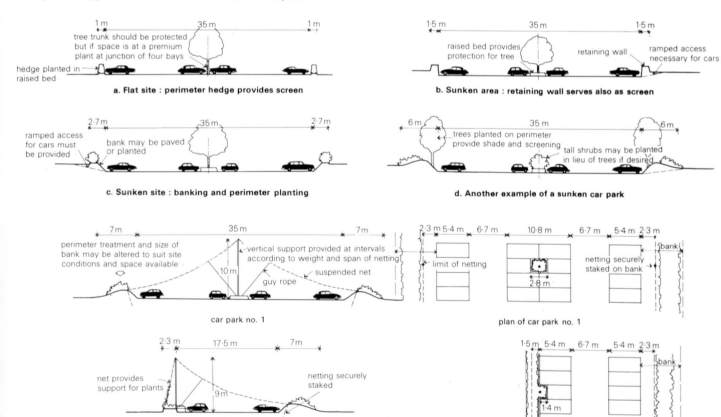

a. Flat site : perimeter hedge provides screen

b. Sunken area : retaining wall serves also as screen

c. Sunken site : banking and perimeter planting

d. Another example of a sunken car park

e. Two examples of a camouflaged car park

Landscaping of car parks

Landscaping depends upon the type of car park adopted. In the case of multi-storey car parks, which are usually sited in the centre of towns and cities, there is seldom much scope for planting trees and shrubs on a large scale. Underground car parks and those set at differing levels provide opportunities for imaginative landscape design, the only restrictions imposed being those governing soil loads, etc., upon the roof structure—as in the design of roof gardens.

Surface car parks, in some ways, are the most difficult to landscape since any space allotted for planting is generally at the expense of car parking bays and for this reason is either kept to a minimum or totally absent.

Initially consideration must be given to the site itself and the relationship between the level of the car park and that of the adjoining ground, the object being to arrive at a solution which enables the cars to be concealed from view, as far as possible. Ways of achieving this may be summarised under the following headings:

(i)   Excavating car park area to a lower level
(ii) Forming banks around the car park
(iii) Retaining the existing level and implementing some form of screening

Existing levels, engineering services, location of nearby buildings or other structures, ground conditions and the siting of existing trees on the site must all be taken into account before a decision is reached.

Excavating to a lower level (Fig.33b, c and d)

Excavation entails the use of earthmoving machinery and the disposal of spoil, either to another part of the site or to a tip some distance away. Drainage of the embankments formed must be included and some kind of treatment of the banks themselves provided. This may be in the form of a retaining wall or other type of retaining structure, grassing or planting. It is also necessary to take into ac-

count the difference in levels between the entrance (and exit) points and the car park itself, making provision for negotiating an inclined route to and from the parking area.

Planting may be confined to the lower level, with trees set amid the parking bays, or also on the banks around the car park. When making a selection, large-leaved trees and those which drop gum or berries should be avoided. These species include:

Limes	*Tilia platyphyllos*
	T. rubra
	T. euchlora
Maidenhair tree	*Ginkgo biloba*
Horsechestnut	*Aesculus spp.*
Sycamore	*Acer pseudoplatanus*
Mountain ash	*Sorbus aucuparia*

Formation of banks

This perimeter treatment is useful where a surplus of soil is near to hand but is costly if this has to be imported onto the site. The problem of providing a ramped exit and entrance does not arise because the level of the car park and that of adjoining ground remains the same, the bank providing a visual barrier which may be grassed, paved or planted.

Retaining existing levels (Fig.33a)

Where no excavation or banking takes place it is necessary to provide screening, either by the construction of a wall or fence or by planting hedging and trees. If hedging shrubs are to be planted it is strongly advisable to include some form of temporary fencing to deter persons from walking through the young plants, thus preventing their proper establishment.

Another approach to screening which might be given some thought is the use of netting. This material is available in a variety of mesh sizes and, comparatively, requires very little support. It may be set vertically or at an angle and in appropriate circumstances can provide the framework for climbing plants (Fig.33e).

Four Water in the Landscape

THE USE OF WATER

The role of water in the outdoor environment

Water in its various forms plays a vital role in our lives and environmentally serves many purposes. Man's most vital need of water is for consumption ; other needs involve the functional use of water : irrigation, transport and the generation of electric power. Increased leisure has highlighted the need for more recreational facilities and water sports of one kind or another are among the main attractions. The trend towards this type of pursuit appears to be increasing and is likely to create further demands on water resources.

The visual and psychological pleasures which water provides are taken for granted and it is not always readily appreciated that some parts of our landscape would lose much of their attraction were it not for the stretches of water that contribute to the scene. Water forms a feature in many different aspects of design ; a glance at the history of garden design shows what an important part water played in many of the great gardens of the past, none of which was considered complete without its lake, pond, canal, basin, or cascade. Moving water creates an impression of activity, a sense of rhythm and purpose ; still water conveys a feeling of tranquility. The reflections of objects

Plate 10
Still water conveys a feeling of tranquillity : land
reclamation scheme at Yateley, Surrey (Brewis Trophy,
1970).

in the water transform the whole surrounding scene, particularly by night where floodlighting or other forms of lighting are used.

Rain or snow falling upon the ground may either seep through the soil (or porous surface) or run off down to a watercourse. Some of the water evaporates but on hard paved surfaces it must be channelled away by means of a drainage installation. Likewise, ground that has poor natural drainage needs to be drained. Liquid waste matter containing human or animal excreta and trade waste effluent, which would otherwise contaminate the watercourses and underground sources of water, must be rendered harmless and disposed of.

The ever-increasing population creates a corresponding demand on water resources. Conservation and intelligent use of those resources demands the application of skill and forethought so that recycling of water may be effected

wherever practicable. In some cases this may give rise to problems beyond the scope of the environmental designer and necessitating the services of a specialist.

Sources of water

Water may be obtained from various sources and, if for human consumption, requires treatment prior to its distribution to the consumers.

Springs (Fig.34a)
Some of the water that percolates through the ground surface flows slowly underground towards the sea and during the course of its journey may encounter geological conditions which cause it to break through the surface of the ground in the form of springs. These frequently occur in

Plate 11
Water employed as a barrier for security purposes:
factory development by Cadbury Schweppes Ltd at
Moreton, Cheshire.
Photo: Stewart Bale Ltd, Liverpool.

hilly country where the surface of the underground water (plane of saturation) is not deep down. Springs also occur on hillsides where a permeable rock stratum overlies an impervious one and, if horizontal, a number of small springs are to be found issuing all along the outcrop. A sloping impervious bed results in a large spring at the lowest point. Geological faults, where the strata on one side of the fault have slipped downwards, causing porous beds to come into contact with impervious beds on the other side of the fault, sometimes result in a spring breaking out in an upward direction.

Because springs are merely an overflow of an underground stream or reservoir they are likely to cease for a time after a spell of dry weather. Some, however, produce a more copious and constant yield than others, depending upon the geological formation of the district. The largest springs originate from the thick beds of limestone, those

from the oolitic beds being the most constant. Although water from a spring is usually more or less organically pure the salts in solution (derived from the rocks) make it generally hard.

Shallow wells
These are wells sunk directly into water-bearing strata and are not very deep—the water level does not generally drop to more than 7·62 m below the ground surface. Their yield is likely to fall off in dry weather and water from this source is liable to contamination, particularly in the vicinity of human habitation, because the subsoil through which it has percolated is not of a sufficient depth to provide an efficient filter. To counter this risk a watertight lining (steining) should be constructed of concrete, brickwork, or cast or wrought iron.

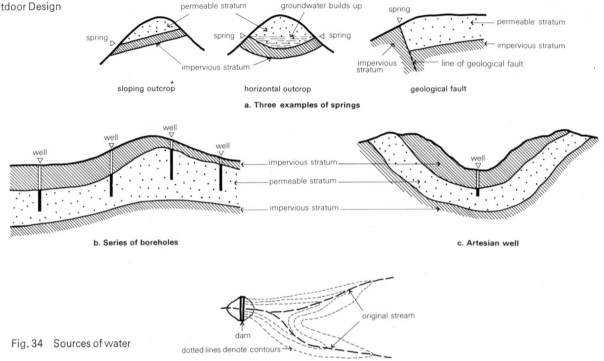

a. Three examples of springs

b. Series of boreholes

c. Artesian well

Fig. 34   Sources of water

d. Upland surface water : impounding reservoir

Deep wells (boreholes) (Fig.34b)
A deep well is one in which the water level is more than 7·62 m from the surface; it is usually bored, rather than dug, and often referred to as a 'borehole'. The water derived by this means comes from strata that are situated between two impervious beds and virtually unaffected by surface impurities. During its passage downwards (which may be a considerable distance) the water undergoes purification by natural filtration while at the same time dissolving soluble mineral matter from the rock through which it flows; consequently it is generally hard water. The collecting surface of such wells can be increased by driving tunnels (adits or collecting galleries) at the bottom in a horizontal direction. The yield from a well is greatest when it is first sunk and then gradually diminishes to a more or less uniform rate.

Artesian wells (Fig.34c)
This type of well (which derives its name from the district of Artois in northern France where many wells of this type are found) is driven into subsoil water which, being at such high pressure (having come from high elevations), immediately rises to the surface as soon as an outlet is provided (i.e. a well is sunk).

Rivers and streams
The consumer source invariably lies close at hand to this supply which provides an ample quantity of water without large capital outlay, although purification and pumping may incur higher running costs than other sources of supply. It is desirable for the intake to be sited upstream from the consumer source in order to avoid undue contamination. Water is pumped from the river or stream into storage tanks and then through the filtration plant into service reservoirs. This prevents pumping of very turbid water from the river during periods of high flood.

Upland surface water (Fig.34d)
Rain is collected near its source and stored in 'impounding reservoirs' (constructed by erecting a dam across a valley) sited well above the consumer source so that the water can be conveyed by gravitation through aqueducts or pipelines without the need for pumping. In most cases legislation prohibits the taking of all the water which falls on gathering grounds since this would deprive other users of their due share.

This is a fairly common source of supply and provides one of the most desirable waters for all purposes on account of its softness.

Methods of creating large expanses of water

An artificially created stretch of water should reflect its function in the landscape and must be sited so that it appears as a natural feature within the context of its surroundings. Its design entails seeking a source of water, assessing the surface area and depth of water required, determining the most economical form of construction and providing the ancillary features associated with the function of the proposed lake. Overriding all these factors is the choice of site, its orientation, physical characteristics and potential.

Methods that may be adopted for creating an expanse of water include:

> Enlarging an existing pool
> Adapting abandoned excavations
> Damming a valley
> Contouring a virgin site

Enlarging an existing pool

Over a period of time a pool may become silted up, giving the impression that it is of much smaller dimensions than is actually the case. By dredging, what appears to be a bog may be transformed into open water and dry land. Methods of excavating under swampy conditions are similar in many ways to those used to enlarge an existing pool.

It is advantageous to dispose of as much water as is practicable, to assist dredging or excavation and to eliminate, wherever possible, the removal of sloppy soil which is of little use for forming banks. The first operation is to seal off any inlets of water and to divert them into a temporary channel while excavation work proceeds. Several weeks before dredging operations are due to begin, a drainage channel should be cut through the silted-up pond to the downstream end, so that the water level gradually falls. If the excavation is carried out during the dry season and at a fairly fast and continuous pace the removal of water may be unnecessary, the level being kept low enough to prevent it from causing any trouble. Unless obstructions are present, excavation should begin at the centre, working outwards towards the edges of the pool with the dragline operating along the longest dimension. The length of the pool can be increased almost indefinitely without any change of excavation method but the width is determined by the reach of the dragline and the depth of the pool.

In general, a strong flow of water through a pool best maintains its condition and appearance. However, the power and potential destructiveness of even a comparatively small stream should not be underestimated; it is at times of flood that the greatest damage occurs and precautions need to be taken to prevent any inflowing stream from breaking out of its channel.

Adapting abandoned excavations

Excavations abandoned by extraction industries may be dry or waterlogged; where operations have been carried out below the level of the water-table they are flooded. The winning of minerals may result in deep pits, such as marlholes, or comparatively shallow excavations like those of many gravel pits. Flooded excavations afford excellent opportunities for adaption to the needs of water sports and recreation provided they are not contaminated by any industrial or harmful waste which cannot readily be eradicated. The waters contained in abandoned mineral workings are generally sterile, tending to be acid and unsuitable for the promotion of plant or animal life.

Soundings should be taken to ascertain the depth of water and the type of strata that lie at the bottom of the excavation.

In planning facilities for water sports, a beach should be provided for waders and swimmers and so that small boats can easily be launched and beached. At least part of the beach should be sited on the northern side of the lake so that the sloping ground receives the maximum amount of sunlight.

Damming a valley

Water runs down mountains and hillsides in a series of streams and finds its way into valleys and from there into rivers flowing down to the sea. By damming the head of the valley a large quantity of water can be retained (impounding reservoir), a method used to supply water to many of our big cities.

A valley may have a narrow defile above which it widens out into a large basin with a fairly flat bottom and, sometimes, steep sides. By the construction of a comparatively short dam across this defile a lake of great area and volume can be created. A suitable site for a dam is to be found, generally, just below the confluence of two streams: water can be ponded up in both valleys. A study of the contours should indicate the likely water level using various dam heights.

Several preliminary site investigations are necessary to ascertain whether a sound and watertight foundation can be obtained at a reasonable cost. Trial holes should be bored along the site of the dam in order to examine sample sections of the strata; from this it is possible to plot a longitudinal section of the subsoil underlying the site and

Plate 12
Water plays an important role in leisure pursuits. This is
an example, at Dorchester-on-Thames, of gravel
workings transformed into a lake for yachting. The
shingle beach at one end provides an area for safe
bathing. *Photo: J. W. Thomas, ARPS, Oxford.*

to form an estimate of the depth to which excavation should be carried out in order to get down to a good foundation.

Although the size of a dam is dictated by the conditions on site it should fulfil the following requirements:

(i) It must be stable enough to withstand the pressures imposed upon it so that there is no risk of its breaking, slumping or moving under any conditions.

(ii) It must be sufficiently high in relation to the over-flow point to prevent water from flowing over any unprotected parts.

(iii) There must be no risk of water leaking through or under the dam.

No dam should be built to retain water of a depth exceeding 1·5 m or any considerable volume, which could cause serious flooding of the surrounding area if suddenly released, without first obtaining the advice of a specialist.

Depending upon its size and the nature of the subsoil a dam may be constructed of earth, concrete, masonry or a combination of the last two. The cement used in the construction should be slow-setting and slow-hardening, using a fairly rich mix (1:5). In a larger dam the interior usually consists of large irregular blocks of stone (plums) set in a stable position with concrete rammed around and between them. This method of construction in a gravity dam helps to increase its weight, stability and resistance to shear. The stone selected for masonry dams must not be affected by the acidity of the water or permit any seepage and the material used for constructing the overflow weir must be capable of resisting the destructive action of water flowing across it. Provision must be made to direct any water passing over the weir into a channel (byewash) from whence it may discharge into a watercourse or other outfall. (See also page 42.)

Contouring a virgin site
A natural pool in the landscape serves as a collecting point for the water which drains from the higher ground surrounding it. The construction of an artificial pool necessitates careful scrutiny of the ground contours of the proposed site; in order to achieve a natural look the pool should be (or appear to be) situated at the lowest point.

Search should be made for a site where a supply of water is at hand, either in the form of springs or a stream, to supply the lake. Alternatively, it may be possible to excavate down to the level of the water-table (if this is not too deep) to obtain a source of supply. In either case it is necessary to carry out preliminary investigations on site.

The excavation operations are comparatively simple. Wherever possible the surplus soil should be deposited on site and graded to levels marrying in with existing contours; this eliminates the expense of carting the material off site. Any existing stream should be channelled through a temporary diversion while excavation proceeds. If for any reason the stream cannot be diverted, the digging of each excavation strip should begin at the upstream end and move downwards so that any loosened soil not picked up is washed downstream, where it is likely to accumulate.

Calculations of the area and depth of a pool are determined to a large extent by its proposed function. The depth is as important as the surface area. At first appearance a large shallow pool gives the most for the outlay incurred but loss of water by evaporation is liable to cause it to silt up more readily than one of greater depth. To overcome the risk of silting and to discourage the growth of bottom weeds deeper excavation needs to be carried out. Sometimes it is possible to achieve similar results by constructing dams or dykes but in this case the surface level of the water would be higher than that resulting from excavations.

Where a watercourse is available to provide the feeder source, measurement of the discharge (volume of water that flows in a unit of time: m³ per hour) must be taken. The velocity of any stream of water is not constant throughout its depth but varies at different levels; when readings are plotted they take the form of a curve (velocity profile). Velocity measurements are recorded at the average point of this curve; the level at which this occurs is 0·60 of the depth of water at the point where the velocity reading is actually taken. If the flow of water is uniform and its cross-sectional area constant, a relationship exists between discharge and time, i.e. discharge is proportional to depth.

Design and construction of small pools

A pool may be nothing more than a hole in the ground filled with water, but in order to retain the water the sides and floor of the cavity must be watertight. The size, shape and layout of the pool depends upon its function, location and the economics of the scheme. The size of a pool basically intended for swimming is governed by the number of persons likely to be using it at any one time. A useful yardstick is to allow 2·50–3·34 m² of surface area per person. For private pools 12×6 m is considered to be the minimum size but 9×4·5 m is usually quite adequate for

Plate 13
A man-made lake lined with heavy-duty plastic:
Birmingham University, Edgbaston.
Photo: Derek Bradshaw.

most private swimming needs. Sizes for public pools are laid down by the Amateur Swimming Association and the International Amateur Swimming Federation, whose regulations should be consulted where this type of pool is planned. Club pools should be not less than 23 × 9 m, which caters for six lanes (each approximately 1·5 m wide). Practically any shape may be selected for a pool, depending upon its site conditions, but the cost of shuttering and formwork must be borne in mind where concrete is used in the construction.

The depth may vary or be uniform throughout the pool ; where aquatic planting is intended a shelf should be provided around the perimeter to accommodate the marginal plants. Where a pool serves only the purpose of a basin for a fountain its depth need be little more than 250 mm but fish need at least 450–600 mm depth in order to survive during the winter. For general swimming activities a depth of 0·91 m is adequate. A depth of not less than 1·82 m is required for diving where the springboard is fixed at a maximum height of 0·76 m above water level (in this case the length of the pool must not be less than 9 m). One-metre springboards require a minimum water depth of 2·6 m; 10 m fixed diving boards not less than 5 m. Provision should also be made for emptying the pool (unless aquatics are planted in the bottom) by sloping the floor towards the outlet.

Materials and methods of construction vary and may be any of the following, depending upon the needs and economics of the scheme.

Concrete

After excavating the site of the pool to the required shape and depth (allowance being made for the thickness of concrete and hardcore) a 100–150 mm layer of hardcore is spread and blinded over the bottom of the excavation, well consolidated to provide a firm foundation for the 100 mm layer of waterproofed concrete (1 : 2 : 5 mix) which is to form the floor of the pool.

The concrete forming the 100 mm thick walls should be of similar mix, reinforced with a suitable size of steel mesh, and the shuttering positioned so that the sides of the pool slope to an angle of not less than 15° from the vertical. This precaution is essential to avoid the risk of damage which is likely to result from water freezing in the pool. When the shuttering has been struck a 1 : 3 waterproof cement rendering should be applied to the whole of the concrete area and finished with a steel trowel to give a smooth surface.

Blockwork construction

Concrete blocks, masonry and brickwork come into this category. The basic construction method is similar to that specified for concrete except that a waterproof finish, in the form of cement rendering, ceramic tiling, chlorinated rubber paint or a plastic lining, is necessary. Alternatively, a waterproof membrane within the structure itself may be provided. The cavities of hollow concrete blocks must be filled with poured grout.

Prefabricated panels

Steel panels or timber, riveted or bolted together in-situ, form a reasonably economic free-standing swimming practice pool. Steel must be protected against corrosion by application of a protective paint unless stainless steel (a more costly material) is used. Timber must be treated with a suitable preservative and a heavy gauge flexible vinyl used as a liner to ensure that the structure retains the water. Replacement of the liner may be necessary after several years, depending upon the intensity of use to which it is subjected.

Glass fibre

Methods of producing moulds for glass fibre units tend to restrict the size that can be manufactured. For small paddling-pools and such uses this material offers an alternative to a plastic liner although it is a little more costly and the shape restricted to that produced by the mould. In theory almost any shape can be manufactured but the high costs of making a mould tend to rule out the specification of 'one-off' products.

The site should be excavated to create a hole slightly larger than the prefabricated unit, which is then placed in position and some of the excavated material backfilled and well firmed around it to ensure that the entire pool is evenly supported. The edge, which is usually lipped, should be concealed by means of paving, rocks or the introduction of plant material to create a natural effect.

Plastic

A flexible type of heavy-gauge plastic material is used to form the basis of a pool of almost any shape. Its major drawback is the risk of the material being punctured, resulting in a leak which may be very difficult to locate. For small pools it has the advantage of being a relatively easy and cheap form of construction. Where a large pool is to be constructed several plastic sheets are welded together in-situ to form a waterproof membrane.

Plastic liners may also be used in the formation of a bog garden by adopting a similar method of construction.

It is important that the surface of the excavated area forming the pool should be smooth and free from any sharp stones that may damage the liner, causing it to leak. In a small pool the liner is placed across the excavation and stretched fairly taut, the edges being secured by weights. As the pool is filled the weight of the water causes the liner gradually to sink down into the excavated area. Once the pool is full the weights can be removed and any surplus material trimmed off, the edge of the liner being nicked as necessary to allow it to lie flat on the ground. The edges of the pool are then camouflaged.

Asphalt
Although an ideal waterproofing material in 'sandwich' construction (e.g. forming 'tanking' to a basement, etc.), asphalt used on its own for the construction of a pool is only suitable for lining shallow saucer-shapes and should be laid to a minimum thickness of 19 mm on a 76 mm (minimum) concrete base or a well-compacted and blinded hardcore foundation.

Puddled clay
The basic material is cheap but its use in the construction of pools has been superseded by quicker methods. The preparation of the clay is carried out by a method similar to that adopted for clay cores in earth dams. Selected clay is spread out and exposed to the action of the elements, causing it to disintegrate, after which it is mixed with a sufficient quantity of water to work it into a plastic condition. The plasticised clay is then placed in layers 100–150 mm thick and tread-and-cut (by means of long spades) to ensure that the fresh layer is bonded to the one beneath. More than one layer may be needed to build up a water-proof lining to the pool.

Soil and bentonite mixture
In the construction of small earth dams a waterproof covering is sometimes applied using a mixture of soil and bentonite, a volcanic clay which, by absorbing large quantities of water, forms a jelly substance that effectively seals the soil against water seepage. A recommended mixture is one part bentonite to four parts sandy soil, or six or eight parts heavy loam. Satisfactory results have also been obtained using leaner mixtures or thinner layers.

Although there appears to be no record of this method having been used to construct a pool it would appear to be quite satisfactory provided that the surface remains intact.

Water as a feature in rock garden construction

Water is particularly attractive when used in association with stone. If it is to be incorporated in a rock garden layout there are one or two rules that must be observed by the designer.

Source of water forming a watercourse
Unless higher ground is visible behind it, water must not be made to gush out at the top of a rock (a stream does not rise to the highest point in order to fall again like a fountain !). In nature, rain drains off the highest points (or rocks) into the ground or into depressions and by gravity finds its way down the hillside, increasing in volume as it collects drainage from elsewhere en route (Fig.60a, page 235).

Rock as a barrier to water
Rock has a tendency to act as a barrier to water and it never flows over a stone if it can channel around it through softer adjacent material. Since water always cuts through the earth rather than the rock the construction of the latter must be continued as a solid on either side of the proposed water channel if it is to present the appearance of a natural watercourse.

Natural routing of a stream
A natural stream channels its way down a rough earth incline by a devious route, winding and turning as each obstruction presents itself. For this reason it is important to pay attention to the lie of the rock so that the water can seek out the weak or easiest places to channel through. Each twist or turn must be visibly accounted for by a construction of rock sufficient to cause the water to take such a course.

Water cascading over rocks
In places where it is desired to channel the water over rocks each piece of stone used for this purpose must show evidence of having been in contact with water in the past. It is not always an easy matter to find exactly the right stone and even water-worn stones are not always suitable if the water which flowed over them did not have much force behind it. The flow of water can be assisted by leaving a small indentation in the concrete channel at the back of the stone so that the flow is given a slight 'kick-off' as it cascades over the rock.

Shape and depth of a stream

A stream always cuts a channel and, except after much rain, it never runs flush (or nearly flush) with the ground surface. In open land its channel flows between earth banks and where it passes among rocks it makes its way through flaws in the rock, sometimes carving its channel so that the rock is exposed in places. At turns in the stream the water is deeper where the current cuts and shallower on the near side; where water falls it digs a hole deeper than elsewhere, according to the force of the water.

To ensure that the finished scheme, when matured, looks perfectly natural the initial excavations for the stream should not be dug too deep and likewise a pool should be shallow to begin with, followed by deeper excavation of the centre where there would, in any case, be more depth of water. The stream (if it is to be successful) ultimately builds itself and concreting of the channel and pool can be carried out as required after the natural watercourse has finally been cut. In all cases earth banks must be at least 150 mm above water level.

Fountains

Nowadays fountains are generally regarded as ornaments but in the past they served a utilitarian purpose and in the sixteenth century were often the only source of water supply for domestic use. In many cases they were not the type of fountain we know today but just simply well-heads or, if more elaborate, basins fed from a nearby stream conducted underground by means of wooden pipes.

A fountain provides an attractive addition to the scene but its size must be in proportion to the basin or pool and it must be sited so that it does not drench passers by. As well as providing interest, a fountain helps to keep a pool fresh by aerating the water—an additional asset where fish are present.

Water jets may be designed to produce either single or multiple sprays of water at a variety of different angles, some being little more than a ripple on the water. The jets may rise vertically at the centre of a pool or, in the case of

Fig. 35   Methods of providing fountains

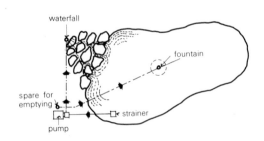

a. Layout for a single fountain and waterfall

Pumps
Two types of pump are employed:
Surface : located outside the pool in a dry, well-ventilated chamber. Water is drawn from the pool by suction pipe and delivered to the fountain(s) and other outlets, such as waterfalls. This type of pump operates more effectively when located below the level of water in the pool, operating with what is known as 'flooded suction' (Fig. 35d).
Submersible : sited completely under water either within the pool itself or housed in a separate flooded chamber. It is very quiet in operation (Fig. 35e).

Motors
A pump may be driven by either a series wound motor or an induction motor. The former runs at relatively high speed developing a comparable high head (pressure)— an advantage for producing a fountain. The induction motor runs at a slower speed and is ideal for the delivery of volumes of water necessary for creating a waterfall.

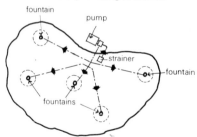

b. Layout for several fountains

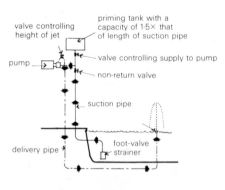

c. Pump located above pool

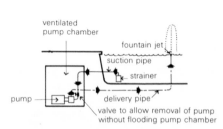

d. Pump located below pool

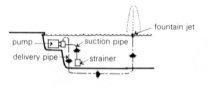

e. Pump located within pool

circular pools, in a series set around the perimeter and focused onto a central feature.

In the majority of cases, where there is no spring near at hand capable of supplying a sufficient pressure of water to produce the water jets to create a fountain, it is necessary to install some kind of prime mover, such as a pump (usually operated by electricity). Water is drawn into the pump via a strainer (to prevent clogging) and ejected through a pipe leading to the fountain jet which is supported just below water level. The pump creates a sufficient pressure of water in the pipe to force it through the jet in the form of a spray; the greater the pressure, the higher the spray if a small bore pipe is used. The output of a pump is reckoned in terms of litres per second against a given head (expressed in metres) which is the resistance it must counter, due to the pull of gravity and friction in the pipe, in order to force the required jet of water to a certain height. The pump may be located either within the pool itself or in a separate chamber but in the latter case it operates more satisfactorily if sited below pool level (Fig.35c, d, e). Where this is not possible, it is essential that a non-return valve is installed in the suction pipe to prevent any water in the pipe and the pump from emptying back into the pool when the pump is shut off.

The pump is operated by an electric motor, its horsepower depending upon its type and capacity and the head it is working against. Advice on these matters and the type of switchgear required should be sought from a specialist. Several pump kits are marketed for use on a domestic scale and readily installed in accordance with the manufacturer's instructions.

THE DISPOSAL OF WATER

Drainage systems

Unwanted water is disposed of by gravitational means in a network of pipes laid underground in a particular pattern (system). These drainage systems may be grouped into three basic types:

> Foul or soil water (sewage)
> Storm or surface water
> Subsurface or subsoil water (land drainage)

In some districts foul and storm water are conveyed together in the same pipes (combined system).

Sewers and drains perform similar functions, the difference lying basically in ownership. Generally speaking, a sewer belongs to the local authority, which is responsible for its maintenance, and a drain belongs to the individual on whose land it is situated.* If a drain serves more than one house it is a sewer, according to the Public Health Act, 1875.

A glossary of sanitation terms is given in BS 4118:1967. Reference should also be made to CP 301:1971 which deals with building and land drainage.

Sewage disposal

A drainage channel used to convey liquid waste matter contaminated by human (or animal) excreta or trade waste effluent to a sewer is classed as a 'soil' or 'foul' drain; the network of pipes conveying it is known as 'sewerage'. The method of sewage disposal depends to a large extent upon the district but, generally, the outfall (main) sewer terminates at a sewage disposal works where the sewage is treated and rendered innocuous. Where no public sewer is available sewage is conveyed by a private sewer to a septic tank situated within the site. Sewage disposal is dealt with in CP 3: Chapter VII: 1950.

Storm (surface) water disposal

A drainage channel which conveys rainwater from roofs (discharging via rainwater pipes) or paved ground surfaces is classed as a 'storm water' or 'surface water' drain. The collected rainwater is conveyed by means of a network of storm water sewers to an existing watercourse or, if there is none within the vicinity, to soakaway pits. In some districts, where the foul and storm water drainage systems are combined, the storm water is permitted to discharge into the foul water drain providing it enters via a water-sealed trap. It is not permissible, however, for a foul drain to discharge into a storm water drain since the latter would then be classed as a foul drain and must be dealt with as such.

The design of a drainage scheme should be kept as simple as circumstances permit and the size and gradient of pipes related to the need so that a minimum amount of maintenance is required.

Trenches for drains must be excavated in straight lines and to correct depths with a firm bottom so that the pipes may be laid to even falls. Table 25 shows the gradients commonly used for various diameters of pipes.

---

*This should be taken as a very broad distinction since it may not apply in the case of some local authorities which have special powers under private or adoptive Acts.

Table 25
Gradients for various pipe sizes

Pipe diameter (mm)	Gradient	Discharge per minute (litres)
100	1:40	636
150	1:60	1432
230	1:90	3237

Conventional drainage practice in the past has resulted in failures of drainage lines due to rigid methods of laying, particularly in the case of inflexible joints. Since 1965 the Building Regulations have therefore been designed to further the use of newer methods of jointing and bedding. Building Research Station Digests Nos. 130 and 131 study the structural design and causes of failure in pipes. Construction methods and bedding of pipes are dealt with in detail in BRS Digest (2nd Series) No.6.

Disposal of subsurface (subsoil) water
A drainage channel which is used for conveying water that percolates through the subsoil is known as a 'subsoil' drain and lowers the water-table underlying a particular area. Drainage is effected by constructing open channels (or ditches) or by laying land drains in prepared trenches at regular spacings to form a drainage pattern—the exact form depending upon the type of subsoil and local topography (Fig.36).

Land drains may be in one of the following forms (Fig.37):

(a) *Tile drain.* Short lengths of clayware or porous concrete pipes laid butt-jointed in a trench. Perforated pitch-fibre pipes and plastic pipes serve the same purpose.
(b) *French drain.* Also known as a 'rubble' (or blind) drain. An excavated trench is filled with selected coarse rubble at the bottom and overlaid with fine rubble. This type of drain is often used for catchwater drains (see below).
(c) *Mole drain.* Underground drainage channels formed in stiff plastic soils (e.g. clay) by using a mole plough.

Spacing of the drains has an effect on the water-table level (Fig.38) and is dependent upon the type of soil (Fig.39). The outfall may be to either a watercourse or a soakaway (Figs 40 and 41).

It is most important that the designer should understand the principles underlying the design of land drainage; these are discussed in some detail below.

Fig. 36   Land drainage patterns

b. Natural

This drainage pattern is adapted to suit the land contours. Drains follow the depressions or valleys, discharging into a main drain.

a. Fan-shaped

No single main drain is used in this system. All drains are laid so that they converge to a single outlet at a particular point. This pattern is often adopted where the site is small.

c. Gridiron

Adapted from the herringbone pattern. Lateral drains discharge into sub-mains which connect to the main drain.

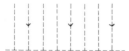

d. Parallel

The main drain is laid alongside one of the boundaries with secondary drains discharging into it.

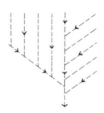

e. Herringbone

This system comprises a main drain into which numerous smaller lateral drains discharge (usually on both sides). The latter are laid parallel to each other and normally should not exceed 60 m in length. Useful pattern where there is risk of settlement following the regrading of contours.

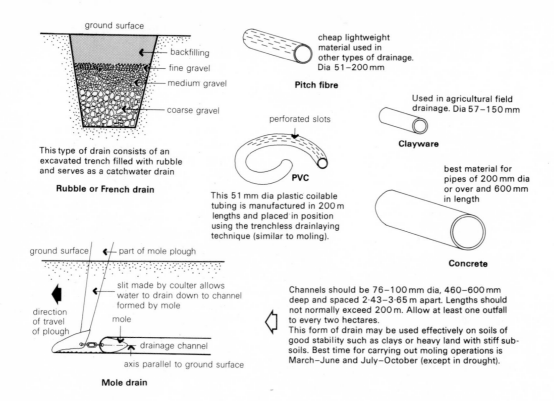

ground surface
backfilling
fine gravel
medium gravel
coarse gravel

This type of drain consists of an excavated trench filled with rubble and serves as a catchwater drain

Rubble or French drain

cheap lightweight material used in other types of drainage. Dia 51–200 mm

Pitch fibre

perforated slots

PVC

This 51 mm dia plastic coilable tubing is manufactured in 200 m lengths and placed in position using the trenchless drainlaying technique (similar to moling).

Used in agricultural field drainage. Dia 57–150 mm

Clayware

best material for pipes of 200 mm dia or over and 600 mm in length

Concrete

ground surface
part of mole plough
slit made by coulter allows water to drain down to channel formed by mole
direction of travel of plough
mole
drainage channel
axis parallel to ground surface

Mole drain

Channels should be 76–100 mm dia, 460–600 mm deep and spaced 2·43–3·65 m apart. Lengths should not normally exceed 200 m. Allow at least one outfall to every two hectares.
This form of drain may be used effectively on soils of good stability such as clays or heavy land with stiff subsoils. Best time for carrying out moling operations is March–June and July–October (except in drought).

Fig. 37   Materials and methods employed in land drainage

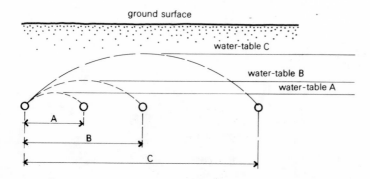

ground surface
water-table C
water-table B
water-table A
A
B
C

Fig. 38   Effect on water-table of spacing of land drains

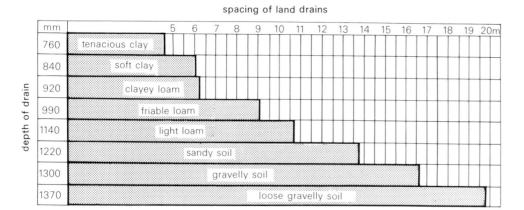

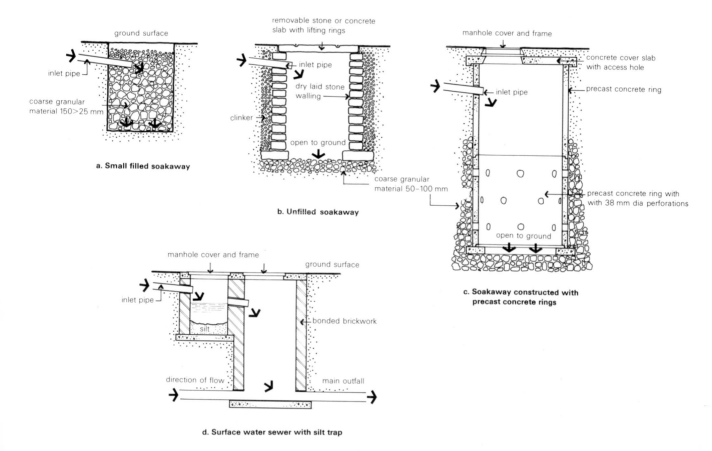

Fig. 39   Spacing and depth of land drains

Fig. 40   Disposal of subsoil water

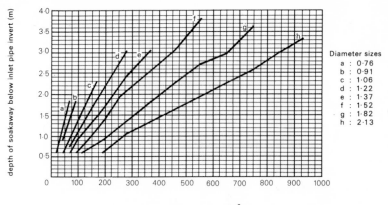

Fig. 41 Capacities of soakaways of various diameters for normal soils

Diameter sizes
a : 0·76
b : 0·91
c : 1·06
d : 1·22
e : 1·37
f : 1·52
g : 1·82
h : 2·13

depth of soakaway below inlet pipe invert (m)

area of ground surface to be drained (m²)

Principles underlying the design of land drainage

The water content of a soil may vary; observation of the ground in wet weather and an examination of the type of vegetation growing there, as well as digging trial holes, should give a good indication of whether land drainage is needed. (See page 19, Soil indicators.)

Rain falling on the soil surface seeps into the ground as gravity water at varying rates, according to the structure and permeability of the subsoil, passing through two distinct zones before reaching the third, and final, zone (Fig.42).

1. *Upper (hygroscopic) zone*
Some of the water in this 'zone of non-saturation' is absorbed by the roots of plants and the remainder percolates through the soil particles on its way to the lower zones.

2. *Middle (capillary) zone*
This 'zone of intermittent saturation', which varies in depth according to the water-table level, extends from the highest point reached by ground water during prolonged wet weather down to the lowest level to which the water-table drops in periods of drought. Under this latter condition air fills the spaces, replacing the water which is

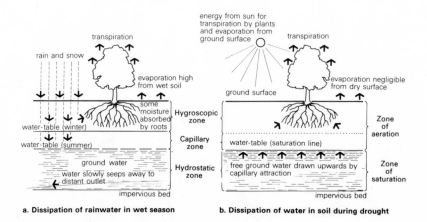

a. Dissipation of rainwater in wet season   **b. Dissipation of water in soil during drought**

Fig. 42 Principles of land drainage

normally percolating downwards among the soil particles in this and the upper zone. Together these two zones (i.e. the strata lying between the ground surface and the water-table level) are then referred to as the 'zone of aeration' During times of drought, free ground water is drawn upwards by capillary attraction into the lower layer of this zone, known as the 'capillary fringe', whose depth varies according to the type of soil but is greater in heavy soils, where the capillary movement is more rapid, than in the finer soils.

3. *Lower (hydrostatic) zone*

The rate of water seepage from the upper zones is related to the cross-sectional area of the pore channels, which decreases with soil depth until a point is reached where all the pore spaces are filled with water (zone of saturation) ; the uppermost limit of the underground pool is known as the 'water-table' and is at its maximum level in winter and during periods of prolonged rainfall. The water is not stagnant but slowly runs out at some distant point, its rate of flow retarded by friction and capillarity. Where the water-table rises above the level of the ground surface it forms stretches of water and swamps.

At the bottom of this zone lies an impervious bed (e.g. clay or shale).

The volume of air present in the soil depends upon the porosity and moisture content and plays an important role in determining the root development of growing plants. Constant diffusion takes place between the air in the soil and that in the atmosphere and, although carbon dioxide is present in both, the activities of micro-organisms within the soil give it a higher carbon dioxide content than the atmosphere, the proportion increasing with the depth of soil due to the restriction of pore spaces at the lower levels, which are often filled with water. If the concentration of carbon dioxide is too high the root hair feeding processes of plants are impeded or unable to function and the plants eventually die. It is in situations where diffusion is limited that a system of land drainage is likely to be needed.

Materials used in the construction of drainage systems

Foul and storm water drains

A foul water drain must have a minimum diameter of 100 mm and a storm water drain at least 76 mm. All pipes used for conveying sewage must conform to the appropriate British Standard.

(i) *Glazed vitrified clay*. Durable but not a flexible material and therefore subject to fracture (see BRS Digests Nos.130 and 131). Bedding of pipes should be in accordance with the recommendations set out in BRS Digest (2nd Series) No.6. Pipes should comply with BS 65 & 540 : Part 1 :1971 ; second quality may be used for storm water installations.

Diameter sizes available : 76, 100, 152 mm and at 76 mm intervals up to 610, 760 mm.

(ii) *Concrete*. Pipes and fittings complying with BS 556 : Part 2 :1972 are used for storm water drains and, where acceptable to the local authority, may also be specified for foul water drains. They are not suitable for conveying acid types of water and should not be laid unprotected in acid soils.

Diameter sizes available : 100, 152 mm and at 76 mm intervals up to 1070, 1220, 1829 mm.

(iii) *Cast iron*. Generally specified for use in poor ground or where drainage runs are suspended but are unsuitable for conveying acid wastes and should not be laid unprotected in acid soils. Pipes and fittings should conform to BS 78 : Part 1 :1961 and Part 2 :1965 or, if subject to low pressure, BS 437 : Part 1 :1970. Where diameters exceed 230 mm, spun cast iron pipes complying with BS 1211 :1958 should be specified.

Diameter sizes available : 51, 76, 100, 150, 230 mm and up to 680 mm in spun cast iron.

(iv) *Asbestos cement*. Not subject to corrosion from acids or chemicals in the soil. It is a lightweight material suitable for suspended drains and is also used for pumping mains. Foul water drains should meet the requirements of BS 3656 :1973. Class 'B' pipes complying with BS 486 :1973 are suitable for use in storm water drainage layouts. The range of fittings tends to be limited and it may be necessary, in some cases, to employ those manufactured from cast iron.

Diameter sizes available : 50, 75, 100, 150, 200, 230, 250, 300, 375, 450, 525, 600, 675, 750, 825 and 900 mm.

(v) *Pitch-impregnated fibre*. An economical material which affords a flexible and simple method of construction. It has a high resistance to acids and chemicals in sewage and any sulphates present in the soil. A wide range of fittings is available. All material should meet the requirements laid down in BS 2760 : 1973.

Diameter sizes available : 51, 76, 100, 130, 150 and 200 mm.

Subsoil drains (Fig.37)

The installation of a land drainage scheme using any of the materials described below may be eligible for a Ministry of Agriculture grant.

(i) *Porous earthenware*. Pipes of this clayware are not of the same quality as those specified for foul water drainage but should conform to BS 1196 : 1971.

Diameter sizes available : 63·5, 76, 102, 152, 229 and 304 mm in lengths up to 610 mm.

(ii) *Porous concrete*. The material should comply with BS 1194 : 1969.

Diameter sizes available : 76, 102, 140, 152, 229, 304, 381, 457, 533, 610, 762 and 914 mm in lengths up to 914 mm.

(iii) *Pitch-impregnated fibre*. Of the same material as that used in foul and storm water drainage schemes to BS 2760. The pipes are perforated to allow subsoil water to percolate into the drainage channel.

Diameter sizes available : 51, 76, 102, 127, 152 and 203 mm in lengths 2·44 to 3·05 m.

(iv) *Polythene*. Has a considerable economic advantage over traditional methods of land drainage installation. There is no British Standard specification for this type of product at present but confirmation regarding those eligible for a grant should be sought from the Ministry of Agriculture.

Diameter sizes available : 51 mm in coils 200 m long.

Five Electricity in the Landscape

THE APPLICATION OF ELECTRIC POWER OUT OF DOORS

Transmission of electricity

Electricity is generated and distributed as a three-phase supply. Transmission is by means of overhead lines or underground cables. Power generated at low voltage (11–15 kV) is raised to a higher voltage (132, 275 or 400 kV) by means of a transformer and transmitted to a point, often many miles away, where another transformer is employed to reduce the voltage to a value suitable for use by the consumer. These transmission lines are in the form of a grid system, operated by the Central Electricity Generating Board, using 132 kV for the National Grid network onto which is superimposed the 275 kV and 400 kV Super Grid. The overhead lines are flexible conductors suspended between tower supports. Single conductors form the transmission lines in the National Grid while the Super Grid employs twin conductors operating at 275 kV and four conductors at 400 kV per phase.

At suitable intermediate points on the network are sub-stations where voltages are stepped down to facilitate local distribution and to allow (if necessary) the current from one circuit to be switched to another. A 132 kV power supply transformed down to 33 kV is further reduced to permit local transmission up to 24 km and loads not exceeding 15 000 kW; This smaller network is then reduced down to 11 kV, transmitting a distance of up to 8 km and loads of 5000 kW; this in its turn is reduced down to 250–360 V to provide transmission over distances of 0·75 km (or less) and loads of up to 40 kW. Finally, the system is reduced to enable distribution to be made to individual consumers, up to a maximum distance of 550 m and loads of 15 kW. This last section of the network takes the form of an underground cable, sited under the footway alongside other engineering services and placed nearest to the back of the footpath (i.e. nearest to the consumer's premises), with gas, water and telephone services (in that order). BS 4727 : Part 2 : Group 04 : 1973 and Group 05 : 1972 include a glossary of terms used for power transmission.

Underground cables are a more expensive means of transmission and are usually adopted only where the provision of overhead lines is physically impracticable or aesthetically undesirable. Three main transmission systems are in use which correspond with those of the National Grid and Super Grid systems :

Super tension	Transmits over long distances and at voltages of 33 000 V and higher.
Extra high tension	Conveys power in the region of 11 000 V or 22 000 V over long distances.
Low tension	Operates at a pressure of around 230 V (for lighting) and 400 V (for heating and electric motors). Cable runs are usually short.

Underground cables need to be fairly flexible while at the same time possessing good conducting qualities. Most systems require at least three cables and to avoid the relatively high cost of laying separate single-core cables the individually insulated conductors are enclosed in one sheath of armouring overall. In high-voltage cables (i.e. above 22 000 V) a pressure of oil or gas is maintained throughout the length in order to eliminate the risk of voids between sheath and insulation.

Temporary supplies of electricity are often required on construction and building sites for the operation of plant and machinery. Reference should be made, in such cases, to CP 1017 : 1969 for supplies operating at voltages up to 650 V, and to BRE Digest No. 179. Reduced voltage may be obtained by means of transformer units (specified in BS 4363 : 1968). The recommendations in BS 4363 cater for single-phase and three-phase. Requirements are included for transformer units for 110 V distribution supplies.

Use of electricity for enclosure and irrigation purposes

Many of the tasks previously undertaken by manual labour have been eliminated and operational methods revolutionised by the application of electricity : electrification of fencing for stock enclosure and automatic watering systems for soil irrigation are two examples of the uses to which electricity may be put.

Electrification of fencing
The cost of erecting stock fencing may be considerably reduced by substituting an electrified fence. This relatively simple means of preventing cattle from straying comprises an electrified wire which is supported on posts set in the ground at specified intervals. The fence may be battery or mains operated, recommendations for which are contained in BS 1222 : 1945 and BS 2632 : 1955, respectively.

The advantages of this type of fence are that it is simple to operate, is readily dismantled and re-erected elsewhere and does not obtrude into the landscape. Although primarily intended as a means of controlling cattle it also acts as a deterrent to would-be trespassers.

Electrically controlled irrigation systems
Electrically controlled irrigation units are a means of providing water when and where it is needed. Apart from crop production, one of the principal problems in times of drought is the watering of grass, particularly on golf-courses, where a considerable amount of time and labour may be expended on manual watering. Underground automatic irrigation systems are of special value here.

By linking each green to an automatic controller, set so that each hydraulic control valve can operate to a predetermined programme, any number of greens may be watered as necessary with little more effort than pressing a button. The system is operated by means of a series of supply pipes laid to feed a number of sprinkler heads sited on the perimeter of each green. When not in operation these sprinkler heads rest slightly below the level of the ground surface so that they do not interfere with mowing or other turf maintenance. Once the water is turned on (in this case by automatic control) the water pressure causes the sprinkler heads to rise out of the ground and rotate, spraying a large area of grass. The sprinklers can be adjusted to water circles of varying diameters; other types may be installed to water a full circle, three-quarter, half or quarter circles according to site requirements.

Another method adopted for automatic irrigation of golfcourses and games pitches is the use of an automatic selftravelling sprinkler. This operates by means of a cable (attached to a coil within the sprinkler) which is drawn out to the distance the unit is intended to travel and anchored to the ground at its free end by means of a steel spike. When the water is turned on (either manually or by an automatic control unit) the pressure of water causes the sprinkler slowly to wind itself along the cable while watering the turf at the same time. When the sprinkler has wound itself to its finishing position the water is immediately cut off by an automatic shut-off valve.

The direction of the prevailing wind must be taken into account when siting fixed sprinklers or irrigation pipes.

Outdoor lighting installations

Lighting may be used for illumination, decoration, and to indicate direction, according to the positions in which the light sources are placed.

Three main factors must be taken into account when considering the provision of outdoor lighting: the purpose it is intended to serve, the quality of installation required and the local character and aesthetic requirements.

(i) Purpose of lighting
Although the principal function of lighting is to enable people to see their way in darkness, local circumstances dictate the level of illumination required. A lighting layout for a street requires a design approach different from that of a car park or pedestrian precinct.

(ii) Quality of lighting
This is particularly important where safety and clear visual perception are deemed essential. Three criteria of quality affect roads in particular, but also apply to other paved surfaces: average luminance of surface, luminance pattern and discomfort glare.

Average luminance of the paved surface. Apart from the reflection properties of a paved surface, the luminance at a particular point depends upon the position and intensity of the light source and the position of the observer.

Average (road) surface luminance = surface-integrated luminance of all points on the (road) surface divided by the surface area.

The visibility of an object 100 m or more away from an observer is determined by the average luminance of the (road) surface behind it, where the paved surface is so shortened by perspective that variations in luminance (being hardly discernible) have no appreciable influence on the visibility of the viewed object. At shorter distances, however, a variation of the paved surface luminance may have a definite effect on perception.

Luminance pattern. Each individual lantern in a lighting installation projects a patch of light onto the paved surface. The luminance and shape of this patch of light depends, to a marked extent, upon the properties of the paved surface. The distribution of dark and light patches resulting from a projection of light onto a uniform surface is described as the luminance pattern. Reflective properties of a dry surface differ considerably from those of a wet one. In a dry state both fine and coarse-textured surfaces give diffuse reflection of light. Although a wet coarse-textured surface also gives a diffuse reflection, a film of water on a fine-textured surface produces a mirror effect (Fig.43).

Discomfort glare. Visual comfort is more important to drivers than to pedestrians and is determined by the level of lighting (sufficient for reliability of perception) and the limitation of glare. The reduction of visual performance, caused by glare, is known as 'disability glare'. Another effect (more difficult to measure) is the discomfort experienced by an observer when subjected to glare for any length of time, referred to as 'discomfort glare'.

(iii) Local character and aesthetic requirements
A lighting installation must be of pleasing appearance by day as well as by night. The height of the mounting (for the lantern) should marry in with the general scale of its surroundings; too low a mounting can make the lighting installation appear insignificant while, on the other hand, lighting columns designed as part of the architectural concept may result in a mounting-height which causes glare or discomfort.

The gentle pace of pedestrian traffic necessitates more attention being given to the details of a design. Glare and uniformity of illumination play a less significant role: the

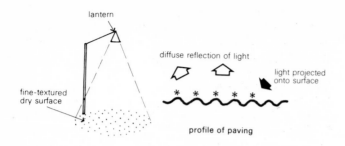

a. Fine-textured dry surface

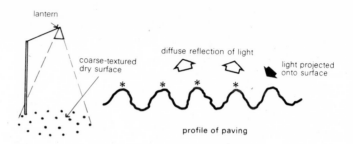

b. Coarse-textured dry surface

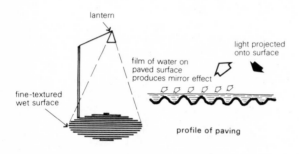

c. Fine-textured wet surface

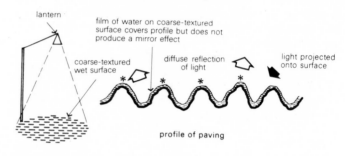

d. Coarse-textured wet surface

Fig. 43   Reflective properties of paved surfaces

emphasis is on good colour-rendering and on the decorative aspect of the lighting.

Choice of light source

Lighting level is based upon the surface luminance of the area; a dark paved surface, such as tarmac, requires twice as much illumination as does a light-coloured surface in order to acquire the same luminance.

Lighting uniformity is determined by luminance values and is of particular importance in street lighting. The impression of uniformity depends upon the distribution of the paved-surface luminance, which differs markedly according to whether the surface is wet or dry.

The choice among the many types of light source, and the variants of each, is usually a compromise since several factors play a part. The principal light sources (lamps) used in public lighting systems are set out below with a brief description of their qualities and application. Although theoretically several types of lamp may be used in one

lantern, the practical result would be considerable optical and mechanical complexity.

(i) *Incandescent lamps*. General lighting service (GLS) Halogen

The radiant energy is distributed continuously throughout the visible spectrum, resulting in good colour-rendering. The halogen quartz lamp has a greater efficiency and twice the life of a GLS lamp. Its high luminance permits accurately controlled light-distribution in a vertical plane, making it particularly suitable for lighting squares and parking areas and for floodlighting.

(ii) *Fluorescent lamps*: 'Short' TL, 'Long' TL

These lamps possess only a low luminance; a suitable light-distribution necessitates the use of large lanterns, making it an uneconomic installation. A more accurate control of light-distribution may be achieved using light-sources having a compact lighting element. Fluorescent lamps are suitable for use in built-up areas and in those places where colour-rendering is important.

(iii) *High-pressure mercury lamps* : Clear bulb (HP ; HP/T)
　　　　　　　　　　　　　　Blended light (MLL)
　　　　　　　　　　　　　　Fluorescent bulb (HPL)
　　　　　　　　　　　　　　Halide lamp (HPI)
The clear-bulb types give a poor colour-rendering and are unsuitable for built-up areas. The blended light is not specified for new installations but is used to replace incandescent lamps in old installations because of its longer life, so reducing operating costs. A reasonable colour-rendering may be achieved with the fluorescent bulb but the halide lamp is 60 per cent more efficient.

(iv) *Sodium lamps:* Low-pressure (SOI)
　　　　　　　　　　Low-pressure (SOX)
　　　　　　　　　　High-pressure (SON)
Low-pressure lamps (SOI and SOX) give very poor colour-rendering and should only be used where this is subordinate to traffic safety. Because of the drab impression created they are unsuitable at very low lighting levels. Although the high-pressure lamp gives a slightly yellowish-white light the colour-rendering is reasonable ; it is one of the most concentrated light-sources.

(v) *Xenon lamps*
Although colour-rendering is excellent the luminous efficiency is low and only large units are competitive with other light-sources. These lamps are suitable for parking and other off-street locations.

Lanterns
The presence of corrosive gases and moisture in the atmosphere means that the components of a lantern must be capable of withstanding corrosion over a long period of time. Corrosive-resistant metals, such as stainless steel and silicon—aluminium alloys, are likely to give better all-round service than that provided by purely protective finishes. If plastic is selected for covers, etc., it is essential to use only those of high quality which are not likely to deteriorate with age or exposure to the elements. Since plastic is unable to withstand high temperatures it is unsuitable for use with higher-wattage lamps. Glass is able to withstand high temperatures and is highly corrosive-proof, but has the disadvantage of weight and is subject to breakage.

It is essential that metal components in contact with one another should be carefully selected from those lying close to each other in the potential series, otherwise electro-

chemical corrosion is likely to result. The construction of the lantern needs to be sufficiently strong to withstand both vibration of the column (due to wind or traffic) and disalignment of the light beams as a result of stormy weather.

Reference should be made to BS 1788:1964 which specifies the performance required for street lighting lanterns and to CP 1004:Part 1:1973 which gives recommendations for mounting heights.

Illuminated signs

Apart from conveying its message (direction, advertisement or identification) a sign must be well-designed, functional and sited so that it does not detract from its surroundings. Statutory regulations govern the siting of signs in relation to traffic safety and general amenity and recommendations for their materials and wiring are set out in BS 559:1955.*

Illuminated signs fall into two main types : visible tubing and panels with superimposed motifs or lettering.

(i) *Visible tubing*. In this type of sign illuminated tubing forms the actual sign which is read at night. It may be fixed to a panel or fascia or set within individual letter shapes in such a manner that the tube is visible. In some cases a continuous tube is constructed to the shape of the lettering and the built-up background to it omitted, but this form necessitates careful design to avoid displaying the somewhat unsightly electrodes and cables during daylight.

If a dramatic or striking effect is desired this type of sign provides plenty of scope for the designer.

(ii) *Panels*. Construction may be of timber, glass, metal or plastic (or a combination of such materials) and the lettering or motif either applied to the face or set within the panel. In some cases, particularly where the face is of plastic, the lettering may be moulded into it and illuminated from behind (e.g. tops to petrol pumps). Consideration must be given to weatherproofing and provision made for ventilation so that the risk of condensation is avoided.

A sign may be a free-standing structure or fixed to a building. If it is suspended from cantilevered brackets,

*S.I.555 Town and Country Planning (Control of Advertisements) Regulations, 1969.

wind action must be taken into account. A lightweight panel may be subject to a considerable amount of pressure and, as a result, suffer damage.

Once the sign is erected in position it must be readily accessible for cleaning and maintenance repairs; where ladders cannot be used either a suspended cradle or framework with platform (as appropriate) may be required in order to reach the sign. Most reputable signmakers offer a maintenance contract which covers regular cleaning and inspection, repainting and any replacements needed. It is generally worth while to take advantage of this type of contract since it is in the interests of all parties concerned that a sign should be kept clean and in good working order.

Light sources
The function and siting of a sign are likely to be the main criteria determining the illumination required. Three types of lighting tube are employed: gas discharge, hot cathode and cold cathode.

(i) *Gas discharge tubes.* Tungsten lamps have been virtually replaced by gas discharge tubes for external purposes. In its simplest form the gas discharge tube is a glass tube filled to a low pressure with neon (an inert gas) through which an electric current is passed, causing the gas to ionise, giving the characteristic red colour. This is the true neon tube. In more sophisticated versions the inner surface of the tube is coated with fluorescent material and a low-pressure gas, such as argon, is used in conjunction with a few drops of mercury. The latter provides a source of ultraviolet radiation which excites the fluorescent coating, the visible light being almost entirely due to this material.

(ii) *Hot cathode tubes.* These fluorescent lamps (mostly made in straight lengths) are sometimes referred to as 'mains voltage' lamps because they are usually operated direct from low voltage AC mains supply through a choke. Their reasonably long life (average 5000 hours) and relatively low cost make their use an economical proposition in situations where only 'white' colours are required. e.g. for back-illumination of sign boxes and fascias. One of their main disadvantages is that after the first 100 hours the light output falls off and thereafter maintains a lower level. Ratings and lengths of lamps range from 20 W (0·61 m) to 125 W (2·43 m). Where it is necessary to use different lengths of tube it is essential that the lengths selected should each have a similar light output per unit length.

(iii) *Cold cathode tubes.* So far as the signmaker is concerned these lamps are by far the most useful because of their very long life (15000 hours) and the ease with which they can be formed into a variety of shapes; the simple robust control gear is also an asset.

Tubes of various diameters are manufactured, the most popular sizes being 9, 11, 15, 20 and 25 mm. A wide range of colours is achieved by the use of different types of fluorescent powder and gas filling: neon and argon/mercury.* The gases combine with the fluorescent powders to give the following results:

Neon combined with	*Colour*
Calcium tungstate and zinc silicate	Flame
Zinc silicate	Amber
Calcium magnesium silicate	Magenta

The true neon tube gives the normal red; for ruby red, the tube is made of ruby-red glass instead of clear glass.

Argon/mercury combined with	*Colour*
Zinc silicate	Green
Calcium tungstate	Blue
Halophosphate	Ice blue, sign white, yellow or apricot
Calcium silicate	Pink

Tubes filled with argon/mercury and fixed externally should be fitted with a cold weather electrode to ensure a constant level of brightness throughout the tube.†

Legibility
Standards of legibility are very difficult to assess because the comprehension of what is portrayed by a sign can be affected by atmospheric conditions and conflicting illuminations nearby; legibility depends also upon a number of interrelated factors, such as height of lettering, its design, spacing of individual letters and their illumination.

Height of letters. A rule-of-thumb method of assessing legibility assumes that 25-mm-high letters are visible (under good conditions) up to a distance of about 15 m

*In practice, a proportion of neon is included to improve the tube characteristics under winter conditions.

†Cold weather can cause the mercury vapour to distil away from the tube ends, causing the tube to appear darker at the ends and bright in the middle.

and that each additional 25 mm of letter height probably extends the visibility limit by a further 15 m (depending upon other factors described below). If legibility is doubtful, the size of the letters should be increased.

Type of lettering. The height of the letters and their face width are interrelated; the ratio of height to width should be approximately 4:3 with a stroke thickness (of an individual letter) of about $\frac{1}{6}-\frac{1}{5}$ of the letter height. Simple block type is more easily read than lettering with serifs; styles using extended or condensed letters tend to reduce clarity. If more elaborate styles are required the height ratio should be increased.

Spacing of letters. Spacing is another method of increasing legibility but it must be in keeping with the scale of the letters and layout. If two upright strokes of a letter are spaced less than 130–150 mm apart they are not discernible as such at a viewing distance of about 457 m. Where the letters are illuminated this spacing must be considerably increased to allow for 'halation' (i.e. 'blurring' or spreading of light from the tube); typographical spacing of letters does not apply in this case.

Illumination. A sign that is legible when not alight must not be assumed to be of equal (or better) legibility when illuminated; factors are in operation quite different from those of normal daylight conditions:
(a) Brightness: the intensity of light diminishes as the distance from which its source is viewed is increased. The light from a sign must be sufficient to make it comprehensible (as opposed to visible) to the human eye at the required distance.
(b) Colour: red gives the best penetration and effect at long range. Amber and green are less, and blue the least effective.
(c) Tube disposition: halation can result if a sign is too bright, making legibility difficult. Where the illuminated tubing is visible, halation may be reduced either by lowering the tube current and using open-trough section letters to channel the light or by enclosing the face in plastic, but this considerably increases the amount of tubing required.

Floodlighting

The purpose of floodlighting is to project light onto a particular object so as to create an illuminated feature. The three principal factors involved in the design of a layout are the nature and surface texture of the object to be floodlit, the level of illumination required and the extent of other lighting in the immediate vicinity.

The dimensions of the surfaces to be floodlit may vary from a single statue to many thousands of square metres of a large building, and affect the layout of the type of floodlighting equipment chosen. Surface texture, another important factor, falls into one of the following categories:

(a) *Matt.* The luminance of this type of surface remains practically constant for a given illumination from whatever angle the observation is made. A good uniformity is obtained by illuminating the surface at an angle that is not too oblique. *Examples:* dressed stone and brickwork.

(b) *Semi-matt.* The appearance of this surface may differ considerably according to both the direction of the light and the point of observation with respect to the surface. *Examples:* painted plasterwork and dull metal.

(c) *Specular.* Light is reflected from this surface as by a mirror, showing a clear image of the light-source; it produces a luminance practically equal to that of the actual source. Buildings close to water may be floodlit to give interesting effects of reflection on the water's surface, but care must be taken to see that only the illuminated surface and not the light-source itself is reflected. *Examples:* marble, glass and polished metal.

The level of illumination may be varied to suit the particular site needs; a piece of sculpture standing on its own against a dark background requires much less light than the façade of a building set in the centre of a brightly-lit town. The darker the surface, the higher must be the level of illumination. Its condition, too, has a bearing on its reflective properties: a dirty surface requires a higher level of illumination in order to give the required luminance. Table 26 gives the reflection factor for a range of materials, based on the use of incandescent lamps as the lighting-source. This should be taken as a guide since different reflection factors are obtained with different types of light-source (e.g. mercury, sodium, etc.). A preliminary test should be made with the light-source selected to ascertain whether the surface reflects sufficient light.

The surface of a building or monument set within a town centre is likely to receive a certain amount of illumination from the public lighting system within its vicinity. A

Table 26
Reflection factors of various facing materials *

Material	Condition of surface	Reflection factor
Brickwork: old	Dirty	0·05
red	New	0·25
yellow	New	0·35
white	New	0·80
Paintwork: imitation stone	Clean	0·50
Stone or concrete: dark	Dirty	0·05–0·10
	Clean	0·25
light	Clean	0·40–0·50
Granite	Clean	0·10–0·15
Marble: white	Clean	0·60–0·65

*The figures given in this table relate to the use of incandescent lamps as the light-source

greater intensity of floodlighting is therefore required to give the same results as that achieved on a building standing on its own, away from a public street.

Floodlighting equipment

Floodlighting is achieved by directing as much as possible of the luminous flux of a light-source in a beam of a particular form. This involves the use of mirrors or prisms (or a combination of both). The light: output ratio of a floodlight depends upon the type and size chosen, the light-source and the form and quality of mirrors employed.

Coloured light may be produced by using incandescent lamps with either filters or coloured metal mirrors or by employing gas discharge lamps. Both types of lamp have their advantages and disadvantages. Incandescent lamps are cheaper to install but their luminous efficiency does not equal that of gas discharge lamps. The main drawback of the latter is that they take at least five minutes to warm up and if put out accidentally cannot be switched on immediately, so that they are unsuitable for quick-change lighting effects.

Incandescent lamps used with filters. The dissipation of heat from these lamps is so great that it is necessary to place filters on the outside of the floodlights or, alternatively, to paint the appropriate colour onto the glass cover. A greater range of colour is achieved by using this method which is flexible, simple and inexpensive to install.

Incandescent lamps used with coloured metal mirrors. With the use of coloured reflectors, only the reflected light is coloured. If the colour is to be pure it is necessary to

prevent the emission of light directly from the lamp by using either a screen in the floodlight or special lamps with internally silvered tops.

Gas discharge lamps

(a) High-pressure mercury–vapour lamps with clear bulb (HP and HP/T): the spectrum of these lamps has a number of blue-green hues. They are useful for lighting white surfaces or where the predominant colour is in the blue-green range, or to give water a cool tint. Quite a narrow beam may be achieved.

(b) High-pressure mercury–vapour lamp with fluorescent bulb (HPL): the overall effect of this light is bluish-white, the very cold colour of mercury light being somewhat warmed by the phosphor which introduces more red. If used for floodlighting foliage it produces a more lifelike effect. Because the emitting surface is larger than that of the HP lamp it gives a rather diffuse beam and is not suitable for illumination sited a considerable distance away from the object.

(c) Mercury–halide lamp (HPI): the advantages of the clear mercury–vapour lamp (giving control of the beam shape) and the mercury lamp with fluorescent bulb (giving better colour-rendering) are combined and make for a very useful lamp for floodlighting purposes.

(d) Blended-light (mercury–incandescent) lamp (MLL): the beam produced by this lamp is not very concentrated, the effect being very similar to that of the mercury (HPL) lamp.

(e) High-pressure sodium–vapour lamp (SON): an ideal lamp where 'warm' colours are required since it produces more natural colour-rendering than the mercury (HPL) lamp. It has similar output to the clear mercury or mercury–halide lamps of the same wattage and a beam-control akin to that possible with the latter type of lamp.

(f) Low-pressure sodium–vapour lamp (SOI and SOX): this lamp needs to be used selectively because it emits a (practically) monochromatic light of an orange–yellow colour which, although ideal for creating the effect of autumnal tints with foliage and for producing interesting displays with white or light-coloured neutral surfaces, often results in black or grey colours if projected onto red brick or similar coloured surfaces.

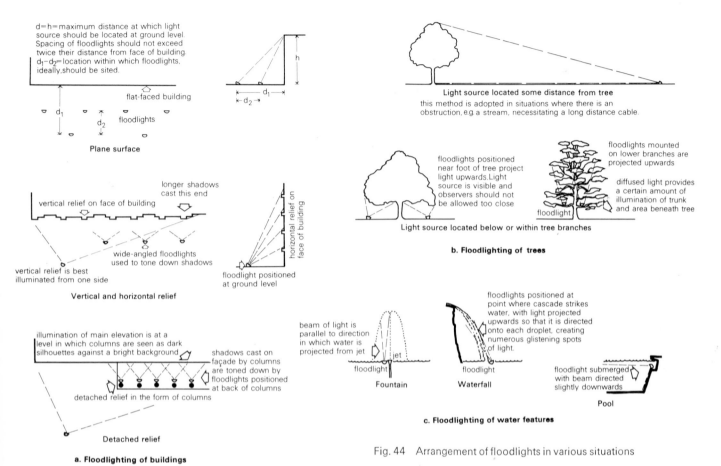

d=h=maximum distance at which light source should be located at ground level. Spacing of floodlights should not exceed twice their distance from face of building.
d_1–d_2= location within which floodlights, ideally, should be sited.

flat-faced building

d_1 d_2 floodlights

Plane surface

longer shadows cast this end

vertical relief on face of building

wide-angled floodlights used to tone down shadows

vertical relief is best illuminated from one side

horizontal relief on face of building

floodlight positioned at ground level

Vertical and horizontal relief

illumination of main elevation is at a level in which columns are seen as dark silhouettes against a bright background

shadows cast on façade by columns are toned down by floodlights positioned at back of columns

detached relief in the form of columns

Detached relief

a. Floodlighting of buildings

Light source located some distance from tree

this method is adopted in situations where there is an obstruction, e.g. a stream, necessitating a long distance cable.

floodlights positioned near foot of tree project light upwards. Light source is visible and observers should not be allowed too close

floodlights mounted on lower branches are projected upwards

diffused light provides a certain amount of illumination of trunk and area beneath tree

floodlight

Light source located below or within tree branches

b. Floodlighting of trees

beam of light is parallel to direction in which water is projected from jet

jet

floodlight

Fountain

floodlights positioned at point where cascade strikes water, with light projected upwards so that it is directed onto each droplet, creating numerous glistening spots of light.

floodlight

Waterfall

floodlight submerged with beam directed slightly downwards

Pool

c. Floodlighting of water features

Fig. 44   Arrangement of floodlights in various situations

(g) Coloured fluorescent lamp (TL) : the long dimensions of this lamp and its fittings, coupled with the fact that only low-powered units are available, restricts its use to schemes requiring continuous line lighting.

Arrangement of floodlights
Before determining the number of floodlights required it is necessary to assess the illumination desired. Allowance must be made for a certain depreciation factor due to the decrease in the luminous output of the lamps during their life, the accumulation of dust and dirt and a decrease in the reflectance of the mirrors that form part of the lights. Once the approximate number of lamps has been determined, consideration can be given to the precise orientation of the various lighting sources. This is dictated by the effect the floodlighting is intended to achieve. The height and angle at which the light-sources are placed can pro-

duce quite a range of different effects, and the shadows cast by relief on a façade create a sense of various depths according to the position of the spectator.

Vertical and horizontal relief (Fig.44a). The relief on a façade is best appreciated with the aid of cast shadows. Vertical relief should be lit from the side and horizontal relief either from above or below (generally the latter is the more practical method). Wherever possible there should be a certain angle between the main direction from which the building is viewed and the direction of the light-source in order to bring out the relief on the façade.

Sometimes the floodlighting of horizontal relief produces long shadows, particularly where there are cornices, and in such cases it may be necessary to compromise between bringing out the relief and the casting of long shadows by concealing a few floodlights to give additional illumination

to those areas insufficiently lit. The shadows may be toned down by placing floodlights to project light beams at right angles to those of the main floodlighting source.

Detached relief (Fig.44a). Where relief is detached from the main façade of a building, for example in the case of a portico, there are two methods of approach:

(a) Direct lighting: additional floodlights are placed in front, at the top or bottom of each detail of relief (e.g. columns) so that the beam, which is in an almost vertical plane, floodlights only that particular item of relief. The main beam of light is projected from some distance away from the facade in order to give a general lighting effect.
(b) Silhouette effect: the main beam of floodlighting is projected in a similar manner to that above except that the additional floodlights are placed behind the relief so that the details appear as dark silhouettes against a brightly lit background.

Vertical features. The character and form of the vertical feature dictate the positioning of floodlights, but care must be taken to avoid symmetrical lighting which is likely to produce equal luminance on adjoining faces. A round feature, such as a tower, should appear round and not as a flat strip. To achieve this, narrow beams are projected at a short distance from it, arranged at intervals of 120° so that the light edges of each beam are tangential to the tower, thereby bringing out the relief.

Most vertical features are viewed from more than one side simultaneously which means that adjoining faces must stand out from one another. If there is relief on each face one floodlight (or a group) is directed at an angle towards each face so that a certain amount of light is also thrown onto the adjoining face, thereby also assisting in toning down any shadows. This method is not suitable where there is no relief since all faces would appear alike.

A piece of sculpture may require only a single floodlight to show it to advantage but may be enhanced by installing subdued lighting in the surrounding area to give the impression of reflected light.

Plate 14
Floodlights used to create different illuminated effects on various parts of a building: *son et lumière* installation at Canterbury Cathedral.
Photo: Studio Jaanus, London.

Floodlighting landscape features
Where gardens, pools, fountains and other natural features in the landscape are the subject of floodlighting the approach depends upon the nature of the object and its setting.

Pools. Floodlighting on still water produces an entirely different effect from that on moving water. The flat surface of still water acts as a mirror, reflecting the floodlit scene surrounding it. In a formal pool underwater lights may be positioned around the perimeter, the beam of light directed downwards, to light the pool itself (Fig.44c).

Fountains. Although fountains may be lit in a similar manner to that used for buildings, a much more attractive effect is achieved by focusing light directly onto the main body of water so that it produces multiple reflections, giving each droplet of water the appearance of a glittering jewel.

For the best results the floodlights should be positioned at the base of the fountain so that each beam is parallel to the direction of the ejected spray of water. Where the water cascades down like a waterfall the floodlight may be directed to where the cascade actually hits the main body of water in the pool or basin (Fig.44c).

Foliage. The method used to floodlight foliage depends upon the effect desired. Foliage may be highlighted to show details or presented as a backcloth to some focal point, such as a building or sculpture (Fig.44b).

Trees may be illuminated by mounting floodlights on the lower branches so that the beams of light are projected upwards through the foliage. The leaves tend to diffuse the light, providing a certain illumination of the ground beneath, rather like that produced by indirect lighting.

Where the light-sources can be concealed, another solution is to place the floodlights at the base of the trees with the beam projected vertically so that the whole height of the tree is illuminated. This method is particularly attractive with plants of a weeping habit. It may also be used in combination with the previously described method, particularly for lighting large trees, and entails fixing high-powered floodlights along the lower branches to produce very strong illumination of the leaves near to the light-source.

If the foliage is to be seen as an effective background to a feature then the light-source should be placed some distance away so that details of the foliage are not observed.

Plate 15
Illumination at ground level of a specimen tree in the
Jephson Gardens, Leamington Spa. Note the additional
illumination of sitting areas near the tree.
Photo: John Maltby Ltd, London.

Plate 16 (opposite)
An example of floodlighting employed to create a
dramatic impact on the landscape : The Glen, Glengoyne
Distillery, Glasgow.
Photo: Ian Hamilton, Glasgow.

LIGHTNING PROTECTION

Effects of lightning

The principal effects of a lightning discharge on any structure are electrical, mechanical and thermal. The discharge may consist of either a single stroke or a sequence of strokes, all following in the same path and conducting separate currents which may last for at least one second.

Damage by lightning is due mainly to thermal effects; the temperature of the core of a lightning channel reaches up to 30 000°C and is capable of setting alight materials of a flammable nature, such as timber. Due to the short duration of the current flow, however, it has very little effect on metals—except thin metal foils which it may cause to fuse or weld.

Electrical effects on a lightning conductor system may cause a flashover (side flash) because of the magnitude of the lightning current and the resistivity of the soil in the vicinity of the point struck. Persons or animals within that area risk injury if the object struck is in an isolated position.

A mechanical effect may also result in damage, e.g. tiles lifted from roofs by the strong air pressure wave which results from the air channel formed between the thundercloud and the lightning conductor being suddenly raised to a very high temperature. There appears to be no means of providing protection against this effect because a lightning conductor is incapable of discharging a thundercloud without a lightning stroke.

Need for protection

Protection against the consequences of a lightning stroke may be approached in two ways: the first is to provide physical means of protection by installing a lightning protector; the second method is to cover the risk of damage occurring by insurance.

The decision as to whether a particular structure should be protected against lightning damage must depend upon the type of structure, its height, location, value, etc., compared with the calculated risk if no protection is provided. The incidence of thunderstorms in Britain is not particularly high, in some areas being less than three days in the year (Fig.45). If the general public are likely to be in the close vicinity of the structure the consequences of its being struck by lightning must be fully appreciated. In some cases the economics of providing physical protection may indicate that insurance cover is the more practical solution.

Structures for which protection is recommended in CP 326:1965 include the following:

Those near to or in which large numbers of persons are likely to congregate.
Essential public services.
Very tall or isolated structures.
Those of historical or other important interest.
Those situated in areas subject to a high incidence of thunderstorms.

Calculating the risk

It is possible to make some assessment of the chance that a particular structure may be struck by lightning. CP 326 gives a 'risk index', on which the risk status of a structure is calculated as a total of scores on seven tables covering:

(i)   Use to which the structure is put.
(ii) Type of construction.
(iii) Contents or type of building.
(iv) Degree of isolation (location of structure).
(v)   Type of country (height above sea level).
(vi) Height of structure above ground.
(vii) Lightning prevalence (number of days in the year on which thunderstorms occur).

For practical purposes a figure of about 40 is generally taken as critical but, although the risk index in some cases may be well below this figure, the problem must be looked at from a common-sense angle: in some cases the risk index may be low but the cost of protection cheap and simple. Any structure exceeding 53 m above ground level requires protection and similarly any part of it, such as a chimney, projecting more than 4·5 m above any adjoining structure, should be protected.

Protective systems and the materials employed

The object of providing a lightning conductor is to cause a lightning stroke to be diverted to it, thereby giving protection to the structure or object against the risk of damage which is likely to arise as a result of a direct lightning stroke. The area to which protection is given by a conductor is termed the 'zone of protection'. It is generally assumed for practical purposes that the protection provided by one conductor takes the form of a cone (the apex of which is the top of the finial) having a radius at the base equivalent to the height of the conductor and giving a protective angle of 45°. Where two or more conductors are spaced at a distance not exceeding twice their height the protective angle may be taken as 60° to the vertical.

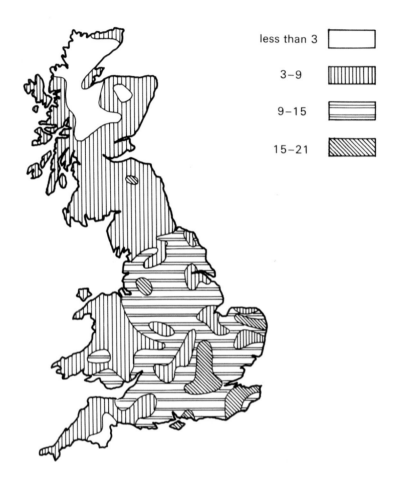

less than 3

3-9

9-15

15-21

Fig. 45   Number of days per year when thunderstorms occur (based on CP 326C : 1965)

Similarly, in the case of horizontal conductors the zone of protection is extended by the length of the conductor. Although the provision of a lightning conductor does not assure complete protection at any point within its zone, the likelihood of an undiverted stroke becomes remote.

Lightning protective systems
A protective system is made up of a number of components whose arrangement largely depends upon the type of structure and the extent of the protection needed. A lightning protective system comprises the following principal components:

(i)   Air terminations: intercept the lightning discharge.
(ii)   Down conductors: act as connectors between air termination and earth.
(iii) Joints and bonds: joints are formed between any two parts of the system; bonds connect underground metal service pipes to the earth termination.

(iv) Earth terminations: allow the lightning current passing down a protective system to discharge into the general mass of earth.

Lightning protection installations are basically of two kinds, both of them static:

Franklin. A lightning conductor system which protects the volume of a cone where the radius of its base is equal to the height of the conductor.

Faraday. A cage installation comprising multiple air terminals fixed at salient points on a roof and bonded together to form a mesh which is connected to down conductors.

Radioactive method of protection
This method is dynamic in operation and basically consists of a container in which are radioactive sources capable of creating ions (extremely small particles) in vast quantities. Because of their excellent conductive properties these ions are drawn up by the intense electric field which exists when a discharge of lightning approaches, so that they form a conductive streamer which meets the lightning discharge and conveys it safely to earth. This means that the effective height of an air terminal, as installed in the Franklin system, is extended and, in consequence, the zone of protection increased.

Under the Radioactive Substances Act, 1960, all premises having radioactive substances must be registered. Exemption of radioactive lightning protectors from the requirements of this Act is contained in Statutory Instrument No. 1835, The Radioactive Substances (Attachments to Lightning Conductors) Exemption Order, 1963.

The radioactive type of protection is not a preferred method for use in Britain and offers no real advantage over the static types.

Materials
Copper and aluminium are the most durable materials used in lightning protection systems but others may also be employed. All materials must comply with the relevant British Standard as set out below:

Aluminium	BS 2898:1970
Copper	
Phosphor-bronze	BS 2874:1969
Naval brass	
Stainless steel	BS 970:Part 4:1970; BS 1449:Part 4:1967

Galvanised mild steel wire	BS 443:1969; BS 1052:1942

The use of some metals externally incurs a risk of corrosion due to chemicals in the atmosphere, particularly where dissimilar metals used in close proximity to each other are not adequately protected against the effects of moisture. Water running over one metal and passing onto another may also lead to corrosion; copper, copper alloys and lead can attack aluminium alloys and zinc.* The presence of sulphur compounds may cause severe corrosion of copper (especially in inaccessible places); a coating of lead should be applied where there is a risk of such corrosion. Joints and bonds may be protected with bitumen or a non-corrosive compound. Where coatings are used, due regard must be given to their durability and non-flammability.

Protection of various outdoor features

In public places the effects of a lightning stroke may easily cause an outbreak of panic in a crowd of people, leading to disastrous results.

The means whereby various features may be protected are described below.

Trees
The economics of providing protection cannot generally be justified unless a tree is of particular historical or botanical importance. CP 326 recommends that a conductor should be positioned to run from the uppermost part of the trunk to the earth termination. The large upper branches should be similarly protected by branch conductors bonded to the main conductor, allowance being made for any swaying action of the tree due to the wind. Two rods driven into the ground opposite each other and close to the tree trunk form the earth termination and, in addition, are bonded by means of two radial conductors to a strip conductor entrenched in the ground, spaced not less than 600 mm from the spread of the overhead branches or with 8 m radius, whichever is the greater.

If several trees growing close together are to be protected, the earth conductor should encircle the group.

An isolated tree adjacent to a structure may be disregarded if it is of a lesser height, but if higher than the structure it can only be considered safe if the distance between them

*See Table 17, Electrochemical series, page 78.

is equal to at least half the height of the structure. If less, the structure should be protected and the air termination or down conductor positioned so that it passes as close as possible to the nearest part of the tree.

Metal fences
Persons or livestock risk injury if in contact with or in close proximity to a metal fence at the moment of a lightning discharge. To counter this risk any continuous length of metal fencing should incorporate 600 mm gaps spaced at 300 m intervals. In practice, such gaps are often made wider to incorporate a gate of timber or other non-conducting material. It is also necessary for the fence to be earthed at regular intervals: 76 m in dry soils or 152 m in permanently damp soils. These earth terminations must be positioned at least 7·62 m from either side of each gap. Earthing may be effected by clamping the fence either to metal uprights set in the ground or to separate earth electrodes.

Marquees
One of the simplest methods of providing protection consists of suspending one or more horizontal air terminations above the marquee from vertical supports. A clearance of at least 1·52 m should be maintained between conductor and fabric; down conductors arranged outside the marquee should be connected to earthing rods, the latter being fixed to a ring conductor (in a position inaccessible to persons using the marquee). Any metal framework forming part of the marquee structure must also be effectively earthed at intervals of not more than 30 m.

Spectator stands
Timber and metal scaffolding are the main constructional elements in the erection of spectator stands and public seating accommodation. Peripheral structural members must be earthed at intervals of not more than 30 m by means of a metal strip (not aluminium) bonded to the base plates carrying the vertical members.

Floodlighting towers and tall metal masts
Tall structures exceeding 30 m should be provided with at least one down conductor. Where stay-wires support a mast, the upper ends of the wire should be bonded to the lightning protective system and the lower ends earthed.

Six Hard Paved Surfaces

The role of hard landscaping

It is not always fully appreciated just how important hard landscaping is to the achievement of good environmental design. The paved surface has a variety of forms each of which must relate to a particular functional need: a motorway, a perambulatory route; a patio; a floorscape to complement a focal feature, or perhaps as a substitute for plants in a location where their survival may be in doubt because of the risk of wear and tear by foot-traffic. It cannot be considered in isolation from all the other elements which together make up the landscape, but must form an integral part of the overall design concept. Although a paved surface is sometimes a useful medium in helping to solve a maintenance problem it should not be adopted arbitrarily without first considering other factors.

Function

To perform its role successfully a paved surface must be capable of resisting the effects of weather, the loads imposed upon it and the surface abrasion to which it is likely to be subjected. The nature and extent of the stresses which the paving must withstand inevitably dictate the type of material to be used in its construction. A road requires a different design technique from that adopted for a footway.* In some instances the function of a paved surface may be that of substitute for vulnerable areas of soft landscaping or to create a defined route for foot traffic. Paving is also employed to provide areas where, for a variety of reasons, people may congregate.

Orientation
Most paving materials are capable of absorbing a considerable amount of solar heat when exposed to the direct rays of the sun, particularly during the summer months, causing physical discomfort. Reflected light may cause glare, depending upon the reflective qualities of the surfacing material. Visual discomfort may be intensified when the surface is wet and in direct sunlight.

In shady locations these kinds of problem are not present but moss or lichen is liable to accumulate, causing the surface to become slippery unless it is regularly swept.

Proximity to other elements
The siting of buildings or other structures has a direct influence upon the microclimate of an area and may in some circumstances be detrimental to the establishment of plant life in a particular location. Although it is possible to assume the direction of wind channelling at the design stage it is often difficult, without recourse to expensive tests in a simulated wind tunnel, to assess the extent of wind eddying that is likely to result. In those areas where plants cannot easily be established, hard paving of some sort is a useful substitute.

Dense shade may also be a problem. Some trees, particularly conifers, are not conducive to the establishment of plants beneath them, causing bare patches of earth to remain. A layer of crushed stone chippings spread there is a better alternative to impervious paving and allows rain to percolate through to the tree roots.

Surface ducts conveying utility services cannot readily be concealed except when incorporated within a paved area. Care is needed to ensure that the positions of access covers coincide as nearly as possible with the pattern of the paving.

*Use of the term 'pavement' to describe a pedestrian path is deprecated since it is a general description applied to any superficial covering for an external surface, such as a road or footway. More specifically it is used to describe a road construction comprising various layers above the subgrade which form a supporting structure for vehicular traffic.

Designing for vehicular traffic

The design of a road is based upon the projected commercial vehicle capacity per day which flows along it. Highway engineering is a discipline beyond the scope of this book; road design should be entrusted to a qualified engineer for all but private access, service and similar minor roads (i.e. up to forty-five commercial vehicles per day).

A road structure (carriageway) may be either rigid (concrete) or flexible (coated macadam) (Fig.46a and b). The latter is more speedily constructed and easier to repair than a rigid one which, although generally designed to carry heavier loads, requires less maintenance. The nature of the materials employed and the depth of the carriageway are dependent upon the load-bearing value of the subgrade (i.e. the subsoil beneath the road structure) which may vary along its route. In weaker areas the subsoil (or other subgrade material) must be strengthened, that of poor load-bearing value being replaced with suitable hardfill to give the required strength.

It is essential that the level of the water-table is kept at least 610 mm below that of the road formation to ensure that there is no risk of damage by frost resulting in a weakening of the structure. Moisture content and density of a soil affect its structural properties and load-bearing capacity. These are of considerable importance where clay is present since its load-supporting power decreases with the increase in moisture and becomes very low when the soil is in a saturated state. To allow the moisture content to remain constant, good waterproofing, particularly of joints, is necessary.

Rigid paving (concrete)

The ability of a concrete carriageway to carry loads over the subgrade without the need for a base makes it comparatively independent of the nature of the subsoil. The structural rigidity of the concrete slab (forming the rigid road structure) allows applied loads to be spread over a large subgrade area. Where the formation of the subgrade is uneven, however, a layer of granular material, capable of being compacted to a depth of not less than 76 mm, should be specified. Where it is found necessary to provide a base, hard, durable, chemically inert material should be used, suitably graded so that it is capable of being compacted to a high density without being affected by frost or liable to deformation due to changes in moisture content or imposed traffic loads.

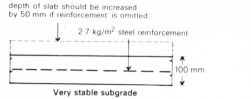

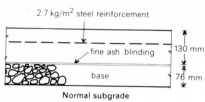

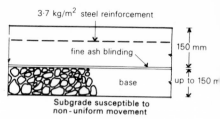

a. Examples of rigid paving (concrete) constructed on various types of subgrade

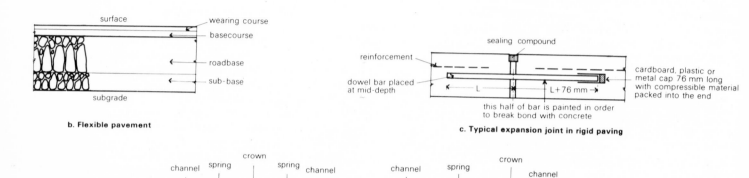

b. Flexible pavement

c. Typical expansion joint in rigid paving

d. Carriageway profiles

Fig. 46   Types of construction and profile of carriageways

Table 27
Concrete slab design for minor roads

Type of subgrade	Slab thickness (mm)	Weight of reinforcement (kg/m²)	Base thickness (mm)
Normal	130	2·7	76
Very stable	100	2·7	no base
Very susceptible to non-uniform movements	150	3·7	up to 150
Embankment more than 1200 mm high	150	3·7	76
Where water-table is within 600 mm of formation	150	3·7	up to 150
Chalks and other soils susceptible to frost heave	150	3·7	up to 355

Concrete slab design (Fig.46a)

The concrete slab is the chief structural component. Its design thickness depends upon the intensity of vehicular traffic using it and the condition of the subgrade. The latter is classified into three categories: normal, very stable and very susceptible to non-uniform movement. For the purposes of calculating the design thickness of the slab and base three other categories are taken into account: embankments more than 1200 mm high; subgrades where the water-table may rise to within 600 mm of the formation; chalks or other soils susceptible to frost heave.

For traffic intensities of up to forty-five commercial vehicles per day the design thicknesses shown in Table 27 are those recommended by the Road Research Laboratory (Table 2, Road Note No.19).

Where a base is necessary a lean-mix concrete, using one part cement to 15–24 parts aggregate, is recommended. An underlay of waterproof paper (to BS 1521:1972, Class B) or polythene sheeting must be spread right across the base material to prevent bonding of the concrete slab to it, thus eliminating the risk of severe cracks developing or friction being set up. It also removes the possibility of any chemical present in the base or subgrade coming into contact with and attacking the concrete, thereby causing a weakening of the structure.

The concrete is deposited in position, either in bays or by what is known as the continuous method, and spread to a level approximately 25 mm above that of the finished surface to allow for compaction. Where coloured concrete is specified only the top 50–76 mm is coloured, the remainder consisting of ordinary Portland cement; pigment should conform to BS 1014:1961. Extra care is needed during the mixing process to ensure that each batch is consistent in colour.

Aggregates may also be used to introduce a particular colour. Reference should be made to the Road Research Laboratory Road Note No.25 which gives a list of sources.

Reinforcement

Steel reinforcement is used for all categories of concrete roads but may be omitted from those shown in Table 27, in which case the slab should be 50 mm thicker than that indicated for reinforced concrete. The main purpose of using steel reinforcement is to minimise the number of cracks developing in the road slab and to prevent any that do occur from opening. Reinforcing mesh should be in accordance with the recommendations laid down in BS 4483:1969 and positioned so that it remains uniform throughout the slab with not less than 50 mm concrete cover. All joints must be lapped and 13 mm expansion joints provided at intervals of 12 m (or 19 mm at 24 m intervals if the subgrade is clay or made-up ground).

The function of expansion joints (transverse joints) is to prevent the development of cracks due to thermal expansion as a result of a rise in the atmospheric temperature. A pre-moulded, compressible, non-extruding material, such as cork or cellular rubber, is used to fill the gap (Fig. 46c).

Flexible pavements (Fig.46b)

The term 'flexible' is applied to those pavements made up of layers of materials comprising individual particles whose interlocking abilities (generally in conjunction with a binding agent) provide a stable structure, capable of supporting superimposed loads, and possessing a low flexural rigidity due to the nature of the constructional materials, which tend to conform to a limited movement once laid and compacted in position.

The function of a flexible pavement is to provide a surface which, by its nature, is capable of carrying the traffic loads imposed upon it and also serves to protect the road foundation from the actions of the weather, by preventing water from penetrating the subgrade so that the risk of frost heave in the subsoil is eliminated.

A flexible road structure is composed of a foundation and a surface. The nature and thickness of the materials employed depend upon the load-bearing value of the subgrade. Where it is necessary to spread the weight of transmitted loads over a wide area of the subgrade the thickness of the road structure is increased by providing a sub-base. The base must be constructed to the full width of the road structure, of uniform thickness throughout, and well compacted using materials which are able to conform to a certain limited movement after being laid in position.

Roadbases

Any of the following materials may be used to form the roadbase:

Hardcore. Most kinds of hard broken stone are suitable. These are spread in layers not normally exceeding 150 mm in thickness and well compacted. Individual stones should not be less than 50 mm along a single dimension and laid so that they interlock and prevent over-riding of others which might result in the transmission of movement to the surfacing material.

Handpitching. The high labour costs involved in laying this type of base preclude its use in all but exceptional circumstances. Depth is governed by the weight and volume of traffic and the load-bearing capacity of the soil and may vary between 115 and 250 mm. A 50–100 mm layer of granular material (e.g. gravel, clinker or shale) is spread over the formation to provide a cushion for the handpitching. The tops of projecting stones are knapped off to give a more even appearance and smaller pieces of stone placed in the interstices between the larger stones. A thin layer of granular material (blinding) lightly spread over the surface further assists in binding together the base and produces an even surface after rolling. The latter operation must be done in a longitudinal direction (i.e. parallel to the channel) because the impact of traffic loads upon a carriageway has a tendency to superimpose forces which cause lateral spreading of the structure.

Waterbound macadam. Coarse aggregate, granular material and stone dust are bound together by the addition of water and then laid in position and compacted to the required depth.

'Wet-mix' consists of 38–50 mm aggregate, stone dust and water, the proportion of fines not exceeding 10 per cent so that the interlocking ability of the aggregate is not impaired.

Coated macadam. Aggregate, binder and filler comprise this material which is defined in BS 892:1967 as graded aggregate coated with a bituminous binder. The latter may be either bitumen or tar, the relevant coated macadams being referred to as bitumen macadam or tarmacadam respectively. Aggregates used are either natural (complying with BS 812:1967) or artificial (e.g. blastfurnace slag). The filler combines with the binder to increase the thickness of the coating to the aggregate, helping to fill the small voids and increasing the viscosity to prevent any run-off. The material is laid by machine and compacted in two layers to an overall depth of 100 mm.

Concrete. A lean-mix concrete using one part cement to 15–24 parts aggregate may be employed as a base, but is unsuitable for a concrete road slab since its compressive strength is not sufficient to provide a wearing surface.

Coarse aggregate should be 38 mm and fine material capable of passing a 5 mm sieve. For a bituminous carriageway a 200–300 mm thick base is laid as two-course material, each layer being compacted in turn.

Cement-stabilised soil. Soil-cement is one of the cheapest materials available for use as a road base and is capable of supporting heavy loads, but its surface is not resistant to abrasion by traffic. The majority of soils may be stabilised with cement, the exceptions being the highly organic types, such as peat and rich agricultural topsoils. Heavy soils generally require the addition of granular material, consisting of up to 20 per cent of their bulk. The proportion of cement needed is determined by tests but is usually about 10 per cent. Lime is sometimes used to assist in the mixing process since it acts as a flocculating agent to break up cohesive soils and assists in stabilising acidic clay soils, i.e. soils most susceptible to shrinkage. Calcium chloride is effective in counteracting the inhibiting effect of organic matter within the soil upon the setting cement.

Surfacing materials

If the carriageway foundation is to give adequate service it must be protected from the elements by a waterproof surface which may be of either one or two courses. Single-course surfacing consists of a single depth of mixed graded material laid directly onto the roadbase. Sometimes the roadbase and basecourse are combined in one structural layer; where a bituminous roadbase is specified no basecourse is required. In two-course work a surface or wearing-course of fine-graded material is laid on a basecourse comprising coarse-graded material. The choice between these two methods of providing a surface depends upon the type of material used for the basecourse and the nature of the traffic to which it is subjected.

The Road Research Laboratory Road Note No.29 gives recommendations for bituminous surfacings for newly constructed roads based on the number of commercial vehicles per day. Reference should also be made to Road Note No.39 which deals with road surface dressing.

Some materials are easier to lay than others, particularly the open- and medium-textured macadams which possess a low fines content. Coated macadams incorporating gravel aggregate are not as satisfactory as those using crushed stone but are less expensive. Although dense bitumen macadam is generally classed as a wearing-course there has been a tendency in recent years to use it for both basecourses and roadbases. It differs from the open- and medium-textured bitumen macadams by reason of its higher content of fine aggregate and the use of a more viscous binder. Together these produce a material which, when laid and compacted, gives a strong and almost impervious structure capable of withstanding heavy traffic loads.

The most expensive types of bituminous material are compressed-rock asphalt and natural rock asphalt; both types are spread by hand and finished with coated chippings. Hot-rolled is the cheapest form of asphalt; when laid either as a single course, two-course, or wearing-course on a dense coated macadam basecourse it provides a very durable surface.

Surface dressings play an important role in carriageway construction by taking the maximum stress imposed by the wheel load. This is transmitted in turn to the base and thence to the sub-base and, finally, the subgrade.

The bearing capacity of a subsoil is determined by tests whose results are expressed as the 'California bearing ratio'. In Road Note No. 29, referred to above, the graph employed for this purpose is fully described and shows the depth of construction necessary for various soil types.

The role played by binders. The term 'bituminous materials' is applied to the various binders used in the construction of flexible pavements. Their ability to resist flow (viscosity) is the chief characteristic which plays a vital role in the manufacture of coated macadams ; the higher the viscosity the stiffer the binder, thus determining the temperature at which the material should be rolled. 'Bituminous' refers to both tar and bitumen binders.

(a) Tar, although cheaper than bitumen, is not so durable for use in open-textured wearing-courses since it is more susceptible to weathering. Tar softens when heated, an advantage for spraying purposes. Its adhesive properties are better than those of bitumen and it is less readily soluble in petrol and fuel oils.

Tar for road use is obtained from crude coal tar, a by-product of those industries producing coke or town gas by carbonisation of coal, subjected to a refinery process. The residue is blended with selected oils to make it sufficiently fluid for use. BS 76 : 1964 classifies tars according to their rate of setting on exposure. Three grades are obtainable :

Rapid setting	For use in close-textured tarmacadams, basecourses and surface dressings.
Medium setting	For use in medium-textured macadams
Slow setting	For use in open-textured macadams

(b) Bitumen : road bitumen is derived from asphaltic petroleum and is produced in the following forms (BS 3690 : 1970) :

Straight-run or residual	A very hard product which can be softened but is only workable at high temperatures. Various grades are available and are grouped according to their penetration ('pen') value.
Cut-back	Volatile oils are added to petroleum bitumen to give it reduced viscosity so that it is more fluid.
Emulsion	The bitumen content is normally 50–65 per cent, dispersed in water with the addition of a small quantity of stabiliser. Although an emulsion may be used without being heated and applied to a damp surface, it cannot be used when the temperature is below freezing point. (BS 434 : 1973.)

Asphalts. These dense, impervious materials, consisting principally or wholly of bitumen and fine mineral filler, are either derived from natural sources or are manufactured mixtures of mineral aggregates and bitumen or natural asphalt.

Natural asphalt occurs in two forms, rock asphalt and lake asphalt (obtained from a lake in Trinidad), and provides the material for the more expensive surfacings. Rock asphalt is a porous limestone impregnated with about 10 per cent bitumen and is the basic material of compressed-rock asphalt. Lake asphalt is a natural deposit containing finely dispersed mineral aggregate.

Manufactured asphalts include rolled asphalt, mastic asphalt and fine cold asphalt. The lifespan of compressed-rock asphalt, rolled asphalt and mastic asphalt is about twenty years ; that of cold asphalt is in the region of eight to ten years.

(a) Compressed-rock asphalt : a dense asphalt which, because of the expense involved, is only used for surfacing areas subjected to exceptionally heavy traffic. The material is in the form of a black powder, laid hot (120 °C), spread to the required level (38–58 mm) and punned to give a heavy-duty surface which is then covered with a layer of precoated chippings. A vibrating roller is used to bed these into the surface ; additional rock-asphalt is brushed in to provide better adhesion for the chippings.

(b) Rolled asphalt (to BS 594 : 1973) : the least expensive and most commonly used asphalt on heavily trafficked roads, this material gives a very durable surface. It consists of a dense mixture of stone (normally less than 5 mm), sand, filler and bitumen or asphalt heated to a temperature of 150–190 °C so that all the aggregate is dry before being mixed. The material is spread and levelled to the depth of a one-course or two-course application (38–76 mm). Full depth compaction of the asphalt must be carried out so that a good riding quality is achieved. The surface may be roughened by rolling in chippings.

(c) Mastic asphalt (to BS 1446 : 1973 and 1447 : 1973) : this material, which has a higher bitumen content than that of rolled asphalt, possesses good abrasive qualities which make it ideally suited to withstand the impact of heavy traffic in vulnerable areas (e.g. bus stops). The mixture consists of rock-asphalt or bitumen and mineral aggregate (6–10 mm) ; this is heated to around 200 °C and laid to a depth of 25–50 mm. Precoated chippings may be spread over the surface and bedded into the asphalt with a smooth roller.

(d) Cold asphalt (to BS 1690:1962): a versatile dense, intermediate material which, although containing less bitumen and not completely impermeable, may be used for a variety of purposes and is capable of being laid by comparatively unskilled labour. It is less susceptible to the effects of bad weather when being laid. Originally it was always laid cold–hence the description–but often it is spread and compacted while still warm and provides a smooth wearing-course. Almost any type of basecourse is suitable for either coarse cold or fine cold asphalt, but a tack coat of bitumen emulsion should be uniformly sprayed on the surface shortly before laying the wearing-course to provide an adhesive film.

Dense tar surfacing (*DTS*). A specification for the work entailed has been prepared by the British Road Tar Association but there is no British Standard Specification for this material, which is similar to rolled asphalt but cheaper and made with tar. The latter is heated before being added to the aggregate and filler and thoroughly mixed until every part of the aggregate is completely covered (not less than 1·5 minutes).

The material may be laid by machine or hand but the latter method must not be adopted when the air temperature falls below 5°C; compaction is by means of a light roller (6–10 tonnes). Where coated chippings are specified for 35 per cent stone content DTS these should be applied across the surface of the wearing-course immediately after the material has been spread and levelled and then rolled while still at the correct rolling temperature. Sizes of the chippings may be 19 mm or 13 mm coated with 2 per cent tar similar to that used for the DTS; 2 per cent filler is often added to ensure that the chippings carry the proportions of tar binder.

Although more expensive than coated macadam, DTS has the advantage of being an impervious material which is resistant to softening caused by oil spillage, making it suitable for car parking areas.

The basecourse and wearing-course may be laid as one operation; where they are two separate layers a uniformly and thinly spread tack coat must be applied to the (dry) surface of the basecourse.

Coated macadams. The stability of these materials lies principally in the interlocking ability of the individual stones which, when compacted, form a major factor in the strength of a roadbase or surface. Graded aggregate is precoated with tar or bitumen to which is added a filler, the material being referred to as either tarmacadam or bitumen macadam according to the type of binder used. Coated macadams are distinguishable from asphalts by their open type of stony structure and classified as either open- or medium-textured coated macadams or dense-coated macadams. Open-textured macadams are fairly easy to lay because they have a low fines content, but are more permeable than the medium- or dense-coated macadams and usually require a surface dressing in order to make the structure waterproof. All these materials are suitable for light traffic and have a lifespan of six to eight years. (BS 4987:1973.)

Open- or medium-textured macadams include:

(a) Tarmacadam (to BS 802:1967): sizes of aggregate (crushed rock or slag) vary according to the type of surfacing; reference should be made to the British Standard which contains tables setting out the sizes required for various types of carriageway surfacing and similar constructions:

Basecourse	Cold or warm laid
Single course	Cold, warm or hot laid
Open-textured wearing-course	Cold or warm laid
Medium-textured wearing-course	Warm laid

(b) Tarmacadam (to BS 1241:1959): used for purposes similar to that above, the aggregate (gravel) is not as satisfactory but its initial cost is less. The rate of coverage varies according to the nominal size of aggregate used and the thickness of the course.

(c) Bitumen macadam (to BS 2040:1953): the mixing temperature varies according to the type of binder used; excessive heating may affect the macadam. Crushed rock, furnace slag or gravel aggregate may be used but the latter, although cheaper, is not as satisfactory as crushed stone.

(d) Tarmacadam 'tarpaving' (to BS 1242:1960): not strictly a road-surfacing material since its use is confined generally to footpaths, playgrounds, etc. It may be laid warm or cold but the operation should not be undertaken during unsuitable weather. Each course must be compacted separately to the specified thickness.

Dense-coated macadams include:

(a) Dense bitumen macadam (to BS 1621:1961):

crushed rock is specified as aggregate; the percentage of binder varies according to the category of traffic using the road surface.

(b) Dense tarmacadam: similar to the open- or medium-textured tarmacadam, described above, but containing a higher percentage of fines and a more viscous binder which provides an almost impervious surface or base that is stronger and able to carry traffic.

Pavings for pedestrian traffic

Some of the materials described below are capable of carrying occasional light wheeled traffic, such as that found in pedestrianised ways in town centres, provided that an adequate foundation is laid which is capable of carrying the imposed loads without damage to the pavement.

Stone flags
The hardness of a stone is the test of its quality as a surfacing material. Laminated rock, which readily splits along the bedding planes and possesses a sufficiently high density to resist spalling by the action of frost, is ideal for use as flagstones. The close-grained sandstones fall into this category, the colours ranging from blue, blue-grey to brown, fawn and buff (the medium and open-grained textured pinks and reds are unsuitable). Perhaps the best and certainly the most popular one which meets all these requirements is York stone (Elland Edge flagrock, known also as 'hard York stone').

Although Portland stone is rather soft (oolitic limestone) it is sometimes used in a formal layout where no excessive wear is anticipated. Purbeck Portland is a harder limestone but more expensive.

The choice of material depends upon several factors, discussed at the beginning of this chapter. In all instances the stone selected must possess hardwearing qualities that prevent its surface from becoming smooth and slippery (particularly when wet) underfoot; riven or axed finish is appropriate for less formal work and sawn face or rubbed for formal paved areas. Thicknesses vary from 50 to 76 mm, depending upon the size of the individual flags and situation in which they are to be used.

On normal soils (i.e. lighter clays, sandy clays, fine sands, sand-and-gravel or gravel) the stone flags are laid on a 76 mm thick foundation of clean hardcore or granular material blinded with sand. They may be laid direct or spot bedded—a traditional method in which a mortar dot is placed at each corner and in the centre of the flag to assist the levelling process. A fairly common alternative is to set the flags on a 25 mm layer of dry sand, care being taken to ensure that there is no risk of the sand being washed out by the action of rain. A crossfall of 1:32 is generally provided to allow surface water to drain away readily.

Joints may be either close-butted or sealed with a grouting comprising five parts fine stone aggregate to one part lime or cement. Sometimes the joints are left open, allowing water to percolate through and alleviating the need for drainage. This is not usually very satisfactory because a gap is left through which weeds may grow and which is a potential risk to pedestrians—a narrow heel or umbrella ferrule may inadvertently lodge there. Instead of using a grout, a dry mixture of similar proportions may be brushed into the joints; this ultimately hardens, performing a similar function to that of grouting.

Slate paving
An expensive material with wearing qualities similar to those of granite; slate is slow to weather and unless riven or frame-sawn has a tendency to become slippery when wet. Thicknesses of slate range from about 13 to 50 mm, depending upon the size of individual slabs; the tendency is to use smaller slabs, in the 450×230 mm range, since these are cheaper. Slate slips are also available for paving odd-shaped areas or as infilling to paving patterns. Offcuts are sometimes used in lieu of setts to form lines of demarcation. Laying techniques are similar to those described for stone flags.

Pre-cast concrete flags (to BS 368:1971)
This is one of the most popular materials used for pedestrian paving and is relatively inexpensive. Sizes of slabs are given in BS 368:1971, thicknesses ranging from 38 mm to 65 mm, depending upon size. Non-slip surfaces are available in a variety of patterns; a non-slip finish is also achieved by casting carborundum into the top surface.

There is no British Standard which deals specifically with reconstructed stone flags but where such material is specified it should generally conform to the recommendations laid down in BS 1217:1945. If pigments are used they should meet the requirements set out in BS 1014:1961; the slab may be coloured throughout its thickness or in a 13 mm surface layer only.

Flags of various shapes are available: reference should be made to manufacturers' catalogues. An inexpensive

Plate 17
A pleasant pedestrian route : stone flags and setts
provide the floorscape pattern in this tree-lined walk
alongside the River Ouse in York.
Photo: George Perkin, ARIBA.

paved surface may be constructed of broken flags laid to a random pattern ('crazy paving').

Bricks and brick pavers

Bricks have been used as a paving material for centuries; some of the finest historical examples of the art of paving in this medium are to be seen in the Netherlands.

A wide range of bricks is manufactured but only those known to be resistant to the action of frost and possessing a low calcium and magnesium content are suitable for paving purposes. Over-firing of bricks in the kiln is not a bad fault in this instance since it serves to reduce the risk of damage due to the action of sulphates within the brick. It is important, however, that sulphate-resistant cement is used for both laying and jointing the bricks, otherwise the presence of magnesium sulphate in the soil may attack and damage the cement.

No British Standard at present exists for paving bricks, as such, but those selected should be hardwearing, with a non-slip surface. A rectangular clay paver is available which conforms to the frost-resistance requirements laid down in BS 3921 : 1974.

The bricks and pavers should be laid on a firm foundation of 100 mm clean hardcore and bedded on a mix of 1 : 4 lime : sand, 1 : 1 : 6 lime : cement : sand or 1 : 3 cement : sand, and pointed in a 1 : 3 mortar. Where traffic is likely to run across the paving the depth of the hardcore base should be increased to 150 mm with 100–150 mm 1 : 2 : 4 concrete laid on top; bedding of the bricks and pavers is as described above.

Setts (to BS 435 : 1931 and BS 706 : 1936)

At one time many town streets were paved with setts. Nowadays, because of the cost of laying them, their use is restricted chiefly to the formation of channels and to pedestrian areas, as a decorative medium.

New granite setts (BS 435 : 1931) are expensive, but where old setts have been taken up and roads resurfaced, they can sometimes be obtained more cheaply secondhand from the local authority. Although granite is the hardest-wearing material, sandstone setts (BS 706 : 1936) are also available and are an adequate substitute.

The setts should be laid on a firm foundation; normally this consists of a layer of coarse clinker, compacted to a depth of 50 mm, blinded with ash, over which is spread a 13 mm layer of sand which acts as a cushion and assists in taking up any irregularities in the setts themselves.

Joints between the smaller setts (150×100 mm) are usually 10 mm wide but this may be increased with the larger sizes according to the designer's choice. Small chip-

pings are brushed into the joints; this is referred to as 'racking up'. The setts are well rammed down 6 mm and the chippings 'prodded' down to the base. Sealing of the joints may be achieved with bitumastic 'hot' liquid, cold emulsion, cement grout, cement mortar, damp sand or soil, depending upon the function and situation of the paving.

Cobbles

Cobbles are a useful means whereby foot traffic may be channelled away from a particular area and encouraged to pursue a defined route. This material is a valuable medium for surfacing odd-shaped small areas and offers scope for a variety of patterns according to the shape and size of individual cobbles employed; these may range up to 100 mm in size or, in some cases, a little larger. Sources are beaches, river beds, flint gravel rejects and surplus wash-mill flints from potteries. Some types of cobble are imported from Normandy.

The traditional method of laying is to set the cobbles in sand or fine gravel so that they are well rammed in. An alternative method is to lay them on a bed of 1 : 4 or 1 : 6 cement (on a clinker base), into which each cobble is individually pressed by hand until set to the required depth. Where vehicular traffic is likely to need to cross the paving, the cobbles should be set on a 100 mm (minimum) concrete base.

Historical examples are to be seen of paths with cobbles firmly rammed into a soil base; this is not the true cobble paving as we know it today.

Woodblocks

First introduced about 1830 as a surfacing material to reduce the noise of horses' hoofs and steel-tyred carriages, woodblocks have not made their mark as a paving material. Like setts, this material calls for high quality laying skills. Jarrah, a very dense hardwood, is probably the most suitable material; yellow deal that has been 'pickled' in creosote may also be employed.

The size of the blocks is usually 76×130×230 mm but smaller ones also may be laid on a concrete foundation, using an adhesive, or bedded on a 6 mm layer of fine sand to produce the required level. The blocks are set close together and consolidated after laying. A crossfall of 1 : 50 is generally sufficient.

Mosaics and tiles

The use of these materials should be restricted to those areas which are partially under cover and not exposed to the full force of the elements. It is essential that they are frostproof, otherwise they are likely to become damaged and gradually disintegrate. Tiles should meet the requirements laid down in BS 1286 : 1945, type A range.

The laying of mosaics is a highly skilled craft involving the assembling of small fragments of marble, fixing them in cement and polishing to give a smooth surface.

Unsealed gravel

This material is available from a wide range of sources and in a variety of colours. It is relatively cheap to lay and maintain. Different sizes of gravel produce various surface textures and may be obtained from either pits or river beds, or produced from crushed stone; local sources are more economical because of transport costs. The larger sizes, e.g. 76–100 mm, are useful as a pedestrian-deterrent surface and ideally suited for spreading around trees where non-porous paving would be undesirable. (BS 1984 : 1967.)

The gravel should be laid on a prepared base of 76–100 mm compacted clean broken hardcore, blinded with ash. Depending upon the size of the gravel, a covering of fine grit or shell may be rolled into the surface to give a finished appearance.

Self-bind gravel

This material possesses self-binding properties and when watered and rolled forms a firmly cemented surface. The gravel is laid on a prepared base, similar to that described for unsealed gravel, and dry rolled to a consolidated depth of 50 mm; it is then wet rolled until the gravel surface becomes covered with a wet slurry (this disappears after a shower of rain, leaving a clear hard surface). It is an economical surfacing material for drives and other areas serving lightweight traffic.

Bituminous surfacing

Some of the materials described for the surfacing of carriageways are suitable for pedestrian use :

    Hot-rolled asphalt to BS 594 : 1973
    Fine cold asphalt to BS 1690 : 1962
    Bitumen macadam to BS 1621 : 1961
    Tarmacadam 'tarpaving' to BS 1242 : 1960

On a stable subgrade the material should be laid on a 100 mm base of clinker or clean broken hardcore blinded with ash. Depth of surfacing depends upon the material used; bitumen macadam, tarpaving and hot rolled asphalt should have a 19 mm wearing-surface laid on a 38 mm basecourse. For fine cold asphalt the wearing-course should be 13 mm thick. The selection of the basecourse

material depends upon the type of wearing-course to be applied; a hot-laid wearing-course requires a hot-laid basecourse.

In children's play areas the hot-rolled asphalt stands up better to wear from scuffing feet than fine cold asphalt.

Disposal of surface water from paved surfaces

Rain falling upon a paved surface must be quickly dispersed to avoid ponding which can be dangerous to wheeled traffic and pedestrians alike. This necessitates laying the surfacing material to crossfalls and gradients which shed the water so that it readily drains away.

Drainage of a carriageway

Normally a carriageway is provided with a barrel camber on straight lengths; where there are horizontal curves the outer one is set at a higher level, the amount of crossfall depending upon the radius of the curve. Generally this should be no flatter than 1 : 48 where tarmacadam to BS 1242 : 1960 is the surfacing material, or 1 : 40 if the surface is open-textured (bitumen macadam to BS 2040 : 1953). Excessive camber reduces the effective riding width, so that high vehicles travelling close to the channel overhang the footway, constituting a danger where there are projections, such as signs on buildings, near to the carriageway.

A carriageway constructed with a barrel camber has its centre (crown) higher than the two edges (channels). To avoid creating a flat triangular section, 'spring' levels are produced at a point midway between the crown and channel on each side. Where the difference in levels makes the forming of a barrel camber unacceptable (e.g. if the buildings on one side of the carriageway have a higher threshold level than those on the other side), it may be necessary to construct a 'hanging' section, i.e. the crown level is sited closer to the higher channel and the spring level produced midway between the crown and lower channel (Fig.46d).

The positioning of road gullies is determined by the surface area of the carriageway, its gradient and the materials used for surfacing. On a cambered section, gullies should be spaced at regular intervals along both channels. On a hanging section, the gullies need to be more closely spaced on the lower channel than on the higher, the actual spacing being determined by the position of the crown. Where horizontal curves occur, the gullies are positioned on the lower channel.

Gulley gratings are made of cast iron (or steel where greater strength is required) and may be set either flush with the channel or within the kerb. In the latter instance the gullies should be closer together and the channel dished to guide the flow of water.

On rural roads, where the kerb race is sometimes omitted, the water which drains off the carriageway is conducted through grips which are cut in the verges separating the carriageway from the drainage ditches. These grips may be either left open or filled with porous granular material. Regular maintenance should be carried out to prevent blockage due to excessive growth of herbage.

Drainage of pedestrian paved areas
While it is important that surface water should readily drain away, no gradient must be so excessive that it causes discomfort to the pedestrian.

Channels may be incorporated where a junction is formed between two areas of paving which slope towards each other. It may be possible to incorporate drainage channels within the paving pattern so that unity of design is achieved in the layout; channel gradients should be a minimum of 1 : 250.

Footways are usually laid with either a crossfall or backfall, necessitating only one line of gullies to take the surface water run-off. In some cases a continuous grating may be incorporated flush with the paving, the channel being set beneath; another method is to omit the grating but leave a narrow gap between the paving (serving a similar purpose). Spacing of the gullies is governed by the surface area of the paving and its gradient. A footway adjacent to a carriageway may be provided with a crossfall enabling surface water to discharge onto the road channel and thence into road gullies.

Surfaces for sports activities

Hard porous surfaces are invaluable, particularly during the winter months, for sporting needs since they permit almost unlimited use provided they are well constructed and regularly maintained. Games pitches, tennis courts and running tracks may all have non-turf surfaces. These consist generally of finely graded, scientifically prepared mineral aggregate combined with a binding agent to produce a material which, when properly laid on a firm foundation, provides a surface capable of withstanding hard use under almost any kind of weather conditions. This type of surface, however, is not considered suitable for games such as rugby or cricket.

Initial site preparation involves stripping off the topsoil and excavating over the area, including a margin of not less than 600 mm, to the depth of the formation level, maintaining a uniform crossfall of 1 : 20 for tennis courts or 1 : 100 for games pitches. The excavated formation should be treated with weedkiller.

Drainage is important; a land drainage system should be installed using 100 mm main drains and 75 mm laterals at 9 m intervals with inverts 300 mm below the base and connected to an outfall.

The foundation should consist of porous filling consolidated to a thickness of 150 mm and blinded with ash. Surfacing may be any of the materials described below.

Tarmacadam
A consolidated depth of 50 mm comprising 19–13 mm nominal size laid at the rate of 7 tonnes per 100 m², to form a basecourse 38 mm thick, and at the rate of 3 tonnes per 100 m² to form a wearing-course.

Bitumen macadam
A 13–19 mm layer of clean broken hardcore is compacted to a depth of not less than 19 mm and then uniformly sprayed with a bitumen solution * at the rate of 0·48–0·72 m²/litre. Bitumen coated 6 > 3 mm graded crushed stone is spread uniformly to a consolidated depth of 13 mm, after which the whole area is lightly sprayed with a tack coat of bitumen solution at the rate of approximately 2·41–4·82 m²/litre, according to the degree of looseness required for play purposes, and dressed with very fine grey-green stone or other suitable chippings.

Hard porous material
Crushed rock, clinker or burnt red shale with binder is laid to a consolidated depth of not less than 38 mm using an adequate quantity of water, before and during the placing of the material in position, to ensure that it is well wetted. A hand roller of not more than 250 kg is used to carry out the consolidating process, which should not be undertaken until a period of approximately half an hour has elapsed after wetting to avoid any risk of 'picking up' the surface.

Proprietary material
A number of brands of surfacing material are available but not all give satisfactory results. It is important, therefore, that only those products of reliable manufacturers are used and that the specifications produced by such firms are carefully examined to ensure that they meet the requirements.

*The grade should be as specified by the manufacturer.

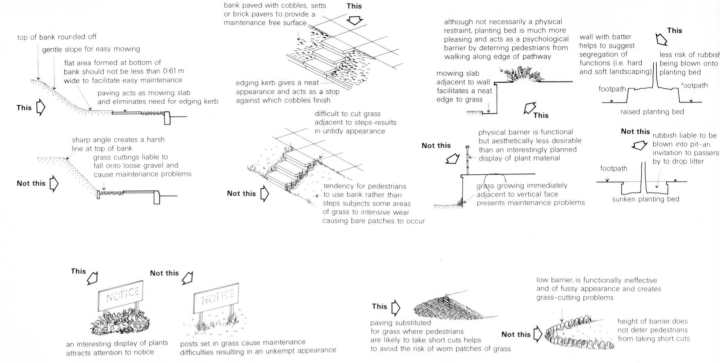

top of bank rounded off

gentle slope for easy mowing

flat area formed at bottom of bank should not be less than 0·61 m wide to facilitate easy maintenance

paving acts as mowing slab and eliminates need for edging kerb

This ⇨

sharp angle creates a harsh line at top of bank

grass cuttings liable to fall onto loose gravel and cause maintenance problems

Not this ⇨

bank paved with cobbles, setts or brick pavers to provide a maintenance free surface

This ⇨

edging kerb gives a neat appearance and acts as a stop against which cobbles finish

difficult to cut grass adjacent to steps-results in untidy appearance

Not this ⇨

tendency for pedestrians to use bank rather than steps subjects some areas of grass to intensive wear causing bare patches to occur

although not necessarily a physical restraint, planting bed is much more pleasing and acts as a psychological barrier by deterring pedestrians from walking along edge of pathway

mowing slab adjacent to wall facilitates a neat edge to grass

This ⇨

Not this ⇨

physical barrier is functional but aesthetically less desirable than an interestingly planned display of plant material

grass growing immediately adjacent to vertical face presents maintenance problems

wall with batter helps to suggest segregation of functions (i.e. hard and soft landscaping)

This ⇨

less risk of rubbish being blown onto planting bed

footpath   footpath

raised planting bed

Not this ⇨

rubbish liable to be blown into pit-an invitation to passers by to drop litter

footpath

sunken planting bed

This ⇗   Not this ⇗

NOTICE   NOTICE

an interesting display of plants attracts attention to notice

posts set in grass cause maintenance difficulties resulting in an unkempt appearance

This ⇨

paving substituted for grass where pedestrians are likely to take short cuts helps to avoid the risk of worn patches of grass

low barrier, is functionally ineffective and of fussy appearance and creates grass-cutting problems

Not this ⇨

height of barrier does not deter pedestrians from taking short cuts

Fig. 47   Junctions between hard and soft landscaping : some typical problems and their solution

Points to check in the specification are :

Aggregate   Quality and type used and grading.
Binder   Type used (if any) and rate of mixing per tonne of aggregate or rate of application per m² where grouted.
Pigment   If colour is used, the type and method of surface marking.

Junctions between hard and soft landscaping

An otherwise admirable design layout may be marred because insufficient thought has been given to the treatment of junctions between the various materials (Fig.47). Grass adjacent to hard paving is the most common problem. To facilitate easy grass maintenance the paving should be set not more than 25 mm below the surface level of the turf. If the turf is set too high above the paving there is a risk that the grass edges may crumble, making for an untidy appearance. Where a mowing strip is provided (e.g. between the grass and a wall or fence) it should not be less than 230 mm wide. Concrete (or other in-situ material) or paving flags are better for this purpose than gravel chippings, for easy sweeping up of grass cuttings.

Paving flags set as stepping stones in grass are best laid flush with the turf surface so that the mower may be run straight across them.

Where planted and paved areas meet it may be desirable to allow some of the low-growing plants to spread beyond the edges of the bed so that the outline is softened. The bed itself may be set flush or raised above the paving.

Plate 18
Junction between hard and soft landscaping. The use of an edging kerb prevents the spilling of soil on to the loose cobbles.
Photo: Blakedown Landscapes Ltd, Kidderminster.

Seven   Soft Landscaped Surfaces

Grass in the landscape

Grass of many different species grows in most parts of the British Isles and thrives in a variety of situations throughout the world. It is the most common form of ground cover and has many advantages:

It provides a green carpet all the year round.

The establishment of grass is generally cheaper than that of any other type of ground cover.

It is relatively simple and cheap to maintain.

Naturalised bulbs can exist quite happily in its midst, providing contrast of colour.

Different cutting techniques can be used to achieve visual textural effects (e.g. close-mown or scythed).

Worn or damaged parts are easily renewed at a comparatively reasonable cost.

Grass is soft and pleasant to walk upon.

It provides one of the cheapest and best surfaces for games pitches and many other sporting activities.

Different grass species may be used in a variety of situations and for different purposes.

In the form of turfs it can be laid to provide an instant ground cover.

Plate 19
Lawns sweeping down
to the water's edge
enhance the setting of
large buildings and
mature trees:
Birmingham
University,
Birmingham.
Photo: Derek
Bradshaw.

Although the advantages of grass outweigh its disadvantages, these must also be taken into account when specifying this form of ground cover:

During the growing season grass requires frequent attention.

In periods of drought some grass species are liable to dry out unless well watered.

It may harbour organisms detrimental to its growth, succumbing to disease which is likely to result in a poor sward.

Grass cannot thrive in areas of very heavy shade or in situations where it is subjected to constant foot traffic.

Because it is one of the cheapest forms of ground cover, grass is abused and often specified for areas where some other form of surfacing material would be a more practical solution. This is particularly noticeable where constant foot traffic passes across defined limits of a grassed area (e.g. short cuts taken across corners), creating unsightly bare patches.

Although a grass verge provides a colourful contrast to the tarmac surface of a carriageway, its purpose is defeated if its width is insufficient. Dust and dirt from the carriageway settling along the grass edges cause a narrow verge to detract from its surroundings because all the fresh green colour is smothered. Maintenance, too, involves edge-trimming operations which are out of all proportion to the area of grass involved.

The design of grass banks also calls for a careful study of maintenance problems since the gradient at which mechanised equipment can be operated satisfactorily is limited. If soil is banked to form a slope greater than its angle of repose there is a risk of erosion and unsightly gullies developing, preventing the grass roots from establishing themselves and binding the soil.

It is a fallacy that grass thrives on any type of soil and in almost any situation. Admittedly there is an endless variety of places where grass is able to establish itself, but to produce a good sward the right species must be selected and the moisture content and texture of the soil must be conducive to healthy growth.

Moisture is necessary for growth, but grass cannot tolerate waterlogged conditions. Where drainage of the soil is too costly in relation to the scheme envisaged the use of a different kind of surfacing medium should seriously be considered. Projections, such as balconies, are a deterrent to grass growth; even if they face the direction of the pre-vailing wind it is no guarantee that driving rain is sufficient to provide the moisture required. The simplest solution is to substitute a paved surface.

Factors affecting the establishment of grass

Grass establishes itself more readily in some situations than in others and its ability to thrive is dependent upon a number of factors which all play an important role, often interacting upon each other. Ecological study of an area of proposed grassland is likely to give a good indication of the species best suited to that particular location.

Obviously the first point to be considered is the purpose for which the grass is intended, since this has a bearing on seed selection, ground preparation, drainage, maintenance, etc. Good grass cannot be produced from poor seed or wrongly selected species and if the proportions used in the seed mixture are incorrect the resultant sward is likely to be disappointing or, in some instances, a failure. Selection of species and their proportions within the mixture specified must be considered in relation to the type of soil and the proposed function of the grassed area. Species suitable for the construction of a fine lawn are not likely to meet the demands required for playing pitches, even though both areas may have the same type of soil.

Fertility, texture and moisture content of soil directly affect plant growth (as discussed earlier) and although the character of soil cannot be changed it is possible for certain modifications to be effected. This may entail the installation of land drainage in order to lower the level of the water-table, since proper drainage of the soil is essential for satisfactory establishment of the young seedlings; the sharper the drainage the less likelihood there is of trouble arising, particularly where the grass is to form a bowling-green. Excessive drainage produces a very dry soil which may be detrimental to the establishment of young plants unless copious watering is carried out during the growing season. Too much water, on the other hand, can also have ill effects upon the plants. In some soils on heavy clay there may be no drainage problems but a lack of good crumb structure (necessary for germination of the seed), causing the soil to adhere in large clods firmly held together except for a few cracks (deflocculation). Clay that appears as small crumbs on drying out (flocculated) makes for better turf establishment.

Aeration of the soil is closely allied to its moisture content and, in conjunction with the mineral nutrients absorbed by plants, is essential for the establishment of young seedlings and their continued healthy growth. The interaction of such factors as sunshine, temperature, rainfall and wind velocity have a direct bearing on plant life. Topographical features contribute to the type of microclimate which a particular location enjoys and altitude directly influences the amount of heat received from the sun which warms the soil (insolation); the bottom of a valley is more subject to late frosts than the slopes of the hills above.

Adequate preparation of the seedbed is essential for the establishment of a fine sward. Since grass is laid down with the object of creating a ground cover, which usually is intended to last for a long time, the ground must first be thoroughly cultivated to produce a fine tilth with the right crumb structure to assist the germination of the seed.

Seed germination depends also upon warmth of the soil. Late summer sowing is likely to be more successful than sowing in the spring when the ground is often cold and wet, because during the summer months the soil has warmed up and this, together with heavy dews, encourages the growth of grass seedlings.

Maintenance operations play an essential part in grass establishment; the initial mowing of the young seedlings helps to encourage the production of vegetative growth from the crown of the plants at ground level (tillering) and so makes for a good covering of grass over the area seeded. The removal of weeds and large stones and rolling to firm the soil surface are also necessary operations in the early stages of grass growth and, later, top-dressing and regular mowing ensure the establishment of a good sward.

Soils and the formation of grass

The type and condition of the soil has a direct bearing upon the grass which ultimately grows there and determines how a particular species is likely to develop. Some grasses are able to thrive on a variety of soil types, but others can only tolerate certain conditions, as indicated in Tables 28–31.

Clay soils
Probably the most difficult soils on which to establish grass are the clays and clay loams, since drainage is generally impeded. During the winter months the surface is sticky and slippery, becoming hard in the dry season with surface cracks and crevices caused by shrinkage of the clay. Drainage of these soils is essential and, in addition

to the installation of a land drainage system, porous material should be incorporated to improve the texture of the soil.

The best remedy for deflocculated soil is the application of calcium salts, in the form of gypsum (calcium sulphate), which assists in promoting good crumb structure at a reasonable cost without radically altering the soil pH, and is non-toxic to plants and animals. Although good results have been obtained by this method it should be remembered that it is not a substitute for aeration or drainage and that in certain areas, notably the Midlands, some soils have failed to respond to this form of treatment.

The amount of gypsum required varies, according to the clay content of the soil; the advice of an agricultural consultant should be sought. Gypsum should be applied after earthmoving operations but before replacement of topsoil, after which a further dressing may be incorporated into the top 50 mm of soil by either rotovating or harrowing. A top-dressing of sharp sand also helps to improve soil texture and drainage.

The *Agrostis* species of fine-leaved grasses (particularly creeping bent) do well on heavy and clayey soils, preferring those of acid reaction; among the coarser-leaved grasses, annual meadowgrass, rough-stalked meadowgrass and timothy are those tolerant of these soils.

Heath and moorland soils
Drainage is often deficient in these thin, light, infertile soils, which may also require an application of lime in order to reduce their acidity. Most cultivated soils fall within the pH range of 4·5 to 7·5. Although plants differ in their ability to withstand acid conditions, many prefer 'slightly acid to neutral' soils. The amount of lime required to bring the pH value to between 6·0 and 6·5 is known as the lime requirement of the soil (LR).

A heavy top-dressing of organic material is essential in the initial preparation of the seedbed and once the grass is established regular top-dressings should be applied in order properly to maintain the sward.

For these soil conditions, brown bent and Chewings fescue are the most suitable fine-leaved grasses, together with the coarse-leaved wavy hairgrass.

Sandy soils
These soils, especially where a proportion of clay is present, are those most favoured for the formation of lawns and sports turf. Where the clay content is low, drainage is generally excessive and the soil poor in mineral

Table 28
Fine-leaved grasses for first-quality turf formation—*Agrostis spp.* (bents)

Genus and species	Habit of growth	Soil preference	Adaptability to various uses
Agrostis tenuis (browntop or common bent)	Small-leaved ; may be tufted or creeping, producing stolons in moist and rhizomes in dry situations. Slow-growing	Does well on most soils—prefers light acid types	One of the most useful grasses in bowling and putting green mixtures. Especially valuable in any mixture for establishing cricket tables
Agrostis stolonifera (creeping bent)	Fine foliage ; long trailing stolons but no rhizomes	Does not thrive in dry soils, preferring moist conditions	Tolerates shaded conditions and resists mowing and grazing. Var. *maritima* is a common constituent of sea-washed turf used for bowling greens
Agrostis canina subsp. (a) *canina* (velvet bent)	Fine-leaved ; stolons with tufted shoots at the nodes. Produces dense sward, springy to walk on	Found in damp and partly shaded areas	Generally too soft for sports turf but suitable for ornamental lawns
(b) *montana* (brown bent)	Densely tufted ; spreads slowly by means of slender rhizomes. Produces rather an open sward	Very drought-resistant ; grows on dry heaths	Valuable constituent in mixtures for bowling and putting greens and tennis courts. Blends well with *A. tenuis* and *Festuca ovina*

Table 29
Fine-leaved grasses for first-quality turf formation—*Festuca spp.* (fescues)

Genus and species	Habit of growth	Soil preference	Adaptability to various uses
Festuca ovina (sheep's fescue)	Dwarf, very tufted habit with almost solid, fine leaves	Survives on majority of soils, prefers acid types of drier sands and gravels	Useful in most playing field mixtures where dwarf grass is required and for tennis court mixtures. Not a particularly good blender
Festuca tenuifolia (awnless or fine-leaved sheep's fescue)	Slightly tufted with very fine narrow leaves. Smallest of the fescues	Found on dry peaty soils and particularly suitable for dry acid soil conditions	Useful in cricket table mixtures and for most sports areas, but should not be sown alone. Hard-wearing
Festuca rubra genuina (red fescue) S.59	Fine-leaved ; extensively creeping rhizomatous habit. Produces many tillers	Successful on most soils but prefers well-drained types	Ideal for games pitches and areas subject to hard wear. A popular grass in luxury turf mixtures
Festuca rubra genuina var. *glaucescens* (Cumberland marsh creeping red fescue)	Slow-developing variety of dwarf creeping habit	Prefers light, well-drained soils	Best sown with other grasses because of its slow development. Excellent in bowling and putting green mixtures
Festuca rubra fallax (Chewing's fescue)	Dwarf tufted habit producing many tillers. Good coloured foliage, except in winter	Grows on most soils but prefers sandy and lighter types	Forms a compact sward which withstands wear and tear and close-mowing. Drought-resistant and a good blender. Useful for bowling and putting greens and fine lawn mixtures

salts and organic material. A top-dressing of peat or compost mixed with the top 300 mm of soil prior to seeding assists in providing an increase in the organic fraction.

The fine-leaved grasses, sheep's fescue and New Zealand browntop, and coarse-leaved hard fescue, thrive on sandy soils.

Chalk soils
In some chalk soils clay pockets are present and, where necessary, should be given the treatment recommended for clays and clay loams. Chalk soils are light, freely drained soils that are usually deficient in plant foods and therefore require regular applications of organic material.

The fine-leaved Chewings fescue and the coarse-leaved hard fescue and crested dogstail are the grasses most suited to these soils.

Types of grass used for turf formation

There is a grass species for almost every type of environment; in the British Isles more than a hundred grasses are indigenous but only a small proportion of this number is used in commercial seed mixtures. Fescues and bents are expensive and are seldom specified for any large expanse of grass which is subject to much use. Coarser mixtures containing perennial ryegrass are more satisfactory for areas that must withstand hard wear, the finer grasses being reserved for bowling-greens and ornamental lawns. The grasses listed below are those which are commercially available and generally in common use.

Fine-leaved grasses (Tables 28 and 29)
Grasses used for ornamental lawns comprise the bents (*Agrostis species*) and the fescues (*Festuca species*). The latter are more tolerant of unfavourable soils and drier conditions, although on highly fertile soils they are likely to be ousted by the more aggressive bents. The fescues have a poor colour during the winter months but are of better appearance during April, May and June; the bents are more noticeable in their colour from July to October.

Agrostis tenuis (New Zealand browntop). The most important bent of all, commonly used in seed mixtures for sports turf. It is found on a wide variety of soils, notably sands and gravels, and although it prefers a dry sandy situation this grass does well on most types of soil. The fescues, especially *Festuca rubra* (Chewings fescue), blend well with browntop and are useful seed mixtures for the formation of bowling-greens and putting-greens. Browntop results in a more even sward than that produced by any other single species and is especially valuable in mixtures for establishing cricket tables. It may be tufted or creeping, producing rhizomes mainly on dry soils and stolons in moist situations.

Agrostis stolonifera (creeping bent or white bent). Grows quickly in rain-soaked soils, is cold-hardy and will grow in shade. There are several varieties:
(a) *maritima*: a common constituent of sea-washed turf, often used for bowling-greens.
(b) *repens*: also known as *var. stolonifera*. Z strain (Z.103) of *Agrostis stolonifera var. stolonifera* is known as 'Emerald Velvet' and produced from stolons.
(c) *palustris*: a tufted creeping bent found on marshland, suitable for heavy soils and sports turf mixtures and useful on poor damp sites.

Seed is hand-collected from salt-marshes and is therefore scarce. Swards are often formed with stolons, especially where 'Emerald Velvet' is used (see below).

Agrostis canina (brown or velvet bent). This species is similar to *Agrostis stolonifera* but the leaves are much finer. It normally grows on heathland and does well on dry soils, spreading more slowly than creeping bent.

There are two varieties which are used in different situations:
(a) *Subsp. canina*, known as velvet bent, is generally found in damp or partly shaded areas and when given sufficient moisture forms a good sward. It is too soft for sports turf but may be used for ornamental lawns since it produces a dense sward which is springy to walk upon and has a pleasant appearance. Seeds, which are hand-collected, come from the Continent and the supply is often limited. Stolons are used or the seed is mixed with *Agrostis tenuis*.
(b) *Subsp. montana*, known as brown bent, is a densely tufted grass which spreads slowly by means of rhizomes. It produces a somewhat open sward which is very drought-resistant and grows on dry heaths. A valuable constituent of putting and bowling-greens, it blends well with *Agrostis tenuis* and *Festuca ovina*. Seed is imported from the Continent.

Festuca ovina (sheep's fescue). A popular grass which grows in distinct tufts and has a dwarf habit. It survives on

Table 30
Coarser-leaved grasses used in turf formation—*Poa spp.* (meadowgrass)

Genus and species	Habit of growth	Soil preference	Adaptability to various uses
Poa pratensis (smooth-stalked meadowgrass)	Creeping habit by means of rhizomes	Prefers medium to light soils and situations where rainfall is low	Drought-resistant; a very useful grass for general recreational ground and games pitch mixtures
Poa trivialis (rough-stalked meadowgrass)	Slightly creeping habit with thin shallow-rooted stolons	Does best on heavy moist soils	Suitable for second-quality lawns, under trees and in shaded situations, but should not be sown alone as in very dry conditions it has a tendency to die out
Poa annua (annual meadowgrass)	Tufted habit. Prolific seed production	Thrives in moist soils and can withstand consolidated conditions. Resistant to waterlogging	Useful in urban situations subject to atmospheric pollution where it is sown with *Poa trivialis* and *Lolium perenne*
Poa nemoralis (wood meadowgrass)	Slightly tufted habit with bright green foliage	Woodland soils	Indigenous to English woodlands. Useful for shady situations where not subject to close mowing

Table 31
Coarser-leaved grasses used in turf formation—Various species

Genus and species	Habit of growth	Soil preference	Adaptability to various uses
Festuca longifolia (hard fescue)	Tufted habit with bluish-green leaves of coarser texture than Chewing's fescue	Successful on most types of soil and more suitable than Chewing's fescue on heavier soils	Withstands hard wear and tear; particularly resistant to cold and drought. Unsuitable for use in fine mixtures for bowling and putting greens but may be used in playing field mixtures. Should not be sown alone
Lolium perenne (perennial ryegrass) S.23	Tufted habit and broad leaved; more leafy and less stalky than other strains. Produces many prostrate tillers	Thrives on all but very dry soils	Covers ground quickly and is very suitable for games pitches and cricket outfields
Phleum pratense (timothy or catstail) S.50	Tufted, dwarf finer-leaved strain of prostrate habit and long runners which root at the nodes	Thrives on majority of soils but prefers heavy types	Improvement on the ordinary timothy strains. Recovers quickly after heavy wear. Only suitable for second-class turf and games pitches
Cynosurus cristatus (crested dogstail)	Dwarf tufted habit with short, dense, broad-bladed leaves that remain remarkably green in winter	Ideal for dry soils, clays and loams	Slow-developing grass. Grows wild on heaths. Not suitable for really fine turf but admirably suitable for playing fields on sand, or gravel, subsoils
Deschampsia flexuosa (wavy hairgrass)	Slightly tufted habit with dark green solid-type leaves	Prefers soils not too rich or alkaline. Grows on poor, sour, heath types of soil	Useful in shaded areas on peaty and heathland soils

most soils but prefers acid conditions. Although used extensively in mixures where dwarf grass is required, it does not blend well with other grasses.

Festuca tenuifolia (fine-leaved sheep's fescue). Also known as *Festuca ovina var. tenuifolia* (and *F. capillata*), this is the smallest of the fescues and has narrow leaves. It is slightly tufted and its dwarf habit of growth makes it an ideal grass for dry, acid soils. Hard-wearing, with very fine leaves that are useful in mixtures for cricket tables and sports areas, it should not be sown alone.

Festuca rubra (red fescue). There are three strains :
(a) Aberystwyth S.59 : extensively used for very fine turf which, when it becomes established, is able to withstand a considerable amount of wear and tear. It is drought-resistant and has excellent recuperative powers, due to its rhizomatous habit. Although this grass prefers well-drained soils it generally succeeds on most types.
(b) *Festuca rubra genuina* (Cumberland marsh creeping red fescue) : a dwarf grass of creeping habit which is excellent for bowling-green mixtures. It prefers light- well-drained soils but is a slow developer and is best sown with other grasses.
(c) F.R. 10 (St Ives creeping red fescue) : a finer-leaved strain than S.59, derived from selected plants and only obtainable from the Sports Turf Research Institute, Bingley, Yorkshire. The dense turf formed by this strain is of a better colour than that of Chewing's fescue and is particularly suitable for use in sea-washed turf bowling-greens and fine lawns.

Festuca rubra fallax (Chewing's fescue). Also known as *F. rubra subsp. commutata* (and *F. rubra duriuscula*), it includes the form known commercially as Chewing's fescue. This grass, which differs from red fescue (chiefly in its dwarf dark green tufted habit producing many tillers), forms a compact sward which can withstand wear and tear, close mowing and drought. It is capable of thriving on the majority of soils but prefers the lighter types and is often used in fine lawn mixtures, being a good blender, although there is sometimes a tendency for it to be pushed out by the more aggressive bent grasses.

Coarser-leaved grasses (Tables 30 and 31)
The fine-leaved grasses are included in mixtures which contain one or more coarser-leaved grasses in order to produce a thick, closely-knit turf.

A number of strains of ryegrass are available commercially and all of them thrive well on a wide range of soils and under various climatic conditions. They are exceptionally vigorous during the summer months.

The common English varieties of meadowgrass are very adaptable, developing by means of underground stems which enable them to withstand a considerable amount of wear and tear and drought. The stalked meadowgrasses should not be sown alone and their proportion in any mixture should be kept on the low side ; they are useful as 'protectors' for the slower-growing grasses.

On heavy clay soils the *Phleum species* are useful because of their quick growth, but unfortunately the majority do not withstand hard mowing.

Although the *Cynosurus species* are unsuitable for forming really fine turf they are useful in medium grass mixtures, particularly on sand or gravel subsoils, because of their deep-rooting habit which enables them to withstand drought. They are hard-wearing and generally retain their colour in winter.

Agrostis gigantea (black bent, red top or emerald green). The use of this grass (also known as *Agrostis stolonifera* var. *major*) is limited to the formation of football pitches. It is loosely tufted with coarse broad leaves and has tough rhizomes.

Festuca longifolia (hard fescue). Also known as *Festuca ovina var. longifolia* and often wrongly named *F. duriuscula* and *F. fallax* (both these names apply to red fescues). This grass has a tufted habit and can withstand hard wear and tear. It is particularly resistant to cold and drought and thrives on most types of soil, but is more suited than Chewing's fescue to heavier soils. Being of coarse texture it should not be used in fine mixtures for bowling or putting-greens, but may be specified for playing-fields. *Festuca glauca* is very similar to *F. longifolia* which has bluish-green leaves.

Lolium perenne (perennial ryegrass). Aberystwyth strain S.23 is by far the best of at least twenty strains that are available commercially and is one of the most important grasses in use for playing pitches and outfields. This grass is easily established and covers the ground quickly after being sown ; its rapid growth excludes weeds and it is quick to recover from adverse conditions. Of tufted habit, but far more leafy and less stalky than most other strains, it has the advantage of being able to grow all the year round. It is capable of standing up to hard wear and constant mowing and produces many prostrate tillers.

Kentish indigenous, Devon eaver and New Zealand mather are other strains. Irish and Ayrshire short-seeded ryegrasses are stalky and less persistent than S.23.

Poa pratensis (smooth-stalked meadowgrass). An ideal species for establishing grass on slopes and embankments. Although valuable for use in dry, sandy situations it is less productive than *Poa trivialis* and prefers medium-to-light soils. Its creeping underground stems enable it to withstand drought and a considerable amount of wear and tear from heavy foot-traffic.

Poa trivialis (rough-stalked meadowgrass). Bright green in colour, this grass grows best in heavy, moist soils and develops well in shady situations and under trees. It grows by means of thin, slightly creeping, shallow-rooted stolons, which depend upon surface moisture more than the rhizomes of *Poa pratensis*, enabling it to cover the ground and fill in the spaces between the more tufted grass (assisting in checking weeds). In dry seasons it loses its colour and takes on a reddish tinge, but is usually green in winter. It is used for the establishment of second-class quality lawns and recreation grounds but does not stand up well to hard wear and should only be used in a mixture.

Poa annua (annual meadowgrass). This grass is often at its best during the winter. Because of its prolific seeding it is a difficult species to eliminate and is usually regarded as a weed. In difficult situations, such as urban areas and in conditions of atmospheric pollution, it is often sown with *Poa trivialis* and *Lolium perenne* and forms a good sward when mixed with a close-knit *Agrostis species*. It is a rapid developer, especially in mild winters, and is resistant to waterlogging, but is not tolerant of drought or dry situations where it loses its colour in summer, causing patchy brown areas to develop; it is susceptible to many fungal diseases.

Phleum pratense (timothy or catstail). The Aberystwyth S.50 strain is a finer-leaved, denser and dwarf variety of timothy whose multi-tillering habit enables it to recover from close-mowing. It grows on most soils but prefers the heavier types. The seed is difficult to harvest and therefore scarce and somewhat expensive. Both this strain and the smaller species, *Phleum bertolinii*, which tillers more freely and forms a more compact turf, are only suitable for use in forming second-class turf.

Cynosurus cristatus (crested dogstail). A slow-developing grass commonly incorporated in seed mixtures. It grows wild on heaths, is ideal for dry soils and does well on chalk pastures, clays and loams, being able to withstand drought. Very similar to perennial ryegrass, it does not creep but grows in dwarf tufts forming short, dense, broad-bladed leaves that retain their colour under conditions of hard wear. It is extremely hard-wearing and invaluable for games pitches, but should not be used in mixtures for bowling or putting-greens. Wiry flowering stems appear in June and require regular mowing to keep them down. When mature, the seeds are a dull brown colour; those that are a canary yellow are immature and should be rejected since they result in even slower growth.

Dactylis glomerata (cocksfoot). The deep-penetrating root system of this densely tufted perennial grass enables it to withstand much drier conditions than some other grasses and to succeed on soils too poor satisfactorily to support perennial ryegrass. It also does well on stiff clays and fertile soils (usually considered the right conditions for ryegrass and timothy). If the seed is sown too thinly the plants develop as isolated clumps, becoming coarse and difficult to control. The Aberystwyth strain S.143 is excellent for use in mixtures for football and rugby pitches, especially on medium-to-light soils, because of its deep-rooting habit, but for similar purposes on heavy soils *Phleum bertolinii*, Aberystwyth S.50, should be substituted.

Grasses of agricultural importance

Classification of agricultural grasses falls into three main groups according to their value to the farmer in seeding-down leys, i.e. grass under rotation (often known as temporary grass) which is generally referred to as 'seeds ley' or 'ley'.

Grasses widely used

Three grasses are commonly used for seeding-down leys and the two important species of ryegrass have different agricultural values.

Dactylis glomerata (cocksfoot). See above.

Lolium multiflorum (Italian ryegrass). Known also as *Lolium italicum*, this grass behaves more or less as a biennial, yielding for one season and then tending to die away rapidly. It forms upright tufts, responds well to large doses of nitrogen and is a valuable grass for leys of one year's duration since it grazes well and produces a good crop of hay. There is no grass that can equal this species for stubble grazing in the autumn and winter of the year of sowing and it is also extremely useful as a pioneer crop in reclaiming poor and hill land.

Lolium perenne (perennial ryegrass). This grass exists in many different strains, all having similar vegetative and floral characters but differing widely in habit. Some are short-lived, erect, stemmy early-flowering types among which are many of the commercial strains; others are prostrate, very leafy, flowering, typified by Aberystwyth S.23, S.101 and Kentish indigenous. The Aberystwyth S.24, which is a superior strain of the commercial class, is more leafy than most and has the early growth and free formation of seed characteristic of the Irish and Scottish strains. These leafy types flower three weeks later than the commercial types and, although slower in their spring growth, are capable of forming a rapidly-knit grass which can adequately withstand the weight of cattle (except in very wet weather)—an important factor on heavy soils. Seed production of these three strains is less than that of the commercial grasses and their cost is therefore higher.

Phleum pratense (timothy). With the exception of the Aberystwyth S.50, timothy is tufted in habit with much shallower roots than those of cocksfoot and therefore more suitable for the moister soils. It is the most palatable of all grasses and exists in both hay and pasture strains, the former being more stemmy and less persistent. Included in the hay strains is Aberystwyth S.51 and in the pasture strains Aberystwyth S.48 and S.50, the latter being a dense super-pasture type.

Useful grasses less frequently used
Apart from annual meadowgrass, which is sometimes a valuable contribution to the grazing of a field because it fills in the bare patches, only two of the numerous species of meadowgrass are of any real agricultural importance.

Poa trivialis (rough-stalked meadowgrass). The ground-covering habit of this species is useful under conditions of low fertility, but on the more fertile soils it is generally undesirable to introduce it in competition with ryegrass or timothy. It can quickly die out in dry situations and is only suitable for moist sites. Although very palatable, its productivity is low compared with that of perennial ryegrass.

Poa pratensis (smooth-stalked meadowgrass). Production of this species is less than that of *P. trivialis* and, except on dry soils, it has little agricultural value; it is more useful as a lawn grass.

Festuca pratensis (meadow fescue). This grass does not compete very well with Italian ryegrass (from which it is not readily distinguished) or cocksfoot, although when it becomes established it may outyield them in hay production over a period of years.

Cynosurus cristatus (crested dogstail). A widely distributed grass, essentially used for grazing purposes, which remains remarkably green in winter. It thrives in a variety of conditions but does best on the less fertile soils, particularly chalky types.

Arrhenatherum elatius (tall oatgrass). The herbage is rather bitter but this grass produces early growth and is erect in habit. On dry light soils it occurs naturally in hedgerows. It does not thrive in competition with perennial ryegrass or cocksfoot and must be heavily sown if a good take is to be obtained.

Agriculturally worthless grasses
The following species may be classed under this heading:

Agrostis spp. (bents). 'Agrostis pasture' denotes unproductive and unpalatable grassland.
Aira spp. (hair grasses).
Brachypodium spp. (false bromes). Totally avoided by grazing stock.
Bromus spp. (brome grasses).
Holcus lanatus (Yorkshire fog). Palatable only in very early spring.
Hordeum spp. (meadow barley grass).
Molinia caerulea (purple moor grass). 'Molinia pasture' implies a very infertile soil.
Nardus stricta (mat grass).
Agropyron spp. (couch; twitch).

Grass nutrition—the purpose and use of fertilisers

The importance of nutrients is such that plants cannot make satisfactory growth in the absence of comparatively large quantities of the major elements; they also require minute quantities of the minor elements. Although the soil may contain adequate supplies of all the required nutrients they are of little use unless present in the form of soluble salts so that they are readily absorbed by the plant roots.

Grass is subject to wear from use and mowing and therefore needs a regular supply of nutrients to counteract the ill-effects. Nutrients may be in the form of either organic or inorganic fertilisers. The former supply the major plant elements and some of the trace elements in a slowly available form over a comparatively long period of time. Inorganic fertilisers comprise those in which inorganic salts (applied as dry solids) provide nitrogen, phosphate and potash and small amounts of trace elements in comparatively quick-acting form.

In Chapter 3 the mineral nutrients essential for plant growth were described in detail. The function and effect of the major nutrients on plant growth are described below. Due regard should be given to the effect of the various fertilisers on the soil reaction; while soils play a large part in providing plant food, they differ in the amount of mineral content which is available to the plant.

Nitrogen

This is the most important mineral element, of which comparatively large amounts are required; unless adequate supplies are maintained, growth is reduced and plants remain undeveloped. Although the leaves and stems of plants are in continuous contact with the nitrogen in the atmosphere (of which it forms four-fifths) they are unable to absorb it directly from this source and it can only reach the plant by root absorption from the soil in the form of chemical compounds (nitrates).

The importance of this element in turf production is its balancing effect against continual mowing by encouraging development of foliage; it also promotes a good colour. When this mineral is deficient the leaves become pale green (chlorotic) due to the presence of pigments in the leaf which are normally concealed by chlorophyll. Nitrogenous fertilisers promote a vigorous growth, giving extra vitality and an increase in foliage growth. Continuous applications of nitrogenous dressings alone would eventually result in soft, weed- and worm-infested grass, readily susceptible to fungal diseases.

For healthy plant growth to continue, the amount of nitrogen absorbed needs to be replaced; this may be from one or more of three sources:

(i) *Natural nitrogen.* Many kinds of beneficial bacteria live in the soil—on the surface of soil particles, between them and in nodules occurring in the roots of leguminous plants—and assist in decomposing the proteins contained in plant and animal remains, converting them from complicated chemical compounds into simpler substances. Gas nitrogen is absorbed from the atmosphere and produces available food for plants—a process referred to as 'fixing'. All these processes are affected by soil conditions; soil that is waterlogged or has inadequate aeration prevents the beneficial bacteria from functioning and so deprives the growing plants of food.

(ii) *Inorganic nitrogen fertilisers.* These rapidly available sources of nitrogen are often required in the spring to encourage fresh growth and are useful for providing a rapid stimulation to poor turf. They are obtainable in the following forms:

(a) *Sulphate of ammonia.* A widely specified and possibly the most generally useful nitrogenous fertiliser. If used on its own, application should be at the rate of 17 g/m^2 and well watered in to prevent scorching of the grass. It may be mixed with superphosphate or potash (a combination which forms the basis of most fertiliser mixtures). Sulphate of ammonia should not be added to basic substances, such as lime or basic slag, which release the ammonia.

When used as a pre-sowing fertiliser it should be applied at the rate of 0·025–0·037 kg/m^2 or, for use as top-dressing, 0·012–0·025 kg/m^2, but is best used with a carrier, such as compost or sterilised soil, in the proportion of one part sulphate of ammonia to five parts compost or sterilised soil.

(b) *Nitrate of soda.* Nitrogen in this form is more costly than sulphate of ammonia but is very quick-acting and of particular value where an immediate result is essential. Since it readily absorbs moisture from the atmosphere, and as a result is liable to cake, it should be stored in a dry place. Being easily soluble, it is rapidly leached from the soil and is therefore wasted if applied in heavy doses. Its continued use may cause deterioration of the soil structure, particularly on heavy soils, due to the formation of a deflocculated 'sodium clay' resulting in a sticky soil texture and a turf that is susceptible to disease and worm and weed invasion. When used as a top-dressing this fertiliser has a tendency to reduce soil acidity. It should be applied at the rate of 0·012–0·025 kg/m^2.

(c) *Nitro chalk.* This fertiliser is useful where the soil is excessively acid, and may be applied as a spring dressing at the rate of 0·004–0·037 kg/m^2, depending upon local conditions. It is quite often bulked with sand in the proportions of one part nitro chalk to six parts of sand (by weight). Nitro chalk must not be mixed with calcium cyanamide, basic slag or oxide lime.

(d) *Nitrate of lime*. A synthetic fertiliser available in two forms—grey or white—and sold as granules. Nitrate of soda is easily leached and may be used in a similar manner to nitrate of soda, particularly where there is acid turf. It is applied at the rate of 0.025 kg/m².

(e) *Urea*. A concentrated nitrogenous fertiliser applied in dry pelleted form at the rate of 0.006–0.012 kg/m². Very even distribution is necessary in order to avoid patchy stimulation of growth.

(iii) *Organic nitrogenous fertilisers*. These fertilisers are slower-acting than inorganic ones and generally larger quantities are necessary.

(a) *Dried blood*. Useful on light soils because it increases drought-resistance; this fertiliser is less liable to scorch turf because the nitrogen content is released more slowly than that of inorganic fertilisers. It possesses good storage properties and for this reason forms an ingredient of many compound fertilisers. Application is generally at the rate of 0.037–0.050 kg/m².

(b) *Hoof and horn meal*. Common ingredients of pre-sowing fertilisers and applied at the rate of 0.072 kg/m². Available in powdered form, these slow-acting fertilisers are by-products of the glue industry.

(c) *Shoddy*. Application of this fertiliser may be made prior to seeding at the rate of 1.50 kg/m². It is slow-acting and particularly useful on heavy land.

Phosphorus
Phosphatic fertilisers stimulate the development of a healthy root system and to a certain extent regulate nitrogen assimilation by plants. Phosphorus is essential for life, being a constituent of protoplasm; its greatest concentration in plants is within the seeds. Although phosphorus is present in the widely distributed mineral apatite (calcium phosphate), it is not in sufficiently large quantities, nor is it found in great abundance within the soil. Sufficient phosphorus in available compounds in the soil promotes rapid plant growth. Better results are obtained if phosphatic fertilisers are applied in small doses at frequent intervals rather than in large doses infrequently.

(a) *Superphosphate of lime*. This fertiliser should not be applied alone because it may cause scorching, but is usually mixed with sand, soil or compost in the proportions of 1:4–6 (by weight) and applied at the rate of 0.037 kg/m² (or more in areas of high rainfall). It is probably the best fertiliser in this category for use on alkaline soils, where it is preferable to bonemeal. In compound fertilisers superphosphate is usually the phosphatic ingredient specified and increases both the density and drought-resisting properties of the sward. It encourages the establishment of seedlings and root formation but must not be mixed with calcium cyanamide, basic slag or oxide of lime.

(b) *Basic slag*. A by-product of steel manufacture consisting basically of the phosphorous impurities removed from pig-iron combined with lime. Basic slag contains 48 per cent quicklime of which, in terms of liming power, 50.8 kg is equivalent to 33.5 kg of lime. It is a very useful fertiliser on very acid, neglected turf but on agricultural grassland is known to encourage the growth of clover. Application should be at the rate of 0.125 kg/m² with up to 0.251 kg/m² on very acid soils. Basic slag must not be mixed with sulphate of ammonia, nitro chalk, superphosphate or ammonium phosphate.

(c) *Bonemeal*. A useful fertiliser which is frequently used in the maintenance of sports turf. Too large an application has a tendency to encourage clover, but bonemeal is often incorporated in seedbed fertilisers as a source of slow-acting phosphate. Annual application to turf should be at the rate of 0.075–0.125 kg/m².

(d) *Boneflour*. A finer texture and a better source of phosphate than bonemeal. It is used in compound fertilisers and is useful on light soils, the rate of application being the same as that of bonemeal.

(e) *Guano*. Materials ranging from bird excreta to dried fish offal are usually referred to as 'guano'; its composition is variable. It is more costly than many of the other phosphatic fertilisers and usually applied at the rate of 0.075–0.125 kg/m².

Potassium
Although potassic fertilisers are not as vital to plants as nitrogen or phosphates they play an important part in stimulating healthy growth and producing turf that is capable of withstanding drought, disease or discolouration. Where plenty of potassium salts (potash) are available for assimilation, healthy plants are produced. Some soils, particularly clays, contain a relatively high level of potassium but total potassium content and quantity available for plant growth are not directly related.

Potassic fertilisers are not often used alone since they tend to encourage clover and other weeds.

(a) *Sulphate of potash*. The safest potassic fertiliser for use on grass. It is slow-acting and is applied to the seedbed or as a top-dressing at the rate of 0.0125–

0·037 kg/m² but, more often, is included in a compound fertiliser.

(b) *Muriate of potash*. This and sulphate of potash are the two most generally accepted fertilisers supplying potash. There are naturally-occurring forms of potash which include carnallite (a mixture of potassium chloride and magnesium chloride) and sylvine (potassium chloride). Various grades of commercial muriate of potash are also available and store comparatively well without deterioration. Application during preparation of the seedbed is at the rate of 0·012–0·037 kg/m², depending upon the potash content of the grades of fertiliser used, and should be carried out in the autumn or winter preceding the sowing season.

(c) *Kainit*. A fertiliser composed of naturally-occurring salts which, because of the chloride and sodium content, is of little value for turf when used on its own, although it may be used during seedbed preparation at the rate of 0·025–0·062 kg/m² applied during the previous autumn or winter. Kainit is frequently included in compound fertiliser mixtures.

(d) *Organic potash*. Ash from various sources, such as burnt hedge trimmings, herbage, weeds, etc., forms a convenient source of organic potash.

Selection of seed mixtures

Basically, six species are used in the formation of grass for recreation and leisure purposes generally:

Agrostis (bents)
Festuca (fescues)
Lolium (ryegrass)
Poa (meadowgrass)
Phleum (timothy)
Cynosurus (dogstail)

Seed mixtures fall into two broad groups: those containing ryegrass and those without it. The non-ryegrass group may be sub-divided into mixtures entirely composed of fescues and bents and those containing timothy and dogstail. Although ryegrass is quick to germinate and of vigorous growth, the appearance of a thick braird of ryegrass seedings merely gives the impression of a good sward. To establish a better grass requires the inclusion of good bottom grasses, such as bent, fescue, meadowgrass, timothy or dogstail. Mixtures which include any of these produce grass of a more pleasant appearance, involving much less maintenance work.

The grass mixtures shown in Table 32 should be taken as a guide only, since local conditions, type of soil and fertility must be taken into account. For the establishment of football and hockey pitches a fairly high proportion of the coarser grasses should be included in the mixture. The Aberystwyth strain S.23 is acknowledged to be the most suitable perennial ryegrass for use in areas subject to hard wear and tear. Other useful alternatives include heraf, pelo and melle (pasture type). The proportion of ryegrass included in any mixture should not exceed 50 per cent and where a fine sward is required it should be excluded altogether, although a small proportion of the S.23 strain may be included in a predominantly bent/fescue mixture to act as a nurse crop which, once the finer grasses become established, progressively dies out due to the constant close mowing.

In shaded areas shade-tolerant species may be used singly or in a mixture (Table 33). The soil in the vicinity of trees is often dry due to the removal of water and nutrients. Overhanging branches may encourage lichen and the deposit of leaves acidify the soil. It is also important to consider the type of tree under which the grass is to be sown; wavy hairgrass is probably the best for growing under conifers, but in some instances it may be better to substitute some other type of ground cover or surfacing material.

In areas of high atmospheric pollution, drippings from trees may be highly toxic and considerably increase the acidity of the soil. Large-leaved grasses exposed to these conditions soon die out; the finer-leaved grasses, particularly the fescues, are more likely to survive provided the correct type of maintenance is regularly carried out. Annual meadowgrass is also a useful species because of its prolific seeding habit. Some of the finer-leaved ryegrasses may also thrive in this type of situation but their shallow-rooting habit necessitates artificial watering during dry spells.

Buying and testing grass seed

Seeds should always be purchased from a reputable supplier. At the time of tendering the contractor should be required to submit a statement giving particulars of purity, germination, year of harvest and origin of the seed; the price per kilogramme should also be given.

The most important points to notice when buying seed are its appearance and smell; the seed should be plump, clean and bright in colour with no musty smell attaching to it. Any seed which does not conform should be rejected.

Table 32
Grass seed mixtures for various purposes in open areas

	Percentages of seeds incorporated in mixture											
Species of grass	Fine lawns		Bowling and putting greens		Tennis courts		Cricket squares		Games pitches		Parks, Golf	
	a	b	a	b	a	b	a	b	a	b	a	b
BENTS : Agrostis tenuis (browntop)	30	10	25	30	10	30	5	10	10	10	10	10
FESCUES : Festuca rubra S.59 (red fescue)	40	—	—	—	30	—	—	—	15	—	15	—
F. rubra fallax (Chewing's fescue)	30	40	50	70	50	45	50	60	15	—	40	15
F. rubra genuina (Cumberland)	—	—	25	—	—	—	—	—	—	—	—	—
F. tenuifolia (fine-leaved fescue)	—	—	—	—	10	—	—	—	—	—	—	—
MEADOWGRASS : Poa trivialis (rough-stalked)	—	10	—	—	—	—	—	10	—	20	—	10
P. pratensis (smooth-stalked)	—	—	—	—	—	—	10	—	—	—	—	—
TIMOTHY : Phleum pratense S.50	—	—	—	—	—	—	—	—	—	10	—	—
DOGSTAIL : Cynosurus cristatus (crested)	—	40	—	—	—	25	35	20	20	10	10	15
RYEGRASS : Lolium perenne S.23 (perennial)	—	—	—	—	—	—	—	—	40	50	25	50

(a) mixture for dry soils
(b) mixture for moist soils

Table 33
Grass species and seed mixtures for shaded areas

			Percentages of seeds incorporated in mixture					
Type of soil	Species of grass		Heavy soils		Medium soils	Medium-to-light soils	Light dry soils	Peaty heathland
			Normal conditions	Polluted atmosphere				
Heavy Moist	RYEGRASS :	Lolium perenne S.23 (perennial)	50	40				
	MEADOWGRASS :	Poa trivialis (rough-stalked)	30	30				
		P. annua (annual)	—	30				
	BENT :	Agrostis stolonifera (creeping)	20	—				
Medium	RYEGRASS :	Lolium perenne S.23 (perennial)			25	25		
	MEADOWGRASS :	Poa pratensis (smooth-stalked)			50	50		
	DOGSTAIL :	Cynosurus cristatus (crested)			—	25		
	FESCUE :	Festuca ovina (sheep's)			25	—		
Light	BENT :	Agrostis tenuis (browntop)					30	
	FESCUE :	Festuca ovina (sheep's)					40	
		Festuca tenuifolia (fine-leaved)					20	
		Festuca rubra S.59 (creeping red)					10	
Peaty heathland	FESCUE :	Festuca tenuifolia (fine-leaved)						30
		Festuca rubra S.59 (creeping red)						30
	HAIRGRASS :	Deschampsia flexuosa (wavy)						40

Seed may be analysed for composition (where a mixture), purity and germination. Any sample taken must accurately represent the bulk of seed from which it is drawn and comply with the sampling requirements laid down in the Seeds Regulations, 1961:

Bulk comprises:

Less than 1 sackful	Bulk must be thoroughly mixed and small portions taken from various parts
1 sackful	Samples must be taken from top, middle and bottom of sack
Several sacks:	
Up to 5	Sample each as directed for 1 sackful
Over 5 and up to 50	Sample 1 sack in 5 (with a minimum of 5 sacks)
Over 50	Sample 1 sack in 10 (with a minimum of 10 sacks)
Heaps or bins	Samples must be taken from various parts of the heap or bin at different depths and not all from the surface

The sample seed obtained must be thoroughly mixed and the final sample which is sent for analysis should weigh not less than 113 g.

Purity tests require a sample of about 3000 seeds taken at random. The impurities found in the sample are classified on a percentage basis into:

> Weed seeds
> Other crop seeds
> Inert matter
> Injurious weeds

For germination tests the seed is subjected to conditions which simulate normal germination temperatures:

> 30 °C for 6 hours
> 18 °–20 °C for 18 hours } each day

The germinated seeds are counted at intervals and their germination capacity determined after a maximum period which varies according to species (e.g. perennial ryegrasss and timothy: 14 days; red fescue S59: 28 days).

Choosing between seed and turf

Turf provides a quick method of forming a lawn and if properly laid the turfs soon knit together. Laying may be done at any time of the year provided the ground is frost-free. Less preparation of the bed is necessary and the turf requires less attention in its early stages than is entailed in the establishment of seedlings.

The drawbacks of using turf instead of seed are that it is expensive and its source is mainly meadowland containing undesirable coarse grasses and weeds. Sea-washed turf, derived from salt marshes and comprising mostly fescues, is recommended for use on bowling-greens because its special nature makes it ideal for play of the ball. Its cost is prohibitive for general lawn use.

The advantages of seed are that the capital outlay is less than that for turf and the resultant sward is more even and closely-knit, especially where the better strains of grass are used. On the other hand, a more thorough preparation of the seedbed is required and the selection of the seed must be carefully made so that the grasses will thrive. Maintenance of the young seedlings must be conscientiously carried out if they are to produce a good sward. Protection of the new grass is necessary to prevent any damage in its early stages of growth. This is particularly important in the establishment of grass in urban areas and is often a factor which determines the use of turf rather than seed in certain locations.

In the construction of bowling-greens the preference for turf is of particular importance because it permits earlier play; if laid during the autumn it is ready for play the following June, whereas autumn-sown seed does not mature until the end of the following season and spring-sown seed is not available for play in the same year.

Establishing grass from seed

Grass swards may be classed into two categories: those that are functional (e.g. games pitches) and those whose purpose is primarily aesthetic (e.g. ornamental lawns). The preparatory work for both is basically the same, although where cost is a primary factor some of the expenditure may be reduced for work which is purely of a utilitarian nature (e.g. rough grassed areas in parkland). It must be stressed that it is false economy to reduce the amount of preparatory work required for areas that are likely to be subjected to wear and tear or where appearance is important.

The operations necessary for the formation of grass fall under the following headings and should generally comply with the requirements set out in BS 4428:1969.

Site levelling

With the exception of golf courses, a level site for sports turf is essential, particularly for such games as hockey, and the adjustment of site gradients must be accurately carried out. Grading and levelling operations should preferably be carried out in the autumn or early winter while the ground is still frost-free. A slight fall on the land facilitates drainage and need be no greater than 1 : 40. For winter games pitches and cricket outfields the optimum fall is 1 : 60–80 across the direction of play. On sites where the gradient is particularly steep it may be necessary to terrace the area surrounding the pitch itself to reduce major grading operations. Attention must be paid to the careful grading of banks surrounding the pitch (or pitches) so that the maximum slope of the bank is not greater than 45°.

Drainage

Good turf cannot be established on poorly drained soil and is not resistant to wear under waterlogged conditions because the lack of aeration which results from impeded drainage causes poor root development, leading to turf deterioration. For bowling-greens a layer of well-washed and graded furnace clinker (winkle clinker), complying with BS 4132 : 1973, should be specified.

Good drainage means that the texture and structure of the soil is better and the soil firmer and warmer, resulting in healthy root development which increases the drought-resistance of the grass and permits better utilisation of fertilisers. In addition, bacterial activity within the soil is promoted by good aeration and leads to active healthy grass growth and a reduction in weeds and turf disorders.

Bad drainage of a site can be recognised by the 'feel' of the soil, which is spongy to the tread. The type of vegetation also gives an indication with the presence of rushes, sedges and certain moss species.

Reference should be made to CP 301 : 1971 which deals with subsoil drainage.

Soil cultivation and preparation of seedbed

When grading and drainage operations are completed the site should be ploughed (or dug) to a depth of 150 mm. In some cases ploughing and grading may be carried out simultaneously. Although the basic character of the soil cannot be altered, it can be modified where necessary. In the case of heavy soils this may mean incorporating gritty material, such as coarse sand or fine coke breeze and ashes. A fertiliser should also be worked into the top 50 mm of soil, at the rate of 0·125–0·187 kg/m², 10–14 days prior to seeding, to ensure rapid germination. One of the many pre-seeding fertilisers may be selected for this purpose since they contain all the essential elements required for the production of healthy turf seedlings. On sandy soils the inclusion of leaf mould or peat helps to improve the water-holding capacity of the soil and also assists in promoting a deeper rooting system.

Wherever possible a period of time should elapse between levelling and sowing the seed in order to clear the site of weeds. This period, known as 'fallowing', allows any dormant weed seeds present to grow into seedlings and subsequently be eliminated. Light harrowing and cross-raking destroys most of these weeds. Stone-picking should also be carried out, either by hand or machine, during the summer months following the grading operations completed in the previous autumn or winter. Fallowing not only enables the weeds to be eliminated, but also allows the soil to settle and consolidate in readiness for seed sowing in early September.

Consolidation

Thorough consolidation of the soil, by rolling in alternate directions three or four times, should follow the initial cultivation so that the ground is firm but not compacted. In small areas consolidation may be carried out by treading with the feet. The surface is then lightly raked to produce a firm seedbed with a fine tilth composed of soil crumbs no larger than wheat grains.

Seed sowing

The best time for seeding is between mid-August and mid-September when the soil is still warm. Seed may also be sown in April, but the soil is not so warm then and subsequent copious watering may be necessary if the summer is dry.

Seeding operations must take place in dry, calm weather, the seed being divided into two equal portions and sown broadcast by hand, portable sower or seed barrow in two directions at right angles to each other. Seeding is generally at the rate of 26–34 g/m². Light raking or harrowing, using a short-spiked chain harrow or bush harrow, should be carried out to cover the seed with not more than 6 mm of soil. A final rolling, though not strictly necessary, is sometimes done, but not where the soil is inclined to be heavy, since this may result in subsequent caking of the surface.

Maintenance

Germination usually occurs about seven to twenty-one

days after sowing, depending upon weather conditions and type of seed. Aftercare of the young seedlings is extremely important if the grass is ultimately to form a good healthy sward. The first job is to pick off all stones exceeding 50 mm diameter; in some areas it may be necessary to remove stones of 13 mm. Light rolling should then be carried out when the grass is about 50 mm high, so that the soil is firmed around the seedlings and the smaller surface stones pushed below the surface. Rolling should be followed a few days later by a light mowing to remove not more than 25 mm of the grass tips. On large areas this is done with a gang mower during dry weather. Mowing should be carried out at regular, but not too frequent, intervals to keep the grass under control, the cutting blades being progressively lowered down to the desired height of cut, which may be 6–19 mm or longer, depending upon the type of turf. Thereafter, mowing should be continued to keep the grass neat and trim.

Weeds that appear after the grass is established and that cannot be removed by hand may be treated with selective weedkillers. Most of the annual weeds succumb to mowing.

After a period of about three months a finely-sieved compost should be lightly worked into the surface at the rate of 1·62–2·16 kg/m² to assist in turf formation; care in application is necessary in order to prevent 'damping-off' (caused by fungal growth).

The year following seeding, an allowance should be made for the application of three dressings of fertiliser—in spring, early summer and autumn. Such fertiliser should take into account the type of soil and its acidity (or alkalinity) since plant nutrients must be absorbed in a balanced proportion. Where this proportion is upset the increase in one element may cause deficiency in another. A balanced fertiliser for normal soils should consist of a granular product containing:

> 10 per cent nitrogen
> 8 per cent phosphate
> 8 per cent potash

Formation of grass using turf

The preparation of the bed for turf is similar to that for the formation of grassed areas from seed, but turf requires much less attention than growing seedlings. Its major drawbacks are its cost and its constituent grass species: much of the turf on the market today is obtained from rough meadow land containing a proportion of undesirable coarse grasses and weeds.

Sources of turf

Apart from meadow turf there are a number of indigenous species to be found in various parts of the country.

Cumberland (sea-washed turf from sea marshes). This fine, even-textured turf is mostly used for bowling-greens and is obtained from the salt marshes of Lancashire, Morecambe Bay and the Solway estuary, near Silloth (Cumbria). The character of this turf varies according to its composition and growing conditions. In some habitats *Festuca rubra genuina* (creeping red fescue) and its varieties are dominant, and in others *Agrostis stolonifera* var.*salina*. Inferior and low-lying sea-marsh turf contains sea meadowgrass or sea poa (*Puccinellia maritima*), which is a difficult grass to maintain away from its maritime habitat.

Thin soils overlying chalk. Good turf may be found in these areas where the predominant species are sheep's fescues, bents and crested dogstail. Typical chalkland weeds may also be present.

Upland heathland and sheep pastures. These areas, particularly in the west, consist of turf predominantly composed of fescues and bents developed naturally. *Nardus stricta* (moor mat grass) and *Sieglingia decumbens* (heath grass) may also be present but, provided fescues or bents predominate, this type of turf is capable of producing a good sward since it is generally weed-free, any weeds present soon disappearing with mowing and proper maintenance.

Poor soils are the natural habitat of the fescues and bents and other fine-leaved grasses and it is important that a certain degree of acidity should be preserved and adequate (but not excessive) fertilisers applied. Whatever source of turf is selected the sods should be checked for the presence of weeds, pests and disease; the turf should meet the requirements laid down in BS 3969:1965.

Turf must be carefully cut and lifted, each sod of uniform size and thickness, to facilitate easy re-laying. Turf-cutting machines are often employed, but where the sods are lifted by hand the turf should be cut into strips 300 mm wide, divided into squares or 1 m lengths, whichever is more expedient. Sods should be laid as soon as possible after lifting and not stored for more than three days.

The bed preparation is similar to that described for the seedbed although a coarser tilth is adequate for turfs. Prior to laying, a fertiliser composed of:

4 parts bonemeal
4 parts superphosphate
1 part sulphate of potash

should be incorporated in the turf bed at the rate of 68 g/m². The sods must be laid in a workmanlike manner; starting along one side of the site and working in straight lines, each sod is laid close to the next to break joint, as in the laying of bricks or tiles. Fine soil or sand is used to fill the joints and the sods well beaten down. Note that the turf layer (standing on a plank) works forward from the area of laid turf to prevent disturbance of the turf bed.

Turf maintenance
When the sods begin to root and knit together, rolling and subsequent top-dressing can be carried out. In the spring a light sandy compost is applied at the rate of 2·45–4·35 kg/m², any mat that has developed in the turf being carefully raked out prior to the application of the fertiliser. Sods that fail to root should be taken out and replaced by fresh ones. A combined turf fertiliser and weed killer may be used. This not only feeds the lawn but also eliminates the weeds, dispensing with weeding operations.

Provision of a turf nursery
It is advisable to set aside an area of ground which can be used as a turf nursery for supplying new turf to areas that have become worn or require replacement. The siting of such an area should be in the open, away from trees and buildings, and maintained in the normal manner along with the rest of the grassed areas.

Vegetative production in the establishment of grass

Vegetative means of producing new swards are not commonly undertaken in Britain (although favoured in America), probably because this method is more costly and laborious than seeding and our climate produces better results by the latter method or by turfing.

Stolons (surface-creeping stems which form roots as they grow) produced from grasses of creeping habit, e.g. Emerald Velvet, are planted 150–300 mm apart on a prepared bed and lightly covered with a fine top-dressing and fertiliser. The grass species generally used is *Agrostis stolonifera,* which produces a sward which is rather coarse and fibrous. It is unsuitable for laying down playing pitches and other areas subject to heavy wear because its shallow-rooting habit makes it susceptible to drought; it may be satisfactory in some cases for the formation of lawns.

Diseases in newly-sown grass

Young grasses are very susceptible to attack by a wide variety of fungi and for this reason it is essential to encourage quick germination and rapid growth of the seedlings at the outset by the application of quick-acting nitrogenous and phosphatic fertilisers. The young grasses may fail to appear due to seed-rot and pre-emergence 'damping-off', or may die at the first or second leaf stage from post-emergence 'damping-off'. Grasses most affected by this type of fungal disease are:

Agrostis (bents)
Festuca (fescues)
Cynosurus cristatus (crested dogstail)
Phleum pratense (timothy)

Pre-emergence 'damping-off'
Cold soils with an excessive water content encourage fungal growth which develops more rapidly than the grass seedlings. Under these conditions spring-sown seed is most susceptible to attack and the disease rapidly becomes established, killing many of the seedlings and resulting in a sward of patchy and poor appearance. The fungi responsible are *Helminth osporium* and *Fusarium* which can be either seedborne or present in the soil. An attack by the soil-borne fungus *Pythium* produces a condition referred to as 'damping-off' (see below). The application of sulphate of ammonia and superphosphate (quick-acting nitrogenous and phosphatic fertilisers) to the seedbed assists in preventing an attack; proprietary seed dressings (whose contents are on the Ministry of Agriculture's current List of Approved Products) may also be applied.

Post-emergence 'damping-off'
Seed sown on poorly prepared heavy soil may die off at the first or second leaf stage giving the appearance of reddish-brown patches in the sward, due to the rotting of the plant stem just below or at soil surface.

Control of the disease by the application of fertilisers depends, to a large extent, upon the type of fungus responsible for the attack. The disease may be caused by *Fusarium culmorum, F. nivale* or *F. avenaceum* where the seed has been densely sown in soil over-fertilised with nitrogen. Soil that is very wet and short of nitrogen and phosphorous is likely to be attacked by *Pythium* and *Cladochytrium caespitis* and in this case a phosphatic fertiliser (e.g. mono-ammonium phosphate) should be applied at the rate of 9–17 g/m² with a suitable carrier.

Cheshunt compound assists in partially controlling this disease and has been used for many years. A number of proprietary brands using this product are available and may be applied at the rate of 2·6 litres/m².

Alternatives to grass as ground cover

A number of indigenous species, although sometimes treated as weeds, are capable of producing an attractive ground cover. For sports turf the use of grass is undoubtedly superior but in other situations subject to much less wear and tear, or where maintenance may be a problem, the planting of alternatives may usefully be considered. The initial establishment of such plants is likely to be more costly than that of grass, but the benefits of lower maintenance costs often far outweigh the capital outlay. The selection of a particular type of plant depends upon the site, its microclimate and the type of soil. The list below gives an indication of the range of plants available ; a browse through any nurseryman's catalogue would provide further suggestions.

Clover. One of the simplest plants to grow and a useful pioneer crop for covering waste tips and poor soils. A member of the leguminous family, it is self-supporting in nitrogen and retains its colour during periods of drought but is susceptible to cold, which causes bare patches. Seeding should be carried out in the spring. Wild white clover and late-flowering red clover are sometimes included in mixtures with ryegrass and timothy.

Chamomile (*Chamaemelum nobile*). A creeping, much-branched herbaceous perennial, normally about 300 mm high. It has a delightful aroma and thrives in ordinary soils. The seedlings should be planted in April at 230 mm centres in rows 300 mm apart, or closer if quick establishment of a sward is required. All weeds must be eliminated until the chamomile has covered the ground. The only maintenance required is clipping once or twice a year either with

shears or with the lawn mower set very high. To encourage branching, all flower-heads should be removed, thereby promoting a bush cover.

Yarrow (*Achillea millefolium*). Another aromatic hardy herbaceous perennial which grows to a height of approximately 900 mm. It is particularly useful for establishing a non-grass ground cover on light soils and is established by the sowing of seed. Although it is regarded as a weed when found growing in the best quality turf, it is capable of blending quite well with turf grasses.

Wild thyme (*Thymus serpyllum*). There are several varieties of this hardy prostrate evergreen aromatic herb suitable for the establishment of a ground cover on light soils.

Pennyroyal (*Mentha pulegium*). A carpeting aromatic herb—native plant of wet heaths—does best on moist loams in partial shade. It requires watering in dry weather and an annual top-dressing. The swards, established by sowing seeds in spring or summer—or by vegetative propagation in spring or autumn—are less persistent than those of chamomile and require annual renovation. *Marjoram hortensis*, a closely related aromatic herb growing up to 610 mm high, is more suited to alkaline soils.

Heather (*Calluna vulgaris*). This type of lawn requires a lime-free soil and is established by cuttings. It is most attractive in flower and essentially an ecological lawn which requires very little maintenance apart from periodic cutting with an old blunt mower. There are many varieties available.

Alpines. Lawns on sloping ground may be established by planting alpines (there are far too many species and varieties to warrant mention here). This type of lawn requires very little maintenance once established and if the right selection is made can provide an interesting and varied feature throughout the year.

Eight Trees: Planting, Care and Protection

TREE PLANTING

The use and misuse of trees

Trees are living plants that are constantly changing and add considerably to the enjoyment of everyday living, providing interesting shapes, movement, sound, colour, texture, patterns of light and shade; they are also a haven for birds. One of their main assets is that they provide scale, contributing to a balanced layout of buildings in relation to the environment. Where no trees exist the buildings often appear stark and unrelated to their surroundings. Even in the centre of a big city the careful siting of just a few trees can transform an otherwise harsh, and often drab, scene.

The selection of trees involves a detailed knowledge not only of the changes which their visual characteristics undergo through the various seasons, but also of the physical form of the plants as they develop and reach maturity. Other factors, such as their compatability with other plants and susceptibility or otherwise to toxic atmospheres or tolerance of lime or acid conditions, must also be borne in mind. Ignorance in these matters may lead to the planting of trees of the wrong species, and may ultimately result in a layout that is grossly out of scale or over-crowded. All too often the remedy adopted is to cut back the trees to such an extent that they appear little more than mutilated trunks. Since trees are the dominant plants and form such an important feature of an environment, it is essential to know at the outset their merits and shortcomings so that they may be wisely chosen and correctly sited.

Plants and their natural habitats

'Plant ecology' is the study of plants as they exist in their natural environments. In nature there is a wide range of habitats which vary according to soil and climatic conditions; each habitat has its own distinctive vegetation (plant community) consisting of plant species that have adapted themselves during the course of time to the particular conditions prevailing (e.g. oakwood community). Under natural conditions various species growing together must have some effect on one another and the result is a 'competition' among the plants whose needs are alike.

Soil plays an important part; on newly-dug ground some plant species grow more vigorously than others and are termed the 'dominant' species of the plant community. The weaker species ultimately either die off or are overgrown by the more successful ones. Others, whose needs are different and not in competition, are termed 'complementary'. A far larger number of these can occupy an area of ground than is possible for competing plants; e.g. in an oakwood there are three tiers of plants:

Tree layer (oak trees)
Shrub layer (hazel and other shrubs)
Field layer (ferns, primroses, etc.)

In time the whole area becomes covered with vegetation and gradually a few species take over and dominate the colony. There is keen competition between tree and tree, shrub and shrub, and between the various carpet plants. Plants may become dominant because they either grow rapidly, are perennials with food reserves or, if large plants, are able to reach the light but, whatever the reason, the vegetation of an area does not always remain the same for an indefinite period; one set of plants may be followed by another of quite a different kind. Such a change of vegetation in any habitat is known as a 'succession'. A natural succession is one brought about by natural causes, not by the activities of man, and may be:

(a) progressive succession, e.g. where a plant community develops from, say, grassland and heath into woodland;
(b) retrogressive succession, e.g. woodland degenerating into scrub and then into grassland.

A succession of communities following each other in a definite (progressive) sequence reaches a stage known as a 'preclimax' community and, finally, a 'climax'. This succession of communities, each fulfilling a definite role in the sequence leading to a climax, is called a 'sere'; it may be primary (prisere) or secondary (subsere). The former is rare (partly due to man's widespread activity) and is a sere which includes all the stages from bare ground to climatic climax, i.e. one that has not been replaced by another sere in recent geological times. If it is known to have been replaced then it is termed a subsere. Some grassland on chalk downs is thought to be prisere because there is no evidence of previous vegetation, unlike other similar areas where there is evidence (fossil or historical) of the former presence of beechwoods.

Factors which determine the special characteristics of a habitat
Four interdependent groups of factors affect the environment of plants:
  (i)   Edaphic: these relate to the nature of the soil (e.g. clay, sand), its texture and composition.
  (ii) Biotic: comprise all the influences exerted by living things such as man, animals, birds, insects and also the influence of plants upon each other and on their surroundings.
  (iii) Climatic: include temperature, intensity and duration of the sun's rays, wind, rainfall and atmospheric humidity.
  (iv) Topographical: these are concerned with altitude, aspect, angle of slope of the ground, proximity to high ground or the sea.
The nature of any habitat stems from a combination of these four factors, different kinds of habitat resulting from variations in the factors. Many of the plants reflect their environmental conditions in their structural modifications.

Woodland communities in relation to their habitats
Much of the woodland of Britain is mixed and the result of planting by man. It is sometimes difficult to find an original plant association, nevertheless there still remains a plant relationship and a study of the changes which take place

is of considerable importance. Types of woodland found in this country are :

Damp oakwoods (pedunculate oak community). These develop on clay loams and fine-grained sandstones and are characterised by mild humus with neutral to slightly acid reaction. The fairly rich shrub layer is dominated by hazel with a rich and abundant field layer. On the outskirts and in more open glades ash, beech, bird cherry and hornbeam are to be found.
   General distribution: typical and abundant on almost all deep soils in south, east and central England ; they also extend into west and north.

Dry oakwoods (sessile oak community). These develop on coarser sands and sandstones with humus of a higher degree of acidity than that of the damp oakwoods. The trees, which may include birch and mountain ash, are often in close canopy and much poorer in the shrub layer, hazel being typically absent. The field layer has few species and is often represented by bracken.
   General distribution: hills of west and north of England ; Wales and Ireland.

Beechwoods. Beechwoods are found on chalky escarpments and other limestone soils, on deep loam overlying chalk plateau and on podzolised loams or acid sands. The chief characteristic of this type of wood is its 'architectural' structure, with little if any ground cover. In more open areas ash and whitebeam may be present.
   General distribution: sides of valleys in southern England, Cotswolds, Wye Valley and Welsh Border.

Ashwoods. These occur on damp chalk soils, sometimes replacing beechwoods, and are light, open-textured woods with abundant subsidiary vegetation. Probably the most striking feature of an ashwood is the uniformity of the carpeting plants ; instead of a mixed vegetation (as in damp oakwoods) there occur large stretches of one kind of plant, which may be dog's mercury, ivy, ground ivy or melic grass, with little else growing in their midst. Trees associated with ash include aspen, crack willow, sallow, wych elm and hawthorn.
   General distribution: limestone hillsides of northern and southern England.

Pinewoods. Pinewoods change very little in appearance throughout the year ; with much of the ground covered with dry pine-needles, there are very few (if any) carpeting plants to be found in areas where the tree canopy is dense. Vegetation occurs in areas where light is able to penetrate and also on the outskirts of woods, and comprises bilberry, ling, wood sage and wavy hairgrass, all of which thrive on the sandy soils typical of pinewoods. A more openly developed pinewood may sometimes support a typical heath community.
   General distribution: southern England.

British native trees

Native trees form the basic tree planting of much of our countryside and are supplemented by others that have been introduced in the past and have established themselves alongside our native species. In preparing planting layouts and, more especially, forestry planting schemes, due regard should be given to preserving and maintaining these indigenous species (see Table 34, page 171).

Factors governing the selection of trees

Planting a tree is an act of faith, since seldom does the planter see the results at maturity.
   The following aspects should be borne in mind when making a selection of tree species (these also apply to other plant material) :

Function	Siting
Visual effect	Ecology
Existing planting	Availability of species
Soil	

An excellent booklet *Trees in town and city* (Ministry of Housing and Local Government, 1958) includes lists and tables which summarise the principal characteristics of each tree listed.

Function (Tables 35–41, pages 172–175)
Trees may be planted for a number of purposes, e.g. :

   to provide timber for commercial gain ;
   to serve as a windbreak or screen ;
   to act as a noise baffle ;
   to provide shade ;
   to give scale to buildings or other structures ;
   to provide colour and form.

Each function necessitates a different approach in the choice of species although two or more needs are often satisfied by the same selection (Figs 48 and 49).

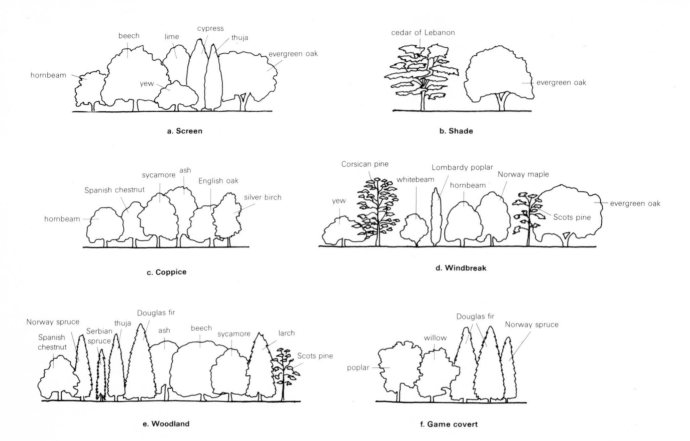

Fig. 48   Use of trees for functional purposes

Visual effect (Tables 42–49, pages 176–180)
Coupled with function is the effect which it is desired to achieve–immediate or long-term. The latter involves the problem of maintenance which in turn affects the economics of the scheme. All these various aspects are interdependent and no single one can be studied in isolation. Sometimes a compromise has to be made to provide an immediate effect, but this must always be seen in relation to a changing long-term process.

The visual characteristics of a planting layout throughout the seasons may be expressed by way of colour, form and texture. The aim should be to provide some kind of interest throughout the year. In winter this may be achieved by coloured bark, branches or formation of the plant; in spring, by blossom and in autumn by leaf colour or fruits of various kinds.

Existing planting
The existing planting often assists in providing some form of immediate landscaped effect and trees should be retained wherever possible, even if only to provide a temporary effect while the newly planted trees establish themselves. The decision to do this rests upon the type, condition and life of the trees in question and the problems of felling and extraction at a later date.

The relationship between new and existing levels must be carefully considered, particularly in the vicinity of existing trees, and precautions taken (Fig.15, page 34).

Soil (Tables 50–54, pages181–182)
Plants obtain from the soil nutrients essential to their growth; the importance of selecting the right type of plant suited to its environment cannot be over-stressed,

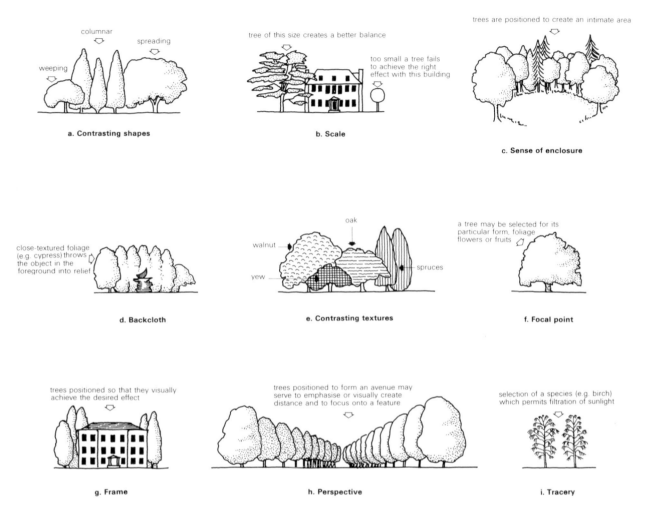

Fig. 49   Use of trees for aesthetic purposes

particularly where highly alkaline or peaty soils are concerned. Soil structure, texture, pH value, drainage and moisture content all play a vital role in plant growth.

Loams are ideal for most plants. Although clay soils are rich in nutrients their cultivation is hard work; they become very sticky when wet and hard and compact when dry. On the other hand sandy soils, although easy to cultivate, do not readily retain water and nutrients are easily leached out. During periods of drought plant loss may result unless watering is regular. It is generally better that plants should be transferred to this type of soil at a fairly early stage of growth. Similarly chalk soils, being usually shallow, are subject to the effects of drought and plants chosen for them must also be alkali-tolerant. Acid peats support a limited range of plant material.

If it is necessary to import topsoil into the area it should conform to that specified in BS 3882:1965. Where there are plants requiring an acid soil, no soil of alkaline reaction must be included.

Siting
Trees intended to give scale to a building must be positioned to achieve the right effect. It is essential to 'sense' the scale of a landscape which varies according to the land form. The height and spread of a tree should be borne in mind since both branches and roots can cause inconvenience or damage, particularly where in close proximity to utility services.

A long-term programme of planting may involve the siting of trees to form a temporary pattern which is altered over a period of years by selective removal of some

of the species, ultimately to produce a well-balanced layout.

A tree which may appear to be of reasonable spread after twenty years can easily become the cause of legal action many years later, due to damage resulting from the spread of its roots or branches onto other property.

Ecology
The ecological approach to the selection of trees necessitates a knowledge of the major plant communities. Certain plants do not always succeed in a natural landscape although they may well do so in a humanised one where natural competition is restricted by the action of man. On the other hand, the reverse may obtain because of atmospheric pollution (Table 40).

Availability of species
The purchase of plants from commercial horticultural sources sometimes means that the planting programme on site has to be geared to receive the plants when lifting operations take place in the nursery.

Trees are available in a number of forms and sizes and may be any one of the following:

Standard	1·67 to 1·82 m straight stem
Three-quarter standard	1·44 to 1·60 m straight stem
Half-standard	1·06 to 1·37 m straight stem
Quarter-standard or bush	0·30 to 0·76 m straight stem
Weeping standard	min. stem height 1·67 m

All these trees (with the exception of quarter-standard) should have a minimum diameter of 19 mm measured

Fig. 50   Forms and sizes of trees available commercially

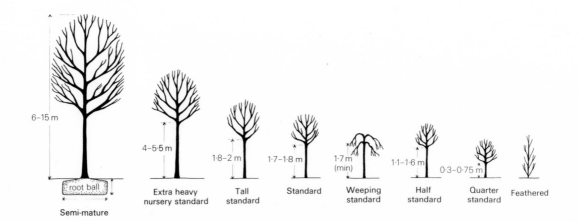

600–900 mm from ground level, as specified in BS 3936 : Part 1 : 1965 (see also BS 3975 : Part 4 :1966) (Fig.50).

Standard trees may sometimes be available in a larger size, termed 'tall standard', 1·90–2·13 m in height with a stem diameter of 25 mm. Feathered trees are also obtainable in varying heights.

Fruit trees may be any one of the following forms (Fig.51) :

    Fan-trained
    Feathered
    Espalier—two, three or four tier
    Cordon
    Grid—three, four, five, six or eight
    'U'—single or double

Trees selected for establishing woodlands are young seedlings ranging from 150 to 610 mm in height. Those sold for forest planting are seldom more than three or four years old. BS 3936 : Part 4 : 1966 recommends sizes and quality of plants, in addition to seeds.

The conventional method used to describe young seedlings is as follows :

1+0   'one-year-old' or 'first year seedling'.
    The young tree has been six to twelve months in the seedbed.
2+0   'two-year-old' or 'second year seedling'.
    The young tree has spent two seasons in the seedbed.
1+1   transplant—'one plus one'.
    One season in the seedbed and another in the transplant lines.

2+1   transplant—'two plus one'.
    Two seasons in the seedbed and one in the transplant lines.
1+1+1   twice transplant—'one plus one plus one'.
    Three-year-old seedling that has spent one year in the seedbed and has been twice transplanted.

The use of semi-mature trees in planting layouts

BS 3975 : Part 4 : 1966 defines a semi-mature tree as '. . . well developed but not mature'.

For the purpose of giving scale and an aspect of maturity to a layout, semi-mature trees are sometimes planted, especially where the area concerned is fairly extensive. They may be incorporated with standard nursery trees (to give a variety of sizes), in groups, or as specimens. All semi-mature trees require special care in transplanting and should meet the requirements set out in BS 4043 :1966 which gives guidance on selection, preparation and lifting operations and also recommends methods of guying and securing a tree, wrapping, watering and spraying.

The essential part of any transplanting technique involving larger trees is to ensure that the root ball remains intact by wrapping and tying it in hessian. This is of even greater importance with light soils than with heavy ones since the latter hold together much better and are easier to move without causing damage.

Some trees transplant much better than others ; only

Fig. 51   Forms of fruit trees

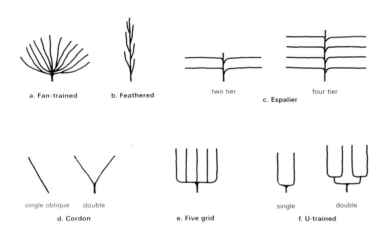

those species that have a good chance of establishing themselves should be selected.

Trees that are difficult to transplant include:

All conifers	Hornbeam
Birch	Oak
Beech	Thorn

Those that are readily transplanted include:

Alder	Maple
Ash	Plane
Chestnut	Poplar
Elm	Sycamore
False acacia	Willow
Lime	

Shallow-rooted trees, such as those growing over chalk or gravelly soils, are more easily moved than those with deep roots growing on clay or sandy soils.

The trees selected should be healthy, vigorous and well-formed with good well-balanced crowns although, if it is a healthy specimen, there is no reason (other than that of appearance) why a tree of irregular form should not be used in places where it is likely to give added interest.

Planting trees in various situations

Certain rules must be observed if successful healthy plants are ultimately to be produced.

1. The tree pit must be larger than the extent of the tree's roots (when spread out) and at least 75 mm deeper than that of the root system.
2. There must be a sufficient quantity of topsoil to allow the tree to obtain adequate nourishment (not less than 0·5 m³). It should be carefully well-firmed around the roots so that no air pockets are left which would prevent the roots from coming into direct contact with the soil.
3. The trees should be well watered at the time of planting, but no such planting should be undertaken in areas of stagnant water or during periods of heavy rainfall.
4. No planting must be carried out during periods of frost and care should be exercised to see that the roots are not exposed to frost, heavy winds or strong sunlight which may cause them to dry out. Where drying out occurs, or is likely to occur, the roots should be soaked in water for a period of twenty-four hours.

Fig. 52   Planting trees and shrubs in ordinary soils

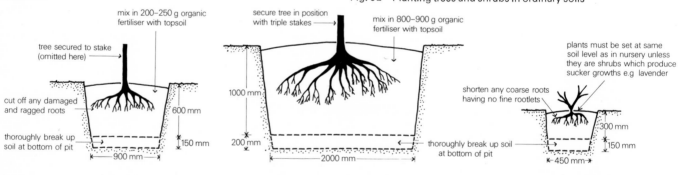

a. Standard tree   b. Extra heavy nursery standard tree   c. Shrub in planting bed

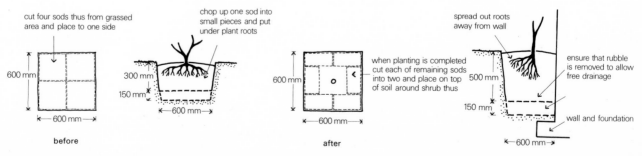

d. Shrub in grass   e. Climbers and wall shrubs

5. Each tree, except seedlings, must be adequately secured to a stout stake (Fig.54).

Careful planting is of no avail if the species selected is unsuitable for the site conditions or soil (Figs 52 and 53).

Planting should be carried out during the dormant season:*

Deciduous trees End October to end March
Conifers   October or April

Any tree planted after February may be subject to the effects of drought which normally follow in spring and early summer, and therefore requires to be watered during the maintenance period. Evergreens are best planted during October while the ground is still warm after the summer sun. Although the soil is usually beginning to warm up in April, sometimes the spring is cold and wet. In areas of high rainfall spring planting is often best done when the ground is less subject to the heavy waterlogging and frost of winter. Light sandy soils in dry areas are subject to spring droughts and here planting is best carried

*This does not apply, of course, to container-grown plants.

out before the end of January and preferably not later than the end of December.

The nurseryman is responsible for lifting, packing and transporting the trees to the site so that they arrive in good condition. Normally, plants are despatched from the end of October until late April–this usually means that no definite delivery date can be given to the customer (although notification is usually sent several days prior to despatch and the earlier the order is placed, the earlier the delivery).

As soon as the trees arrive on site they should be unpacked and placed in a previously dug trench–two spades wide and of the same depth–and the roots well covered with moist soil (heeled in) unless they are to be planted immediately in position. The plants can then be safely left in the trench until ready to be placed in their final planting stations.

Groups of trees on virgin soil
The area should be cultivated to a depth of not less than 230 mm and cleared free of all weeds, rubbish and large stones. These sites are without the beneficial leaf mould

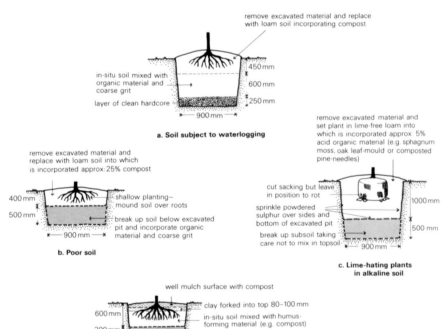
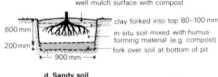

Fig. 53 Planting methods adopted where soil conditions are unsatisfactory

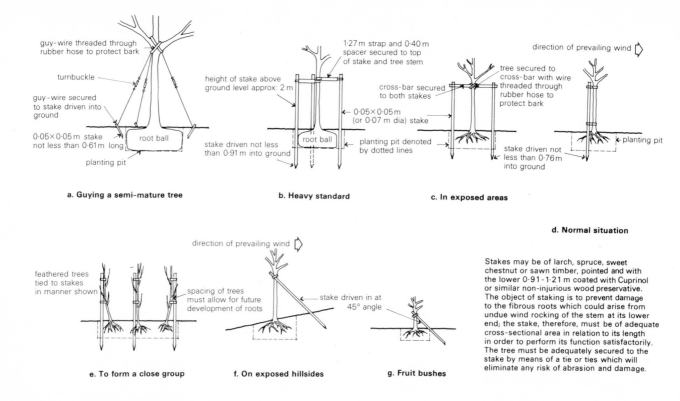

Fig. 54   Various methods of staking trees

and humus normally found in woodland areas and often require the addition of a good all-round fertiliser applied at the rate of 68 g/m².

Trees at individual stations
BS 4428 : 1969, Section 7, describes the planting method which should be adopted. Precautions are necessary in grassed areas to prevent damage to the turf.

New woodlands and shelter-belts (Fig.55)
The sites selected for woodland planting are often difficult areas of established grassland, hillsides or moorland and in each case young seedling trees are planted—usually three-year-old transplants.

Established grassland requires ploughing or the vegetation and top layer of roots scraping away (screefing) so that a bare patch of soil is left; approximately 450–600 mm square provides sufficient space in which to plant a tree. Ploughing is a more effective form of preparation since it helps to suppress the vegetation. Where screefing

is done an application of Dalapon can be effective for this purpose. Hillside planting generally has little preparation since the sites are often too steep to allow machines to operate. The young seedling is either 'notch' or 'mattock' planted. Where the slope of the hillside permits ploughing, better results are often obtained; this also applies to moorland and heathland, especially in the more difficult areas such as wet peaty highland. An application of fertiliser should also be given. The ridges and furrows produced by ploughing must follow natural drainage requirements so that no ponding occurs and the surface water is allowed to drain along the furrows to open ditches along the contours. Conversely, in dry soils the furrows should be formed so that they conserve any surface water to prevent drying out of the soil.

Turf planting (a Belgian method) involves the cutting of ditches 1·52 m wide. Turfs are removed and placed grass face downwards alongside the ditches and left for at least a month to allow the sandwiched vegetation to become partially rotted to form a suitable rooting medium

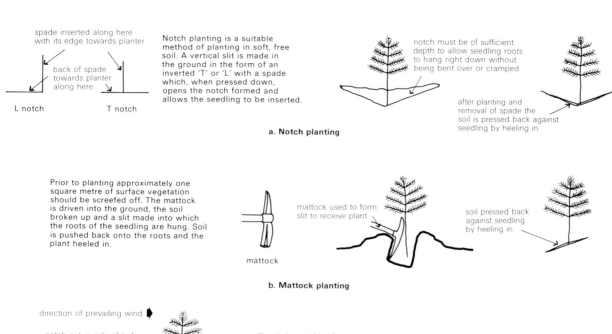

spade inserted along here with its edge towards planter

back of spade towards planter along here

L notch   T notch

Notch planting is a suitable method of planting in soft, free soil. A vertical slit is made in the ground in the form of an inverted 'T' or 'L' with a spade which, when pressed down, opens the notch formed and allows the seedling to be inserted.

notch must be of sufficient depth to allow seedling roots to hang right down without being bent over or cramped

after planting and removal of spade the soil is pressed back against seedling by heeling in

a. Notch planting

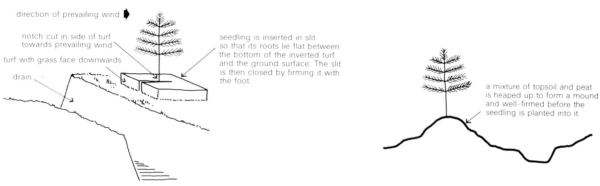

Prior to planting approximately one square metre of surface vegetation should be screefed off. The mattock is driven into the ground, the soil broken up and a slit made into which the roots of the seedling are hung. Soil is pushed back onto the roots and the plant heeled in.

mattock

mattock used to form slit to receive plant

soil pressed back against seedling by heeling in

b. Mattock planting

direction of prevailing wind

notch cut in side of turf towards prevailing wind

turf with grass face downwards

drain

seedling is inserted in slit so that its roots lie flat between the bottom of the inverted turf and the ground surface. The slit is then closed by firming it with the foot.

c. Turf planting

a mixture of topsoil and peat is heaped up to form a mound and well-firmed before the seedling is planted into it.

d. Mound planting

Fig. 55 Methods of planting tree seedlings

for the plants. Alternatively, deeper turfs (approximately 230 mm deep) may be cut and the seedlings planted in them. The method of planting involves cutting a notch in the side of the turf towards the direction of the prevailing wind; the tree is inserted so that its roots lie between the bottom of the inverted turf and the ground.

Replacing trees in existing woodland

Poor specimens and dead trees should first of all be removed and preferably the tree stumps and roots taken out, although this latter task is not always necessary. The essential preliminary operation is to remove scrub and undergrowth to provide space and sufficient light for the new trees. Attention to drainage is necessary where this has become choked or damaged. Minimal preparation is needed and fertilisers are seldom required since there is ample leaf litter and humus within the soil already.

Street planting

The (usually) limited space and close proximity of public utility services place a restriction on the maintenance operations normally adopted for tree planting. Adequate preparation is essential, therefore, to ensure the satisfactory establishment of a newly planted tree in these circumstances. A hole not less than 2 m diameter by 0.75 m deep should be dug and prepared in accordance with the recommendations set out in BS 4428:1969, Section 7. If the excavated material is of poor quality at least two-thirds of it should be replaced with soil complying with BS 3882:1965.

No hard surfacing should be laid within a radius of 1 m of the tree, otherwise surface water and air may be prevented from penetrating to its root system, resulting in poor growth or death. A developing tree needs room to expand; paving sited too close is liable to disruption and failure, caused by roots growing near to its surface.

Wasteland

Industrial wasteland is perhaps the most difficult type of site on which to give advice since much depends upon the ground composition and origin. More research is still needed in this field but, generally, any plants that are able to establish and colonise themselves (even if only weeds) should be retained since any sort of vegetation cover is valuable; screefing or ploughing should not be carried out.

It has been found that tree seedlings are more tolerant of a variety of soil conditions than older trees, provided the pH value of the material when mixed with a quantity of topsoil is within a tolerable range. Since topsoil is generally in short supply in such situations this is of considerable advantage. The material should be analysed so that any deficiencies can be counter-balanced by the application of the correct amount of chemical. On water-logged sites it may be desirable to form a mound of topsoil at each tree station to facilitate drainage.

Tree spacing

The spacing of trees (except for commercial woodlands) should be governed by the spread of their overhead canopies. When two or more trees are placed in close proximity to one another the general rule is that the distance between two trees should be equivalent to the sum of half the diameter of the spread of each tree.

In the planting of commercial woodlands this rule does not apply, since the trees are spaced for the purpose of producing timber rather than for their amenity value (although this latter point should always be borne in mind when selecting a mixture of species). Spacing varies according to the planting technique adopted and the species used. This also applies to the spacing of trees within shelter-belts. Since thinning is one of the forestry maintenance operations, close spacing of 1·50×1·50 m may readily be adopted.

TREE SURGERY AND PROTECTION

The care and management of trees

The early stages of a tree's life after planting in its permanent station are the most important if a healthy vigorous tree is to become established. Careful maintenance is essential, particularly in the case of transplanted semi-mature trees. Watering should be regularly carried out but any waterlogging, which could ultimately result in the death of the tree, must be avoided. Mulching and weeding the area around the tree are also important maintenance operations.

In the establishment of plantations, maintenance includes the following operations:

Beating up

This is carried out during the first year after planting and involves replacing any trees that have died, where this constitutes more than 10 per cent of the total or where deaths have occurred in groups or patches.

Weeding

This operation is carried out for the first two years after planting and may, in some cases, be necessary for a further year—usually where light-demanding trees are planted (e.g. pines).

Cleaning

When the side branches become interlaced with those of adjoining trees, referred to as the 'thicket stage' (from eight to ten years after planting), it is necessary for all the surplus and undesirable growth to be cut back. The latter often includes species, other than those originally planted, that have established themselves and those trees of the planted crop that have grown more quickly than the others, developing an overlarge crown, poor shape and being generally coarse ('wolf trees').

Brashing

Cleaning and brashing operations are carried out simultaneously. The latter consists of removing the side branches of the young trees up to a height of 1·82 m (head height).

Thinning

A very necessary maintenance operation intended to reduce the number of trees growing on the site in order to provide more growing space and less root competition for the remainder. It also has a financial benefit, giving an intermediate monetary return between planting and the maturity of the final crop.

Thinning takes place when the trees have reached a height of about 9 m, or earlier where the trees are spaced at 1·50 m or less.

Pruning

This is a continuing operation from that of brashing and consists of removing side branches to prevent the formation of knots in the timber. The maximum height to which this is carried out is usually 9 m. The earlier pruning takes place, the smaller the resulting knot in the mature tree. Reference should be made to Section 54 of BS 3975 : Part 5 : 1969 for the definitions of forestry terms.

The practice of tree surgery and other work

Trees are valuable (priceless in some instances !); it is important that they are well looked after and any damaged or decaying limbs either correctly treated or skilfully removed so that the appearance of the tree is in no way spoiled. There are many examples which provide us with stark evidence of the lack of understanding and practice of correct tree surgery in this country. The results of such ignorance show only too clearly that this most important operation is frequently left in the hands of fools and Philistines.

Trees are liable to be attacked by disease and decay, especially when they grow old. They may also suffer damage by wind, flood, animals or insects—to say nothing of damage by vandalism ! The retention of trees in a building development may necessitate the pruning of certain limbs or roots to prevent damage either to the tree or to the building and its services. Tree surgery helps to keep trees healthy and provides proper treatment to enable them to fit into a new environment (where they are retained in a layout). The life of a tree may be extended by proper care and treatment being given at the right time, especially where there is attack by disease.

The operations involved in tree surgery vary according to the needs of each individual tree; those most frequently undertaken may be summarised under the following headings :

> Pruning and removal of limbs
> Bracing of limbs
> Treatment of hollows
> Feeding

They should generally conform to the requirements set out in BS 3998 : 1966 (shortly to be revised).

Only skilled men should be employed and it is essential that all of them are covered by third party and public liability insurances since much of this work involves tree-climbing and operating above ground level.

Safety is an extremely important factor in all tree work ; on no account must an operative be left to work completely on his own, even at ground level, because of the risk of accident. No tie, scarf or casual shoes should be worn or loose-fitting clothing permitted. A safety rope or harness is always used by experienced operatives. Knots are important; three types are in general use : bowline, timber hitch and prussic knot.

The charge for tree surgery operations may be by one of the following methods :

(i) *Lump sum price.* This method requires the preparation of a clearly defined specification which should include a provisional sum to cover any work necessary to deal with hidden defects that may arise during the course of operations.

(ii) *Bill of quantities.* Although this method provides the designer with a schedule of rates for carrying out the work, the pricing of such items in the Bill must rely on average sizes of trees and average conditions prevailing. It is necessary, therefore, to include a fairly substantial contingency sum to cater for any abnormal and unforeseeable items likely to be encountered during the course of operations.

(iii) *Daywork rates.* Rates for various operations are agreed prior to carrying out the work ; many reputable firms undertake tree surgery on this basis.

Expert advice should be sought from an arborist * prior to the carrying out of any development so that the trees can be inspected and proper precautions taken to ensure their continued healthy existence.

Pruning and removal of limbs

This is the most common operation undertaken by tree surgeons and may involve anything from simple pruning and thinning of minor branches to the removal of a large limb. The important point to remember in this type of work is that wherever possible the limb which is being removed should be cut back to the main trunk or, in the case of a branch, to the main one. If it is cut so that a short stub remains this usually dies and rots back into the tree, especially where situated in a shady position. The cutting back of the limb (or branch) to provide a clean finish not only gives a better appearance to the tree but also gives the wound a much better chance of healing and thus prevents the risk of any disease arising.

*Aboricultural Association, 59, Blythewood Gardens, Stansted, Essex.

The removal of a big limb of a tree should only be resorted to when absolutely necessary, as after damage by storm, and undertaken at a time when the sap is low, the safest time generally being in November. If branches are removed in the spring it can cause much debility especially in the more sappy woods such as horse chestnut, lime, birch, walnut and many of the maples and conifers. Large branches should always be removed in at least two pieces (the actual number being decided on the site and depending upon the size and situation of the branch); the last piece to be sawn off should be light in weight and preferably not more than 300–460 mm long. This method of working not only makes the removal easier but also helps to eliminate the risk of damage to the tree which may easily result if a heavy branch is sawn close to the trunk in one cut, since the branch is liable to break away when the saw is half-way through the cut, thus tearing part of the bark away.

Bark is the protective layer of a tree and when severed or damaged becomes an exposed wound liable to attack by fungi and disease. For this reason, and because the growth (callus) that forms naturally over any wound in the tree takes years to develop, it is essential that such wounds are given immediate protection by the application of either Stockholm tar * or one of the commercial preparations on the market, such as 'Arbrex 805' (a bitumen emulsion, with a fungicide added to give protection against organisms and disease, supplied ready for use and applied by brush). When dried out it forms a protective seal or artificial callus. All cuts greater than 25 mm diameter should be given this protective treatment.

Bracing of limbs

Trees whose trunks have divided when young often constitute a danger when they reach maturity; during high winds the various parts of the tree do not always sway in unison and eventually cracks appear where the trunks fork. Dampness and fungoidal spores can then penetrate the sound wood and set up disease. To prevent damage, the two trunks or limbs should be braced together with a steel wire rope. Modern cabling is generally unnoticeable.

As an alternative to the use of artificial supports for heavy branches their weight may be reduced by pruning, but it is recommended that this method is resorted to only where the tree contours would remain unspoilt.

*A special type of tar obtained from pine trees which, unlike ordinary tar, has no harmful effect on plant tissues and seals over the wound completely.

Treatment of hollows

Where hollows already exist, all rotting wood must be removed and the whole area of the cavity cleaned and scraped with a suitable tool to remove any decayed matter, especially the soft, brown, crumbling wood and spongy mass found at the bottom. The surface of the wood should then be thoroughly cleaned with an antiseptic such as 'Presotim' to destroy the fungi and arrest, as far as possible, the decaying process.

In some cases hollows may be in the form of water-holding pockets and these must be thoroughly drained.

After cleaning and draining, the hollows and pockets must be allowed to dry out. These may be filled, but current practice favours leaving them open, particularly the larger ones, so that they may be readily inspected and kept clean to allow air to circulate. For medium and smaller hollows a non-rigid filling is generally used, such as 'Arbrex 805' mixed with hardwood chippings and sawdust, applied inside the cavity in layers and then weathered off to enable callus growth to cover it.

Tree feeding

Where trees have been neglected or subjected to ill use over a period of time the application of fertiliser is often specified. This should consist of the following (by weight):

    5 parts sulphate of ammonia
    5 parts superphosphate
    1½ parts sulphate of potash

The amount of fertiliser required for each tree is based on the following formula:

$$W = g \times f$$

where W = total amount of fertiliser required
  g = girth of tree in metres measured at breast height
  f = 18 kg of fertiliser

Holes 230 mm deep are made (using a crowbar) at 600 mm centres in a ring around the tree coinciding with the outermost spread of the branches. Two further rings of holes are made at 600 mm intervals beyond this first outer ring and three rings are likewise made at the same intervals within the perimeter of this first ring, making a total of six rings of holes in all.

The fertiliser is then divided and allocated equally between the prepared holes, and poured into each individual hole, which is then filled up with soil to the level of the adjacent ground.

Protection of newly planted trees

Trees are subject to the ravages of wind as well as abuse and damage by humans and animals and in their early stages of growth need some kind of protection if they are to survive such perils. Protection may be in the form of galvanised or plastic coated wire mesh 1520 mm high by 760 mm wide, rolled to a diameter of 230–300 mm around the stem and secured to the tree stake by means of galvanised wire staples. Where several trees are closely planted to form a group it may be simpler and more economical to erect a protective fence for the group.

In rural areas such protection must also include rabbit-proof fencing. Where there are grazing animals in the vicinity of young trees the protective guard must be substantial and sited in a position to prevent the animals from stripping leaves or bark. A simple and relatively cheap guard may be constructed using three stout posts to form a triangle with stout horizontal rails. Metal guards are manufactured from vertical mild steel flats fabricated to diameters ranging from 300 to 760 mm and in heights of 1·52, 1·67, and 1·82 mm. The tops of the slats are curved outwards and the bottom of each alternate one is in the form of a cranked foot for fixing into the ground. A similar type of guard for use with more mature trees is available: 1–1·37 m high and of 1·22 m diameter (and upwards). Both types are pre-fabricated in two or more sections to facilitate easy erection, and secured by bolts.

Table 34
Trees native to Britain

Botanical name	Family	Common name	Habitat	Height (m)
Acer campestre	Aceraceae	Field maple	Hedgerows	3–12
Alnus glutinosa	Betulaceae	Alder	Streams and damp woods	12–15
Arbutus unedo	Ericaceae	Strawberry tree	S. W. Ireland	4·5–7·6
Betula nana	Betulaceae	Dwarf birch	Scottish highlands	3–6
Betula pendula	Betulaceae	Silver birch	Hillsides	12–23
Carpinus betulus	Carpinaceae	Hornbeam	Wales, C. and S. England	15–23
Corylus avellana	Corylaceae	Hazel	Hedges, copses and woods	3–6
Crataegus monogyna	Rosaceae	Hawthorn	Hedgerows	6–12
Crataegus oxycantha	Rosaceae	Hawthorn	Hedgerows	6–12
Euonymus europaeus	Celastraceae	Spindle	Hedgerows	3–7·6
Fagus sylvatica	Fagaceae	Beech	Calcareous soils	18–30
Fraxinus excelsior	Oleaceae	Ash	Fields and woodlands	21–27
Ilex aquifolium	Aquifoliaceae	Holly	Hedgerows	3–15
Malus sylvestris	Rosaceae	Crab-apple	N. England and Scotland	4·5–9
Mespilus germanica	Rosaceae	Medlar	S. England	3–4·5
Populus alba	Salicaceae	White poplar	Streams and damp woods	18–28
Populus canescens	Salicaceae	Grey poplar	S. England	24–30
Populus tremula	Salicaceae	Aspen	Moist situations	12–15
Prunus avium	Rosaceae	Gean	Copses and woodland	15–21
Prunus cerasus	Rosaceae	Sour cherry	Copses and hedgerows	3–6
Prunus padus	Rosaceae	Bird cherry	Copses and hedgerows	9–15
Pyrus communis	Rosaceae	Wild pear	Hedges and woods	6–18
Quercus petraea	Fagaceae	Sessile oak	Woods and fields	18–24
Quercus robur	Fagaceae	English oak	Woods and fields	18–27

continued

Table 34 *Continued*

Salix alba	*Salicaceae*	White willow	Wet meadows and streams	18–24
Salix cinerea oleifolia	*Salicaceae*	Common sallow	Woods, hedges and streams	6–9
Salix fragilis	*Salicaceae*	Crack willow	Streams and wet meadows	9–24
Sorbus aria	*Rosaceae*	Whitebeam	Chalky soils, England	6–12
Sorbus aucuparia	*Rosaceae*	Mountain ash	Hillsides	9–18
Sorbus torminalis	*Rosaceae*	Wild service tree	S. and C. England	12–15
Tilia cordata	*Tiliaceae*	Small-leaved lime	Woods	6–30
Tilia platyphyllos	*Tiliaceae*	Broad-leaved lime	Woods	30–37
Ulmus glabra	*Ulmaceae*	Wych elm	Fields and woods	24–30
Ulmus procera	*Ulmaceae*	English elm	Fields and woods	36–38
Viburnum lantana	*Caprifoliaceae*	Wayfaring tree	Hedgerows	2·5–6
Juniperus communis	*Cupressaceae*	Juniper	Arid hills and downs	1·8–12
Juniperus c. nana	*Cupressaceae*	Dwarf juniper	N. England and Scotland	0·30
Pinus sylvestris	*Pinaceae*	Scots pine	Peaty soils	18–30
Taxus baccata	*Taxaceae*	Yew	Hilly areas	4·5–15

Table 35
Trees for timber production

Broadleaved

Acer pseudoplatanus (sycamore)
24–28 m. Strong shade-bearer when young but light-demander later. It is best planted on fairly good soils and is suitable for planting in coastal or town locations, but should not be planted in poor moorland areas (except as a shelter belt).

Alnus glutinosa (common alder)
12–15 m. Light-demanding but will grow on very infertile wet soils and can be used as nurse or pioneer species with other more valuable species such as *Picea sitchensis* (Sitka spruce).

Betula pendula (silver birch)
12–23 m. Light-demanding but very hardy. Volume of timber produced is small though of good quality. Tolerant of wide variety of soils.

Castanea sativa (Spanish chestnut)
18–30 m. Strong light-demander after twentieth year but will stand moderate shade when young. Best planted for coppice on well-drained loams and sandy loams; unsuitable for lime-rich soils.

Fagus sylvatica (beech)
18–30 m. Strong shade-bearer suitable for underplanting where there is sufficient soil moisture but is difficult to establish where there is no overhead shade. *Pinus sylvestris* (Scots pine) or *Pinus nigra maritima* (Corsican pine) are ideal nurse species, growing faster than beech which grows very quickly when young. Ideal on fertile loams overlying calcareous formations; unsuitable for heavy waterlogged soils.

Fraxinus americana (N. American white ash)
21–27 m. One of the fastest growing of the American hardwoods.

Fraxinus excelsior (common ash)
21–27 m. Light-demander except when very young. To provide good quality timber it must be planted on lime-rich soils where there is plenty of free-moving soil moisture.

Populus alba (abele or white poplar)
18–28 m. Valuable for exposed coastal locations.

P. berolinensis (Berlin poplar)
18–22+ m.

P. Eugenei (hybrid poplar)
24–45 m. Probably the best poplar to grow commercially in Britain.

P. Gelrica (hybrid poplar of Continental origin)
21–27 m. One of the best poplars for commercial production.

P. Pacheri (hybrid poplar)
21–27 m.

P. Robusta (hybrid poplar)
27–30 m.

P. Serotina (black Italian poplar)
24–30 m. Hardy fast-growing trees which prefer a loamy soil in a sheltered situation but may be planted on clays (slower growth rate). They do not like acid peats or old woodland sites where there is dense regrowth and must be kept free from weeds to prevent any competition for the available soil moisture.

continued

Table 35 *Continued*

Quercus petraea (durmast or sessile oak)	18–24 m. Grows at higher elevations than *Q. robur* (common or pedunculate oak), the other native species, and is more shade-tolerant, but needs to be kept weed-free for the first few years of growth. Best timber produced on deep, porous, well-drained soils.
Q. rubra (red oak)	24–28 m. Much less exacting than other oaks although producing timber of inferior quality. It will tolerate poor acid soils but dislikes calcareous soils. Useful as a short rotation pioneer species.
Salix Caerulea (cricket-bat willow)	Up to 30 m. Excellent for growing in places too damp for other trees, is of considerable commercial value and used in the manufacture of cricket bats.
S. triandra (almond-leaved willow)	Up to 9 m. Used in the manufacture of many forms of basketry.

Coniferous

Abies alba (common silver fir)	12–45 m. Best timber produced on deep, well-drained moist loamy soils in locations not subject to intensive frost.
A. grandis (giant or grand silver fir)	30–60+ m. Light shade-bearer but not used much for underplanting. Prefers deep well-drained moist loamy soils and areas not subject to heavy snowfall. It is fairly frost-tender and must not be planted in frost hollows or poor acid soils.
A. procera (noble fir)	30–45 m. Prefers well-drained loamy soils and will tolerate more acid conditions than other silver firs. It is not suitable for calcareous soils and dislikes very poor soils and exposed situations.
Cupressus macrocarpa (Monterey cypress)	15–30 m. Very light shade-bearer but difficult to establish (young plants subject to damage in cold areas) and does better in warm moist locations, particularly on the coast.
Larix decidua (common or European larch)	24–42 m. Fairly hardy and strong light-demander. Prefers moist well-drained loams on open site not too exposed. Dislikes poorly-drained or very dry soils and does not tolerate smoky atmospheres or coastal exposure. Suitable for planting with oak or pine.
L. eurolepis (Dunkeld larch)	18–30 m. Light-demanding and fast-growing. Tolerates poorer soils than *L. decidua* and is moderately frost-resistant and fairly wind-resistant.
L. kaempferi (Japanese larch)	23–30 m. Strong light-demander but fairly resistant to snow damage. May be planted on a wide variety of soils. Tolerant of industrial atmospheres but dislikes dry locations. Quality of timber produced does not warrant planting on fertile soils.
Picea abies (common or Norway spruce)	15–30 m. Moderately shade-bearing and fairly frost-hardy, but in real frost hollows *Pinus sylvestris* (Scots pine) should be planted as a nurse. It is more suitable for planting in low-lying areas than *P. sitchensis* (Sitka spruce). It prefers moist soils and will thrive on shallow peat. On clay or dry soils it is liable to suffer disease and it should not be planted on heather sites or areas of atmospheric pollution. It is not windfirm.
P. omorika (Serbian spruce)	18–24 m. Thrives in similar conditions to those of *P. abies* but is even more tolerant of exposed situations, although its rate of growth is somewhat slower.
P. sitchensis (Sitka spruce)	30+ m. May be planted on a wide variety of soils and at high elevations. Although not very windfirm it withstands exposure well and is tolerant of atmospheric pollution. It is better than *P. abies* on poorer types of moorland. Turf or shallow planting is best.
Pinus contorta latifolia (lodgepole pine)	21–24+ m. Wind-resistant and frost-hardy but does not tolerate shade or smoke-polluted atmospheres. Will thrive on sandy or peaty soils and may be used as a nurse on poor soils.
P. nigra maritima (Corsican pine)	30–45 m. Light-demanding, frost-hardy and resistant to coastal gales. It will thrive practically anywhere, except high elevations, but prefers light sandy soils near sea level in areas of low rainfall. Tolerates smoky atmospheres and is better than *P. sylvestris* on chalky soils.
P. sylvestris (Scots pine)	18–30 m. Slow-growing light-demander which grows on a variety of sites but prefers light sandy soils in areas of low rainfall. Used as a nurse for beech on limestone formations. Does not tolerate smoky atmospheres and is subject to damage by insects.
Pseudotsuga menziesii (Oregon Douglas fir)	30–60 m. Rapid growth produces a timber which is not of very high quality, particularly on fertile soils. Prefers well-aerated sandy soils and will thrive on rocky areas and at the bottom of slopes where there is ample fresh moisture. Reasonably shade-tolerant but will not stand polluted atmospheres.
Thuja plicata (western red cedar)	27–45+ m. Shade-tolerant and may be used for underplanting. Does well on good loamy soils and clays but dislikes poor soils and areas subject to frost. Very windfirm.

Table 36
Trees for forming screens and windbreaks

Broadleaved

Acer platanoides (Norway maple)	15–24 m
A. pseudoplatanus (sycamore)	24–28 m
Ailanthus altissima (tree of heaven)	15–21 m
Arbutus unedo (Killarney strawberry tree)	4·5–7·6 m
Betula pendula (common silver birch)	12–23 m
Carpinus betulus (hornbeam)	15–23 m
Populus alba (white poplar)	18–28 m
P. nigra Italica (Lombardy poplar)	18–30 m
P. Serotina (black Italian poplar)	24–30 m
Prunus Pissardii (purple-leaf plum)	6–7·6 m
Quercus ilex (evergreen oak)	18–27 m
Sorbus aria (whitebeam)	6–12 m
Tilia platyphyllos (broad-leaved lime)	24–30 m
*Ulmus angustifolia cornubiensis (Cornish elm)	24–30 m
*U. glabra (wych elm or Scotch elm)	24–30 m

Coniferous

Chamaecyparis lawsoniana (Lawson's cypress)	15–30 m
†Larix decidua (common larch)	24–42 m
Pinus nigra (Austrian pine)	24–30 m
P. n. maritima (Corsican pine)	30–45 m
Bad transplanter.	
P. pinaster (maritime pine)	27–30 m
P. radiata (Monterey pine)	18–21 m
P. sylvestris (Scots pine)	18–30 m
P. thunbergii (black pine)	24–30 m
Taxus baccata (English yew or common yew)	9–18 m
Thuja occidentalis (American arbor-vitae)	9–12 m
T. plicata (western red cedar)	27–45+ m

*Prone to elm disease
†Deciduous conifer

Table 37
Trees with dense foliage for forming a noise baffle

Broadleaved

Acer platanoides (Norway maple)	15–24 m
A. pseudoplatanus (sycamore)	24–28 m
Aesculus hippocastanum (horse chestnut)	21–30 m
Catalpa bignonioides (Indian bean tree)	9–15 m
Carpinus betulus (hornbeam)	15–23 m
Juglans nigra (black walnut)	18–30 m
Quercus ilex (evergreen oak)	18–27 m
Q. robur (common oak)	18–27 m

Coniferous

Taxus baccata (English yew or common yew)	9–18 m

Also most evergreen conifers

Table 38
Wind-resistant trees for exposed situations

Broadleaved

Acer pseudoplantanus (sycamore)	24–28 m
Alnus glutinosa (common alder)	12–15 m
Crataegus oxycantha (thorn)	4·5–9 m
Populus alba (white poplar)	18–28 m
P. canescens (grey poplar)	24–30 m
One of the best on chalky soils.	
P. Serotina (black Italian poplar)	24–30 m
Prunus spinosa (blackthorn)	3–6 m
Quercus ilex (evergreen oak)	18–27 m
Q. robur (common oak)	18–27 m
*Ulmus glabra (wych elm or Scotch elm)	24–30+ m

Coniferous

Araucaria araucana (Chile pine or monkey puzzle)	30–45 m
Cupressus macrocarpa (Monterey cypress)	15–30 m
†Larix kaempferi (Japanese larch)	23–30 m
Picea abies (common spruce or Norway spruce)	15–30 m
P. sitchensis (Sitka spruce)	30+ m
Rapid-growing.	
Pinus mugo (mountain pine)	3–20 m
P. muricata (bishop pine)	15–27 m
Not suitable for chalky soils.	
P. nigra (Austrian pine)	24–30 m
P. n. maritima (Corsican pine)	30–45 m
Bad transplanter.	

*Prone to elm disease
†Deciduous conifer

Table 39
Trees for planting in seaside locations

Broadleaved

Acer pseudoplatanus (sycamore)	24–28 m
Arbutus unedo (Killarney strawberry tree)	4·5–7·6 m
Crataegus oxycantha (thorn)	4·5–9 m
Fraxinus excelsior (common ash)	21–27 m
Laburnum alpinum (Scotch laburnum)	6–19 m
L. anagyroides (common laburnum)	4·5–9 m
Populus alba (white poplar)	18–28 m
P. nigra Italica (Lombardy poplar)	18–30 m
P. Serotina (black Italian poplar)	24–30 m
Prunus spinosa (blackthorn or sloe)	3–6 m
Quercus cerris (Turkey oak)	15–30 m
Q. ilex (evergreen oak)	18–27 m
Salix alba (white willow or Huntingdon willow)	18–24 m
Sorbus aria (whitebeam)	6–12 m
S. aucuparia (rowan or mountain ash)	9–18 m
*Ulmus glabra (wych elm or Scotch elm)	24–30+ m

*Prone to elm disease

Table 39 *Continued*

Coniferous

Cupressus macrocarpa (Monterey cypress)	15–30 m
†*Larix kaempferi* (Japanese larch)	23–30 m
Pinus mugo (mountain pine)	3–20 m
P. nigra maritima (Corsican pine)	30–45 m
P. pinaster (maritime pine)	27–30 m
P. radiata (Monterey pine)	18–21 m
P. sylvestris (Scots pine)	18–30 m

†Deciduous conifer

Table 40
Trees tolerant of atmospheric pollution

Broadleaved

Acer (maples)	6–30+ m
but not *Acer palmatum* (Japanese maple) and cultivars.	
Aesculus carnea (pink horse chestnut)	7–15 m
Aesculus hippocastanum Baumannii	21–27 m
(double flowered white horse chestnut : no conkers)	
Ailanthus altissima (tree of heaven)	15–21 m
Betula pendula (silver birch)	9–23 m
Carpinus betulus (hornbeam)	15–23 m
Catalpa bignonioides (Indian bean tree)	9–15 m
Crataegus (thorn)	4·5–9 m
Fraxinus (ash)	7–30 m
Roots extend for a great distance.	
Juglans regia (walnut)	9–30 m
Laburnum wateri Vosii	4·5–7·6 m
Malus (flowering crab)	2·5–12 m
Platanus (plane)	18–30 m
Populus (poplar)	6–45 m
Prunus (Japanese cherry)	3–16 m
Prunus avium (gean or wild cherry)	15–21 m
Prunus cerasifera (myrobalan or cherry plum)	6–7·6 m
Pyrus (pear)	4·5–10 m
Sorbus aria (whitebeam)	6–12 m
Sorbus aucuparia (mountain ash)	9–18 m
Tilia (lime)	15–36 m

Coniferous

Abies veitchii (Japanese silver fir)	15–21 m
*Ginkgo biloba (maidenhair tree)	15–24 m
Picea omorika (Serbian spruce)	18–24 m
Pinus nigra (Austrian pine)	24–30 m
Taxus (yew)	3·6–18 m

*Deciduous conifer

Table 41
Fast-growing trees

Broadleaved

Acer negundo (box elder)	12–18 m
A. platanoides (Norway maple)	15–24 m
A. pseudoplatanus (sycamore)	24–28 m
A. saccharinum (silver maple)	27–30 m
Ailanthus altissima (tree of heaven)	15–21 m
Alnus glutinosa (common alder)	12–15 m
Carpinus betulus (hornbeam)	15–23 m
Fairly fast.	
Fraxinus (ash)	7–30 m
Roots extend for some distance.	
Liriodendron (tulip tree)	21–45 m
Populus (poplar)	6–45 m
Pterocarya (wing nut)	18–30 m
Pyrus betulaefolia (Chinese pear)	6–9 m
Quercus palustris (pin oak)	15–24 m
Salix (willow)	6–30 m
*Ulmus (elm)	12–36 m

Coniferous

Abies grandis (giant fir)	30–60+ m
Cupressocyparis leylandii (Leyland cypress)	9–12+ m
Ideal for quickly forming a screen.	
Cupressus macrocarpa (Monterey cypress)	15–30 m
Pinus strobus (white pine or Weymouth pine)	24–30 m
Metasequoia glyptostroboides (dawn redwood)	21–33 m

*Prone to elm disease

Table 42
Trees with grey or silvery coloured foliage

Broadleaved

Acer saccharinum (silver maple)	27–30 m. Leaves silvery-white beneath.
Alnus incana (grey alder)	18–21 m. Grey down on undersurface of leaves.
Malus tchonoskii (crab)	9–12 m. Leaves on young shoots covered with fine silvery-white 'felt'.
Populus alba (white poplar)	18–28 m. White woolly undersurface of leaves.
P. canescens (grey poplar)	24–30 m. Undersurface covered with grey 'felt'. One of the best poplars for planting on chalky soils.
P. tremula (aspen)	12–15 m. Wavy-edged greyish leaves perpetually quiver.
Pyrus nivalis (pear)	6–9 m.Conspicuous early in season when pure white flowers in abundance are produced simultaneously with white-woolly young leaves.
P. salicifolia Pendula (weeping willow-leaved pear)	4·5–7·6 m. Willow-like leaves covered with silky white down.
Salix alba Sericea (silver willow)	12–15 m. Very striking silvery-white leaves.
Sorbus aria Decaisneana (whitebeam)	9–14 m. Silvery-grey effect in spring, leaves white underneath.
S. a. Lutescens (whitebeam)	9–14 m. Upper surface of leaves covered with creamy-white hairs, giving them a silvery appearance. Excellent street tree.
S. folgneri (whitebeam)	6–9 m. Leaves vivid silvery-white underneath ; assume rich colours in autumn.
S. intermedia (Swedish whitebeam)	6–12 m. Undersurface covered with close grey 'felt'. Excellent tree for street planting and industrial areas.
Tilia tomentosa (silver lime)	18–30 m. Leaves have silvery-white 'felted' undersurface.

Coniferous

Abies delavayi forrestii (Chinese silver fir)	9–18 m. Milky-white underside of leaves contrasts well with dark upper surface.
A. procera (noble fir)	30–45 m. Silvery-blue leaves. Unsuitable for planting on calcareous soils.
A. veitchii (Japanese silver fir)	15–21 m. Leaves silvery-white underneath. Thrives better than most other species in vicinity of large towns.
Cedrus atlantica Glauca (blue cedar)	24–30 m. Silvery-blue leaves.
Chamaecyparis lawsoniana Elegantissima (Lawson's cypress)	6–9 m. Silvery-grey leaves.
C. l. Fraseri (Lawson's cypress)	Up to 4·5 m. Grey-green leaves.
C. l. 'Silver Queen' (Lawson's cypress)	6–12 m. Young foliage silvery-white in early summer.
Juniperus virginiana Glauca (pencil cedar)	12–15 m. Leaves silvery-grey during spring and early summer, changing to green.
Picea pungens Glauca (blue spruce)	15–23+ m. Leaves covered with a bluish-white bloom.
Pinus wallichiana (Bhutan pine or Bhotan pine)	21–30+ m. Greyish-green leaves.

Table 43
Trees with golden or yellow coloured foliage

Broadleaved

Acer cappadocicum Aureum (maple)	12–21 m. Broad glossy leaves red when young, turning golden-yellow.
A. negundo Auratum (box elder)	12–18 m. Leaves bright golden-yellow.
A. pseudoplatanus Worlei (golden sycamore)	12–15 m. Soft yellow foliage April–July.
A. saccharinum Lutescens (silver maple)	18–21 m. Young leaves soft yellowish-green in summer.
Alnus incana Aurea (grey alder)	15–18 m. Young shoots and foliage yellow.
Catalpa bignonioides Aurea (golden Indian bean tree)	3–6 m. Velvety-yellow leaves which retain their colour throughout the season.
Fagus sylvatica Zlatia (golden beech)	6–12 m. Leaves soft yellow, turning green in late summer. Slow-growing.
Laburnum anagyroides Aureum (golden-leaved laburnum)	4·5–7·6 m. One of the prettiest golden-leaved trees. Sometimes apt to revert.
Liquidambar styraciflua Aurea (yellow-leaved sweet gum)	15–23 m. Yellow leaves throughout the season.
Populus Serotina Aurea (golden poplar)	18–24 m. Leaves clear golden-yellow in spring and early summer.
Robinia pseudoacacia Frisia (false acacia)	9–15 m. Leaves remain rich golden-yellow throughout season.
Sorbus aria Chrysophylla (whitebeam)	9–14 m. Upper surface of leaves yellow.

Table 43 *Continued*

Coniferous

Chamaecyparis lawsoniana Hillieri	10–18 m. Light feathery habit, bright golden foliage.
C. l. Lane	Up to 12 m. Dense golden foliage, more compact that *C. l. Stewartii*.
C. l. Lutea (Lawson's cypress)	Up to 12 m. Feathery sprays of golden-yellow foliage.
C. l. Stewartii	Up to 12 m. Similar to *C. l. Lutea* but looser and broader in habit. Tendency to lose colouring with age.
C. l. Westermanii	10–18 m. Foliage old gold : spreading, somewhat pendant branches.
C. nootkatensis Lutea (Nootka cypress)	16–18 m. Foliage suffused soft yellow-green.
Cupressus macrocarpa 'Donard Gold'	18–20 m. Foliage rich deep golden-yellow.
C. m. Lutea	18–20 m. Foliage soft yellow, less dense than *C. m. 'Donard Gold'*.
Juniperus communis Depressa Aurea	1·8–6 m. Young shoots and leaves golden ; bronze-tinted in winter.
Picea orientalis Aurea	Up to 6 m. Young shoots creamy-yellow.
Thuja occidentalis Aureospicata	3·5–5 m. Young shoots tipped golden-yellow. Erect-growing variety.

Table 44
Broadleaved trees with purple foliage

Acer cappadocicum Rubrum (maple)	15–18 m. Expanding young leaves are red, becoming green and later turning golden. Colours well on chalk soils.
A. palmatum Atropurpureum (Japanese maple)	4–6 m. Leaves bronzy-crimson throughout summer.
A. platanoides 'Goldsworth Purple' (purple-leaved Norway maple)	18–21 m. Rich dark crimson-purple leaves throughout summer. Bright red keys. This is the deepest shade of crimson-purple of all large-leaved big trees and is ideal when associated with *A. p. Drummondii*.
A. p. Reitenbachii (maple)	18–21 m. Leaves red at first, becoming bronze/green then turning dark red in autumn.
A. p. Schwedleri (purple Norway maple)	15–20 m. Leaves and young growth rich crimson-purple. More vigorous than *A. p. Reitenbachii* and most effective when pruned hard every other autumn.
A. pseudoplatanus Spaethii (sycamore)	15–18 m. Purple underside of leaves effectively displayed in breeze.
Betula pendula Purpurea (purple leaf birch)	13–18 m. Purple leaves provide a pleasing contrast among greens. Purple bark. Slow-growing tree of somewhat weak constitution.
Catalpa erubescens Purpurea (Indian bean tree)	7·6–10 m. Young leaves and shoots very dark purple, becoming green.
Fagus sylvatica Purpurea (purple beech)	23–30 m. Familiar rich bronzy-purple leaves are pale red when young.
Malus Aldenhamensis (flowering crab)	9–11 m. Reddish-purple foliage is accompanied in spring by large wine-red flowers.
M. Eleyi (flowering crab)	6–9 m. Attractive young copper-coloured downy leaves accompanied by masses of purple-red flowers in spring.
M. Lemoinei (flowering crab)	7·6–9 m. Bronze-tinted foliage and deep wine-red flowers. Vigorous spreading habit.
M. purpurea (flowering crab)	9–11 m. Young leaves bronze-coloured, accompanied in spring by a wealth of rosy-crimson flowers.
M. 'Profusion' (flowering crab)	7·6–9 m. Young leaves coppery-crimson, accompanied by wine-red fragrant flowers in spring. Habit similar to that of *M. Lemoinei*.
Prunus cerasifera Atropurpurea (purple-leaf plum)	6–7·6 m. Young leaves rich ruby-red, darkening to purple. Small single white flowers in early spring.
P. c. blireiana (flowering plum)	3–4·5 m. Coppery-purple foliage retains its colour throughout summer. Semi-double rosy-pink flowers in early spring.
P. c. Nigra (flowering plum)	3–4·5 m. Similar to *P. c. Atropurpurea* but foliage is a richer colour.
Quercus petraea Purpurea (durmast oak)	15–24 m. Leaves reddish-purple when young, changing to green-flushed red.

Table 45
Broadleaved trees with variegated foliage

Acer negundo Elegantissimum (box elder)	6–9 m. Bright yellow variegation.
A. n. Variegatum (box elder)	6–7·6 m. Leaves conspicuously margined white. Very attractive small tree.
A. platanoides Drummondii (Norway maple)	18–21 m. Leaves margined white. For contrast plant with *A. p. 'Goldsworth Purple'*.
A. pseudoplatanus Leopoldii (sycamore)	15–18 m. Leaves yellowish-pink, mottled white and cream.
Fagus sylvatica Tricolor (beech)	23–27 m. Purplish coloured leaves edged and striped with rose-pink and pinkish-white.
Fraxinus pennsylvanica Variegata (N. American red ash)	15–18 +m. Silvery-grey leaves margined and mottled creamy-white.
Liriodendron tulipifera Aureo-marginatum (tulip tree)	9–14 m. Leaves edged golden-yellow.
Quercus cerris Variegata (Turkey oak)	15–23+ m. Leaves bordered by a white band of varying width.

Table 46
Trees which display good autumn foliage colour

Broadleaved

Acer campestre (hedge maple)	3–12 m. Clear yellow. Round-headed tree.
A. carpinifolium (Japanese hornbeam maple)	Up to 7·6 m. Hornbeam-like leaves, old gold.
A. cissifolium (Japanese tree)	6–9 m. Red and yellow. Not suitable for chalk soils.
A. ginnala (a bushy maple)	4·5–6 m. Vivid crimson. One of the best for autumn colour.
A. griseum (paperbark maple)	4·5–12 m. Red and scarlet. Trunk and primary branches peel and reveal orange-coloured bark beneath.
A. grosseri *A. hersii* (snake-bark *A. henryi* maples) *A. pennsylvanicum*	6–9 m. Rich red and crimson.
A. macrophyllum (Oregon maple)	24–30 m. Bright orange. Not suitable for colder areas.
A. platanoides (Norway maple)	15–24 m. Clear yellow.
A. p. Reitenbachii (maple)	18–21 m. Dark red.
A. rubrum Schlesingeri (scarlet Canadian maple)	21–24 m. Red.
Carpinus caroliniana (American hornbeam or blue beech)	6–12 m. Orange-yellow and scarlet. Bushy type of tree.
Crataegus crus galli (cockspur thorn)	3–6 m. Shades of orange and scarlet.
C. lavallei (hawthorn)	6–8 m. Orange-red.
C. pedicellata (scarlet haw)	3–6 m. Shades of yellow to scarlet.
C. prunifolia (thorn)	3–5 m. Shades of orange and scarlet.
Fraxinus excelsior Jaspidea (golden bark ash)	21–27 m. Clear yellow.
F. oxycarpa 'Raywood' (ash)	15–23 m. Smoky-purple.
F. velutina coriacea (Arizona ash)	9–12 m. Purple.
Liquidambar styraciflua (sweet gum)	15–23 m. Crimson and gold. Not suitable for shallow chalky soils.
Liriodendron tulipifera (tulip tree)	21–45 m. Golden-yellow.
Malus tschonoskii (crab)	9–12 m. Yellow and scarlet.
Parrotia persica	9–12 m. Gold, orange and crimson. One of the finest for autumn colour.
Prunus hillieri 'Spire' (flowering cherry)	7·6–9 m. Red and orange.
P. 'Pandora' (flowering cherry)	7·6–9 m. Purplish-red.
P. sargentii (flowering cherry)	7·6–11 m. Brilliant vermillion and deep red.
P. serrulata pubescens (flowering cherry)	9–12 m. Coppery-purple.
Quercus coccinea Splendens (American scarlet oak)	21–24 m. Scarlet-crimson tints. A comparatively slow-growing tree.
Sorbus alnifolia submollis (Chinese whitebeam)	6–9 m. Yellow.
S. aucuparia (mountain ash) and varieties	9–18 m. Red and orange.
S. folgneri (whitebeam)	6–9 m. Red and orange.

Table 46 *Continued*

Coniferous

Ginkgo biloba (maidenhair tree)	15–21 m. Clear yellow.
Metasequoia glyptostroboides (dawn redwood)	21–33 m. Tawny-pink to red.
Taxodium distichum (deciduous cypress or swamp cypress)	15–30 m. Bronzy-yellow.

Table 47
Broadleaved trees with coloured bark and stems

Acer capillipes (maple)	6–11 m. Bark striped with white, jagged lines. Young growths coral red.
A. davidii (David's maple)	6–11 m. Bark striped with white, jagged lines.
A. griseum (paperbark maple)	4·5–12 m. Mahogany-brown peeling bark, orange beneath.
A. grosseri (Grosser's maple)	6–9 m. Striated bark and young shoots remain yellow through to second year, ultimately also becoming striped.
A. hersii (Hers's maple)	7·6–9 m. Bark and twigs olive-green striped white.
A. pennsylvanicum (moose wood or snake-bark maple)	7·6–9 m. White striated bark and stems.
Betula spp. (birch)	9–23 m. Most of these have whitish bark and stems.
Fraxinus excelsior Jaspidea (golden-bark ash)	21–27 m. Yellow of wood outstanding in winter.
Platanus hispanica (London plane)	18–30 m. Peeling bark reveals light ochre colour beneath.
Prunus serrula (flowering cherry)	9–15 m. Bright reddish-brown peeling bark.
Salix alba Chermesina (scarlet willow)	15–18 m. Orange-scarlet young shoots
S. a. Chrysostella (willow)	15–18 m. Golden-yellow shoots shading to orange-scarlet.
S. a. Tristis (golden weeping willow)	15–18 m. Younger branches bright yellow in winter.
S. a. Vitellina (golden willow)	18–19 m. Yolk-of-egg coloured shoots in winter.
S. daphnoides (violet willow)	Up to 12 m. Shoots purple-violet with white 'bloom'. Extremely effective in winter if pollarded occasionally.
S. purpurea (purple osier)	Purple shoots.
Tilia platyphyllos Rubra (red-twigged lime)	18–30 m. Bright brown-red shoots and red buds in winter.

Table 48
Broadleaved trees of weeping form

Acer saccharinum Pendulum (weeping silver maple)
Betula pendula Youngii (Young's weeping birch)
Caragana arborescens Pendula
Crataegus monogyna Pendula (weeping hawthorn)
Fagus sylvatica Pendula (weeping beech)
Fraxinus excelsior Pendula (weeping ash)
Gleditschia triancanthos Bujoti (honey locust)
Laburnum anagyroides Pendulum (weeping laburnum)
L. watereri 'Alford's Weeping'
Malus 'Echtermeyer' (flowering crab)
Populus tremula Pendula (weeping aspen)
Prunus invensii
P· 'Kiku-shidare Zakura' (Cheal's weeping cherry)
P. Moerheimii (weeping Fiji cherry)
P. subhirtella Pendula (weeping spring cherry)
Pyrus salicifolia Pendula (weeping willow-leaf pear)
Salix alba Tristis (golden weeping willow)   9–15 m
S. blanda (Wisconsin weeping willow)
S. purpurea Pendula (weeping purple willow)
S. sepulcralis (weeping willow)   12–18 m
Sophora japonica Pendula (weeping pagoda tree)
Sorbus aria Pendula (weeping whitebeam)
Tilia petiolaris (weeping silver lime)

Note. Unless a tree is naturally of pendulous habit its height depends to a large extent upon the training up of the leading shoots until the desired height is attained, otherwise the growth in height is extremely slow.

Table 49
Broadleaved trees of fastigiate or columnar habit

Acer platanoides Columnare (Norway maple)	16–18 m
A. p. Cucullatum (Norway maple)	16–18 m
A. pseudoplatanus Erectum (sycamore)	22–30 m
Betula pendula Fastigiata (birch)	12–18 m
Lombardy poplar habit.	
Carpinus belululus Columnare (hornbeam)	12–21 m
Spire-like when young.	
Crataegus monogyna Stricta (hawthorn or quick)	6–8 m
Excellent small tough tree for planting in confined areas.	
Fagus sylvatica Dawyck (Dawyck beech)	12–15 m
Malus prunifolia Fastigiata (flowering crab)	7–10 m
M. tschonoskii (flowering crab)	9–12 m
M. 'Van Eseltine' (flowering crab)	9–12 m
Populus alba Pyramidalis (white Bolleana poplar)	15–21 m
Erect branches, resembling in habit the Lombardy poplar.	
P. nigra Italica (Lombardy poplar)	18–30 m
Extensive root system.	
Prunus Amanogawa (Lombardy cherry)	4·5–7·6 m
P. hillieri 'Spire' (flowering cherry)	7·6–9 m
Quercus robur Fastigiata (fastigiate oak)	12–18 m
Robinia pseudoacacia Pyramidalis (false acacia)	15–18 m
Sorbus aucuparia Fastigiata (mountain ash var.)	9–15 m
S. commixta (mountain ash or rowan)	7·6–9 m
Excellent street tree.	
S. 'Joseph Rock' (mountain ash)	6–12 m
Upright but later spreading.	
S. thuringiaca Fastigiata	6–10 m
Tilia platyphyllos Fastigiata (lime)	18–22 m

Table 50
Trees that will grow on chalk soils

Broadleaved

Acer campestre (field maple)	3–12 m
A. negundo (box elder)	12–18 m
A. platanoides (Norway maple)	15–24 m
A. pseudoplatanus (sycamore)	24–28 m
Carpinus betulus (hornbeam)	15–23 m
Crataegus (thorn)	4·5–9 m
Fagus (beech)	6–30 m
Fraxinus (ash)	7–30+ m
Juglans regia (walnut)	9–30 m
Laburnum (golden chain)	4·5–9 m
Prunus (almond, peach, plum, cherry, etc.)	3–16 m
Quercus cerris (Turkey oak)	15–30 m
Quercus ilex (evergreen oak)	18–27 m
Robinia (false acacia or locust)	3–24 m
Sorbus aria (whitebeam)	6–12 m

Coniferous

Abies cephalonica (Grecian fir)	12–30 m
A. pinsapo (Spanish fir)	Up to 30 m
Chamaecyparis lawsoniana (Lawson's cypress)	7·6–15+ m
Cupressus macrocarpa (Monterey cypress)	15–30 m
Ginkgo biloba (maidenhair tree)	15–21 m
Juniperus (juniper)	0·3–18 m
*Larix decidua (common larch)	24–42 m
Picea (spruce)	15–30+ m
Pinus mugo (mountain pine)	3–20 m
P. nigra (Austrian pine)	24–30 m
Thrives better than any other pine on chalky soils.	
P. sylvestria (Scots pine)	18–30 m
Sequoia sempervirens (redwood)	39+ m
Will thrive on calcareous formation if there is at least 600 mm depth of soil.	
Taxus (yew)	3·6–18 m

*Deciduous conifer

Table 51
Trees that will grow on acid soils

Broadleaved

Acer negundo (box elder)	12–18 m
A. palmatum (Japanese maple)	Up to 6 m
Ailanthus altissima (tree of heaven)	15–21 m
Betula (birch)	9–23 m
Castanea (sweet chestnut)	18–30 m
Gleditschia (locust)	12–36 m
Populus alba (white poplar)	18–28 m
Robinia (false acacia)	3–24 m
*Ulmus (elm)	12–36 m
Roots spread through a large area of soil.	

Coniferous

Abies (silver fir)	12–60 m
Picea (spruce)	15–30+ m
Pseudotsuga menziesii (Oregon Douglas fir)	30–60 m
Tsuga (hemlock)	15–30 m

*Prone to elm disease

Table 52
Trees that will grow on clay soils

Broadleaved

Acer (maple)	6–30 m
Except snake-bark maple and those species forming small- to medium-sized trees.	
Alnus (alder)	4·5–27 m
Betula (birch)	9–23 m
Carpinus (hornbeam)	15–23 m
Crataegus (thorn)	4·5–9 m
Fraxinus (ash)	7–30+ m
Laburnum (golden chain)	4·5–9 m
Malus (flowering crab)	2·5–12 m
Populus (willow)	6–45 m
Prunus (almond, peach, plum, cherry, etc.)	3–16 m
Quercus (oak)	7·6–30 m
Salix (willow)	6–30 m
Sorbus (mountain ash and whitebeam)	7·5–12 m
Tilia (lime)	15–36 m

Coniferous

Abies (silver fir)	12–60 m
Chamaecyparis (false cypress)	7·6–15 m
Juniperus (juniper)	0·3–18 m
Pinus (pine)	3–45+ m
Taxus (yew)	3·6–18 m
Thuja (arbor-vitae)	4·5–45+ m

Table 53
Trees that will grow on dry, poor soils

Broadleaved	
Acer pseudoplatanus (sycamore)	24–28 m
Betula (birch)	9–23 m
Caragana arborescens (Siberian pea tree)	3–6 m
Robinia (false acacia)	3–24 m
Sorbus aucuparia (mountain ash or rowan)	9–18 m
Ulmus (elm)	12–36 m
Roots spread through a large area of soil.	
Coniferous	
Juniperus communis (common juniper)	1·8–12 m
Pinus banksiana (Canadian jack pine)	6–13+ m
Unsuitable for chalky soils but will grow in almost pure sand.	
P. contorta (beach pine)	6–9+ m
Used for fixing sand dunes in maritime exposures.	
P. halepensis (Aleppo pine or Jerusalem pine)	9–15 m
Withstands hot, dry conditions.	
P. nigra maritima (Corsican pine)	30–45 m
Bad transplanter.	
P. pinaster (maritime pine)	27–30 m
Suitable for sandy soils and coastal areas.	
P. sylvestris (Scots pine)	18–30 m

*Prone to elm disease

Table 54
Trees that will grow on moist soils

Broadleaved	
Alnus (alder)	4·5–27 m
Betula nigra (N. American river birch)	15–27 m
B. pendula (common silver birch)	12–23 m
Crataegus oxycantha (thorn)	4·5–9 m
Fraxinus (ash)	7–30+ m
Roots extend for a great distance.	
Liquidambar styraciflua (American sweet gum)	15–23 m
Populus (poplar)	6–45+ m
Pterocarya (wing nut)	18–30+ m
Salix (willow)	6–30 m
Sorbus aucuparia (mountain ash or rowan)	9–18 m
Coniferous	
Abies alba (silver fir)	12–45 m
A. procera (noble fir)	30–45 m
Unsuitable for calcareous soils.	
Picea abies (common spruce or Norway spruce)	15–30 m
P. omorika (Serbian spruce)	18–24 m
P. sitchensis (Sitka spruce)	30+ m
Rapid growing, also thriving in dry soils.	
Taxodium distichum (deciduous cypress or swamp cypress)	15–30 m
Thuja occidentalis (American arbor-vitae)	9–12 m
T. orientalis (Chinese arbor-vitae)	4·5–9 m
Tsuga heterophylla (western hemlock)	21+ m
Rapid-growing but unsuitable for shallow chalk soils.	

Nine Shrubs, Bulbs, Herbaceous and Alpine Plants

SHRUBS

Use of shrubs in landscape design (Tables 55–75, pages 190–218)

Plants are one of nature's most valuable assets, enjoyed by all living creatures. There is a plant for virtually every kind of environment and perhaps none is more varied in size, form, colour and texture than that vast group of woody perennials classified under the broad heading of 'shrubs'.

Shrubs range in size from a few millimetres to the height of a small tree and are specified as laid down in BS 3936 : Part 1 :1965. They may be classified as follows :

Large	Higher than 1·82 m
Medium	0·90–1·82 m high
Small	0·45–0·90 m high
Sub-shrub	Less than 0·45 m high

Shrubs play a prominent role, both functional and aesthetic, in the environment and provide a wealth of material sufficient to satisfy even the most fastidious designer. Choice of size and selection of species depend upon the scale of the layout. The larger specimens may be used to create a frame or backcloth for other plants or planted as a feature to give focal emphasis in a design. Some grow tall quite quickly, forming a screen, windbreak or enclosure, and those armed with spines or prickly leaves make formidable barriers; others are ideal for planting against a wall or covering a pergola. Low spreading plants are excellent weed suppressors and provide ground cover. Creeping or cascading species may be used to cover banks that are too steep for grass maintenance.

Where it is desired to emphasise perspective in a layout the adroit siting of shrubs is a useful means of contriving vistas and helping to create an illusion of breadth or depth. Undulations in the local topography may be concealed or punctuated, according to choice, by careful disposition of the planting. Groupings of close-textured varieties assist in highlighting the contrast between solid and void; those whose foliage possesses a bold and interesting sculptural quality complement the architectural features in a design.

The texture, form and differing hues revealed by shrubs during their development follow a seasonal cycle that ensures a changing scene throughout the year. Many have delightful blooms and possess a fragrance which makes them particularly attractive to bees and other insects which participate in the life cycle of the plants. Fruits, the culmination of floral development, provide a valuable source of food for birds and other wild life.

Factors affecting the choice of shrubs

The principal factors governing plant selection may be summarised under the following headings.

Function
The purpose for which a shrub is required is the foremost consideration since this has an important bearing on its size and form. The choice may also need to satisfy other requirements which, although of secondary importance, are often interrelated.

A single specimen may be used to create a focal point; a group of shrubs to provide a screen, enclosure or barrier; climbers to clothe a wall; low spreading varieties to serve as ground cover or cascade down a bank.

Effect
The conception of a design is reflected in the process of its implementation which, in the case of plants, is never static. Plant selection must take into account, therefore, the changes that occur throughout the seasons and with the passage of time; the size and role of the plant at maturity must be borne in mind when considering the effect which it is intended to achieve in the various stages of the implemented design.

The form and structure of a plant serve to emphasise a particular aspect of the design: if a vertical theme is to predominate shrubs of columnar habit should be chosen; low spreading ones serve to accentuate the horizontal dimensions. Both the selection and arrangement of the plants enhance different aspects of the design at various times of the year.

Sensual perception
The impact of plants upon the senses differs according to the stimulus encountered: colour, form and texture are perceived by the eye; the aroma of flowers, fruit or leaves by the nose; the sound of swaying branches and rustling leaves by the ear; the feel of barbs, spines and prickles by the body.

In plant selection the visual aspect is usually given primary consideration, but the role of the other senses in the overall conception, although perhaps relatively of secondary importance, must not be overlooked.

Form. The structure of a plant is revealed in its silhouette, changing in character as it matures. Plant forms range from horizontal to vertical, columnar to weeping, erect to prostrate, with complex variations.

Fig. 56   Examples of plant form

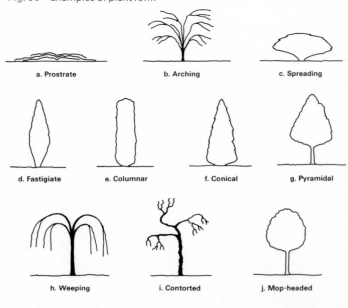

a. Prostrate   b. Arching   c. Spreading

d. Fastigiate   e. Columnar   f. Conical   g. Pyramidal

h. Weeping   i. Contorted   j. Mop-headed

Texture. The combination of silhouette, size and shape of the leaves, their arrangement, their surface and that of the branches and shoots, produces an overall effect which differs between one kind of shrub and another (Fig.57). Small, closely-spaced leaves along much of the length of the branches give a dense effect (ideal for hedges) very different from that of large-scale, widely-spaced foliage (Fig.58).

Variations in texture are valuable; in a small layout interest must lie in detail, whereas in the larger landscape the planting is viewed as a whole.

Colour. The attraction of most plants lies not so much in their form or texture as in the colours which they reveal at different times of the year. The seasonal colours of the natural landscape in Britain are:

Spring (April–May)	Bright yellow-greens of young leaves and shoots Dewy fresh-green grass Silver-grey, pink, white and gold blossom
Summer (June–August)	Dark green leaves Varying shades of reds and blues prominent in flowers
Autumn (September–October)	Rich reds, browns, gold and softer yellow hues of leaves
Winter (November–March)	Browns and greys of woodlands Purple-grey-rust shades of hedgerows Black-blue silhouettes in blazoned winter skies Glistening gold, white and red stems or bark in streaks of low-angled sunshine

Warm colours stand out as the predominant hues in any setting, while the cool ones appear to recede into the background. When opposite colours in the spectrum are placed together, their effect is mutually enhanced. It is therefore advisable to restrict to a minimum the number of colours in a planting layout in order to achieve the maximum effect.

Fig. 57   Examples of plant texture

Fig. 58   Use of plant texture to provide contrast

enly balanced relationship tween each leaf creates an erall dense effect, e.g. beech

a less dense but evenly balanced relationship between leaves permits filtration of light and creates an open texture, e.g. birch

this type of plant texture relies upon strong directional form of leaf pattern to create an overall effect, e.g. fishbone cotoneaster

the size of the individual leaves and their relationship to each other produces a plant texture which contrasts well with the brickwork against which it is set

Close even texture   b. **Open even texture**   c. **Texture with directional emphasis**

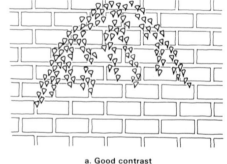

a. **Good contrast**

he bold outline of the leaf structure creates a pattern of coarse texture, e.g. horse chestnut

the arrangement of the needle-like leaves produces a feathery type of texture, e.g. Douglas fir

the foliage in this illustration produces a texture which bears a similar scale relationship to that of the brickwork and therefore does not create any contrast but tends to blend in with the background

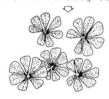

d. **Coarse texture**   e. **Feathery texture**

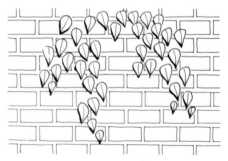

b. **Insufficient contrast**

Climatic conditions

Although most of the shrubs grown in Britain possess a wide range of climatic tolerance, not all of them are completely hardy and some may fail under adverse conditions. If an environment similar to that of their natural habitat can be provided they are able to thrive quite happily; this usually necessitates local climatic adjustments in the form of shelter from wind and frost.

Climate (sunshine, wind and rain) may be considered in terms of a large region (macroclimate) or quite a small local area (microclimate). Each aspect of climate influences the growth of plants and, indirectly, their selection.

Sunshine. Some plants revel in the full sun, while others become parched and dry without shade. On a hot, dry site only those plants capable of withstanding arid conditions are able to survive.

Wind. Drying wind can be disastrous for those plants requiring shelter; in exposed places the shallow-rooted, less resistant species may be uprooted by gales. In coastal districts salt-laden winds have a detrimental effect on those plants unable to withstand marine conditions.

Rain. Moisture in the atmosphere and percolating through the soil assists in creating growing conditions for the plants. Although no shrub is able to thrive in stagnant water there are many useful species (e.g. willows and dogwoods) which prefer moist conditions.

Topography

Climate and topography are interrelated (the higher the altitude, the lower the ground temperature): the aspect of the ground and its angle of slope have an important bearing on the amount of sun radiation it receives at different seasons (see Fig.10):

North	Coldest slope all the year round
South-west	Warmest from October to April
South-east	Warmest from June to August
South	Warmest in May and September

Fluctuations in temperature are much greater in valleys than on mountain tops. Cold air in a valley moves downwards and the warm air rises; it is here that frost pockets occur. The warmest location is about two-thirds of the way up a hillside (an important point to remember when siting plants which produce blossom in April–May, the danger months when late frosts are liable to occur).

Ecological balance

In nature certain groups of plants exist alongside one another and form their own individual type of community which is readily identifiable with a particular kind of soil. Much of the planting carried out today is maintained by man and the natural competition between plants controlled, but the selection of shrubs for the creation of a semi-wild landscape must provide an ecological balance in order that some of them do not crowd out their neighbours and take over the community. The purest plant community in a natural landscape is to be found at its centre where conditions are at their most stable. Towards the edges of the area the distribution becomes less pure and the influence of various outside factors is discernible.

The three principal shrub communities are described below.

(i) *Heaths.* Heath soils occur in parts of the New Forest, Ashdown Forest, large areas of Dorset, Surrey, Cornwall and Eastern Scotland, and are often quite shallow, made up of a thin layer of unrotted peat and several millimetres of rotted humus and sand overlying a subsoil of sand or gravel dry and deficient in salts. It is not a favourable soil for most plants and only those able to endure drought conditions survive. The shrub layer includes:

ling	broom
heather	dwarf willow
gorse	brambles
bracken	bilberry

Larch (*Larix decidua*) and pine (*Pinus sylvestris*) are also found growing in the community. If the ling grows high, casting shade, it tends to exclude all other plants and only mosses (*Polytrichum* and *Hypnum*) and lichens (*Cladonia*) are able to grow there. Leguminous plants thrive in these soils because they are able to make use of nitrogenous food produced by bacteria in their root nodules.

(ii) *Moorland.* Of the three types of moorland found in Britain—grass, cottongrass and heather—only the latter contains shrubs within the plant community. The sandy, shallow soil overlies impervious rock, producing waterlogged conditions which hinder the decomposition of humus. The result is an accumulation of peat 0·30–1·22 m thick.

Although it is sometimes difficult to distinguish a dry heather moor from a damp heath, their fundamental difference lies in the accumulation of peat due to high rainfall and lack of drainage. Whereas heaths occur mostly on wide, gently undulating ground exposed to sun and wind, the heather moors are usually on high ground, often wild, with rocky outcrops. The rainfall in these areas is high and low cloud fairly persistent, characteristic of the West of England where moist winds blowing from the Atlantic deposit their moisture on the hills. Bilberry is often co-dominant with heather in these areas and on better-drained sites becomes the dominant plant. At high elevations extensive areas of cowberry (*Vaccinium vitis-idaea*) are found.

Shrubs typical of a heather moor include:

> ling (*Calluna vulgaris*)
> bell heather (*Erica cinerea*)
> cross-leaved heath (*Erica tetralix*)
> dwarf willow (*Salix repens*)
> bramble (*Rubus*)
> gorse (*Ulex*)

Although heather moors are typically found on wet soils and heaths on dry, both are characterised by a poor supply of nitrates and both are inhabited by those species that can tolerate this deficiency, so that they hold much of their plant life in common.

(iii) *Chalk scrub.* Many of the plants found on chalk downland are small-leaved surface rooters, whose existence is determined to a large extent by the grazing of sheep and rabbits. In parts of the chalk downs, particularly on the periphery of beechwoods, plant communities form what is known as 'chalk scrub' which mostly comprises dwarf trees and shrubs typical of the calcareous soils. The plants include:

> whitebeam (*Sorbus aria*)
> wayfaring tree (*Viburnum lantana*)
> juniper (*Juniperus communis*)
> dogwood (*Cornus sanguinea*)
> box (*Buxus sempervivum*)
> elder (*Sambucus nigra*)
> brambles (*Rubus spp.*)
> roses (*Rosa rubiginosa*)
> hawthorn (*Crataegus spp.*)
> clematis (*Clematis vitalba*)
> ivy (*Hedera*)

Hawthorn predominates in chalk down scrub where associated with beechwoods containing dog's mercury as the dominant carpeting plant. If wood sanicle is the dominant carpeter in a similar type of association, then juniper is more frequently found there.

Horticultural requirements

Most shrubs tolerate a wide range of soils and conditions but there are some whose existence depends upon a particular type of environment. Those plants which thrive in the same type of soil and require similar cultural methods should, ideally, be grouped together in the same area.

The quality and condition of a plant is more important than its size in the nursery. All shrubs supplied should meet the requirements set out in BS 3936: Part 1:1965, which also includes a list of forms and sizes normally supplied by the trade.

Planting

The main planting season in Britain, allowing slight variations for different latitudes, is broadly as follows:

Deciduous plants	End of October to end of March or early April
Evergreens and dwarf conifers	End of September or early May
Pot or container grown plants	Ideally, end of September to early May, but may be done at any convenient time of year

The first task is to break up the soil to a depth of at least 230 mm below the surface of the subsoil, using heavy tines. Where the topsoil has previously been stripped it must be replaced on top of the subsoil, taking care not to mix the two. Any topsoil imported onto the site should comply with BS 3882:1965 and care must be taken to see that it is of the correct pH value for the plants which are to grow in it. Soil samples should be taken and the appropriate tests made; it may also be necessary to specify the required lime content, depending upon the plant material envisaged. Any nutrient deficiencies within the soil must be rectified before planting is undertaken.

Bulky organic manures, such as farmyard, should be mixed with the topsoil during preliminary cultivation at the rate of 135 g/m²; bonemeal and other concentrated organic manures, at 68–135 g/m²; inorganic fertilisers (e.g. lime), at 135–271 g/m².

The planting hole, which should be dug just before

planting, must be large enough to accommodate the plant's roots without cramping or disturbing them and of a sufficient depth to allow the plant to be set in the ground at the same level as that at which it grew in the nursery.* The soil at the bottom of the hole should be broken up to a depth of at least 150 mm to prevent any hard pan and to assist drainage. Care must be taken to see that enough room is allowed in the holes prepared for those plants with a root-ball (balled-up) to prevent any damage to them during the actual planting process (Figs 52 and 53, pages 164 and 165).

Plants must never be left out of the ground with their roots exposed to frost or drying wind. Bundles of plants should be untied and opened immediately upon arrival and either planted in their permanent stations, or, if this is not possible, heeled-in in a trench so that their roots are in direct contact with the soil, taking care to see that the plants are correctly labelled. Any that appear unduly dry should be stood in water for twenty-four hours.

Planting is best carried out during dull, cloudy weather when there is little or no wind and no strong sunlight. In some cases support may be required; stakes should be straight and adequate in size and driven well into the bottom of the hole prior to planting. On no account must wire be used to tie the plant to its support since this is likely to cause damage to the stem which may ultimately prove fatal.

Pot-grown plants are treated in the same manner as those that are balled-up and, after being soaked in water, are removed from the pot with the root-ball intact. Where necessary the young roots may be lightly loosened before planting. Where the plant has become pot-bound the pot may have to be broken in order to prevent the roots from being damaged.

The planting distance between shrubs depends upon their height and spread. Generally, the distance between two adjacent shrubs is taken as the sum of half the ultimate diameter of each. Plants are spaced closer for hedges or for groups of the same species. Larger shrubs required for immediate effect are sometimes planted close together and after a few years each alternate one is taken out to enable the remainder to grow on to maturity. Reference should be made to BS 4428:1969, Section 8.

*There are a few exceptions to this rule, e.g. lavender.

Maintenance

The care of newly planted shrubs during the first growing season in their new environment is most important. They must be watered to ensure that the roots do not dry out (evergreens are particularly susceptible to drought) and any shrub loosened by frost must be carefully firmed-in by treading.

Beds should be kept clean and friable, but no digging or indiscriminate forking undertaken since damage may be done to feeding roots near the surface. Light forking, sufficient to assist the penetration of rain water, need be done only once or twice a year, when additional manure or fertiliser may also be incorporated into the soil during early spring.

Weeds should be kept under control by hoeing at regular intervals until the shrubs become established; thereafter weed control may be effected by the application of weed-killing chemicals. If the soil is treated in late winter or early spring it helps to prevent the establishment of annual weeds.

Feeding should be just sufficient to maintain healthy growth; usually only those plants growing on the lighter soils require annual feeding and the enrichment of the soil with leaf litter until they establish themselves.

In the early stages of plant growth, pruning normally involves shortening the longer shoots to balance root loss and disturbance (due to transplanting) and removing damaged branches or shoots. Some shrubs require cutting back hard in their early growth in order to encourage new growth to develop from the base.

Shrubs for forming hedges

Tables 55–59 (pages 190–192) give details of shrubs suitable for the establishment of various kinds of hedge. The function of a hedge is likely to dictate the type of plants to be used and its maintenance depends upon whether the hedge is a formal or informal one.

A hedge is a living barrier which is effected by means of closely spaced plants set along a defined line. The width of an established formal hedge may reach 460–600 mm and an informal one 200 mm or more—a point to remember when planting alongside a path or boundary. If adjacent to a fence the plants should be planted 300–460 mm away from it. Where a thick hedge is required a staggered double row should be set out, thus:

```
*    *    *    *    *    *    *    *    *
   *    *    *    *    *    *    *    *
```

It is better, usually, to specify smaller sizes of hedging shrubs because they establish themselves more readily than the larger ones and are cheaper to purchase.

A trench 460 mm wide by 380 mm deep is dug and the bottom broken up for a further 150 mm. Planting is carried out in the same manner as for shrubs generally.

Careful maintenance during the early formation of the plants is important, particularly in a formal hedge, in order to lay the foundation for healthy, sturdy, mature and well-furnished growth (Fig.2). Pruning and trimming is part of the after-care operation : in the first year after planting the hedge should be cut back hard to encourage new growth from the base ; flowering hedges should be pruned immediately the blooms are over.

At some phase in a development it may be found necessary to move a plant. The transplanting of a mature hedge involves considerable risk because of the intertwining growth. Root pruning is a vital pre-moving operation which should be carried out one season (or preferably two) beforehand. It is better to lift several plants simultaneously rather than each individual plant and the root pruning should be carried out with this in mind. As much root-ball as is practicable should be kept intact and the trench dug sufficiently wide to accommodate it without causing disturbance to the roots. Watering is essential in order to prevent drying out.

Shrubs in tubs and window boxes

The shrubs selected should be in scale with their surroundings and also with the size of container used. The height ratio, generally, of shrub to tub should not exceed 3:2 if a reasonable balance is to be achieved.

One of the advantages of growing shrubs in containers is that ideal soil conditions for the plants may be created and maintained without the influence of factors detrimental to growth or development. Free drainage is important ; a layer of clean hard rubble, such as broken bricks or the larger stone chippings, should be placed at the bottom of the tub and covered with sphagnum moss or thin grass turfs set grass-side downwards. On no account must there be any trace of lime present (e.g. mortar rubble) if lime-hating shrubs are to be planted. The remainder should be filled with good quality topsoil (to BS 3882:1965), allowed to consolidate to within 25 mm of the rim prior to planting. The containers are best placed in their final positions before being filled with soil since, once filled, rollers and additional manpower may be required to move them.

Window boxes are, of necessity, comparatively small containers and therefore require small low-growing or trailing plants. These are often supplemented by bulbs and other herbaceous plants or alpines. Preparation of the boxes is similar to that of tubs but the size of rubble is smaller—gravel or ashes are suitable as a base. The soil or planting medium is best covered with a layer of moss to prevent splashing of the windows or adjacent walls.

Plant containers, particularly window boxes, are liable to suffer the effects of drought because of the constant circulation of air around them, and the plants require more frequent watering than those in open ground. Even when ideal soil is prepared it is desirable to change the growing medium every other year to prevent waterlogging and also to dispense with any toxic residues derived from fertilisers applied as top-dressing.

Planting in roof gardens

A roof garden is akin to a patio but has no background, only an enormous expanse of sky. Often strong winds prevail and protection for the plants must be provided. Since the soil of a roof garden is liable to dry out rather quickly, a good layer of peat should be incorporated and the plants should be given fairly frequent top-dressings. Materials used for the construction of a roof garden for the planting of trees, shrubs and grass are shown below. The finished surface of the supporting roof structure should be laid to falls to facilitate drainage.

	Trees (mm)	Shrubs (mm)	Grass (mm)
Soil surface			
Topsoil	1500	600	250
Peat	200	150	80
Fibreglass	25	25	25
Gravel	250	150	130
Roof structure			

Table 55
Shrubs suitable for forming formal hedges

Botanical name	Common name	Evergreen or deciduous	Height (m)	Spacing (mm)
Buxus sempervirens	Box	E	2·43	460
Carpinus betulus	Hornbeam	D	6·00	300
Cupressocyparis leylandii	Leyland cypress	E	6·00	460
Fagus sylvatica	Beech	D	4·57+	300
Ligustrum	Privet	E	1·82–3·00	300
Lonicera nitida Yunnan	Lonicera	E	2·13	300
Prunus lusitanica	Portugal laurel	E	6·00	600
Rosmarinus officinalis	Rosemary	E	1·21	460
Taxus baccata	Yew	E	7·62	460
Thuja plicata	Western red cedar	E	4·57	600

Table 56
Shrubs suitable for forming an impenetrable barrier

Botanical name	Common name	Evergreen or deciduous	Height (m)	Spacing (mm)
Crataegus spp.	Hawthorn	D	4·57+	230
Ilex aquifolium	Holly	E	6·00+	460
Prunus spinosa	Blackthorn	D	3·65	300
Pyracantha spp.	Firethorn	E	2·43+	600
Rosa rugosa vars.	Ramanas rose	D	1·82	600
Ulex europaeus	Gorse	E	1·82	460

Table 57
Shrubs suitable for forming low hedges

Botanical name	Common name	Evergreen or deciduous	Height (mm)	Spacing (mm)
Artemisia abrotanum	Southernwood	E	600–900	460
Berberis buxifolia Nana	Dwarf barberry	E	600–900	230
Buxus sempervirens	Box	E	460	230
Erica spp.	Heathers	E	600–1200	230–300
Euonymus fortunei radicans	Euonymus	E	900+	230
Hypericum moserianum	Rose of Sharon	E	500	300
Lavandula spica	Lavender	E	900	230
Potentilla fruticosa	Potentilla	D	900	300
Rosa pimpinellifolia	Scotch rose	D	600	380
Rosmarinus officinalis	Rosemary	E	900	300
Santolina chamaecyparissus	Lavender cotton	E	460	230

Table 58
Shrubs suitable for forming large informal screens

Botanical name	Common name	Evergreen or deciduous	Height (m)	Spacing (mm)
Acer pseudoplatanus	Sycamore	D	6·09	900
Arundinaria japonica	Bamboo	E	3·65	900
Buddleia davidii	Buddleia	D	2·43	760
Corylus avellana	Hazel	D	4·57	460
Prunus laurocerasus	Laurel	E	6·09	900
Rhododendron spp.	Rhododendron	E	3·00	900
Syringa spp.	Lilac	D	4·57	900

Table 59
Shrubs suitable for forming flowering hedges

Botanical name	Common name	Evergreen or deciduous	Height (m)	Spacing (mm)
Berberis spp.	Barberry	E or D	1·82–2·43	300
Chaenomeles japonica	Japonica	D	1·52	460
Cotoneaster spp.	Cotoneaster	D	0·90–2·43	300–460
Cytisus spp.	Broom	D	0·90–2·13	460
Deutzia spp.	Deutzia	D	2·43	600
Elaeagnus spp.	Oleaster	E or D	1·52–3·00	600
Escallonia	Chilean gum box	E	1·82	380
Forsythia spp.	Forsythia	D	2·43–3·00	460–600
Hippophae rhamnoides	Sea buckthorn	D	3·00	600
Kerria japonica Pleniflora	Jew's mallow	D	1·82	600
Mahonia aquifolium	Oregon grape	E	1·21–1·82	300
Olearia haastii	Daisy bush	E	2·13	380
Philadelphus spp.	Mock orange	D	1·82–2·43	600
Prunus cerasifera	Myrobalan	D	1·21–3·00	380
Rhododendron spp.	Rhododendron	E	2·43–3·00	900
Rosa hugonis ; R. rubiginosa	Roses	D	1·52–3·00	600
Viburnum spp.	Viburnum	D	2·42–3·00	600
Weigelia spp.	Weigelia	D	1·82	600

Table 60
Shrubs for walls and pergolas

(E=evergreen, T=twining habit, SC=self-clinging)		
E	*Acacia dealbata* (silver wattle)	3·65–4·57 m. Silvery fern-like foliage ; yellow flowers.
T	*Actinidia chinensis* (Chinese gooseberry)	Bold heart-shaped leaves and red, hairy stems. Ideal foliage plant for a large wall or tree.
TE	*Akebia quinata*	Up to 12 m. Oval deep-green leaflets arranged in fives. Chocolate-purple pendent flowers. Useful for pergola with S.E. or W. aspect.
T	*Aristolochia macrophylla* (Dutchman's pipe)	Up to 9 m. Large heart-shaped bright green leaves ; insignificant flowers. Suitable for any aspect.
E	*Camellia williamsii 'J. C. Williams'*	3 m. Matt green leaves : single clear pink flowers with yellow stamens. Plant of arching habit, ideal for N. or W. wall that is not windswept.
SC	*Campsis radicans* (trumpet vine)	6–8 m. Clusters of tubular vermilion flowers. Suitable for S. or W. wall.
	Caryopteris clandonensis (blue spiraea)	0·91–1·52 m. Grey-green aromatic leaves (remaining dormant until late April) ; clusters of long-stemmed rich blue flowers. Suitable for S. or W. wall.
	Ceanothus 'Autumnal Blue	1·52–1·82 m. Oval, glossy green leaves ; large spikes of soft blue flowers. Late-flowering variety for S. or W. wall.
T	*Celastrus orbiculatus*	9–12 m. Leaves turn clear yellow in autumn, providing a vivid contrast to the orange and scarlet capsules and seeds of fruits (borne by female plants). Ideal for creating winter effect on pergola of any aspect.
	Chaenomeles (japonica or flowering quince)	0·91–3·65 m. Apple-like blossoms of varying colours from pure white to brilliant red. Ideal for walls of any aspect.
	Chimonanthus praecox (winter sweet)	2·43–3·04 m. Fresh green willow-like leaves ; primrose-yellow flowers are produced on bare twigs in winter. Suitable for S. or W. wall.
E	*Choisya ternata* (Mexican orange flower)	1·82–2·13 m. Bright green foliage ; clusters of starry, white flowers. Suitable for N., S. or W. wall.
TE	*Clematis armandii 'Snowdrift'*	3·65–6·09 m. Dark green, pointed leathery leaves. Clusters of white flowers in abundance. Needs a warm, sheltered wall.
T	*Clematis macropetala 'Markham's Pink'*	3·65–4·57 m. Soft-pink semi-double blooms.
T	*Clematis montana rubens*	6·09–9·14 m. Delicate mauve-pink flowers with yellow anthers borne in profusion.
	Cotoneaster horizontalis (fish-bone cotoneaster)	0·76–1·37 m. Herringbone-branching with small oval, glossy green leaves which persist until December–January. Flowers insignificant but attractive to bees ; abundant red berries. Suitable for walls of any aspect.
	Cytisus battandieri (broom)	2·43–4·57 m. Silvery-green laburnum-like leaves ; pineapple-scented golden-yellow flowers. Vigorous, upright shrub throwing shoots up from base. Does best in warm, sheltered locality on S. or W. wall.
	Deutzia rosea Carminea	1·22–1·52 m. Shrub of bushy, arching habit with soft rose-pink flowers freely borne. Suitable for E., S. or W. wall.
E	*Escallonia 'Donard Seedling'*	2·74–3·65 m. Shrub of bushy, arching habit with white flowers suffused pink and pink in bud. Good shrub for bees and suitable for S. or W. walls.
E	*Euonymus fortunei Variegatus*	0·76–1·06 m. Silver variegated foliage. Useful for planting against low walls or under windows. Ideal for associating with heathers and suitable for any aspect.
E	*Ficus 'Brown Turkey'* (fig)	4·57 + m. Attractive foliage. May be planted against walls of any aspect but fruits best on S. or W. wall.
	Forsythia suspensa sieboldii	2·43–3·65 m. Shrub of pendulous habit with primrose-yellow flowers along its shoots. Excellent for N. wall.
E	*Garrya elliptica*	2·43–3·65 m. Oval, matt, grey-green leaves with wavy margins. Silvery-grey catkins hang in clusters, November–February (male catkins twice as long as the female). Ideal winter shrub for walls of any aspect.
	Hamamelis mollis (Chinese witch hazel)	3·65–5·48 m. Upspreading branches bear bright yellow strap-like petalled flowers, January–February. Suitable for any aspect and ideal for associating with *Erica carnea 'King George'*.

continued

Table 60 *Continued*

ESC	*Hedera* (ivy)	Self-clinging climbers suitable for walls of any aspect. Hardiest of all climbers.
	Hibiscus syriacus (bush mallow)	Up to 3 m. Upright branching habit with greyish bark. Large 'hollyhock' flowers. Suitable for S., E. or W. aspect.
SC	*Hydrangea petiolaris*	Up to 18 m. Bold, heart-shaped rich green leaves turn delicate lemon-yellow in autumn. Large, flattish corymbs of white flowers. Stems rough with reddish-brown peeling bark. Ideal self-clinging climber for large area of walling with N., E. or W. aspect.
	Jasminum nudiflorum (winter jasmine)	Up to 4·57 m. Bright yellow flowers, November–February. Succeeds in all aspects but flowers may be subject to frost damage on exposed E. walls.
T	*Jasminum officinale* (jasmine)	3·04–3·65+ m. Clusters of white, sweetly scented flowers in summer. Suitable for pergolas with E., S. or W. aspect.
	Kerria japonica Pleniflora (batchelors' buttons)	2·43–3·04 m. Double, button-type orange-yellow flowers; fresh green foliage and apple green shoots. Shrub with semi-upright habit for any aspect.
T	*Lonicera periclymenum Serotina* (late Dutch honeysuckle)	Reddish-purple flowers outside, yellow within. Vigorous climber suitable for pergolas with N., E. or W. aspect.
	Lycium chinense Carnosum (Duke of Argyll's tea tree)	1·52–2·13 m. Small, narrow, grey-green leaves on grey twiggy growths. Soft purple starry flowers followed by clusters of pendent, oval, orange fruits which bow down the arching branches. Succeeds in any aspect and will thrive in shade.
E	*Magnolia grandiflora Exmouth*	9–12 m. Large, glossy oval leaves; globular white flowers 0·20–0·25 m across. A magnificent shrub for large walls with S. or W. aspect.
T	*Muehlenbeckia complexa*	Up to 6 m. Small, heart-shaped leaves spangle the fine wiry black mesh of thriving growths. Unusual climbing plant of vigorous habit for pergolas with S. or W. aspect. Ideal for seaside locations.
E	*Osmanthus delavayi* (holly-olive)	2·13–3·04 m. Small, dark glossy green, heart-shaped, toothed leaves; pure white tubular flowers produced in abundance.
SC	*Parthenocissus quinquefolia* (Virginia creeper)	Five-lobed leaves which turn brilliant scarlet in autumn. Self-clinging climber suitable for walls of any aspect but colour best in sunny situations.
T	*Passiflora caerulea* (passion flower)	Flowers with creamy-white sepals and blue centre are sometimes followed by egg-shaped orange fruits. Suitable only for growing on pergolas in warm, sheltered locations with S. or W. aspect.
T	*Polygonum baldschuanicum* (Russian vine)	Feathery sprays of creamy-white flowers smother the whole plant, giving it a lacework appearance. Attractive red stems in spring. A rampant climber which succeeds on pergolas with any aspect.
	Prunus triloba (Chinese dwarf almond)	2·13–3·04 m. Branches wreathed with rosette-shaped double pink flowers. Its dense, twiggy habit stands out well against a wall. Suitable for S. or W. aspect.
E	*Pyracantha rogersiana Flava* (firethorn)	2·43–4·56 m. Bright green foliage; masses of cream coloured flowers followed by orange-yellow berries.
E	*Rosa 'Alberic Barbier'* (rambler rose)	Glossy foliage. Double creamy-yellow blooms turning to white when fully out. Suitable for pergola with sunny aspect.
	Rosa 'Mme. Alfred Carrière' (climbing rose)	Double white blooms tinted blush. Does well on a north-facing wall.
	Rubus phoenicolasius (Japanese wineberry)	2·43–3·04 m. Stems covered with red hairs. Bright orange-red edible fruits borne in clusters on arching stems. Suitable for training on pergolas, poles or wires with E., S. or W. aspect.
T	*Vitis coignetiae* (ornamental vine)	Bold, dark green, shield-shaped wrinkled vine-like leaves (downy beneath) turn brilliant orange and red in autumn. Excellent for covering unsightly sheds or over trees. Suitable for S. or W. walls but requires training.
T	*Wistaria floribunda Macrobotrys*	Tapering racemes of soft lavender flowers up to 0·91 m long. Ideal for pergolas, balconies or trellis with S. or W. aspect.

Table 61
Hardy shrubs for planting on banks

(E=evergreen)		
	Berberis wilsonae (Mrs Wilson's barberry)	0·61–0·91 m. Semi-prostrate, spreading habit ; soft green semi-evergreen foliage, purplish in winter. Masses of coral-red berries.
E	*Calluna vulgaris* and vars. (Scottish ling heather)	0·61–0·76 m. Requires lime-free soil.
	Cotoneaster adpressa	0·30–0·46 m. Rigidly branched shrub of close-growing habit, spreading widely over ground. Obovate leaves turn scarlet in autumn. Bright red berries.
	Cotoneaster dammeri	0·051–0·076 m. Prostrate habit ; growths trail over ground in all directions, shaping themselves to contours.
	Cotoneaster horizontalis (fishbone cotoneaster)	0·76–1·37 m. Herringbone-branching ; abundant red berries.
	Cotoneaster salicifolia 'Autumn Fire'	0·10–0·15 m. Bold, willow-like foliage ; clusters of red berries.
E	*Erica carnea* and vars. (heather)	0·12–0·30 m. Flowers range in colour from white to deep carmine, produced November–March. Thrives on lime or acid soils.
E	*Erica cinerea* (bell heather)	0·30–0·61 m. Urn-shaped, rosy-purple flowers produced June–August/September. Thrives on poor, thin, acid soils but dislikes lime.
E	*Euonymus fortunei Variegatus*	0·76–1·06 m. Broad-spreading silver-variegated foliage plant. Ideal for associating with heather.
	Genista lydia (broom)	0·76–0·91 m. Pendulous green shoots 0·61 m long, bent like a sickle, are clothed with golden-yellow flowers.
E	*Hedera helix* and vars. (ivy)	Very adaptable plants with a variety of leaf shapes and colour.
E	*Helianthemum nummularia* and vars. (sun rose)	0·15–0·30 m. Saucer-shaped, crimped flowers in a variety of colours.
E	*Hypericum calycinum* (Rose of Sharon)	0·30–0·46 m. Shrub of low, dense habit ; large bright yellow flowers and striking boss of stamens. Tolerates shade.
E	*Lavandula spica Hidcote* (lavender)	0·30–0·46 m. Silvery foliage ; deep purple-blue flowers.
E	*Mahonia aquifolium* (Oregon grape)	0·91–1·52 m. Dark green foliage turns red or plum-purple in autumn. Golden-yellow flowers in racemes and an abundance of small, plum-like purple berries. Ideal for shady banks.
E	*Pachysandra terminalis*	0·15–0·20 m. Bright green foliage. Ideal for shady banks.
	Potentilla fruticosa Mandschurica	0·30–0·46 m. Shrub of dense, semi-prostrate habit with arching growths. Grey leaves ; cream-coloured flowers.
E	*Rhododendron impeditum*	0·30–0·38 m. Compact habit. Saucer-shaped mauve flowers.
E	*Rhododendron keleticum*	0·30–0·46 m. Small, dark green leaves ; large, saucer-shaped, deep purple flowers with centres heavily spotted with black. Suitable for semi-shaded banks.
	Rosa Macrantha (rose)	0·61–0·91 m. Long sprays of blush pink, single flowers with orange-yellow stamens.
	Rosa micrugosa (rose)	0·91–1·22 m. Broad-spreading shrub of dense habit. Large, saucer-shaped, single, shell-pink flowers.
	Rosa nitida (rose)	Up to 0·61 m. Low-spreading shrub with pinnate foliage which turns brilliant crimson before dropping. Rosy-red, single flowers followed by scarlet fruits.
E	*Rosmarinus lavandulaceus* (rosemary)	0·46–0·61 m. Low-arching shrub with wide-spreading branches. Narrow fresh green leaves ; lavender flowers. Excellent for dry soil.
E	*Salvia officinalis* (sage)	0·76–0·91 m. Low-spreading shrub. Soft grey-green foliage.
E	*Santolina chamaecyparissus Corsica* (lavender cotton)	0·25–0·46 m. Frosted white foliage ; small yellow flowers.
E	*Sarcococca humilis* (Christmas box)	0·31–0·46 m. Bluish-green, willow-like foliage ; small white flowers.
E	*Senecio cineraria*	0·61–0·76 m. Low-spreading shrub with white-felted foliage ; yellow, daisy-like flowers. Suitable for dry banks in full sun.
E	*Senecio laxifolius*	0·91–1·22 m. Bushy, spreading shrub with grey foliage ; bright yellow disc-shaped flowers in clusters.
	Ulex gallii (gorse)	0·15–0·20 m. Dense, prostrate shrub with green spiny shoots and miniature gorse flowers. Ideal for hot banks.
	Vinca spp. (periwinkle)	0·30–0·61 m. Plants of carpeting habit with white or blue flowers. Ideal for shady banks.
	Also conifers of broad-spreading or prostrate habit.	

Table 62
Shrubs for providing ground cover

E=evergreen, SE=semi-evergreen

E	*Berberis candidula* (barberry)	0·76–0·91 m. Dense, wide-spreading habit. Small, dark, shiny green leaves produced in tufts in axils of the spines. Bright yellow flowers followed by oval fruits with purple bloom, 13 mm long.
SE	*Berberis wilsonae* (Mrs Wilson's barberry)	0·61–0·91 m. Spreading habit. Oblanceolate leaves, less than 0·02 m long, turn rich red in autumn. Small, roundish, coral or salmon-red somewhat translucent berries are borne in profusion and persist into winter.
E	*Calluna vulgaris* and vars. (Scottish ling heather)	0·61–0·76 m. Minute, scale-like leaves. Flowers, white, pink or shades of purple, in thin terminal spikes.
E	*Cistus corbariensis* (rock rose)	0·91–1·22 m. Oval leaves, 0·05 m long. White flowers, with yellow blotch at base of each petal, 0·04 m across.
	Cotoneaster dammeri	0·05–0·07 m. Prostrate habit; growths trail over ground in all directions, shaping themselves to the contours. Globose, coral-red fruits, 6 mm across, persist into winter.
	Cotoneaster horizontalis (fishbone cotoneaster)	0·76–1·37 m. Herringbone-branching; abundant red berries studded along branches.
	Cotoneaster Hybridus Pendulus	0·61 m. Prostrate habit. Glossy green, long leaves. Brilliant red berries in abundance during autumn and winter.
E	*Cotoneaster microphylla*	0·61–0·91 m. Low-spreading, often prostrate habit. Glossy green, small, oval leaves. Scarlet berries, 6 mm across.
	Cotoneaster salicifolius 'Autumn Fire'	0·10–0·15 m. Spreading habit. Bold, willow-like foliage; clusters of red berries.
	Cytisus beanii (dwarf broom)	0·30–0·46 m. Small linear leaves. Deep golden-yellow flowers.
	Cytisus kewensis (dwarf broom)	0·46 m. Procumbent, spreading habit. Pale sulphur-yellow single flowers, 13 mm long, borne two or three together.
	Cytisus procumbens (dwarf broom)	0·02–0·05 m. Prostrate, mat-forming habit. Whip-like shoots mould themselves to ground contours. Bright yellow flowers in abundance.
E	*Erica spp.* (heath or heather)	0·12–0·61 m. Distinct among hardy shrubs for smallness and great number of linear leaves. Spikes of tiny flowers of white or various shades of purple.
E	*Euonymus fortunei* (spindleberry)	0·76–1·06 m. Trailing habit; aerial roots. Dull green oval leaves, 0·04 m long, with pale broad veins. Pinkish fruits.
E	*Gaultheria itoana*	0·15–0·23 m. Low-spreading, carpeting habit. Tiny oval leaves. Small, urn-shaped white flowers followed by moth-ball type bright red berries. Ideal for shady positions.
E	*Gaultheria procumbens* (checkerberry)	0·07 m. Carpeting habit. Glossy, dark green leaves. Urn-shaped white flowers followed by bright red berries. Ideal for shady positions.
	Genista lydia (broom)	0·76–0·91 m. Pendulous green shoots, 0·61 m long, bent like a sickle, are clothed with golden-yellow flowers.
	Genista sylvestris (Dalmatian broom)	0·15 m. Forms neat, dense hummocks. Thin angular branches with stiff, sharp spines. Terminal racemes of golden-yellow flowers.
E	*Halimiocistus sahucii*	0·23–0·38 m. Prostrate habit. Dainty, deep green foliage. Saucer-shaped white flowers, 25 mm across, borne in profusion.
E	*Hedera colchica* (Persian ivy)	0·10–0·15 m. Spreading habit; aerial roots. Bold, heart-shaped dark green leaves, often exceeding 200 mm in length and 100 mm in width.
E	*Helianthemum nummularium* (sun rose)	0·15–0·30 m. Semi-shrubby plant. Older stems prostrate, younger ones erect, somewhat hairy. There are a number of varieties with various coloured flowers.
E	*Hypericum calycinum* (Rose of Sharon)	0·30–0·46 m. Shrub of low, dense habit; large bright yellow flowers and striking boss of stamens. Tolerates shade.
E	*Lavandula spp.* (lavender)	0·30–0·91 m. Bushy, grey-leaved plants bearing fragrant blue or various shades of violet or lilac flowers.
	Lithospermum diffusum (gromwell)	0·15 m. Creeping habit, forming mats of semi-herbaceous trailing shoots covered with gentian-blue flowers.
E	*Pachysandra terminalis* (Japanese spurge)	0·15–0·20 m. Dense carpeting habit. Bright green foliage. Spikes of greenish-white flowers borne in late winter.
	Potentilla arbuscula Beesii (shrubby cinquefoil)	0·30–0·46 m. Bushy habit; forms mounds of silvery-coloured foliage. Buttercup-yellow flowers.

Table 62 *Continued*

	Potentilla fruticosa Mandschurica (shrubby cinquefoil)	0·30–0·46 m. Dense shrub of semi-prostrate habit; arching growths. Grey foliage; cream-coloured flowers. Thrives in shade.
SE	*Rubus tricolor* (bramble)	Prostrate habit. Round stems (devoid of prickles and spines) covered with yellowish-brown bristles, 3 mm long. Heart-shaped leaves. White flowers, 25 mm across. Large, bright-red edible fruits.
	Salix repens (creeping willow)	0·30–0·46 m. Creeping habit, spreading by underground stems. Lanceolate leaves, 0·02 m long, dull grey-green above, silvery below.
E	*Santolina spp.* (lavender cotton)	0·25–0·61 m. Narrow, closely-set, saw-edged leaves on semi-woody stems. Masses of small yellow flower heads.
E	*Sarcococca humilis* (Christmas box)	0·30–0·46 m. Dense, spreading habit. Bluish-green willow-like foliage; small, white flowers. Excellent in shade. Goes well with *Elaeagnus* or *Osmanthus*.
	Vinca spp. (periwinkle)	0·30–0·61 m. Plants of carpeting habit with white or blue flowers. Excellent in shade.

Table 63
Shrubs with bold or sculptural-type foliage

E = evergreen

	Actinidia kolomikta	1·82–6·04 m. Climbing habit. Heart-shaped leaves, up to 0·15 m long and 0·10 m wide, are purplish when young, some later developing pink and white variegation.
	Ampelopsis megalophylla (vine)	9 m. Climbing habit. Large pinnate or bi-pinnate leaves, 0·30–0·61 m long; the ovate-oblong leaflets have toothed edges and are up to 0·15 m long and 0·07 m wide. One of the most striking of all climbers, but does not generally display any autumn colour.
	Aralia chinensis (Chinese angelica tree)	3·04+ m. Trunk armed with stout spines. Bi-pinnate leaves, up to 1·22 m long and 0·61 m wide, somewhat resemble those of angelica, comprising numerous leaflets. Plant throws up suckers over a wide area and is best planted at back of border so that its rather gaunt stems may be partly hidden. Thrives in sandy soil in a sunny position.
	Aristolochia macrophylla (Dutchman's pipe)	10+ m. Rampant climbing habit. Heart-shaped, somewhat coarse leaves, up to 0·23 m long and 0·20 m wide. Useful plant for clothing an unsightly structure or a dead tree.
E	*Elaeagnus pungens Maculata*	1·52–3·04 m. Vigorous, spreading and dense habit. Leathery oblong-ovate leaves, 0·10 m long and 0·05 m wide, brilliant golden-yellow with green margins.
E	*Fatsia japonica* (Japanese aralia)	1·82–4·57 m. Spreading habit. Shiny, bright green palmate leaves, up to 0·35 m wide, divided into 7–9 segments. One of the largest-leafed hardy shrubs providing a 'tropical' effect. Does best in semi-shade; useful for seaside locations.
	Ficus carica (fig)	Up to 10 m. Leaves ovate in general outline. 0·20 m long with heart-shaped base, 3–5 lobed and palmately nerved. Makes a handsome wall shrub.
	Hydrangea sargentiana	1·82–2·12 m. Gaunt, leggy habit. Dark green velvety broadly ovate heart-shaped leaves, up to 0·23 m long and 0·17 m wide. Requires sheltered, shady position.
E	*Magnolia delavayi*	Up to 10 m. Ovate leaves, 0·30–0·35 m long and 0·20 m wide, dull grey-green above and greyish-white underneath. Best grown on W. or N.W. wall. Tolerates chalk soils.
E	*Magnolia grandiflora Exmouth*	Up to 12 m. Dark green, shiny leathery oblong-oval leaves, 0·23 m long and 0·10 m wide, felted with orange underneath.
	Paeonia suffruticosa (Moutan peony)	1·52–1·82 m. Bi-pinnate leaves 0·46 m long, often with a red petiole, match the floral display in quality.
	Parthenocissus henryana	4·5+ m. Climbing habit. Leaves composed of 3–5 oblanceolate leaflets, up to 0·13 m long and 0·05 m across, dark velvety green with attactive pink and silver variegation (these are more prominent when plant is grown in partial shade). Fine red autumn colour.
	Paulownia tomentosa (foxglove tree)	Up to 15 m if left to develop, but best pruned back hard each winter leaving only one or two shoots which will produce annual growths of 3–4 m. Long-stalked, ovate leaves, heart-shaped at base and often 3- to 5-lobed, up to 0·91 m across. Size of leaves diminishes as plant becomes more tree-like (if left to develop naturally, leaves are up to 0·23 m across and shallowly-lobed).
E	*Rhododendron basilicum*	Up to 10 m. Dark green leaves, up to 0·30 m long and 0·15 m wide, shiny on the surface and covered underneath with dense short hairs (*indumentum*).

continued

Table 63 *Continued*

E	*Rhododendron macabeanum*	6 m. Oblong-eliptical leaves, up to 0·30 m long and 0·15 m wide, dark green on surface and greyish-white underneath. Reasonably hardy where provided with some shade and protected from wind.
E	*Rhododendron sinogrande*	Up to 10 m. Mature leaves dark shining green, silver or fawn underneath, up to 0·91 m long and 0·30 m across. Young leaves silver. Needs protection from wind. Slow-growing.
	Rhus typhina Laciniata (stag's-horn sumach)	Up to 3·65 m. Pinnate leaves, 0·61 m long and up to 0·23 m wide ; deeply incised leaflets turn orange in autumn.
	Salix magnifica (shrubby willow)	Up to 6 m. Straggly habit. Oval or obovate leaves on young specimens, up to 0·23 m long and 0·13 m wide (less on mature plants), grey-green upper surface and glaucous underneath.
	Sambucus racemosa Plumosa Aurea	3–4·5 m. Finely-cut, golden 5- to 7-foliate leaves. Slow-growing.
E	*Trachycarpus fortunei* (Chusan palm)	Up to 7·5 m. Fan-shaped leaves, up to 0·76 m long and 1·22 m across, divided into numerous segments approximately 0·05 m across. General effect somewhat exotic ; individual leaves are handsome.
E	*Viburnum cylindricum*	Up to 15 m. Dark green oblong-oval leaves, 0·20 m long and 0·10 m wide, covered with a waxy film.
E	*Viburnum davidii*	0·61–0·91 m. Spreading habit. Dark green, narrowly obovate, leathery leaves, up to 0·15 m long and 0·06 m wide. *Viburnum cinnamomifolium* resembles it in foliage but grows much taller.
	Vitis coignetiae (vine)	Vigorous climbing habit. Dark green ovate leaves, 3–5 lobed, brown-felted on under surface, up to 0·30 m long and 0·20–0·23 m across. Magnificent crimson autumn colours.
	Vitis pulchra (vine)	Climbing habit. Bronzy-green three-lobed leaves, 0·20 m long and 0·11–0·14 m across, are reddish when they first unfurl ; undersides woolly. Gives the most brilliant autumn display of all vines.
	Vitis vinifera Purpurea (Teinturier grape)	Climbing habit. Young leaves claret-coloured, turning deep purple with age ; 3- to 5-lobed, up to 0·15 m long and the same across.

Table 64
Hardy shrubs with coloured foliage
E=evergreen, SE=semi-evergreen

Silver or grey foliage

E	*Artemesia arborescens*	1·22–1·82 m. Finely divided, very silvery foliage. Likes a warm sunny situation.
SE	*Atriplex halimus* (tree purslane)	2·43–3·04 m. Loose, bushy habit ; long silvery leaves on arching branches. Thrives near sea and in well-drained soils.
E	*Cistus 'Silver Pink'* (rock rose)	0·61 m. Silvery-grey foliage ; delicate pink flowers.
E	*Cotoneaster buxifolia vellaea*	0·30–0·61 m. Low, arching and spreading habit ; dainty, frosted grey foliage.
	Cotoneaster wardii	1·82–2·74 m. Erect branching habit ; greyish ovate leaves.
	Cytisus battandieri (broom)	2·43–4·57 m. Three-lobed, shining silvery foliage ; thick clustered racemes of bright yellow flowers with pineapple scent. Fast-growing shrub ; ideal on walls.
E	*Elaeagnus angustifolia* (oleaster)	2·74 m. Silvery-grey, willow-like leaves ; oval, silvery-amber berries.
E	*Erica tetralix Alba Mollis* (cross-leaved heath)	0·23–0·38 m. Pearly-white frosted foliage ; pure white flowers. Unsuitable for very dry areas.
E	*Halimium lasianthum*	0·61–1·06 m. Silvery foliage ; bright yellow flowers, 0·038 m across, with maroon-crimson blotch at base. Ideal for sunny position on rock garden or at front of border.
E	*Helianthemum nummularium 'Henfield Brilliant'* (sun rose)	0·15–0·30 m. Wide-spreading habit. Silvery foliage and deep copper-orange flowers. Thrives best in sunny position ; ideal for banks and dry walls.
E	*Helianthemum nummularium 'White Queen'* (sun rose)	0·15–0·30 m. Silver foliage ; white flowers with primrose centre.
E	*Helichrysum lanatum* (everlasting)	0·46–0·61 m. Broad, cushion habit. Silver-grey lavender-like leaves ; bright lemon-yellow flowers. One of the best grey-foliaged shrubs.
E	*Helichrysum splendidum* (everlasting)	0·76–0·91 m. Broadly rounded habit. Narrow, grey-felted leaves ; clusters of yellow flowers. Useful foliage shrub.
	Hippophae rhamnoides (sea buckthorn)	4·57–6·09 m. Narrow leaves, silvery-white undersides ; masses of translucent orange berries in autumn. Ideal for seaside locations and arid soils. Should be planted in groups so as to include both sexes.
E	*Lavandula spica* and vars. (English lavender)	0·30–0·91 m. Grey foliage ; long spikes of greyish-blue or purple flowers. Thrives in light and well-drained soils ; does best in sunny positions.
E	*Lavandula spica Vera* (Dutch lavender)	0·76–0·91 m. Broad silvery leaves ; long spikes of soft blue flowers. The source of 'oil of lavender'.
E	*Olearia macrodonta* (New Zealand holly)	2·13+ m. Greyish holly-like leaves. White flowers in large terminal clusters, up to 0·15 m across, smother the plant. Excellent for seaside locations ; resistant to gales.
	Perovskia atriplicifolia 'Blue Spire' (Russian sage)	0·91 m. Deeply cut aromatic foliage ; whole plant (except flowers) enshrouded in silvery-white down. Requires sunny position.
	Potentilla arbuscula Beesii	0·30–0·46 m. Bushy habit. Silvery foliage ; buttercup-yellow flowers.
	Potentilla fruticosa Mandschurica (shrubby cinquefoil)	0·30–0·46 m. Silvery foliage ; creamy-white flowers with small yellow centres.
	Rubus thibetanus (bramble)	1·22–1·52 m. Low, wide-spreading habit. Fern-like 'frosted' silver-grey leaves on arching stems with white waxy 'bloom'.
	Salix repens Argentea (willow)	1·22–2·13 m. Wide-spreading, prostrate habit. Silver twigs and foliage ; dainty yellow catkins.
E	*Salvia officinalis* (sage)	0·61–0·76 m. Bushy habit. Grey foliage ; bright wistaria-blue flowers.
E	*Santolina chamaecyparissus Corsica* (lavender cotton)	0·25–0·46 m. Narrow, closely-set, saw-edged 'frosted' white foliage. Small yellow flowers. Ideal for edging or plant containers.
E	*Senecio laxifolius*	0·91–1·22 m. Bushy, spreading habit. Large oval, felted grey leaves. Bright yellow daisy-like flowers.

Yellow foliage

	Acer japonicum Aureum (Japanese maple)	2·43–3·65 m. Classified as a tree but more often adopted as a shrub. Clear gold, lobed leaves retain their colour throughout summer.
E	*Calluna vulgaris Aurea* (Scottish heather or ling)	0·61–0·76 m. Soft golden foliage on feathery sprays, turning pink in winter.
E	*Calluna vulgaris 'Golden Haze'* (Scottish heather or ling)	0·61 m. Bright golden foliage all year round.
	Corylus avellana Aurea (golden nut)	1·82 m. Golden foliage.

continued

Table 64 *Continued*

E	*Erica cineria 'Golden Hue'* (Scotch heath or grey heath)	0·30–0·61 m. Slender, upright shoots covered with soft golden foliage. Ideal for winter effect.
E	*Hedera helix 'Buttercup'* (ivy)	1·82 m. Small, bright golden leaves.
E	*Ilex aquifolium 'Mme Briot'* (holly)	3·96–5·48 m. Golden leaves shaped like those of the common holly.
E	*Ligustrum ovafolium Aureum* (golden privet)	1·52+ m. Bright yellow foliage. Useful for hedging.
	Philadelphus coronarius Aureus (mock orange)	1·22+ m. Bright yellow foliage in spring, turning greenish-yellow ; creamy-white semi-double flowers.
	Sambucus nigra Aurea (golden cut-leaf elder)	1·82–2·13 m. Intense golden foliage, deepening with age. Particularly striking when grown on moist soils.

Purple or red foliage

	Acer palmatum Atropurpureum (Japanese maple)	1·82+ m. Classified as a tree but more often adopted as a shrub. The deeply-divided five-lobed purple leaves are rich red-purple when the sun shines through them.
	Acer palmatum Dissectum Atropurpureum (Japanese maple)	1·82+ m. Very finely-cut purple foliage. Classified as a tree ; picturesquely gnarled, spreading habit.
	Berberis thunbergii Atropurpurea (purple-leaved barberry)	0·91–2·43 m. Rich bronzy-red foliage in spring and summer, turning vivid red in autumn. One of the best purple-foliaged shrubs.
	Corylus maxima Purpurea (purple-leaf filbert)	3·65–6·09 m. Leaves rival those of the copper beech in colour. Purple catkins in early spring. Ideal for planting with the golden nut.
	Cotinus coggygria Foliis Purpureis (Venetian sumach or smoke tree)	1·52–2·43 m. Dark maroon foliage.
E	*Mahonia aquifolium Atropurpurea* (Oregon grape)	0·91 m. Foliage is deep purple for most of the year. Golden-yellow flower spikes.
	Rosa rubrifolia	2·13–2·74 m. Spraying habit. Leaves and stems purple, coated with plum-like bloom. Dainty, pink flowers followed by purple heps. Ideal foliage shrub ; almost thornless.
E	*Salvia officinalis Purpurascens* (purple sage)	0·61–0·91 m. Pastel-shaded soft purple foliage.
	Weigelia florida Foliis Purpureis	1·22–1·52 m. Purple foliage ; rose-pink flowers.

Bluish-green foliage

E	*Bupleurum fruticosum*	1·22–1·82 m. Dark, shiny, blue-green oval leaves ; pale lemon-yellow flowers in large umbels. Excellent evergreen shrub for exposed seaside locations or chalk soils.
	Cercis siliquastrum (Judas tree)	3·04 m. Classified as a tree but often adopted as a shrub. Blue-green oval leaves ; pea-like bright purplish-rose flowers in clusters.
E	*Coronilla glauca*	1·52–1·82 m. Glaucous foliage ; pea-like yellow flowers in clusters. Requires warm sunny position or near S. wall.
E	*Daphne collina*	0·30–0·46 m. Low cushion habit. Oval-shaped, deep bluish-green leaves ; soft purple tubular flowers. Ideal for rock garden ; slow-growing.
	Decaisnea fargesii	Up to 3·04 m. Handsome, large, pinnate bluish-green leaves, 0·61 m long. Panicles of yellow flowers are followed by clusters of long, cylindrical, indigo-blue seedpods. Interesting and uncommon shrub ; likes a rich loamy soil in a shady situation.
E	*Hebe cupressoides* (shrubby speedwell)	1·22–1·52 m. Cypress-like, glaucous-blue foliage, resembling a dwarf conifer. Pale mauve flowers.
E	*Hebe pinguifolia Pagei* (shrubby speedwell)	0·23–0·38 m. Glaucous-blue oval leaves ; pearl-white flower spikes. Excellent for ground cover.
E	*Rhododendron Prostigiatum*	0·23–0·45 m. Dense cushion of blue-green foliage, smoky-purple in winter. Abundance of rich violet flowers. Attractive shrub for rock garden.
E	*Rhododendron 'Sapphire'*	0·61–0·91 m. Compact, cushion-like habit. Bluish-green foliage ; small soft clear blue flowers with dark, contrasting stamens.
	Romneya trichocalyx (Californian tree poppy)	1·52–2·13 m. Blue-green poppy-like foliage ; large white flowers with golden stamens.
	Rosa pimpinellifolia 'Spring Gold'	0·91–1·22 m. Upright but spraying habit. Blue-green foliage ; branches spangled with creamy-yellow semi-double flowers.
E	*Ruta graveolens 'Jackman's Blue'* (rue or herb of grace)	0·61–0·91 m. Compact, bushy habit. Opalescent-blue foliage ; bright yellow flowers. Does best in sunny position on light soils. Makes a good dwarf hedge. Fresh leaves are beneficial to poultry

Table 64 *Continued*

E	*Sarcococca humilis* (Christmas box)	0·30–0·46 m. Dense, spreading habit. Willow-like bluish-green leaves; small white flowers. Excellent as ground cover in shady situations.
	Tamarix pentandra 'Pink Cascade'	3·04–4·57 m. Glaucous-green foliage; long arching sprays of rose-pink flowers.
E	*Vinca minor* 'Miss Jekyll's White' (dwarf periwinkle)	0·15–0·20 m. Deep bluish-green foliage provides a contrast for the small, pure white flowers. Ideal over-carpet to dwarf bulbs in shady situations.
E	*Yucca flaccida* 'Ivory'	0·61–1·22 m. Glaucous lanceolate leaves; ivory-white flowers.

Variegated foliage

E	*Buxus sempervirens Elegantissima* (box)	0·91–1·22 m. Dainty, silver-edged, grey-green leaves which retain their colour even in dense shade.
E	*Buxus sempervirens Marginata* (box)	0·61–0·76 m. Leaves margined with golden-yellow. Useful for low hedges; grows in any soil, including chalk, and shady situations.
	Cornus alba Sibirica Elegantissima (dogwood)	2·43–3·04 m. Soft jade-green leaves with silver edges. One of the best variegated shrubs.
	Cornus alba Spaethii (dogwood)	1·52–1·82 m. Golden-edged foliage which retains its colour throughout season. Should be planted in a sunny situation.
	Cotoneaster horizontalis Variegatus (fishbone cotoneaster)	0·76+ m. Leaves attractively edged with white, suffused with red in autumn.
E	*Daphne odora Aureo-marginata*	0·76–1·22 m. Lanceolate, apple-green leaves have yellow variegations. Reddish-purple flowers. Should be sheltered from N. and E.
E	*Elaeagnus pungens Dicksonii*	2·43–3·04 m. Leaves have a broad band of gold round edges. A more stable variety than *Maculata* since it seldom reverts to green.
E	*Elaeagnus pungens Maculata*	1·52–3·04 m. Striking, golden variegated shrub with yellow in middle of leaves. Slow-growing.
E	*Euonymus fortunei* 'Silver Queen'	0·76–1·06 m. Green leaves variegated with silver; assume pretty rose tints in winter.
E	*Euonymus japonica Aureo-picta* (spindle tree)	1·22–1·52 m. Leathery, polished green leaves with golden variegations.
	Hibiscus syriacus Meehanii (bush mallow)	0·91–1·22 m. Upright-branching habit. Variegated silver foliage. Single mauve flowers.
E	*Ilex altaclarensis* 'Golden King' (holly)	1·82+ m. Broad leaves with bright golden margin, few spines.
E	*Ilex aquifolium Argenteo-marginata* (holly)	1·82+ m. Broad leaves margined silver. Berries well.
	Kerria japonica Variegata (Jew's mallow)	0·91 m. Silver variegated leaves; single yellow flowers.
E	*Osmanthus heterophyllus Variegatus*	1·22–1·52 m. Compact, holly-like shrub; leaves bordered creamy-white. Small white flowers.
E	*Pachysandra terminalis Variegatus* (Japanese spurge)	0·15–0·20 m. Carpeting habit. Leaves variegated with white. Slower spreading than the type.
E	*Pieris japonica Variegata*	0·61–1·82 m. Leaves variegated with creamy-white, flushed pink at first. Slow-growing.
E	*Salvia officinalis Tricolor*	0·38–0·53 m. Sage-grey leaves edged with soft gold and with purple-pink marbling. A lime-loving plant.
E	*Vinca major Maculata* (periwinkle)	0·30–0·61 m. Carpeting shrub. Leaves variegated golden-yellow, diffused outwards towards edges. Light red stems and bright blue flowers.
E	*Vinca major Variegata* (periwinkle)	0·30–0·61 m. Leaves blotched creamy-white.
E	*Vinca minor Aureo-variegata* (dwarf periwinkle)	0·20–0·46 m. Golden variegated leaves.
	Weigelia floridia Variegata	1·82–2·43 m. Silver-edged foliage; rose-pink flowers. Rather slow-growing.
E	*Yucca filamentosa Variegata*	0·61–0·76 m. Foliage less stiff than the type, arching outwards around edge of plant. Soft colourings of sea-green, apple-green, grey and golden stripes all occur on each leaf.

Table 65
Shrubs for providing winter effect
E=evergreen, SE=semi-evergreen

Winter-flowering shrubs

E	*Camellia sasanqua* and vars.	2·13–3·04 m. Twiggy, arching growth. Small pointed leaves ; single or semi-double, white or blush-pink flowers. Needs a north-facing wall in a sheltered position.
	Chimonanthus praecox and vars. (winter sweet)	2·43–3·04 m. Open-branching habit. Pale, waxy, yellow flowers, stained purple at centre, appear on leafless branches. Pointed, willow-like fresh green leaves. Excellent shrub for S. or W. walls.
E	*Clematis cirrhosa*	3·04 m. Coarsely-toothed foliage. Yellowish-white flowers, 0·03 m across. Needs mild conditions to give of its best.
	Cornus mas (cornelian cherry)	3·04–4·57 m. Spreading, open habit. Masses of small, yellow flowers produced on bare branches. Red fruits and bronzy-red autumn tints. Useful for hedging.
	Corylopsis spicata	1·52–2·13 m. Spreading, hazel-like shrub ; roundish, leathery, glaucous leaves. 0·15 m long spikes of primrose-yellow flowers. Needs shelter from frost to avoid damage to blooms.
	Daphne mezereum (mezereon)	1·06–1·37 m. Erect-branching habit. Purplish-red flowers along bare branches, followed by scarlet berries.
	Daphne odora Aureomarginata	0·76–1·22 m. Low, wide-spreading shrub (hardier than the type). Soft reddish-purple flowers in terminal clusters, noted for their scent. Oval, apple-green leaves with marginal variegation.
E	*Erica carnea* and vars. (heath)	0·12–0·30 m. Low and tufted habit forming hummocks of evergreen foliage covered with small spikes of white, pink, red or carmine flowers.
E	*Erica darleyensis*	0·30–0·46 m. Bushy, rounded habit. Soft purple-rose flowers. Does well on lime or chalk.
E	*Erica mediterranea* 'Silver Beads'	0·30–0·46 m. Dense bush covered with white flowers.
E	*Garrya elliptica*	2·43–3·65 m. Bushy habit. Matt, grey-green, oval leaves. Soft jade-green catkins touched with pink. Useful wall shrub for any aspect.
	Hamamelis mollis (Chinese witch hazel)	3·65–5·46 m. Twisted strap-like, bright yellow petals, red at the base. Hazel-like leaves turn golden-yellow in autumn. Attractive contrast achieved by planting *Erica carnea* vars. underneath.
	Jasminum nudiflorum (winter jasmine)	Up to 4·57 m. Long slender, drooping branchlets. Bright yellow flowers. Ideal for walls of any aspect.
SE	*Lonicera purpusii*	2·13–2·74 m. Arching, bushy habit. Creamy-white short, tubular flowers on bare branches.
E	*Mahonia japonica*	1·52–2·13 m. Bushy habit. Bold, pinnate, leathery, soft green foliage. Clusters of long, pendulous racemes of lemon-yellow flowers.
	Osmaronia cerasiformis (osoberry)	0·91–1·52 m. Forms a thicket of erect stems. Drooping racemes of small, greenish-white flowers borne from leaf axils, giving way to purple plum-like fruits later.
E	*Rhododendron* 'Christmas Cheer' (hybrid rhododendron)	0·91–1·22 m. Pink in bud but turning to white on opening.
E	*Ribes laurifolium*	0·61–1·22 m. Spreading habit. Large, leathery, drooping leaves ; hanging racemes of small, greenish-yellow flowers.
E	*Sarcococca humilis* (Christmas box)	0·30–0·46 m. Dense, spreading habit. Willow-like, bluish-green foliage ; small, white flowers followed by blue-black fruits.
	Viburnum bodnantense 'Dawn'	2·74–3·65 m. Vigorous habit. Arching sprays of rose-flushed tubular flowers in rounded clusters freely produced over several weeks and remarkably frost-resistant.
	Viburnum farreri	2·74–3·65 m. Bushy, upright-branching habit. Young growth bronze coloured. White flowers, tinted pink, produced in terminal clusters appear intermittently over a long period. One of the most attractive winter-flowering shrubs.
E	*Viburnum tinus* (laurustinus)	1·82–3·04 m. Bushy, rounded habit, much branched and furnished to the ground. Dark glossy green foliage. Clusters of pinkish buds opening to white flowers throughout the winter.

Shrubs displaying coloured stems

	Berberis dictyophylla	1·82–2·13 m. Graceful shrub. Young red stems covered with white 'bloom'.
	Berberis virescens	1·82–2·74 m. Erect-branched shrub. Bright red stems.
	Cornus alba Sibirica (Westonbirt dogwood)	1·82–2·73 m. Sealing wax red stems. One of the finest shrubs for winter colour.

Table 65 *Continued*

	Cornus stolonifera Flaviramea (yellow-stemmed dogwood)	1·82–2·43 m. Butter-yellow stems. Provides good contrast if planted in conjunction with the red-stemmed dogwoods.
	Kerria japonica (Jew's mallow)	1·22–1·82 m. Close clumps of bright green twigs.
	Leycesteria formosa (flowering nutmeg)	1·82–2·43 m. Vivid, sea-green stout stems.
	Rubus biflorus (white-wash bramble)	1·82–2·74 m. Stems have thick white waxy coating.
	Rubus cockburnianus	2·43–2·74 m. Throws up stems of 1·82–3·04 long coated with a pure white wax.
	Rubus lasiostylus	1·22–1·82 m. Thick bluish-white wax coating on stems.

Shrubs bearing catkins in winter

	Corylus avellana (hazel)	3·04–6·09 m. Forms a dense thicket of erect, much-branched stems. Male catkins 0·03–0·06 m long.
	Corylus maxima Purpurea (purple-leaf filbert)	3·65–6·09 m. Has same habit as *C. avellana*. Male catkins purple, 0·05–0·07 m long.
E	*Garrya elliptica*	2·43–3·65 m. Of bushy habit and rapid growth. Slender, pendent, silky male catkins 0·07–0·15 m long in cold districts but may be 0·30 m or more in warmer localities.
	Salix aegyptiaca	3·65–5·43 m. Shrubby species producing showy yellow catkins.
	Salix caprea (goat willow, palm or sallow)	4·57–6·09 m. Conspicuous native shrub. Female catkins, silvery, 0·05 m or more ; male catkins very silky and yellow provide a yellow glow when caught in late sunlight.
	Salix cinerea oleifolia (common sallow)	1·82–3·04 m. Silky catkins 0·02–0·03 m long.
	Salix discolor (pussy willow)	Up to 7·62 m. Young shoots purplish-brown. Cylindrical male catkins up to 0·03 m long ; female catkins up to 0·07 m long in fruit.
	Salix gracilistyla	1·82 + m. Very showy male catkins, yellowish-grey suffused with red 0·02–0·03 m long.
	Salix smithiana	Up to 6·09 m. Male catkins, 0·02–0·05 m long, produced in abundance.
	Salix viminalis (common osier)	Up to 6·09 m. Catkins up to 0·02 m long.

Shrubs bearing ornamental fruits which persist into winter

	Berberis aggregata (barberry)	1·22–1·52 m. Dense habit. Roundish ovoid fruits, approximately 6 mm long, red with a bloom.
	Berberis gagnepainii (barberry)	1·82–2·43 m. Dense, erect habit. Oval fruit, 9–16 mm long and 6 mm wide, black covered with a blue bloom. Does well on chalk soils.
SE	*Berberis wilsonae* (Mrs Wilson's barberry)	0·61–0·91 m. Semi-prostrate, spreading habit. Coral-red berries borne in clusters.
E	*Cotoneaster dammeri*	0·05–0·07 m. Prostrate habit (shoots root where they touch the soil). Sealing-wax-red globose berries 6 mm wide.
SE	*Cotoneaster distichus*	1·22–2·43 m. Stiff, upright habit. Obovate fruits 13 mm long, bright scarlet.
	Cotoneaster frigida	4·57–6·09 m. Rounded habit. Clusters of pea-like, bright red berries. Fast-growing shrub.
	Cotoneaster horizontalis	0·61–1·37 m. Spreading habit with 'herring-bone' branches. Globose bright red fruits, 5 mm wide.
E	*Cotoneaster wardii*	1·82–2·74 m. Stiff, erect branches. Bright orange-red obovoid berries, 10 mm wide.
	Euonymus europaeus (spindle tree)	3·04–7·62 m. Bright red fruits, 13–19 mm across, open to emit orange-red seeds.
	Euonymus latifolius	3·04–4·57 m. Spreading, loose head of branches. Pendulous fruits, 19 mm across, rich rosy-red, with 4–5 winged lobes which open to emit orange coloured seeds.
	Euonymus sachalinensis	3·04–4·57 m. Of similar habit and closely akin to *E. latifolius*. Rosy-red 4- to 5-lobed fruit with conical top.
E	*Pernettya mucronata* (prickly heath)	0·91–1·52 m. Dense, bushy habit (spreads freely by suckers). Globose fruits, 5–13 mm diameter, varying in colour from white, pink to deep plum-purple. One male plant should be included with every three female plants.
	Rosa moyesii	1·82–3·04 m. Erect stems. Bright crimson bottle-shaped fruits, 38 mm long, crowned by erect sepals.
E	*Stranvaesia davidiana*	3·65–5·48 m. Vigorous, upright-branching with spreading side shoots. Scarlet globose fruits, 6–8 mm wide, borne in clusters.

Table 66
Shrubs displaying autumn colour
E = evergreen, SE = semi-evergreen

Autumn foliage

	Acer circinatum (vine maple)	Up to 9·14 m. Usually little more than a shrub, although classified as a tree. 7- to 9-lobed leaves, 0·07–0·13 m wide, turn orange and crimson.
	Acer ginnala (maple)	Up to 6 m. Large shrub or small tree of bushy habit. 3-lobed leaves, 0·09 m long and 0·06 m wide, turn vivid crimson before falling. This species is one of the best for autumn colour.
	Berberis morrisonensis (Mt Morrison barberry)	Up to 1·82 m. Compact habit. Obovate leaves, 0·01–0·02 m long, in clusters of 3–8, turn brilliant shades of scarlet and gold.
	Berberis thunbergii (Thunberg's barberry)	0·91–2·43 m. Close, compact habit. Obovate or spathulate leaves, 0·01–0·03 m long and crowded in tufts along branches, assume brilliant shades of scarlet-crimson and orange-yellow.
	Berberis virescens (barberry)	1·82–2·74 m. Tall, erect habit. Obovate leaves, 0·02–0·03 m long, turn crimson and orange-yellow.
	Berberis vulgaris (common barberry)	1·82–3·04 m. Erect stems branch and spread outwards at top into graceful, arching form. Oval or obovate leaves, 0·02–0·05 m long in tufts, assume brilliant shades of crimson.
SE	*Berberis wilsonae* (Mrs Wilson's barberry)	0·61–0·91 m. Spreading habit. Oblanceolate leaves, less than 0·02 m long, turn rich red.
	Berberis yunnanensis (Yunnan barberry)	0·91–1·82 m. Rounded habit. Obovate leaves, 0·02–0·04 m long, turn crimson.
	Berchemia racemosa	Up to 4·57 m. Climbing habit (if trained), otherwise spreading and tangled. Ovate leaves, 0·04–0·07 m long, turn clear yellow.
	Celastrus orbiculatus	9–12 m. Strong, vigorous, climbing habit. Shallow-toothed, variably-shaped leaves, 0·05–0·13 m long, turn clear yellow.
	Clethra barbinervis	1·82–3·04 m. Bushy habit. Oval or obovate leaves, 0·05–0·13 m long, often clustered at the end of the twig, assume red and yellow shades. Requires a lime-free soil.
	Cornus baileyi (N. American dogwood)	Up to 3·04 m. Erect-branching habit. Ovate or lanceolate leaves, 0·05–0·13 m long, assume brilliant autumn hues. Usually found on sandy shores; does best on light soils.
	Cornus sanguinea (common dogwood)	1·82–3·65 m. Erect habit. Ovate leaves, 0·04–0·07 m long, turn rich purple.
	Cotinus coggygria and vars (Venetian sumach)	3·65–4·57 m. Round bushy habit. Simple, orbicular or obovate leaves, 0·04–0·07 m long, turn red and orange.
	Cotinus obovatus (*syn. Rhus cotinoides*) (smoke tree)	Up to 4·57 m. Simple obovate or oval leaves, varying much in size but generally 0·05–0·07 m long, turn various shades of scarlet, claret and orange. Does not colour well if grown in a rich soil.
	Cotoneaster bullatus Floribundus	3·04–3·65 m. Somewhat spare habit, few branches. Ovate or oblong leaves, 0·04–0·13 m long, assume rich autumnal hues.
	Cotoneaster dielsiana	1·82 m. Slender, arching or pendulous branches. Ovate leaves, 0·01–0·02 m long, assume brilliant red tints.
	Cotoneaster foveolata	2·43–3·65 m. Oval to ovate leaves, 0·04–0·10 m long, turn brilliant scarlet and orange.
	Cotoneaster lucida	1·82–3·04 m. Bushy habit. Ovate or oval leaves, 0·02–0·05 m long, assume brilliant autumn colours.
	Cotoneaster nitens	Up to 1·82 m. Dense, leafy habit. Roundish-oval leaves, 0·01–0·02 m long, assume brilliant autumn colours.
	Disanthus cercidifolius	2·43–3·04 m. Resembles witch hazel in habit. Ovate to roundish leaves, 0·05–0·11 m long, turn claret-red suffused with orange.
	Enkianthus spp.	0·91–6·09 m. In habit these shrubs are marked by their branches and leaves which are arranged in whorls. The saw-edged oval or lanceolate foliage, up to 0·10 m long, assumes brilliant shades of red and orange which is not excelled in any other group of shrubs. Requires a lime-free soil.
	Euonymus alatus (winged spindle tree)	1·82–2·43 m. Stiff, open habit. Narrowly oval or obovate leaves, 0·02–0·13 m long, turn rich rosy scarlet. Will thrive on chalk.
	Euonymus europaeus (spindle tree)	3·04–7·62 m. Spreading, bushy habit. Narrowly oval leaves, 0·02–0·07 m long, assume bright red hues. Will thrive on chalk.
	Euonymus latifolius	3·04–4·57 m. Loose, spreading habit. Oval, oblong or obovate leaves, 0·07–0·13 m long, turn bright red. Will thrive on chalk.

Table 66 *Continued*

Euonymus sachalinensis	3·04–45·7 m. Of similar habit to that of *E. latifolius* ; leaves take on similar hues. Will thrive on chalk.
Euonymus yedoensis	1·82+ m. Flat-topped habit. Minutely-toothed obovate or oval leaves, 0·05–0·13 m long, turn purplish-red. Will thrive on chalk.
Fothergilla gardenii	0·61–0·91 m. Thin habit and weak, spreading branches. Oval or obovate leaves, 0·02–0·06 m long, turn rich crimson before falling. Requires lime-free soil.
Fothergilla major (American witch hazel)	1·82–3·04 m. Rounded bush with generally erect stems. Roundish oval or broadly ovate leaves, 0·05–0·10 m long, turn orange-yellow. Slow-growing ; requires lime-free soil.
Fothergilla monticola	Up to 1·82 m. Habit more open and spreading than *F. major*. Roundish to obovate leaves, 0·05–0·10 m long, turn red before falling. Slow-growing ; requires lime-free soil.
Oxydendrum arboreum (sorrel tree)	Up to 6 m. Tree-like shrub. Oblong-lanceolate leaves, 0·10–0·20 m long, turn bright crimson. Thrives best in conditions suitable for rhododendrons.
Parrotia persica	May develop into a small tree up to 12 m if trained up, but often treated as a shrub. Horizontal, wide-spreading branches. Ovate, oblong or obovate leaves, 0·06–0·13 m long, assume glorious tints of crimson and gold.
Parthenocissus spp. (Virginia creeper)	Leaves divided into 3–7 leaflets. Brilliant autumn foliage.
Photinia villosa	4·57 m. Sometimes forms a broad-headed small tree. Obovate or ovate-lanceolate leaves, 0·03–0·09 m long, turn scarlet and gold. Leaves of var. *Flava* turn clear yellow, providing contrast with bright red berries.
Rhus copallina (shining sumach)	Up to 1·22 m. Prominently winged, pinnate leaves comprising 9–15 lanceolate leaflets, each 0·05–0·09 m long, turn rich reddish-purple.
Rhus glabra (smooth sumach)	1·22–1·82 m. Pinnate leaves, 0·30–0·46 m long, comprising 15–29 oblong-lanceolate toothed leaflets, each 0·05–0·11 m long, turn a bright rich red.
Ribes americanum (American blackcurrant)	0·91 m. Closely akin to the common blackcurrant. Irregularly-toothed 3- to 5-lobed leaves suffused with brilliant shades of crimson and yellow.
Staphylea bumalda (bladder nut)	0·91–1·82 m. Leaves comprise three leaflets, 0·03–0·07 m long, ovate-lanceolate and sharply toothed, which assume bright autumnal tints.
Stephanandra tanakae	1·82 m. Twiggy habit. Broadly ovate or triangular double toothed leaves, 0·05–0·13 m long, turn deep yellow or orange.
Vaccinium corymbosum (swamp blueberry)	1·22–3·65 m. Forms dense thicket of much-branched, erect stems. Ovate leaves, 0·02–0·09 m long, turn brilliant shades of red.
Viburnum alnifolium (hobble bush)	1·82–3·04 m. Strong-growing shrub with erect central shoots, the lower ones prostrate. Roundish, irregularly-toothed leaves, 0·10–0·20 m long, turn deep claret-red.
Viburnum opulus (guelder rose)	3·04–4·57 m. Native shrub forming a thicket of erect stems. Maple-like leaves, 0·05–0·10 m long, coarsely toothed, assume brilliant hues of red.
Viburnum plicatum tomentosum	3·04–4·57 m. Bushy habit ; horizontal-branching. Ovate or oval, toothed leaves, 0·02–0·03 m long, turn ruby-crimson.
Vitis amurensis (Amurland grape)	Strong-growing, climbing habit. 5-lobed leaves, 0·10–0·25 m wide, assume fine crimson and purple hues.
Vitis coignetiae (ornamental vine)	Vigorous climbing habit. Roundish, 3- to 5-lobed leaves, up to 0·30 m long, display hues of orange and crimson.
Vitis vinifera 'Brandt' (grape vine)	Vigorous climbing habit. Coarsely-toothed 3- to 5-lobed leaves, 0·07–0·15 m wide, assume pink, crimson and orange tints.

Autumn flowers

Caryopteris clandonensis (blue spiraea)	0·91–1·52 m. Violet-blue flower spikes. Ideal subject for mass effect at the front of the border.
E *Ceanothus 'Autumnal Blue'* (Californian lilac)	1·52–1·82 m. Spikes of soft blue flowers.
Ceanothus 'Gloire de Versailles' (Californian lilac)	3·04–3·65 m. Branching habit. Spikes of soft powder-blue flowers.
Ceratostigma willmottianum (plumbago)	0·61–1·22 m. Plumbago-blue phlox-shaped flowers.
Clematis orientalis (orange-peel clematis)	3·04–6·09 m. Climbing habit. Yellow flowers, 38–50 mm across.
Clematis rehderiana	Up to 7·62 m. Climbing habit. Soft primrose-yellow bell-shaped flowers.
Clematis songarica	1·22–1·52 m. Low, rambling shrub. Creamy-white flowers, 19–25 mm across, followed by feathery seed heads.
Clematis viticella	2·43–3·65 m. Climbing habit. Violet, purple or red-purple flowers, 38 mm across.

continued

Table 66 *Continued*

	Clethra alnifolia (sweet pepper bush)	Up to 1·82 m. White flower spikes.
	Elsholtzia stauntonii	1·52 m. Semi-woody plant. Narrow-cylindrical, grey woolly panicles of purplish-pink flowers, 100–200 mm long.
	Erica tetralix (cross-leaved heath)	0·23–0·38 m. Older stems prostrate ; erect young flower-bearing stems with dense heads of rose-coloured flowers.
E	*Erica vagans* (Cornish heath)	0·30–0·61 m. Spreading habit. Spikes, 100–175 mm long, of pinkish-purple flowers.
E	*Escallonia Iveyi*	3·04 m. White flowers, each 13 mm across, in pyramidal panicles, 130–150 mm high, approximately 100 mm wide at base.
E	*Fatsia japonica* (Japanese aralia)	1·82–4·57 m. Spreading habit. Milky-white flowers in panicles of globose heads, each 50–76 mm across.
	Fuchsia magellanica Riccartonii	0·91–1·82 m. Straight, vigorous branches. Sealing-wax red and purple flowers. One of the hardiest and best fuchsias.
	Hibiscus syriacus and vars. (bush mallow)	1·82–3·04 m. Bushy habit. Hollyhock-like flowers, 63–100 mm across, ranging in colour from white, pink and red to mauve and purple.
SE	*Hypericum forrestii*	0·91–1·22 m. Golden-yellow saucer-shaped flowers, 50–63 mm across.
E	*Hypericum galioides*	0·61–0·91 m. Dense, rounded habit. Clusters of small, yellow flowers.
SE	*Hypericum 'Hidcote'*	1·52–2·13 m. Dense, bushy habit. Large, golden-yellow saucer-shaped flowers.
SE	*Hypericum kouytchense*	0·61–1·22 m. Rounded bush. Rich yellow flowers, up to 56 mm across.
	Indigofera gerardiana	0·61–1·22 m (higher if grown against a wall). Graceful, wide-spreading habit. Racemes of pea-shaped, purplish-rose flowers, 13 mm long.
E	*Lonicera alseuosmoides*	Climbing habit. Yellow and purple flowers, 13 mm long.
	Lonicera periclymenum Serotina (late Dutch honeysuckle)	6·09 m. Twining habit. Flowers reddish-purple outside, yellow within. Ideal for N., E. or W. aspects.
E	*Mahonia fortunei*	1·52–1·82 m. Erect, unbranching stems. Bright yellow flowers in erect cylindrical racemes, 50–76 mm long.
E	*Osmanthus heterophyllus*	3·04+ m. Rounded, dense, bushy habit. Small white flowers, 3–4 mm across.
	Perovskia atriplicifolia (Afghan sage)	0·91–1·52 m. Semi-woody plant with long, stiffly erect branches. Violet-blue flowers in spikes, 50–130 mm long.
E	*Pileostegia viburnoides* (evergreen schizophragma)	3·04+ m. Self-clinging climber. Creamy-white flowers, each 9 mm across, are borne in panicles 100–150 mm long.
	Polygonum baldschuanicum (Russian vine)	Vigorous, rampant, twining habit and quick-growing. Innumerable panicles of white flowers, flushed with pink. Ideal for covering unsightly objects.
	Romneya coulteri (Californian tree poppy)	1·22–2·43 m. Semi-shrubby plant with herbaceous stems. White flowers, 100–130 mm across, with golden-yellow centres.
E	*Salvia microphylla* (Graham's sage)	0·91–1·22 m. Rich red flowers, 25 mm long, turn later to magenta-purple.
	Schizandra propinqua sinensis	Twining habit. Yellowish flowers borne in clusters in leaf axils.
	Senecio scandens	Rampant, rambling habit. Small bright yellow, daisy-like flowers in compound panicles. One of the most conspicuous flowering plants in late autumn.
E	*Viburnum tinus* (laurustinus)	1·82–3·04 m. Dense, much-branched shrub bearing white flowers, 6 mm across.

Autumn fruits

	Actinidia chinensis (Chinese gooseberry)	Up to 9 m. Vigorous climber. Edible fruit shaped like a walnut, up to 50 mm long, covered, more or less, with reddish-brown hairs.
E	*Aucuba japonica* (variegated laurel)	1·22–1·52 m. Rounded, bushy habit. Bright scarlet, roundish oval fruits, each 13–16 mm long, borne in compact clusters 50–76 mm long. Include one or more male plants with females to ensure production of berries.
	Berberis aggregata (barberry)	1·22–1·52 m. Dense habit. Masses of small, ovoid red fruits, each 6 mm long, with a bloom. Fruits persist into winter.
	Berberis 'Barbarossa' (barberry)	1·52–1·82 m. Vigorous shrub. Scarlet berries in profusion.
	Berberis 'Bountiful' (barberry–a hybrid of *B. wilsonae*)	0·91 m. Spreading habit and arching branches. Clusters of coral-red berries.
	Berberis 'Buccaneer' (barberry–raised from *B. aggregata*)	1·82 m. Erect habit. Large clusters of pearl-pink berries which later turn bright red.
	Berberis chitria (barberry)	3·04–3·65 m. Spreading habit. Oval-oblong dark red fruits, up to 13 mm long, with bloom on them, hang in drooping bunches.
	Berberis koreana (Korean barberry)	Up to 1·82 m. Small, ovoid, bright red, waxen berries.

Table 66 *Continued*

	Berberis morrisonensis (Mt Morrison barberry)	Up to 1·82 m. Compact shrub. Globose-ovoid, somewhat translucent red berries, 10 mm long, in clusters.
	Berberis rubrostilla (barberry)	1·82 m. Compact shrub. Oblong-ovoid translucent coral-red fruits, 16 mm long, are borne 2–4 on a main stalk and hang in profusion. The fruits are among the largest in the genus.
	Berberis vulgaris (common barberry)	1·82–3·04 m. Erect habit, arching at the top of stems. Bright red ovoid berries, up to 13 mm long, occur in profusion.
SE	*Berberis wilsonae* (Mrs Wilson's barberry)	0·61–0·91 m. Spreading habit. Small, roundish coral or salmon-red, somewhat translucent, berries are borne in profusion. Fruits persist into winter.
	Billardiera longiflora	Up to 1·82 m. Twining habit. Brilliant deep blue, oblong-globular berries (dry capsules), 19–25 mm long.
	Callicarpa bodinieri giraldii	1·82–2·74 m. Erect habit. Globose glossy rose-madder fruits, 3–5 mm across.
	Celastrus spp. (staff tree)	3·65–12 m. Shrubs of spreading habit, many of them vigorous climbers. Large clusters of golden-yellow, pea-size fruits which, when ripe, open to reveal scarlet-coated seeds.
	Clerodendron trichotomum (glory tree)	3·04–6·09 m. Bushy habit. Bright blue, pea-size berries, later turning black, are surmounted by crimson calyces whose lobes have become fleshy and spreading.
	Cotoneaster bullata	3·04–3·65 m. Long, arching branches bear bright red, cherry-like or pear-shaped fruits, 8 mm across.
E	*Cotoneaster buxifolia*	0·30–0·61 m. Low-spreading shrub. Obovoid, orange-red fruits, 6 mm long, create a brilliant display.
E	*Cotoneaster conspicuus Decorus*	0·91–2·43 m. Semi-prostrate branches studded with shiny, bright scarlet globose berries, 10 mm across.
	Cotoneaster 'Cornubia' (a hybrid of *C. frigida*)	Up to 6·09 m. Spreading habit. Enormous crops of bright red berries weigh down the branches.
E	*Cotoneaster dammeri*	0·05–0·07 m. Prostrate shrub with creeping stems which trail over the ground shaping themselves to the contours. Globose, coral-red fruits, 6 mm across, persist into winter.
	Cotoneaster frigida	4·57–6·09 m. Rounded shrub. Bright red, pea-like fruits borne in large clusters persist into winter.
	Cotoneaster horizontalis (fishbone cotoneaster)	0·76–1·37 m. Flat habit ; horizontally-spreading branches studded with small, scarlet berries which persist into winter.
E	*Cotoneaster microphylla*	0·61–0·91 m. Low-spreading shrub, often of prostrate habit. Scarlet-red berries, 6 mm across.
SE	*Cotoneaster prostrata*	0·91–1·22 m. Long arching branches spray out fanwise from base. Scarlet-red berries, 13 mm long, in abundance, persist into winter.
SE	*Cotoneaster salicifolia*	Up to 4·57 m. Spreading habit. Bright red berries, 6 mm across, in clusters.
	Cotoneaster wardii	1·82–2·74 m. Stiff, erect habit. Bright orange-red berries, 8–10 mm long, in abundance, persist into winter.
	Elaeagnus multiflora	1·82–3·04 m. Wide-spreading habit. Edible, deep orange, scaly fruits, 13 mm long.
	Elaeagnus umbellata	3·65–5·48 m. Wide-spreading habit. Globose fruits, 6–8 mm across, are silvery at first becoming ox-blood red later.
	Euonymus europaeus (spindle tree)	3·04–7·62 m. Spreading, bushy habit. Rosy-red capsules and orange-red seeds, 13–19 mm across. Fruits persist into winter.
E	*Gaultheria miqueliana*	0·23–0·30 m. Low and spreading habit. Globose, edible, white or pink berries, 8 mm wide.
E	*Gaultheria shallon* (salal or shallon)	0·61–1·82 m. Forms dense thicket of stems. Dark purple, edible berries, 8 mm wide.
	Gaulthettya wisleyensis	0·91 + m. Bushy habit. Laden with bunches of ox-blood red, globose fruits, 6 mm wide.
	Hippophae rhamnoides (sea buckthorn)	4·57–6·09 m. Sometimes forms a tree. Orange coloured, ovoid berries, 6–8 mm long.
SE	*Hymenanthera crassifolia*	0·91–1·82 m. Dense, rounded habit with stiff, flat-growing branches. Globular berries, 6 mm diameter, are pure white, often stained with purple and abundantly produced.
	Hypericum androsaemum (tutsan)	0·61–0·91 m. Bushy habit. Pea-size, berry-like capsules are purplish-red at first, turning black later.
	Lycium spp. (box thorn)	1·22–3·04 m. Loose habit. Globose, oval or ovoid orange or scarlet fruits, up to 25 mm long, are very ornamental.

continued

Table 66 *Continued*

	Menispermum canadense (Canadian moonseed)	3·65–4·57 m. Fast-growing climber of twining habit. Clusters of blackcurrant-like fruits.
	Pernettya mucronata and vars. (prickly heath)	0·91–1·52 m. Forms dense low thicket. Globose berries, up to 13 mm across, range in colour from pure white to deep plum purple.
	Photinia villosa	4·57 m. Scarlet, haw-like fruits. Does not thrive on shallow, chalky soils.
E	*Pyracantha spp.* (firethorn)	1·82–6·09 m. Globose fruits, 5–8 mm across, are bright red, orange or yellow, borne in clusters. Many of them persist into winter.
	Rhus typhina (stag's-horn sumach)	7·62 m. Flat-topped shrub or tree. Female plants bear showy fruit clusters thickly covered with crimson hairs.
	Rosa canina (dog rose)	1·82–3·65 m. Strong-growing habit. Ovoid or roundish bright red fruits with sepals fallen away.
	Rosa davidii (David's rose)	2·43 m. Erect-branching habit. Scarlet-red, bottle-shaped fruits, 19 mm long.
	Rosa moyesii	1·82–3·04 m. Sturdy habit; erect stems. Bottle-shaped, bright crimson fruits, 38 mm or more long, crowned by erect persistent sepals.
	Rosa nitida	Up to 0·61 m. Erect stems. Globose, scarlet bristly fruits, 8 mm wide.
	Rosa pendulina	0·61–1·22 m. Robust shrub devoid of prickles. Bright red, narrowly pear-shaped fruits, 19–25 mm long, surmounted by erect, persistent sepals.
	Rosa roxburgii (burr rose)	1·82–2·43 m. Stiff-branched shrub. Tomato-shaped, spiny yellowish-green fruits, 38 mm diameter.
	Rosa rugosa (Ramanas rose)	1·22–1·82 m. Bright red, tomato-shaped fruits crowned with the sepals.
	Rosa villosa (apple rose)	1·22–1·82 m. Sturdy habit. Apple-like crimson fruits, 25–38 mm long.
	Salix bockii (willow shrub)	0·91–1·52 m. Catkins produced from leaf-axils of current year's growth, up to 38 mm long.
E	*Skimmia spp.*	0·30–1·22 m. Slow-growing shrubs whose chief attraction is their bright red berries which are borne in clusters. To obtain fruits of *S. japonica* one male plant should be planted with every six females.
E	*Stranvaesia spp.*	3·65–6·09 m. Generally globose fruits, 6–8 mm wide, ranging in colour from pale to brilliant red.
	Symphoricarpus rivularis (snowberry)	0·91–1·82 m. Forms dense thickets of erect stems which are weighed down by masses of marble-like snow-white berries, 13 mm or more across.
	Viburnum betulifolium	Up to 3·04 m. Long branches bent over by weight of bunches of red currant-like berries, 6 mm long, which persist into winter. One of the best berrying shrubs.
E	*Viburnum davidii*	0·61–0·91 m. Low, compact habit. Bright turquoise, narrow oval fruits, 6 mm long, on female plants.
	Viburnum opulus (Guelder rose)	3·04–4·57 m. Forms a thicket of erect stems. Bright red, currant-like fruits which persist into winter.

Table 67
Shrubs which tolerate atmospheric pollution
E=evergreen

E	*Aucuba japonica* (variegated laurel)	1·22–1·52 m. Oval, glossy green, leathery leaves; bright scarlet berries borne on female plants. Tolerates deep shade.
	Berberis spp. and vars. (barberry)	0·30–3·65 m. Large group of deciduous and evergreen shrubs. Thorny stems; orange or yellow flowers followed, in many cases, by red, purple or black fruits. Colourful foliage displayed by some deciduous types in autumn.
	Colutea arborescens (bladder senna)	1·82–2·43 m. Pinnate foliage; pea-shaped bright yellow flowers followed by bladder-like pods.
	Cornus spp. (dogwood)	1·52–3·04 m. Foliage of varying shades of green, some variegated. Coloured stems provide interesting winter effect.
	Corylus avellana (hazel nut)	3·04–6·09 m. Long yellow catkins provide winter interest. Golden foliage tints in autumn.
	Cotoneaster spp.	0·30–3·65 m. Ornamental deciduous and evergreen shrubs varying greatly in their habit. Small, white inconspicuous flowers followed by red or black berries.

Table 67 *Continued*

	Daphne mezereum (mezereon)	1·06–1·37 m. Erect-branching habit. Purplish-red flowers before leaves appear ; scarlet berries later. Must not be pruned.
	Deutzia scabra and vars.	3·04–3·65 m. Erect-branching habit. White or pinkish flowers in erect panicles.
	Elaeagnus spp. (oleaster or wild olive)	1·52–5·48 m. Deciduous and evergreen shrubs with silvery scales on undersides of leaves. Excellent wind-resister.
E	*Escallonia spp.* (Chilean gum box)	1·82–5·48 m. Rich glaucous green saw-edged foliage. Terminal clusters of hawthorn-like or waxy tubular white, pink or red flowers.
E	*Euonymus japonica* (evergreen spindle tree)	1·22–1·82 m. Leathery, polished green leaves. Thrives in sun or shade ; makes a useful hedge plant.
	Forsythia spp.	1·22–3·65 m. Open habit. Small, golden-yellow bell-like flowers. Thrives in sun or partial shade ; does not object to exposed situation.
E	*Hedera helix* and vars. (common ivy)	Climbing habit ; makes excellent ground cover. Leaves of some are variegated.
	Hypericum spp.	0·30–1·82 m. Evergreen and deciduous flowering shrubs. Bright yellow single flowers. Thrive in any soil and hot dry situations.
	Hydrangea paniculata Grandiflora	1·82–2·43 m. Semi-arching habit. Broad, tapering panicles of white flowers, fading to pink. One of the best late-flowering shrubs.
E	*Ilex aquifolium* and vars. (common holly)	3–15 m. Glossy green leaves with prickly edges, some variegated. Bright red berries.
	Jasminum nudiflorum (winter jasmine)	Up to 4·57 m. Long, slender, drooping branchlets. Bright yellow flowers. Ideal winter-flowering shrub for walls of any aspect.
	Kerria japonica (Jew's mallow)	1·22–1·82 m. Bushy, wide-spraying habit. Light green lanceolate leaves ; bright green twigs. Arching branches wreathed with golden-yellow 'buttercup' flowers.
E	*Ligustrum spp.* (privet)	1·22–3·65 m. Larger-leaved useful for foliage effect and smaller-leaved for hedging. Will thrive in shady situations.
	Philadelphus spp. (mock orange)	0·91–4·57 m. Fragrant flowering shrubs, often with long arching branches. White or yellowish-white flowers, some of them with large purplish-crimson blotches at base of petals. Broadly-oval, saw-edged leaves.
E	*Pyracantha spp.* (firethorn)	1·82–6·09+ m. Smallish narrow, oval foliage, usually saw-edged. Masses of small, white flowers followed by attractive red, orange or orange-yellow berries. Useful wall shrub for any aspect.
E	*Rhododendron spp.* and vars.	0·15–12 m. One of the most handsome group of flowering shrubs. Thrive best in positions sheltered from N. and E. winds.
	Ribes spp. (flowering currant)	0·91–2·43 m. Large genus of spring-flowering shrubs, thriving in most soils in shade or semi-shade.
	Sambucus nigra and vars. (common elder)	4·57–9·14 m. Vigorous habit. White flowers followed in autumn by purple or black berries.
E	*Senecio spp.* (groundsel or ragwort)	0·15–1·52 m. Many resemble the olearias with their silvery-white foliage and daisy-like flowers. Thrive in sunny, sheltered positions.
	Spiraea spp.	0·30–5·48 m. Deciduous flowering shrubs providing interest over a long period. Small individual flowers are arranged in closely packed heads, white, pink or crimson.
E	*Skimmia japonica*	0·91–1·52 m. Broadly dome-shaped bush ; aromatic glossy leaves. Large scarlet berries borne on female plants. Plant one male to every three female plants. Thrives in shade.
	Symphoricarpus albus (common snowberry)	1·82–2·43 m. Rounded leaves ; pink flowers followed by white 'mothball' berries. Thrives in dense shade.
	Viburnum spp.	0·45–4·15 m. Deciduous and evergreen shrubs with white or pinkish flowers followed, in many cases, by handsome fruits and brilliant autumn foliage.
	Vitis spp. incl. *Ampelopsis* and *Parthenocissus* (ornamental vines ; Virginia creepers)	Climbing shrubs, notable for their wealth of variation in foliage form. Among the most brilliant autumnal tints. Self-clinging species ideal for walls ; tendril-climbing species suitable for pergolas, etc.

Table 68
Shrubs for seaside locations
E=evergreen, SE=semi-evergreen

SE	*Atriplex halimus*(tree purslane)	2·43–3·04 m. Loose, bushy habit. Arching branches clothed with long silvery leaves. Makes a first-class hedge.
E	*Aucuba japonica* (variegated laurel)	1·22–1·52 m. Oval, glossy green, leathery leaves ; bright scarlet berries borne on female plants. Tolerates deep shade.
E	*Berberis darwinii* (barberry)	1·82–2·43 m. Deep green, glossy foliage. Masses of rich orange-yellow flowers ; bluish-purple round berries.
	Buddleia davidii and vars.	1·82–3·65 m. Long-pointed, finely toothed foliage, white-felted beneath. Large panicles of pink, violet blue, purple or white flowers.
SE	*Buddleia globosa* (orange ball tree)	2·43–3·04 m. Robust shrub of loose habit. Long, tapering, dark green leaves, grey underneath. Orange-yellow ball-like flowers.
SE	*Bupleurum fruticosum*	1·22–1·82 m. Bluish-green foliage. Small, yellow flowers in clusters make an effective contrast.
E	*Cistus laurifolius* (rock rose)	1·22–1·82 m. Stiff, erect, open habit. Dark, dull green foliage ; white flowers 0·06–0·07 m across. Considered the hardiest species.
E	*Cistus pulverulentus* (rock rose)	0·45–0·61 m. Compact habit. Sage-green foliage ; vivid rose-pink flowers.
	Colutea arborescens (bladder senna)	1·82–2·43 +m. Pinnate foliage ; pea-shaped bright yellow flowers followed by bladder-like pods.
	Cornus sanguinea (common dogwood)	1·82–3·65 m. Erect habit. Dull, dark green leaves assume a rich reddish-purple in autumn. Useful background plant but of undistinguished character.
E	*Corokia virgata*	3·04–4·57 m. Twiggy habit. Shoots slightly zig-zagged but not tortuous or interlaced. Dark, glossy green foliage ; small yellow flowers, followed by orange-yellow egg-shaped fruits.
E	*Cotoneaster lactea*	2·43–3·65 m. Bold, olive-green foliage on arching branches ; creamy-white flowers, followed by large clusters of orange-red berries which persist throughout winter. Ideal for hedging or wall planting ; quickly makes an effective barrier.
	Escallonia spp. (Chilean gum box)	1·82–5·48 m. Rich glaucous green, saw-edged foliage. Terminal clusters of hawthorn-like or waxy tubular white, pink or red flowers.
E	*Euonymus fortunei* (spindleberry)	0·76–1·06 m. Procumbent habit. Oval/ovate leaves 0·02 m long. Good for providing ground cover in sun or shade.
E	*Euonymus japonica* and vars. (evergreen spindle tree)	1·22–1·82 m. Leathery, polished green leaves. Thrives in sun or shade ; makes a useful hedge plant.
	Fuchsia magellanica Riccartonii	0·91–1·82 m. Straight, vigorous branches. Scarlet and purple flowers. One of the hardiest species.
E	*Garrya elliptica*	2·43–3·65 m. Bushy habit. Matt, oval, grey-green leaves. Abundant clusters of soft jade green catkins touched with pink appear on male plants.
E	*Griselinia littoralis*	3·04–6·09 m. Rounded habit. Apple-green leathery foliage. Chalk-tolerant ; dislikes heavy clays.
E	*Hebe spp.* (speedwell)	0·30–1·52 m. Evergreen ornamental summer and autumn-blooming shrubs. Handsome spikes of white, pink, red, purple or blue flowers.
	Hippophae rhamnoides (sea buckthorn)	4·57–6·09 m. Open branching habit when young, becoming dense and rounded with age. Narrow leaves, silvery-white underneath. Abundance of translucent orange berries.
	Hydrangea macrophylla and vars.	0·91–1·22 m. Dense, rounded shrub. Large, oval, saw-edged leaves. Rounded heads or flat, lacy corymbs of white, pink or blue florets.
E	*Hypericum calycinum* (Rose of Sharon)	0·30–0·46 m. Low, dense and creeping habit. Leaves take on purplish shade in autumn. Large bright yellow flowers. Excellent ground cover for sun or shade.
	Ilex aquifolium and vars. (common holly)	3–15 m. Glossy green leaves with prickly edges, some variegated. Bright red berries.
E	*Lavandula spica* (Old English or Mitcham lavender)	0·30–0·91 m. Bushy habit (if trimmed annually). Grey foliage ; long spikes of pale greyish-blue flowers. Thrives in full sun.
	Leycesteria formosa (flowering nutmeg)	1·82–2·43 m. Vivid sea-green stems and deep green pointed leaves. Clusters of flesh-pink flowers with pendulous purple bracts.

Table 68 *Continued*

E	*Ligustrum ovalifolium* (oval-leafed privet)	1·82+m. Small oval leaves. Makes ideal hedge plant.
E	*Lonicera nitida* (Chinese bush honeysuckle)	0·91–1·52 m. Erect habit. Small, oval, glossy green leaves. Used extensively for hedging.
	Lycium chinense Carnosum (Duke of Argyll's tea tree)	1·52–2·13 m. Rambling habit. Vigorous and quick-growing. Purple flowers, followed by scarlet berries.
E	*Mahonia aquifolium* (Oregon grape)	0·91–1·52 m. Foliage bronze in spring, turning red or plum-purple in autumn. Broad, golden-yellow flower spikes, followed by purple plum-like berries. Makes a dense carpet under trees.
E	*Olearia albida* (daisy bush)	3·04+ m. Dark green oval leaves, white-felted underneath ; white flower heads. One of the best hedging plants for maritime exposure.
E	*Olearia haastii* (daisy bush)	0·91–2·43 m. Bushy, spreading habit. Small dark green heart-shaped leaves ; masses of white daisy-like flowers.
E	*Olearia traversii*	4·57+ m. Oval dark green foliage, silver-felted underneath, silver-felted young shoots. Considered one of the best and fastest-growing evergreens for forming wind-breaks in S.W. coastal areas ; will thrive in sand.
E	*Phillyrea angustifolia*	Up to 3·04 m. Compact, rounded, olive-like bush with linear leaves, small, dull white flowers, followed by roundish-oval blue-black fruits.
	Rosa canina (dog rose)	1·82–3·65 m. Strong-growing shrub with prickly stems. White or pinkish flowers in clusters, bright red egg-shaped fruits. One of the commonest and most beautiful of wild shrubs.
	Rosa pimpinellifolia (Scotch rose or burnet rose)	0·91–22·1 m. Dwarf bush with creeping roots ; erect, short-branched stems covered with slender spines. Leaves closely set on branches. White or pale pink solitary flowers ; dark brown globose fruits.
	Rosa rubiginosa (sweet briar)	1·82–3·65 m. Erect bush with arching branches ; prickly stems. Single pink flowers borne in profusion ; bright red egg-shaped fruits.
E	*Rosmarinus officinalis* (rosemary)	1·52–1·82 m. Aromatic grey-green linear leaves, felted on undersides. Useful herb.
	Sambucus nigra (common elder)	4·57–9·14 m. Pinnate foliage. Yellowish or dull-white flowers, followed by shiny black globose berries. Ideal for out-of-the-way damp, dark corners where little else will thrive.
E	*Senecio reinoldii*	1·52+ m. Forms a dense dome of shiny, roundish-ovate leathery leaves. White-felted young shoots ; small flower heads in terminal clusters of corymbs 0·12–0·25 m wide.
E	*Skimmia japonica*	0·91–1·52 m. Broadly dome-shaped bush, aromatic glossy leaves. Large scarlet berries borne on female plants. Plant one male to every three female plants. Thrives in shade.
	Spartium junceum (Spanish broom)	1·82–3·04 m. Gaunt habit. Almost leafless rushlike stems ; pea-shaped yellow flowers. Thrives on light or chalky soil.
	Symphoricarpus albus (common snowberry)	1·82–2·43 m. Rounded leaves ; pink flowers, followed by white 'mothball' berries. Thrives in dense shade.
	Tamarix spp.	1·22–3·65 m. Deciduous or evergreen graceful shrubs with scale-like or feathery leaves. Very hardy and quick-growing. Thrive in sun ; ideal for quickly forming a good thick high hedge.
	Ulex europaeus (common gorse)	1·22–1·52 m. Spiny, scale-like foliage. Masses of yellow, broom-like flowers.
E	*Viburnum tinus* (laurustinus)	1·82–3·04 m. Bushy, rounded habit, much branched and furnished to the ground. Narrowly-ovate dark glossy-green leaves. White flowers ; deep blue ovoid fruits.
	Yucca gloriosa (Adam's needle)	Up to 2·43 m. Usually a single, thick, fleshy stem crowned with many straight, spine-tipped leaves. Creamy-white flowers in large panicles 1·22 m high.
	Yucca recurvifolia	0·91–1·82 m. Broad bluish-green sword-shaped leaves bend downwards from the middle. Bold spikes of large, pendent cream flowers.

Table 69
Shrubs for game coverts*
E=evergreen, SE=semi-evergreen

Shrubs to provide food

	Cornus alba (dogwood)	1·52–3·04 m. Forms a wide-spreading thicket of crimson-red stems. Whitish or tinted steel-blue 'peas'.
	Cotoneaster frigida	4·57–6·09 m. Vigorous and spreading habit. Large mid-green leaves ; bright crimson berries in autumn.
E	*Cotoneaster microphyllus*	0·61–0·91 m. Slender, rigid branches shrouded in dark green leaves. Large, bright crimson berries.
SE	*Cotoneaster simonsii*	2·43–3·65 m. Vigorous, straight-branching and semi-upright habit. Fine autumn foliage. Scarlet berries in profusion, often remaining into early spring.
	Leycesteria formosa (flowering nutmeg)	1·82–2·43 m. Vivid sea-green stems ; deep-green pointed leaves. Flesh-pink flowers with purple bracts. Small gooseberry-like fruits.
SE	*Ligustrum vulgare* (common privet)	3·04 m. Oval foliage ; white flowers in panicles. Small black berries.
	Mahonia aquifolium (Oregon grape)	0·91–1·52 m. Foliage assumes spring and autumn tints. Golden-yellow flower spikes, followed by purple plum-like berries.
	Rosa rugosa (Ramanas rose)	1·22–1·82 m. Vigorous, rounded shrub. White flowers followed by red heps.
	Rubus idaeus (wild raspberry)	1·22–1·52 m. Large red, juicy fruits.
	Sambucus nigra (common elder)	4·57–9·14 m. Vigorous habit. White flowers, followed by purple or black berries in autumn.
	Symphoricarpus albus (common snowberry)	1·82–2·43 m. Rounded leaves ; pink flowers, followed by white 'mothball' berries.

Shrubs to provide cover

E	*Hypericum calycinum* (Rose of Sharon)	0·30–0·46 m. Low, dense habit. Leaves take on a purplish shade in autumn. Large, bright yellow flowers.
E	*Lonicera nitida* (Chinese bush honeysuckle)	0·91–1·52 m. Erect habit. Small, oval, glossy green leaves.
E	*Lonicera pileata*	0·61–0·91 m. Horizontal branches. Bright green foliage.
E	*Prunus laurocerasus* (common laurel)	Up to 6·09 m. Vigorous dense habit. Dark green leathery foliage.
E	*Prunus lusitanica* (Portugal laurel)	3·04–4·57 m. Dense, bushy habit. Oval, deep green leaves.
E	*Rhododendron ponticum*	2·43–3·65 m. Dark green leathery foliage ; mauve flowers.
E	*Ruscus aculeatus* (butcher's broom)	0·91–1·22 m. Forms dense clumps ; stiff, spiny leaves which, on female plants, sprout bright red marble-like fruits.

*See also Table 95, page 249.

Table 70
Shrubs which grow in shady positions
*E=evergreen; *may be planted under trees*

	Acer palmatum (Japanese maple)	Up to 6 m. Classified as a tree but more often adopted as a shrub. Deeply 5- to 9-lobed leaves, long-pointed and double-toothed.
E	*Aucuba japonica* (variegated laurel)	1·22–1·52 m. Oval, glossy green, leathery leaves. Bright scarlet berries borne on female plants. Tolerates smoky atmosphere.
	Azalea spp. and vars.	0·76–1·82 m. Large group of deciduous and evergreen shrubs which form part of the rhododendron genus but are often treated separately in catalogues. Colourful display of flowers ranging from white, yellow, pink, orange, red to deep purple.
	Berberis spp. and vars. (barberry)	0·30–3·65 m. Large groups of deciduous and evergreen shrubs. Thorny stems ; orange or yellow flowers—some of them showy. Red, purple or black fruits borne by many in autumn when some of the deciduous types display gorgeously-tinted foliage.
E	*Buxus spp.* (box)	0·46–2·43 m. Mainly of erect habit. Small, rounded leaves. Yellowish-green insignificant flowers ; grown principally for its dense foliage.
E	*Camellia spp.* and vars.	2·13–3·65 m. Group of shrubs requiring soil conditions similar to those for rhododendrons. Shiny, somewhat leathery leaves. Flowers large and showy, white, pink or red.
	Chaenomeles spp. (Japonica or flowering quince)	0·91–3·65 m. Much-branched and generally spreading habit. Flowers range in colour from white to scarlet and are followed by quince fruits in autumn.
E	*Choisya ternata* (Mexican orange blossom)	1·82–2·13 m. Glossy, finger-like, aromatic foliage. Clusters of white, star-like flowers. Requires shelter from cold winds.
	Cornus alba and vars. (dogwood)	1·52–3·04 m. Foliage of varying shades of green, some variegated. Coloured stems provide interesting winter effect.
	Cotoneaster dammeri	0·05–0·07 m. Prostrate habit ; growths trail over ground in all directions, shaping themselves to the contours. Globose, coral-red fruits persist into winter.
	Cotoneaster microphylla	0·61–0·91 m. Low-spreading, often prostrate habit. Glossy green, small, oval leaves. Scarlet-red berries.
	Cotoneaster salicifolius 'Autumn Fire'	0·10–0·15 m. Spreading habit. Bold, willow-like foliage ; clusters of red berries.
	Cotoneaster simonsii	2·43–3·65 m. Vigorous, straight-branching and semi-upright habit. Foliage turns shades of crimson and scarlet in autumn ; scarlet berries in profusion, often remaining into early spring. Excellent hedging shrub ; attractive to bees.
	Elaeagnus spp. (oleaster or wild olive)	1·52–5·48 m. Group of deciduous and evergreen shrubs with silvery scales on underside of leaves. Excellent wind resisters.
E	*Euonymus japonica* and vars. (evergreen spindle tree)	1·22–1·82 m. Leathery, polished green leaves. Useful hedging plant.
E	*Fatsia japonica* (Japanese aralia)	1·82–4·57 m. Spreading habit. Shiny, bright green, palmate leaves, up to 0·35 m wide, divided into 7–9 segments. Useful for seaside locations.
E	*Gaultheria shallon* (salal or shallon)	0·61–1·82 m. Forms dense thicket of stems. Dark purple, edible berries, 8 mm wide.
	Genista tenera (Madeira broom)	3·65 m. Grooved stems. Small grey-green, lanceolate leaves. Yellow flowers in terminal clusters.
E	*Hedera helix* (ivy)	Self-clinging shrub. Thick, leathery, oval 3- to 5-lobed leaves, 0·10 m long. Greenish-yellow flowers in clusters ; black berries.
	Hypericum calycinum (Rose of Sharon)	0·30–0·46 m. Low, dense habit ; large, bright yellow flowers and striking boss of stamens. Sometimes fails during first year, but hardy when established.
E	*Ilex spp.* (holly)	1·82–15 m. Variety of shrubs ranging from the small, prickly-leaved types to those having smooth leaves. Golden-leaved varieties are not suitable for growing under trees.
	Jasminum nudiflorum (winter jasmine)	Up to 4·57 m. Whip-like stems. Bright yellow flowers, November–February.
E	*Kalmia latifolia* (American calico bush)	2·43–3·04 m. Glossy green, ovate-lanceolate leaves 0·12 m long. Pink flowers in clusters.
E	*Laurus nobilis* (sweet bay)	2·43–3·04 m. Dense, pyramidal habit. Aromatic leaves ; stands clipping well. Thrives in coastal areas.
E	*Ligustrum spp.* (privet)	1·22–3·65 m. Larger-leaved species useful for foliage effects and smaller-leaved for hedging.
E	*Leycesteria formosa* (flowering nutmeg)	1·82–2·43 m. Vivid, sea-green stout stems. Oval, long-pointed leaves, 0·15 m long. Purplish funnel-shaped flowers with claret-coloured bracts.

continued

Table 70 *Continued*

E	*Lonicera pileata*	0·61–0·91 m. Spreading, purplish stems. Small glossy green, oval, blunt-ended leaves. Yellowish-white minute flowers followed by translucent bluish-purple berries. Excellent for woodland planting.
	Mahonia aquifolium (Oregon grape)	0·91–1·52 m. Foliage bronze in spring, turning red or plum-purple in autumn. Broad spikes of golden-yellow flowers followed by purple plumlike berries. Makes a dense carpet.
E	Osmanthus spp.	1·22–6·09 m. Spine-toothed leaves. Small, white or yellowish flowers in small clusters followed by dark blue berries.
E	*Pachysandra terminalis (Japanese spurge)	0·15–0·20 m. Dense, carpeting habit. Bright green foliage. Spikes of greenish-white flowers borne in late winter.
E	*Pernettya mucronata and vars. (prickly heath)	0·91–1·52 m. Forms dense, low thicket, stems suckering freely. Small, oval, spiny-pointed, toothed, leathery leaves. Globose berries, up to 13 mm across, range in colour from pure white to deep plum-purple.
	Philadelphus spp. (mock orange)	0·91–4·57 m. Fragrant flowering shrubs, often with long, arching branches. Broadly oval, saw-edged leaves. White or yellowish-white flowers, some of them with large purplish-crimson blotches at base of petals.
E	Phillyrea decora (jasmine box)	1·52–3·04 m. Hard, firm, ovate-lanceolate leaves, 0·12 m long, with bevelled edges. Small, greenish-white flowers, in axillary clusters, followed by blue-black berries.
E	Prunus laurocerasus (common laurel)	3·04–4·57 m. Vigorous, dense habit. Dark green leathery leaves, 0·15 m long. Short, erect racemes of minute white flowers, followed by black fruits.
E	Prunus lusitanica (Portugal laurel)	Up to 6·09 m. Dark glossy green leaves, 0·12 m long, with wavy margins. Long, erect racemes of white flowers.
E	Pyracantha spp. (firethorn)	1·82–6·09+ m. Smallish, narrow oval foliage, usually saw-edged. Masses of small, white flowers followed by attractive red, orange or orange-yellow berries.
E	Rhododendron spp.	0·15–12 m. Large group of lime-hating flowering shrubs. Generally leathery-type foliage. Associate happily with deep-rooting plants but should not be planted in close competition with hungry trees.
	Ribes spp. (flowering currant)	0·91–2·43 m. Large genus of spring-flowering shrubs. Palmately lobed, toothed leaves. White, greenish or purple flowers. Juicy berries.
	Rubus spp. (bramble)	0·61–3·04 m. Shrubs of ornamental value either for flowers, fruit, foliage or colour of stems. Thrive in poorest soils ; many make useful ground cover.
E	Ruscus aculeatus (butcher's broom)	0·91–1·22 m. Forms dense clumps ; stiff, spiny leaves which, on female plants, sprout bright red marble-like fruits.
	*Sambucus nigra (common elder)	4·57–9·14 m. Vigorous habit. White flowers followed by purple or black berries in autumn.
E	Sarcococca spp. (Christmas box)	0·61–1·82 m. Glossy green, leathery leaves ; small white flowers followed by purple or bluish-black berries.
	Skimmia japonica	0·91–1·52 m. Broadly dome-shaped bush ; aromatic, glossy leaves. Large scarlet berries borne on female plants (three female to one male should be planted).
	*Symphoricarpus albus (common snowberry)	1·82–2·43 m. Rounded leaves ; pink flowers followed by white 'mothball' berries.
E	*Viburnum tinus (laurustinus)	1·82–3·04 m. Bushy, rounded habit, much branched and furnished to the ground. Dark glossy green foliage. Clusters of pinkish buds opening to white flowers throughout the winter.
E	*Vinca spp. (periwinkle)	0·30–0·61 m. Plants of carpeting habit with white or blue flowers.

Table 71
Shrubs for dry, sunny positions
E = evergreen, SE = semi-evergreen

E	*Artemisia abrotanum* (southernwood or lad's love)	0·90–1·22 m. Old-fashioned shrub with soft, greyish green, aromatic, fern-like foliage. Small, yellow flower heads.
SE	*Atriplex halimus* (tree purslane)	2·43–3·04 m. Loose, bushy habit with arching branches of ovate, pointed, silvery leaves. Greenish, insignificant flowers.
	Berberis spp. (barberry)	0·30–3·65 m. Some of the deciduous forms of this large group thrive in dry, sunny locations. Thorny stems ; orange or yellow flowers followed by red, purple or black fruits. Some display outstanding autumn foliage tints.
	Caryopteris clandonensis and vars. (blue spiraea)	0·91–1·52 m. Spreading and bushy habit. Grey-green foliage (remains dormant until late April). Violet-blue flower spikes.
E	*Cistus corbariensis* (rock rose)	0·91–1·22 m. Low-spreading habit. Fresh green crenulated leaves. Saucer-like flowers with yellow blotch at base. One of the hardiest *Cistus* ; thrives on chalky soils.
	Colutea arborescens (bladder senna)	1·82–2·43+ m. Pinnate foliage ; pea-shaped bright yellow flowers, followed by bladder-like pods.
	Cytisus spp. (broom)	0·03–4·57 m. Lime-tolerant group of exceptionally free-flowering shrubs which do best in sandy soils. Poor transplanters.
	Genista spp. (broom)	0·02–4·57 m. Closely related to *Cytisus*. Foliage is insignificant but wiry stems are wreathed in small, yellow flowers.
	Hedysarum multijugum	1·22 m. Long pinnate foliage. Upright racemes of rosy magenta pea-shaped flowers.
E	*Helianthemum nummularium* and vars. (sun rose)	0·15–0·30 m. Low-spreading habit. Dainty saucer-shaped, crimped flowers in a variety of colours.
E	*Helichrysum lanatum* (everlasting)	0·46–0·61 m. Broad cushion habit. Silver-grey lavender-like foliage ; bright lemon flowers.
	Hippophae rhamnoides (sea buckthorn)	4·57–6·09 m. Open-branching habit when young, becoming dense and rounded with age. Narrow leaves, silvery-white underneath. Translucent orange berries in abundance. Plant in groups so as to include both sexes.
	Hypericum spp. (St John's wort)	0·30–1·82 m. Evergreen and deciduous shrubs. Bright yellow single flowers.
E	*Lavandula spp.* (lavender)	0·30–0·91 m. Grey linear foliage. Spikes of greyish-blue or violet-blue flowers.
E	*Olearia spp.* (New Zealand daisy bush)	0·91–6·09 m. Stiff, leathery leaves, usually green above and white, silvery or grey beneath. Small flower heads, white or purplish, in branched clusters.
	Perovskia atriplicifolia (Afghan sage)	0·91–1·52 m. White-felted shoots and small, oval, grey-green leaves. Spikes of violet-blue flowers.
SE	*Phlomis fruticosa* (Jerusalem sage)	0·91 m. Broad-spreading and bushy habit. Grey-green sage-like foliage. Spikes of bright yellow hooded flowers.
	Potentilla spp. (shrubby cinquefoil)	0·15–1·52 m. White or yellow single flowers like those of small, single roses, displayed over a long period.
	Rosa pimpinellifolia and vars. (Scotch or burnet rose)	0·91–1·22 m. Creeping roots ; short-branched, erect, thorny and bristly stems. Leaves deep green, closely set on branches. Pink, white or yellow flowers.
E	*Rosmarinus officinalis* (rosemary)	1·52–1·82 m. Loose habit (unless trimmed). Aromatic grey-green linear leaves, felted on underside. Small, bluish-lilac flowers.
	Rubus spp. (bramble)	0·61–3·04+ m. Group of shrubs noted for their prickly or bristly stems which are often long and trailing ; many have stems with a thick, white waxy coating. Flowers white or pink, generally in terminal racemes or panicles. Fruits are blackberry-like.
E	*Santolina spp.* (lavender cotton)	0·25–0·61 m. Narrow, closely-set, saw-edged leaves on semi-woody stems. Masses of small, yellow flower heads.
E	*Senecio spp.*	0·15–1·52 m. Important group of grey-leaved shrubs with thick leaves, usually felted on one or both sides. Yellow or white daisy-like flowers.
	Spartium junceum (Spanish broom)	1·82–3·04 m. Erect, reed-like growth. Linear bluish-green leaves. Pea-shaped yellow flowers.
	Tamarix spp.	1·22–3·65 m. Deciduous or evergreen, graceful shrubs with scale-like or feathery leaves. Very hardy and quick-growing. Ideal for quickly forming a good thick, high hedge.
	Ulex europaeus (gorse)	1·22–1·52 m. Spiny, scale-like foliage. Masses of yellow, broom-like flowers.

Table 72
Shrubs for moist (not waterlogged) sites

Arundinaria spp. (bamboo)	1·22–7·62 m. Group of shrubs with straight cylindrical stems and whorled branchlets. Admirable for screen planting but E. winds may cause temporary browning of foliage.
Cornus alba and vars. (dogwood)	1·52–3·04 m. Forms a wide-spreading thicket of crimson-red stems which provide winter interest.
Cornus stolonifera and vars. (red osier dogwood)	0·91 m. Prostrate suckering stems. Dark green, ovate leaves.
Leycesteria formosa (flowering nutmeg)	1·82–2·43 m. Vivid sea-green stems and deep-green pointed leaves. Clusters of flesh-pink flowers with pendulous purple bracts.
Philadelphus spp. (mock orange)	0·91–4·57 m. Fragrant flowering shrubs, often with long, arching branches. White or yellowish-white flowers, some of them with large purplish-crimson blotches at base of petals. Broadly oval, saw-edged leaves.
Phyllostachys spp. (bamboo)	2·43–6·09 m. Group of shrubs with woody, zigzagged stems, flattened above joints.
Salix spp. (shrubby willow)	0·15–3·04+ m. Catkin-bearing shrubs, some of which may develop into trees. Many have attractively coloured bark.
Sambucus spp. and vars. (elder)	2·13+ m. Compound foliage and clusters of white flowers. The common species *S. nigra* and its varieties are useful shrubs for industrial locations.
Viburnum opulus and vars. (guelder rose)	3·04–4·57 m. Bushy habit. Foliage takes on rich red tints in autumn. Flat cymes of white flowers followed by translucent red berries which persist long into winter.

Table 73
Shrubs for peaty (acid) soils
E=evergreen

E	*Calluna vulgaris* and vars. (Scottish ling heather)	0·61–0·76 m. Compact, upright habit. Minute, scale-like leaves. Terminal spikes of white, pink, crimson or purple flowers.
E	*Camellia spp.*	1·82–3·65 +m. Shiny, somewhat leathery foliage. Large, showy flowers of white, pink or red, borne singly or in few-flowered clusters. Do best in light shade, sheltered from cold winds.
E	*Clethra alnifolia Paniculata* (sweet peppermint)	1·22–1·82 m. Erect branches, arching at tips, clothed with fairly long, fresh green leaves. Long, pointed white flower spikes.
E	*Daboecia cantabrica* (Irish heath)	0·30–0·61 m. Bushy and spreading habit. Dark, glossy green foliage, white-felted below. Terminal racemes of pendent, bell-shaped purple or white flowers.
	Enkianthus spp.	0·91–6·09 m. In habit these shrubs are marked by their branches and leaves which are arranged in whorls. The saw-edged foliage assumes brilliant tints in autumn (not excelled in any other group of shrubs).
E	*Erica spp.* (heath or heather)	0·12–0·61 m. Distinct among hardy shrubs for smallness and great number of their linear leaves. Spikes of tiny flowers of white or various shades of purple.
E	*Gaultheria spp.*	0·15–1·82 m. Zigzagged branchlets. Toothed, ovate leaves. Small, pinkish white flowers followed by white, pink, red, dark blue or black berries.
E	*Kalmia latifolia* (American calico bush)	2·43–3·04 m. Glossy green ovate-lanceolate leaves, 0·12 m long. Pink flowers in clusters.
E	*Pieris spp.*	0·61–6·09 m. Attractive glossy green foliage. Showy panicles of urn-shaped, white flowers in terminal racemes or panicles.
E	*Rhododendron* (inc. *Azalea*) *spp.*	0·15–12+ m. Very large group of shrubs, some developing into trees, with conspicuous, many-scaled buds which open into showy, bell-shaped or funnel-shaped flowers, solitary, in pairs or terminal clusters.
E	*Skimmia spp.*	0·30–1·22 m. Small group of shrubs with leathery, aromatic foliage, radially grouped. Small, white, yellow or yellowish white flowers in terminal panicles followed by bright red or dull crimson berries.
	Vaccinium spp.	0·15–3·65 m. Group of evergreen and deciduous shrubs bearing small white, or pinkish flowers followed by greenish-yellow, red, purple or bluish-black berries.

Table 74
Shrubs for clay soils
E = evergreen, SE = semi-evergreen

E	*Berberis darwinii* (barberry)	1·82–2·43 m. Deep green, glossy foliage. Masses of rich orange-yellow flowers ; bluish-purple round berries.
E	*Berberis stenophylla* (barberry)	3·04–3·65 m. Arching habit ; dark, narrow foliage. Cascades of orange-yellow flowers. Unequalled dog-proof hedge.
	Berberis thunbergii and vars. (barberry)	0·91–2·43 m. Broad, bushy habit. Pale straw-coloured flowers, suffused red ; bright red fruits. Foliage turns brilliant red in autumn. Superb hedging subject and unsurpassed in its display of coloured foliage.
	Cotoneaster frigida	4·57–6·09 m. Vigorous and spreading habit. Large, mid-green leaves ; bright crimson berries in autumn.
SE	*Cotoneaster simonsii*	2·43–3·65 m. Vigorous, straight-branching and semi-upright habit. Foliage turns shades of crimson and scarlet in autumn ; scarlet berries in profusion, often remaining into early spring. Excellent hedging shrub ; attractive to bees.
	Forsythia intermedia and vars.	2·43–3·65 m. Erect-branching with semi-pendulous side shoots. Broad-petalled rich yellow flowers.
	Forsythia viridissima	1·52–2·43 m. Erect-stemmed ; lanceolate leaves. Yellow flowers which appear later than most other forsythias.
	Kerria japonica (Jew's mallow)	1·22–1·82 m. Bushy, wide-spraying habit. Light green lanceolate leaves ; bright green twigs. Arching branches, wreathed with golden-yellow 'buttercup' flowers.
E	*Mahonia aquifolium* (Oregon grape)	0·91–1·52 m. Foliage bronze in spring, turning red or plum-purple in autumn. Broad, golden-yellow flower spikes followed by purple plum-like berries. Makes dense carpet under trees.
	Philadelphus spp. (mock orange)	0·91–4·57 m. Fragrant flowering shrubs, often with long, arching branches. White or yellowish-white flowers, some of them with large purplish-crimson blotches at base of petals. Broadly-oval saw-edged leaves.
E	*Pyracantha spp.* (firethorn)	1·82–6·09+ m. Smallish, narrow oval foliage, usually saw-edged. Masses of small, white flowers followed by attractive red, orange or orange-yellow berries. Useful wall shrub for any aspect.
	Ribes sanguineum and vars. (flowering currant)	1·82–2·43 m. Vigorous erect habit. Five-lobed, tooth-edged foliage ; rosy-red flowers.
	Rosa spp. and vars. (rose)	0·61–1·52+ m.
	Salix spp. (shrubby willow)	0·15–3·04+ m.
	Sambucus canadensis (American elder)	2·13–5·48 m. Vigorous, low-branching habit. Pure white flowerheads 0·10–0·20 m across. Excellent for providing quick effect in any soil.
	Sambucus nigra and vars. (common elder)	4·57–9·14 m. Vigorous habit. White flowers followed in autumn by purple or black berries. The type is widely distributed along hedgerows, especially on chalk soils.
	Viburnum opulus (guelder rose)	3·04–4·57 m. Bushy habit. Foliage takes on rich red tints in autumn. Flat cymes of white flowers followed by red translucent berries which persist long into winter.

Table 75
Shrubs for chalky soils
E=evergreen, SE=semi-evergreen

E	*Aucuba japonica* (variegated laurel)	1·22–1·52 m. Oval, glossy green, leathery leaves ; bright scarlet berries borne on female plants. Tolerates smoky atmosphere and deep shade.
	Berberis spp. and vars. (barberry)	0·30–3·65 m. Large group of deciduous and evergreen shrubs. Thorny stems ; orange or yellow flowers—some of them showy. Red, purple or black fruits borne by many in autumn when some deciduous types display gorgeously-tinted foliage.
	Buddleia spp.	2·74–6·09 m. Flowering shrubs much loved by butterflies. Valuable for quick effect. Flowers usually carried in nodding panicles.
E	*Buxus sempervirens* (common box)	0·61–2·43 m. Luxuriant dark green foliage. Much used for clipped specimens.
	Chaenomeles speciosa and vars. (japonica)	0·61–2·43 m. Much-branched, spreading habit. Flowers vary from pure white to pink, vermilion and scarlet ; edible quince fruits in autumn. Ideal as wall shrubs for any aspect.
E	*Choisya ternata* (Mexican orange blossom)	1·82–2·13 m. Glossy, finger-like, aromatic foliage ; clusters of star-like white flowers. Needs a warm corner or wall.
E	*Cistus spp.* (rock rose)	0·45–2·43 m. Flowers resemble those of a large single rose. Thrive on poor dry soils and are hardier when starved.
	Clematis spp. and vars.	Climbing habit. Flowers of a wide range of colours. Thrive in full sun with cool root run.
	Cornus spp. and vars. (dogwood)	1·52–3·04 m. Foliage of varying shades of green, some variegated. Many have coloured stems, providing winter effect.
SE	*Cotoneaster franchetii*	2·43–3·65 m. Bushy, arching habit. Graceful branches clothed with sage-green leaves. Fire-red berries in profusion in autumn.
	Cotoneaster simonsii	2·43–3·65 m. Vigorous, straight-branching and semi-upright habit. Foliage turns shades of crimson and scarlet in autumn ; scarlet berries in profusion, often remaining into early spring. Excellent hedging shrub ; attractive to bees.
	Deutzia spp. and vars.	0·91–3·65 m. Most are of upright growth with lanceolate or longish-oval, saw-edged leaves. Clusters of white, rose or purple flowers. Thrive best in sheltered positions.
E	*Elaeagnus pungens* and vars. (oleaster or wild olive)	1·52–3·04 m. Vigorous, spreading habit. Narrow oval or lanceolate leaves, some variegated. A good evergreen for providing shelter. Tolerant of most conditions.
E	*Erica carnea* and vars. (heath)	0·12–0·30 m. Forms hummocks of evergreen foliage covered with small spikes of white, pink, red or carmine flowers. Useful winter-flowering plant.
E	*Erica darleyensis* (heath)	0·30–0·46 m. Bushy and rounded habit. Masses of soft purple flowers.
E	*Erica mediterranea* and vars. (heath)	0·30–0·46 m. Dense habit. Rose-red flowers.
E	*Escallonia spp.* and vars. (Chilean gum box)	1·82–5·48 m. Rich glaucous green saw-edged foliage. Terminal clusters of hawthorn-like or waxy tubular white, pink or red flowers.
E	*Euonymus japonica* (evergreen spindle tree)	1·22–1·82 m. Leathery, polished green leaves. One of the best evergreens for coastal or town planting ; thrives in sun or shade. Useful hedge plant ; stands clipping well.
	Forsythia spp.	1·22–3·65 m. Open habit. Small, golden-yellow bell-like flowers. Thrives in sun or partial shade and does not object to an exposed site.
E	*Hebe spp.* (speedwell)	0·30–1·52 m. Ornamental flowering shrubs, invaluable for seaside planting. Purple, mauve, red, pink or white flower spikes.
	Hibiscus syriacus and vars. (shrubby mallow)	1·82–3·04 m. Upright branching habit. Small, hollyhock-like flowers. Thrives in full sun.
SE	*Hypericum beanii*	0·91–1·22 m. Neat habit. Good autumn foliage colour. Saucer-shaped golden-yellow flowers 0·05–0·63 m across.
E	*Ilex aquifolium* and vars. (common holly)	3–15 m. Glossy green leaves with prickly edges, some variegated. Bright red berries.
	Kerria japonica (Jew's mallow)	1·22–1·82 m. Bushy, wide-spraying habit. Light green lanceolate leaves ; bright green twigs. Arching branches wreathed with golden-yellow 'buttercup' flowers.
E	*Laurus nobilis* (sweet bay)	2·43–3·04 m. Dense pyramidal habit. Aromatic leaves ; stands clipping well. Thrives well in coastal areas and in shade.
E	*Ligustrum spp.* (privet)	1·22–3·65 m. Larger-leaved species useful for foliage effects and smaller-leaved for hedging. Will thrive in shade.
E	*Mahonia aquifolium* (Oregon grape)	0·91–1·52 m. Foliage bronze in spring, turning red or plum-purple in autumn. Broad, golden-yellow flower spikes followed by purple plum-like berries. Makes dense carpet under trees.

Table 75 *Continued*

E	*Osmanthus heterophylla* and vars.	1·52–3·04 m. Compact habit. Holly-like foliage, some variegated ; small white flowers.
	Philadelphus spp. (mock orange)	0·91–4·57 m. Fragrant flowering shrubs, often with long, arching branches. White or yellowish-white flowers, some with large, purplish-crimson blotches at base of petals. Broadly-oval saw-edged leaves.
	Potentilla spp. (shrubby cinquefoil)	0·15–1·52 m. White or yellow single flowers like those of small, single roses, displayed over a long period.
	Ribes spp. (flowering currant)	0·91–2·43 m. Large genus of spring-flowering shrubs, thriving in most soils in shade or semi-shade.
E	*Rosmarinus officinalis* (rosemary)	1·52–1·82 m. Aromatic, grey-green linear leaves, felted on undersides. Useful herb.
	Rubus spp. (bramble)	0·61–3·04 m. Shrubs of ornamental value either for flower, fruit, foliage or colour of stems. Thrive in poorest soils and in shade ; many make useful ground cover.
	Sambucus spp. (elder)	2·13+ m. Compound foliage and clusters of white flowers. The common species, *S. nigra* and its varieties, are useful shrubs for industrial locations.
E	*Senecio laxifolius*	0·91–1·22 m. Bushy, spreading habit. Oval to lanceolate grey leaves, 0·03–0·05 m long ; white felted shoots. Ideal foliage plant for dry soil in sunny situations.
	Spiraea spp.	0·30–5·48 m. Deciduous flowering shrubs providing interest over a long period. Small, individual flowers are arranged in closely packed heads, white, pink or crimson in colour.
E	*Ulex europaeus* and vars. (common gorse)	1·22–1·52 m. Spiny, scale-like foliage. Masses of yellow broom-like flowers.
	Viburnum spp.	0·45–4·15 m. Deciduous and evergreen shrubs with white or pinkish flowers followed, in many cases, by handsome fruits and brilliant autumn foliage.

BULBOUS PLANTS

Bulbous and tuberous plants are distinguished by two main characteristics : each possesses an underground food store and during the dormant period is capable of being preserved out of the ground.

The term 'bulb' in its widest sense includes corms, tubers, rhizomes and tuberous roots, all of which are described below (see also BS 3975 : Part 4 : 1966).

Bulb

A complete plant, ovoid or conical in shape, comprising a modified shoot with a disc-like basal plate supporting roots on its underside. The several layers of graded fleshy leaves (scales) on its upper surface are often enveloped in protective dry leaves (tunic) and provide protection for the following year's bud.

In all but a few cases bulbs are classed with perennial plants although different in root structure. A bulb stores most of its food before it begins to flower whereas a perennial plant, as such, stores few nutrients, relying on those absorbed directly from the soil in order to make growth.

The small bulbs, known as 'bulbils', are those borne in the axils of the leaves of some plants ; 'bulblets' are the small bulbs which develop close to a mature bulb.

Examples: narcissus, tulip.

Corm

A swollen underground stem of rounded or flattened shape with a basal plate and roots. Unlike most bulbs, a corm is not a perennial and once flowering is completed it begins to shrivel up, becoming a mere husk. Simultaneously with this process a new corm is formed above the old one to take its place. In many cases a number of cormlets (spawn) are formed and these provide the basis for the following year's flowers. Corms are neither scaly nor tunicated.

Examples: crocus, gladiolus.

Tuber

A more or less thickened underground stem of roundish or irregular shape (sometimes of knobby appearance) which serves as a storehouse for the plant. It has no tunic but a rough leathery type of skin and is furnished with latent buds (in the form of eyes) from which growth develops ; its roots are widespread.

Examples: cyclamen, begonia.

Rhizome

A thickened creeping stem (thinner and more elongated than a tuber) which spreads widely underground, developing roots and flowering or producing leafy shoots at fairly definable intervals and then spreading further beyond them.

Examples: flag iris, *Anemone nemorosa.*

Tuberous roots

Modified true roots. The buds are seldom supported by the roots themselves but are to be found around the collar or base of the stem.

Examples: Dahlia, Ranunculus (includes the common buttercup).

The value of bulbs in the outdoor environment

There are bulbs for every season, displaying an amazing range of colour, shape and size. By introducing them into a layout, particularly one that is newly constructed, a rewarding floral array is provided in the early stages of development when other plants are not yet mature or producing their blooms. The bulb-blooming sequence is shown in Table 76.

Bulbous plants range from the smallest, such as crocus, snowdrop and chionodoxa (which may reach less than 25 mm in height), to the largest lilies whose blooms tower above the tallest man. Some of these plants are ideal subjects for particular uses or situations: tulips and hyacinths for formal bedding; narcissi, expecially some of the trumpet daffodils, naturalised in grass; bluebells in woodland. Carpets of these and other spring bulbs provide one of the glories of the sylvan scene and many of the smaller exotic species display their blooms to advantage when set among rocks or grown in planting bowls and window boxes. Others thrive quite happily in drifts set among shrubs and at the front of herbaceous borders. The water's edge makes an interesting setting for some of the moisture-loving plants, such as the rhizomatous *Iris sibirica.*

Selecting bulbs for various purposes

Although many bulbs thrive in a variety of situations, some are happier in certain types of environment.

Grass

The selection of bulbs for naturalising is dependent upon the nature of the grass and its maintenance. In rough grass which may be cut only two or three times a year selection should be from among the taller, more robust narcissus species such as the golden trumpet daffodils and short-capped white forms of the *poeticus.*

In shorter grass the older varieties of daffodil with their shorter stems and tough constitution or the large-flowered hybrid crocus are best. Colchicums are among some of the more showy autumn bulbs but they must not be planted anywhere within the reach of grazing animals. The yellow varieties of crocus are best kept apart from the purple and white ones but the latter may be mixed together. The smaller bulbs are suitable for growing in ornamental lawns that are regularly maintained or beneath trees where the grass is sparse and therefore receives less attention.

It is generally desirable that the bulbs should be allowed to die back naturally to preserve their vigour for the next flowering season. Inevitably this means an untidy array of plants for part of the season (until May for crocuses and June for daffodils) and it is advisable, therefore, to site the bulbs in areas which are of lesser visual importance and where there is no need for early grass-cutting.

Woodland

In woodland, as in grass, the best effects are obtained by selecting and massing one variety. Apart from winter aconites, few bulbs thrive in deep shade but many tolerate semi-shade or an open glade provided the soil is not too dry. Under beech trees *Cyclamen neapolitanum* is the only satisfactory plant because its leaves are active during winter and early spring before the beech tree comes into leaf.

Aconites, crocuses and snowdrops form the main display early in the year; by careful selection of species and varieties a display of snowdrops may be extended over several months. These are supplemented by other woodland bulbs such as fritillaries, bluebells, daffodils and anemones. Lilies make superb subjects and colchicums are ideal for autumn display at the edge of the woodland.

Wild garden

The native plant Solomon's seal (*Polygonatum multiflorum*) and its companion the false Solomon's seal (*Smilacina*) are naturally at home in the wild garden. Wake Robin (*Trillium*) also naturalises well with ferns and native plants.

Rock garden

Many of the smaller bulbs provide colour at those times of the year when few rock plants are at their best. Two of the hardiest free-flowering plants for the rockery—meadow saffron of spring (*Bulbacodium vernum*) and Glory of the

Table 76
Hardy bulbous plants and their flowering seasons

Botanical name	Common name	Height (mm)	Jan	Feb	Mar	Apr	May	June	July	Aug	Sep	Oct	Nov	Dec	Planting time	Form
Allium		150–300					—	—	—	—					Sept–Nov	bulb
Anemone	Windflower	76–300			—	—									Oct, Feb–Mar	rhizome
Bulbocodium		76–150			—										Sept–Oct	bulb
Camassia	Quamash	600–900						—	—						Oct or Feb	bulb
Chionodoxa	Glory of the Snow	100–150		—	—										Sept–Oct	bulb
Colchicum	Autumn crocus	76–230			—	—				—	—	—			July–Sept	corm
Convallaria majalis	Lily of the valley	150				—	—								Sept–Oct	rhizome
Corydalis		76–300			—	—									March	rhizome
Crocosmia	Montbretia	600–1200								—	—				Mar–April	corm
Crocus		19–100	—	—	—	—					—	—			July, Sept–Oct	corm
Cyclamen	Sowbread	76–150	—	—	—	—						—	—		Mar, June–July	tuber
Eranthis	Winter aconite	50–100	—	—	—										Sept–Oct	rhizome
Erythronium	Dog's tooth violet	150–300				—	—								Aug–Sept	bulb
Fritillaria	Fritillary	100–460				—	—								Sept–Oct	bulb
Galanthus	Snowdrop	150–300	—	—	—	—							—	—	Sept–Nov; Mar–April	bulb
Hyacinthus	Hyacinth	100–200				—	—								Sept–Oct	bulb
Iris tall bearded		460–900					—	—	—						July, Oct, Mar	rhizome
dwarf bearded		100–380					—	—							July, Oct, Mar	rhizome
beardless		100–1520	—	—	—		—	—	—						Oct, Mar	rhizome
Japanese		380–760						—	—						Oct, Mar	rhizome
cushion		50–600					—								Oct	rhizome
bulbous rooted		25–600	—	—	—						—		—		Aug–Oct	bulb
Ixia	African corn lily	300–460					—	—	—						Sept–Jan	corm
Leucojum	Snowflake	100–300					—	—			—	—			Aug–Nov	bulb
Lilium	Lily	230–1830						—	—	—	—				Aug–Sept, Oct–Nov	bulb
Muscari	Grape hyacinth	150–200		—	—	—	—	—							Aug–Nov	bulb
Narcissus																
daffodils		300–600			—	—									Aug–Nov	bulb
miniature & spp.		76–300	—		—	—						—			Aug–Nov	bulb
other types		400–600				—	—								Aug–Nov	bulb
Ornithogalum		300–600			—	—	—	—	—						Aug–Nov	rhizome
Oxalis	Wood sorrel	25–230					—	—	—	—	—				Aug–Nov	rhizome or tuber
Pancratium	Corsican lily	300–600					—	—							Oct–Nov or Mar	bulb
Polygonatum	Solomon's seal	300–900		—	—	—	—	—							Oct, Feb–Mar	rhizome
Puschkinia	Striped squill	100–150		—	—	—									Oct–Nov	bulb
Ranunculus	Buttercup ; Crowfoot	250–360					—	—	—						Dec–April	rhizome
Roscoea		150–300						—	—	—	—				March	tuberous root
Schizostylis	Kaffir lily	300–900									—	—	—		Oct–Mar	bulb
Scilla	Squill	76–380		—	—	—	—	—	—	—	—	—			Aug–Nov	bulb
Sternbergia		150										—			Oct–Nov	bulb
Trillium	Wood lily	150–600				—	—								Aug–Oct	tuberous root
Tulipa	Tulip															
tall-growing spp.		250–860				—	—								Sept–Nov	bulb
fosteriana		300–600				—									Sept–Nov	bulb
greigii		180–360				—									Sept–Nov	bulb
kaufmanniana		100–200			—										Sept–Nov	bulb
botanical spp.		76–460		—	—	—									Sept–Nov	bulb
Zephyranthes	Zephyr lily	130–300								—					Aug–Nov	bulb

Jan Feb Mar Apr May June July Aug Sep Oct Nov Dec

Snow (*Chionodoxa*)—bloom early in the year and are best planted in small clumps. The daintier and smaller botanical tulip species, like *T. linifolia* (and its companion *T. batalinii*), *T. hageri*, *T. tarda* and *T. urumiensis* and the miniature species of narcissi give a fine display in the sunnier positions along with other sun-loving plants such as *Oxalis*, Californian hyacinth (*Triteleia*), harlequin flower (*Sparaxis*), crocus species and the choicer species of bulbous iris, e.g. *I. danfordiae* and *I. histrioides Major*.

The semi-shady positions on the rockery should be reserved for *Fritillaria*, *Puschkinia*, snowdrops, *Sarana* (ideal for planting in clay soils) and those which do not enjoy full sunlight. Many of these plants are also at home in the shrub bed or border. The more vigorous bulbs, such as the grape hyacinths (*Muscari*), are ideal for growing through carpeting perennials but (as in the case of some of the alliums and *Anemone nemorosa*) should be kept apart from the choicer plants because of their capacity to seed so readily. *Crocus speciosus* and *C. tomasinianus* also tend quickly to swamp other crocuses if planted nearby and the large summer foliage of the colchicums is liable to smother smaller plants when it dies off.

Shrubbery
Shrubs serve as a backcloth and protection for many of the bulbs that also thrive in the shadier parts of the rock garden, referred to above. *Ipheion uniflorum* is a pretty little plant which is ideal for planting in drifts between shrubs (or in a pocket in the rock garden) but is not suitable for exposed situations; Star of Bethlehem (*Ornithogalum*) is an adaptable, hardy choice for naturalising in shrubberies, woodland or grass. The snakeshead fritillaries (*F. meleagris*) make charming groups in semi-shaded positions. Snowdrops, grape hyacinths and crocuses are also useful subjects for planting in drifts.

Herbaceous border
A narrower border sheltered at the foot of a warm wall is an excellent home for the more desirable, though less hardy, species of bulbs which include the Guernsey lily (*Nerine bowdeni*), sea lily (*Pancratium maritimum*), Californian hyacinth (*Triteleia*) and Belladonna lily (*Amaryllis belladonna*).

In the more open herbaceous border the taller kinds of *Narcissus*, *Tulipa*, *Camassia*, *Gladiolus* and bulbous iris provide a range of colour, and for the front of the border the smaller bulbous plants suggested for the shrub bed make an added attraction.

Plant containers and window boxes
Selection should be from among the shorter-stemmed varieties unless large containers are used. For these, daffodils, tulips and hyacinths are the most popular. If the larger daffodils are planted they need to be removed once their display is over in order to make room for other plants that are to follow. The miniature wild types (species) e.g. the hoop petticoat daffodil (*Narcissus bulbocodium*) do not present the problem of concealing dying foliage since their small leaves are less conspicuous when the plant fades.

Some of the shorter-stemmed tulip species are ideal. They include the *kaufmanniana* tulips and the *greigii* hybrid tulips, whose dazzling scarlet or deep golden-yellow flowers are in most cases further enhanced by the beautifully marked and mottled leaves.

The tulip family comprises a number of sections, each distinguishable by its habit and time of flowering; the earliest blooms are those of the botanical species. They include the *kaufmanniana*, *greigii* hybrids and the *fosteriana* tulips. Although taller (except the variety 'Rockery Beauty' which is a dwarf sport from this particular group) the latter group are quite suitable for larger containers. The early double tulips (250–380 mm) are also useful and make a fine display in April.

Hyacinths give both colour and fragrance and are quite happy grouped with daffodils and tulips or planted on their own. Second-size bulbs are recommended since they do not require support. The miniature hyacinths throw smaller spikes which produce a beautiful effect in the smaller containers and window boxes.

The choice of small bulbs for planting in window boxes, pans, pots, jardinières, etc., is wide and various, enabling a colourful display to be enjoyed at all seasons of the year. With few exceptions most of the subjects that are suitable for general garden planting are able to thrive in containers of one kind or another. Crocuses top the list of popular spring bulbs but some autumn flowering varieties should also be included. Although they are one of the easiest plants to grow crocuses must be positioned in full sun, otherwise their flowers remain unopened.

Another readily adaptable group are the grape hyacinths (*Muscari*); because of their tendency to increase rapidly it is necessary for them to be divided periodically. Other choice subjects include the Siberian squill (*Scilla siberica*), Glory of the Snow (*Chionodoxa*), Dog's tooth violet (*Erythronium*), *Fritillaria*, miniature iris (*I. danfordiae* and *I. histrioides Major*), *Oxalis*, snowdrop (*Galanthus*) and its almost identical later-flowering companion snowflake (*Leucojum*).

Purchasing bulbs

All bulbs should meet the requirements set out in BS 3936 : Part 9 : 1968 and are best purchased from a bulb specialist, since the performance of bulbs reflects the preparation and treatment given to them during the previous year. Healthy bulbs are firm and weighty with a plump appearance. Any that are shrivelled or damaged or have a musty smell should be rejected. Only the best stocks give the best flowers; it is therefore essential that they should be obtained from a reliable source where the bulbs have been handled carefully and not cropped in the field for flowers. Cheap lots invariably result in the purchase of useless bulbs.

Grading of tulips and narcissi
Tulip bulbs are graded according to their circumference. Planting sizes generally are 70, 80, 90 and 100 mm but bulbs up to 130 mm may be used; those measuring 60–70 mm are often referred to as 'seed'.

Grading of narcissi is according to the type of bulb produced, as described below. Although the bulbs are sold by weight to the retail trade it is usually more satisfactory to buy by the count since the weight of a particular variety differs from district to district.

Mother bulbs. A cluster of bulbs, arranged in a fan-shaped group, with a number of offsets (chips) attached to it at the base and on either side. Occasionally the bulbs grow in a circular fashion, encircling the central bulb and are referred to as 'broody' or 'hen and chickens', the offsets producing long thin leaves but no flowers.

Large and small chips. These are the portions removed from the mother bulb. The remaining bulb may be single or double-nosed, and is often flat-sided and cannot, therefore, be sold as a round or a double-nosed bulb. It is nevertheless suitable for flowering out of doors.

Large and small rounds. Completely round single-nosed bulbs, much sought after for forcing since they produce good flowers and relatively little foliage. The best rounds result from the planting of large chips which are lifted at the end of one year.

Double-nosed bulbs. Ordinary trade size are used for normal retail and mail trade; extra-large trade double-nosed are used in very high-class retail trade. Similar to rounds, they produce at least two flowers with abundant foliage.

As lifted. These bulbs are as they are lifted from the field— i.e. assorted, but in practice many of the best planting sizes, such as the mother bulbs and chips, are often removed prior to sale.

Bulb soils and planting preparations

The ground should be dug through and allowed to settle for at least seven to ten days prior to planting any bulbs in it. Most bulbs are capable of adapting to a range of soils but thrive better in some than others.

Narcissi prefer a well-drained, open loam while tulips require the addition of leaf-mould; autumn crocus, *Chionodoxa*, *Muscari* and *Scilla* also like a leaf-mould mixture. Horticultural peat should be incorporated in soils into which *Eranthis* is planted so that the soil retains moisture. Hyacinths are more demanding in their requirements; soil mixtures for these plants should consist of loam, leaf-mould, peat and sand in equal proportions. The Spanish and Dutch irises, on the other hand, do best in a drained light sandy soil, while the English irises prefer a slightly heavier mixture. Crocuses and snowdrops thrive in any good all-round soil mixture.

The incorporation of a small amount of well-rotted manure or compost into the soil is generally beneficial, particularly where plants have previously been growing there, but a large quantity of fresh manure is undesirable because it is inclined to encourage disease. An application of bonemeal in autumn or dried blood in early spring is also recommended (according to the planting season).

Where narcissi are planted in existing turf a dressing of sulphate of ammonia should be sprinkled over the surface at the rate of 17 g/m² and the dosage repeated three or four weeks later.

Planting holes in heavy soils should have a small quantity of sharp sand placed at the bottom, underneath each bulb.

HERBACEOUS AND ALPINE PLANTS

The role of herbaceous and alpine plants in landscape design

Herbaceous plants, unlike shrubs, have soft, non-woody stems which generally die to the ground at the end of a season. They form the mainstay of the flower border, one of the glories of the traditional English cottage garden, and are mostly seen at their best during the summer months, providing fragrance and a colourful array of blooms. Their range is wide enough to meet the needs of almost any kind of situation: ground cover, infill for shrub beds, flowers for cutting or providing nectar for bees, edging to borders or the surround to a pool, trailing blooms for hanging baskets, climbers for a trellis fence, etc. Many herbaceous plants thrive quite happily alongside shrubs; some (e.g. lily-of-the-valley) are happier away from the heterogeneous border plants.

In their native habitat alpine plants are found in alpine meadows or growing on mountainsides at altitudes where trees are unable to survive. Mostly dwarf and compact in habit, they thrive best in full sun on well-drained soil. Although alpines are generally associated with rock gardening there are other means of displaying them. For those that thrive in vertical crevices, dry stone walling or gaps between paving flags provide an ideal home; others are suitable for planting on steep banks, in borders, paths, window boxes or to provide an alternative to a grassed area. Alpines that enjoy a hot, dry situation may be grown quite easily and cheaply in a scree, but those plants needing the protection of an alpine house are relatively costly to maintain.

Herbaceous borders

At one time it was customary for herbaceous plants in borders to be grown in rows with the tallest plants at the back, the shorter ones in the next row and so on, down to the front row which comprised the smallest plants. This formality of design gradually disappeared when writers such as William Robinson and Gertrude Jekyll advocated that there should be more natural freedom in garden layouts, with plants disposed as in their native haunts. Although formal beds are still to be seen in some civic and classical gardens, they are generally con-

sidered to be a hangover from the Victorian era of park design and, because of the labour involved in their maintenance, have been superseded by plants or other features requiring less attention.

Herbaceous borders may be of any size, shape or aspect, although if north-facing this may impose restrictions on plant selection. Depth is more important than length, since a narrow border also places limitations on the choice of plants. Generally, the height of the tallest plants should not exceed half the width of the border; contrast of shape and form must be matched by careful combination of colours to produce an artistic composition.

Most herbaceous plants are indifferent to all but extreme soil conditions and therefore suitable for growing in a wide variety of situations. Although cheap to stock initially, particularly if the plants are grown from seed, the herbaceous border generally requires more attention than the shrub bed (Tables 77–80).

The border must be prepared several weeks before planting in order to give the ground a chance to settle and consolidate. The ground should be dug two spits deep and manure or compost incorporated at all levels, with the addition of bonemeal in the top one. Ideally, the work should be done in autumn, ready for planting in the following spring, although in frost-free and reasonably dry conditions planting may take place from early November until the end of March. December and January are not always good planting months and, although plants slacken their rate of growth during the early autumn, late September or October is often better for planting, since the natural warmth of the soil encourages the plants to make growth. On cold heavy clays planting is best deferred until the spring. Plants that are slow to make new roots to establish themselves, if planted in winter, are in danger of rotting if the soil remains very wet for long periods.

The ultimate height and spread of the plants must be borne in mind when setting them out so that sufficient space is allowed for proper growth without cramping. Planting distances between herbaceous plants are recommended as follows:

Dwarf growing (e.g. *Primula*)   230–300 mm
Medium growing (e.g. *Erigeron*)   300–380 mm
Stronger growing (e.g. *Delphinium*) 460–600 mm

The planting hole for each plant must be large enough to accommodate the roots spread out and the crown or growth points set in their proper positions relative to the soil surface.

Table 77
Hardy herbaceous perennials for sunny positions

Anaphalis triplinervis (pearl everlasting)	0·30–0·45 m. Bold, silvery, woolly leaves with prominent veins. Creamy-white blooms resembling everlasting flowers.
Anchusa azurea 'Loddon Royalist'	0·91–1·52 m. Large intense blue flowers.
Anthemis tinctoria (ox-eye chamomile)	0·61–0·76 m. Feathery-type foliage ; yellow flowers.
Arnebia echioides (prophet flower)	0·23–0·30 m. Narrow, hairy leaves. Tubular primrose-yellow flowers with black spot at base of each petal.
Aster spp.	0·30–1·52 m. Wide range of coloured flowers.
Campanula spp. (bell flower)	0·30–0·91 m. Flowers white and varying shades of blue.
Coreopsis verticillata Grandiflora (tickweed)	0·46–0·61 m. Yew-like foliage ; golden-yellow starry flowers.
Delphinium brunonianum	0·25–0·38 m. Kidney-shaped, hairy leaves ; violet-blue flowers.
Dicentra formosa 'Bountiful' (bleeding heart)	0·30–0·46 m. Fern-like leaves ; deep pink flowers.
Doronicum caucasicum (leopard's bane)	0·30–0·46 m. Kidney-shaped, deeply toothed leaves. Deep-yellow flowers, 0·05 m across. The earliest perennials to flower.
Erigeron spp.	0·23–0·61 m. Flowers range in colour from pink, coppery-orange to deep violet-blue.
Euphorbia epithymoides (cushion spurge)	0·30 m. Fresh green foliage ; bright golden flowerheads.
Galega Hartlandii (goat's rue)	1·37–1·52 m. Bushy habit ; deeply-lobed pea-green leaves and blue and white wistaria-like flowers.
Gypsophila paniculata 'Bristol Fairy' (baby's breath)	0·91 m. Large hummocks of foliage covered with a shimmering multitude of tiny double white flowers on wiry stems.
Helenium spp. (sneezeweed)	0·30–1·22 m. Shades of orange, red and yellow flowers. Succeeds on poor soils.
Heliopsis scabra 'Golden Plume'	1·22 m. Resembles a large zinnia ; coarsely-toothed leaves and double golden-yellow 'sunflowers'.
Incarvillea delavayi (trumpet flower)	0·46–0·61 m. Dark green, 'mountain ash' foliage. Bright rosy-pink gloxinia-like flowers.
Iris unguicularis	0·30 m. Winter-flowering species which likes a limy soil. Flowers, sky-blue with yellow markings.
Kniphofia spp. (tritoma or red hot poker)	0·46–1·52 m. Striking plants with brightly coloured 'torches'.
Liatris spicata (gay feather or blazing star)	0·46–0·61 m. Striking plant with small, dark green lance-shaped leaves and long-lasting, reddish-purple flowers. Does well on poor, light soils.
Linum narbonnense 'Six Hills' (flax)	0·46 m. Small, narrow leaves. Panicles of clear blue flowers on slender, erect stems.
Meconopsis cambrica (Welsh poppy)	0·30 m. Deeply cut leaves 0·20 m long ; yellow or orange flowers 0·03 m across.
Paeonia spp. (paeony)	0·76–0·91 m. Handsome plants, flowers range in colour from white to deep plum-purple. Require well-manured, deeply-cultivated soil.
Papaver orientale (oriental poppy)	0·91 m. Brilliantly coloured giant flowers, ranging from white to rich crimson.
Pyrethrum roseum	0·76–0·91 m. Fern-like foliage. Single or double flowers in colours ranging from white to crimson.
Salvia superba	0·46–0·91 m. Sage-like foliage 0·07 m long. Violet-purple flower spikes.
Sedum spectabile (stonecrop)	0·30–0·46 m. Oval glaucous leaves. Rose-pink flowers in flat heads. Tolerant of dry conditions and useful for planting in tubs or containers.
Serratula shawii (saw-wort)	0·15–0·23 m. Finely-cut dark green leaves ; bright purple 'cornflowers'.
Solidago canadensis (golden rod)	0·30–1·82 m. Narrow leaves 0·07–0·15 m long. Panicles of yellow flowers. Dwarf hybrids are excellent foil for michaelmas daisies.
Trollius europaeus (globe flower)	0·30–0·61 m. Deeply-cut fresh green leaves. Flowers pale lemon to bright orange in colour.
Verbascum hybridum (mullein)	0·91–1·52 m. Thick woolly leaves. Tall flower spikes.
Veronica incana (speedwell)	0·30 m. Lance-shaped silver-grey leaves ; spikes of dark blue flowers.

Table 78
Hardy herbaceous perennials for shady positions
E=evergreen

	Anemone hupehensis 'September Charm'	0·61–0·91 m. Soft pink, cup-shaped flowers.
	Artemesia lactiflora (white mugwort)	1·37–1·52 m. Spikes of foam-like, cream-coloured flowers.
	Aruncus dioicus (goat's beard)	1·22 m. Imposing fern-like foliage. Creamy-white plumes on branching stems. Attractive plant near water.
	Astilbe spp. (false goat's beard)	0·61–0·91 m. Feathery, plume-like foliage, often bronze-tinted in spring. Flowers arranged on spikes, ranging from white to deep red in colour.
E	*Helleborus niger Grandiflorus* (Christmas rose)	0·30–0·46 m. Deep green leathery, toothed leaves. Snowy-white saucer-shaped flowers. Useful winter-flowering plant.
	Iris foetidissima	0·61 m. Bright green glossy foliage. Purple flowers ; brilliant scarlet seeds.
E	*Lamiastrum galeobdolon Florentium* (yellow archangel)	0·15 m. Startling white variegated leaves. Good for providing ground cover ; will thrive in shade, even if soil is dry.
	Paeonia spp. (paeony)	0·76–0·91 m. Handsome plants ; flowers range in colour from white to deep plum-purple. Require well-manured, deeply-cultivated soil.
	Polygonatum multiflorum (Solomon's seal)	0·61–0·91 m. Broad, smooth, greyish-green leaves ; arching sprays of tubular creamy white flowers. A woodland plant which also grows in shallow water.
	Primula florindae	0·91 m. Large, tongue-shaped leaves ; pendent whorls of primrose-yellow flowers on stout stems.
	Scrophularia nodosa (knotted figwort)	0·30–0·91 m. Oval, toothed leaves. Small, brownish-red inconspicuous flowers.
	Smilacina racemosa (false spikenard)	0·61–0·91 m. Slender pointed leaves, 0·15–0·23 m long. Creamy-coloured feathery clusters.
E	*Tiarella cordifolia* (foam flower)	0·23 m. Dense mass of heart-shaped leaves. Spikes of white fluffy flowers. Good weed-suppressor.
	Viola gracilia 'Grandeur'	0·15 m. Masses of violet-blue flowers.

Table 79
Hardy herbaceous perennials for ground cover
E=evergreen

	Ajuga pryamidalis (pyramidal bugle)	0·23 m. Dark green oval leaves, semi-evergreen ; compact pyramidal, gentian blue flower spikes 0·15 m long.
	Alchemilla mollis (lady's mantle)	0·30–0·46 m. Kidney-shaped, wavy-edged, grey-green leaves ; dainty, yellowish-green sprays of flowers. Native of damp meadows and open woodland.
	Anaphalis triplinervis (pearl everlasting)	0·30–0·46 m. Bold silvery, woolly leaves with prominent veins. Creamy-white blooms resembling everlasting flowers.
	Astrantia carniolica (masterwort)	0·30–0·61 m. Sprays of greenish-white flowers in terminal bosses. Thrives in sun or shade where there is adequate summer moisture.
	Bergenia purpurescens 'Ballawley' (pig squeak)	0·30 m. Large rounded glossy, semi-evergreen leaves ; bright rose-red flowers borne on red stems. Thrives on chalk soils in sun or partial shade. Excellent foil for dwarf conifers and ideal plant for tubs or other containers.
	Brunnera macrophylla	0·30–0·46 m. Heart-shaped leaves, up to 0·15 m. across ; blue, forget-me-not flowers. Does best in moist soil and partial shade.
	Centaura dealbata 'John Coutts'	0·46 m. Pointed, coarsely-toothed leaves, bright pink flower with yellow eye.
E	*Epimedium niveum 'Rose Queen'* (barrenwort)	0·30 m. Elegant foliage, reddish autumn tints ; slender spikes of rose-pink flowers.
	Geranium macrorrhizum var. *Ingwersen* (crane's-bill)	0·38 m. Light green foliage develops bright autumn colours. Soft pink flowers.
	Geum borisii	0·30 m. Deeply-toothed, wedge-shaped leaves ; rich orange-scarlet flowers.
	Hosta spp. (plantain lily)	0·30–0·91 m. Bold foliage, often with variegation ; white, mauve or lavender lily-like flowers.
	Hypericum linarioides	0·076 m. Foliage turns reddish-brown in autumn ; golden-yellow flowers.
	Lamium spp. (dead nettle)	0·15 m. Flowers borne on short spikes. Will thrive in shade, even if soil is dry.
	Ligularia spp.	0·61–1·82 m. Large-leaved, strong-growing, weed-suppressing plants ; ideal for the wild garden and waterside.

Table 79 *Continued*

	Lotus corniculatus (bird's-foot trefoil or bacon and eggs)	Procumbent plant with bright yellow flowers.
	Maianthemum bifolium (May lily)	0·10–0·20 m. Fresh green lily-of-the-valley type leaves. Fluffy white flower spikes. Native woodland plant.
E	*Nepeta faassenii* (catmint)	0·30–0·46 m. Small, serrated, silvery-grey, scented foliage. Enjoys light soil and sun but will not thrive in heavy, poorly-drained soil.
	Oenothera missouriensis (evening primrose)	0·15–0·23 m. Lance-shaped leaves on trailing stems ; large, funnel-shaped lemon-yellow flowers.
	Polygonum spp. (knotgrass)	0·23–1·06 m. Dense mass of narrow leaves ; stiff, small spikes of creamy-white, pink or crimson flowers.
	Potentilla alba	0·10 m. Finger-like greyish-green leaves ; small white flowers.
E	*Stachys lanata 'Silver Carpet'* (lamb's tongue or lamb's ear)	0·30 m. Silvery-white felt-like foliage. Thrives in sun or light shade.
	Viola cornuta (horned violet)	0·10–0·23 m. Broad oval leaves ; long-flowering plant except during drought.

Table 80
Hardy herbaceous perennials with interesting foliage
E = evergreen

E	*Acanthus mollis Latifolius*	0·91–1·22 m. Deeply lobed, shiny, bright green leaves 0·61 m long. Stiff spikes of lilac-pink 'foxglove' flowers.
	Achillea 'Moonshine' (yarrow)	0·61 m. Silver, fern-like foliage. Soft sulphur-yellow flowers in flat heads, 0·07–0·10 m across.
	Artemesia lactiflora 'Silver Queen'	0·91 m. Pointed, willow-like leaves, silvery on both surfaces.
	Ballota pseudodictamnus	0·61 m. Heart-shaped white, woolly leaves.
	Buphthalmum speciosum	1·52 m. Bold, heart-shaped leaves ; large panicles of golden, disc-like flowers.
E	*Eryngium spp.* (sea holly)	0·46–1·06 m. Rosettes of divided leaves of greyish-green or jade-green ; blue flowers.
	Filipendula ulmaria Aurea	0·30 m. Mounds of golden foliage April–October.
	Geranium renardii	0·30 m. Greyish-green, vine-like, felted foliage with finely etched veins which produce an embossed effect.
	Gunnera manicata (prickly rhubarb)	1·82–2·43 m. Gigantic, deeply lobed leaves, 1·52+ m across. Unique plant for sunny, sheltered margin of pools.
	Hosta spp. (plantain lily)	0·30–0·91 m. Very useful range of plants producing clumps of broad, striking foliage.
	Iris monnieri	1·22 m. Bright green sword-like foliage ; rich yellow flowers. Strong-growing plant for damp situations.
	Ligularia dentata 'Desdemona	1·22–1·52 m. Large, heart-shaped, dark mahogany-green leaves with plum-coloured undersurface.
	Lobelia fulgens 'The Bishop'	1·22–1·52 m. Beetroot-coloured foliage ; rich vermilion flowers. Does best on damp soils.
	Macleaya cordata 'Coral Plume'	1·82–2·13 m. Bold grey-green leaves produced on upright stems ; spikes of delicate coral-pink spiraea-like flowers.
	Peltiphyllum peltatum (umbrella plant)	0·61–0·91 m. Large rounded, lobed leaves. Very invasive plant ; requires deep, moist soil—suitable beside pool or stream in sun or light shade.
	Rheum palmatum (sorrel rhubarb)	1·52–1·82 m. Large, five-lobed leaves ; creamy-yellow flowers on imposing spikes.
	Rodgersia tabularis	0·91–1·22 m. Large, round, scalloped leaves ; creamy-white astilbe-like flowers.
	Scrophularia nodosa Variegata (knotted figwort)	0·61–0·91 m. Light green leaves with yellowish markings.
	Sedum spectabile	0·46 m. Oval, pastel glaucous green foliage ; rose-pink flowers in broad umbels.
	Senecio 'White Diamond'	0·61–0·91 m. Silvery-white much-divided leaves ; bright yellow flowers.
	Stachys spicata (woundwort)	0·30–0·46 m. Long, pointed, bluish-green wrinkled leaves ; lilac-pink flowers.
	Symphytum officinale Argenteum (comfrey)	0·61–1·23 m. Lanceolate, variegated leaves 0·15–0·25 m long ; blue flowers.

Alpines in the rock garden

Rocks provide plants with a cool root-run and the crevices and pockets of soil between the rocks are ideal for those species which thrive in this kind of home. The crags and higher parts of a rock garden are the driest spots and suitable for plants enjoying such conditions.

Most alpines prefer a gritty soil containing sharp sand (to ensure good drainage), a certain amount of humus (to hold moisture) and loam (to act as a binding factor and as a supplement to the food provided by the humus). John Innes seed compost, by coincidence, is a good general alpine soil often used for this purpose. This seed-raising mixture is composed of

> two parts loam
> one part peat
> one part sand
> superphosphate (measured quantity)
> chalk (measured quantity)

It should always be obtained from a reputable dealer because the loam content, as well as the efficiency of the steaming process, is liable to vary in quality.

There is no reason, of course, why any good garden soil should not be used in conjunction with the following additions to provide a basic mixture:

> three parts soil
> one part loam
> two parts leaf-mould
> one part coarse sharp sand
> one-eighth part bonemeal
> one-eighth part ground chalk (or limestone flour)

This mixture may be adjusted to suit site conditions: on heavy clay soils an extra one-half part should be substituted for the loam content and on poor sandy soils the amount of loam doubled.

Most alpines tend to prefer a neutral or alkaline soil and for the lime-loving species the quantity of ground chalk should be doubled. Lime-hating alpines require a basic mixture comprising

> two parts leaf-mould
> one part acid peat
> one part gritty sand
> one part loam
> one-eighth part bonemeal

For woodland plants the following richer leafy mixture is recommended:

> three parts leaf-mould
> one part sand
> two parts loam
> one-eighth part bonemeal

These soil mixtures are given as basic guides only, since many plants thrive quite happily if extra lime or leaf-mould (according to need) is dug in during the planting operations.

Alpines range in size from tiny cushions to bushy clumps and spreading mats. It is important to ensure that one type of plant does not smother another. The small tufts, cushions and smaller bushy plants should be planted on the higher parts of the rock garden while the mat-forming and wide bushlets occupy the lower parts. Shrubs may be planted to complement the alpines in a rock garden; a

Table 81
Shrubs suitable for planting with alpines in the rock garden
D=deciduous, E=evergreen

			Approximate height (mm)	Colour	Period of maximum interest
ED	*Azalea*	in variety	760–1800	Range through white, yellow, orange, pink, red	Spring
E	*Berberis* (barberry)	dwarf varieties	450–900	Yellow	Spring, some berries in autumn
ED	*Cotoneaster*	dwarf varieties	300–900	Red berries	Autumn/winter
D	*Cytisus* (broom)	dwarf varieties	230–900	White, yellow	Spring/summer
E	*Daboecia* (Irish heath)	in variety	600–750	White, pink, purple	Summer/autumn
D	*Daphne*	dwarf varieties	450–900	Pink, purple	Early spring
E	*Erica* (heather)	in variety	120–300	White, pink, purple	Winter–summer
D	*Genista* (broom)	dwarf varieties	25–900	Yellow	Spring/summer
E	*Hebe* (speedwell)	dwarf varieties	300–900	White, blue, purple	Summer/autumn
D	*Potentilla fruticosa*	varieties	600–1200	White, yellow	Summer/autumn
E	*Rhododendron*	dwarf varieties	450–1200	All colours	Spring/autumn/summer
E	*Santolina chamaecyparissus*		250–600	Yellow	Summer
E	*Viburnum davidii*		600–900	Turquoise blue berries	Autumn

selection is given in Table 81.

Planting time for alpines depends largely upon the local climate. In districts where spring and early summer is dry and the soil of a dry nature (e.g. sand or gravel), September and October are ideal months because the plants are able to establish themselves before the winter sets in. In areas of high rainfall where the soil is inclined to be wet (e.g. clay or heavy loam), planting is best delayed until March or April to avoid the plants being subjected to cold, damp conditions before they have a chance to re-root. Careful attention must be given to watering, however, in order to counteract the adverse effects of the cold drying winds usually experienced during this period.

Alpines in association with dry stone walling

Most of the plants which thrive in the crevices between rocks may be readily accommodated in the vertical positions provided in the construction of dry walls where there is no risk of their becoming saturated with moisture. Dry walling is built without the use of any kind of mortar, but where plants are to be incorporated a layer of soil is placed between each course of stones. Construction of the

wall and planting should, ideally, be carried out simultaneously. Both sides of a free-standing wall may be studded with plants but it is important to select species which enjoy those particular aspects (Fig.59).

Dry walls forming part of the construction of raised beds need not be higher than 610 mm but should not be less than 300 mm in width. The hollow interior, between the two walls, should be filled with a soil mixture similar to that specified for rock garden construction, well compacted as construction proceeds; planting of the wall faces should be done at the same time.

The more rampageous species should be set at the lower part of the wall and those capable of withstanding drought conditions planted nearer the top. A thin layer of soil is placed over the course of stones and the roots of each plant spread out and then covered with a further layer of soil to give a total overall depth of approximately 25 mm.

Where it is not possible for planting to proceed during the construction of the wall, a layer of turf or heavy loam should be incorporated between the stones to form the joints. Planting should then take place during September or October, because sufficient watering of the alpines is almost impossible if they are planted in the spring. A hole is gouged out with a narrow trowel and the roots

put daintier alpine species and those capable of thriving in drought conditions towards top part of wall—see detail

soil

plant the more rampageous species at bottom of wall

a. Section

spread thin layer of soil over stones and place roots of plant on top, covering them with more soil to give overall depth of 25 mm approx

in dry stone walling soil is used instead of mortar

c. Planting alpine in joint

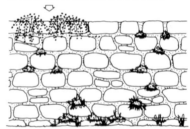

set plants of spreading or pendulous habit on top of wall so that they cascade over it

selection of plants for wall depends upon its aspect, e.g. if north-facing the plants must be shade-tolerant if they are to thrive

b. Elevation of wall

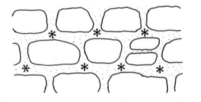

* roots of plants are less liable to dry out if set here

d. Positioning of plants

Fig. 59 Planting alpines in dry stone walling

Table 82
Alpines suitable for planting in dry walls

	Height (mm)	Colour	Period of maximum interest
Aethionema 'Warley Rose' (stone cress)	100	Rosy-red	May–June
Alyssum saxatile Citrinum (gold dust)	230	Lemon yellow	May–June
Androsace lanuginosa Leichtlinii	100	White	June–July
Androsace sarmentosa	100	Soft pink	June–July
Anthyllis montana Rubra	75	Crimson	May–June
Arabis caucasia Flore Pleno	150	White	April–May
Armeria juniperifolia	50	Silvery-pink	April–June
Aubretia vars.	50	Variety of colours	April
Campanula fenestrellata	100	Light blue	May–Sept
Campanula poscharskyana	100	Light blue	June–Oct
Cheiranthus cheiri 'Harpur Crewe' (wallflower)	230	Yellow	April–June
Chiastophyllum oppositifolium	100	Golden-yellow	July–Aug
Dianthus 'Aubrey Pritchard'	150	Shell pink	June
Dianthus knappii	230	Yellow	July–August
Dryas octopetala (mountain avens)	130	White	May–June
Erodium corsicum Album	75	White	May–August
Geranium dalmaticum (cranesbill)	150	Pink	May–July
Hypericum empetrifolium	75	Orange-yellow	June–August
Hypericum polyphyllum	150	Yellow	July–September
Iberi 'Little Gem' (candytuft)	150	White	May–June
Phlox douglasii 'Boothman'	50	Mauve	May–June
Phlox douglasii 'Eva'	25	Rosy-mauve	May–June
Phlox subulata 'Temiscaming'	100	Reddish-purple	May–June
Polygonum vaccinifolium	150	Pink	August–October
Pterocephalus parnassi	75	Mauve-pink	April–June
Tunica saxifraga	150	Pink	June–August

of the plants spread out and teased into the soil as far as possible using a thin wedge-shaped piece of wood. A small quantity of water is squirted into the hole, which is then carefully plugged with rotted turf or heavy loam.

Alpines suitable for planting in dry walls are listed in Table 82.

The alpine bank, lawn and path

In some situations a steep slope need not necessarily be retained by either rocks or walling but may be ideal for the planting of those alpines whose habitats are not to be found among the rock outcrops. The idea of an alpine bank is to select plants which are capable of retaining the soil and which produce a colourful display of blooms. Such plants are those whose qualities make them unsuitable for use as rock plants (e.g. *Helianthemum*). Choice may be limited if the bank does not enjoy full sun for most of the day.

The height of a bank may range from one to several metres; on high banks provision should be made for reaching the upper parts. This may be effected by setting wooden or concrete posts in holes, formed at an angle running downwards into the bank itself, and left projecting 150–200 mm beyond the face to provide a hand- or foothold.

Planting is best carried out during the period February to April, depending upon weather conditions. Care must be taken to ensure that all weeds are eliminated beforehand and preparation of impoverished soils should consist of the application and digging in of a complete fertiliser at the rate of approximately 68 g/m^2.

Where the slope of a bank is firm but too steep for normal digging, holes for plants should be formed about 300 mm deep, pointing downwards at right angles to the slope of the bank, and spaced at approximately 230 mm in staggered rows. Just over half the depth of each hole should be filled with leaf-mould well mixed with about one heaped tablespoonful of bonemeal. Where the gradient permits normal digging in of humus there is no need to take out holes and fill them with leaf-mould.

All plants must be well soaked prior to planting and when set in their respective holes the soil should be

Table 83
Carpeting plants for alpine lawns and paths

	Height (mm)	Colour	Period of maximum interest
Quick-growing			
Acaena buchananii	50	Red seedheads, grey foliage	June–September
Acaena inermis	50	Khaki leaves, spineless	June–September
Acaena microphylla	50	Red, spiny bronze foliage	June–September
*Arenaria balearica (sandwort)	13	White, light-green foliage	May–June
Cotula squalida	25	Frondlike bronzy-green foliage	
Hutchinsia alpina	50	White, dark green foliage	May–June
Mazus reptans	25	Mauve	May–June
Minuartia verna Aurea	75	White, golden-green foliage	June–September
Sedum album Murale	100	Pink, bronzy-purple foliage	June–July
Sedum sexangulare	50	Yellow, bronzy-green foliage	June
Medium- or slow-growing			
Campanula pusilla Alba	100	White	June–September
Campanula pusilla 'Miranda' (fairies' thimbles)	100	Silvery-blue	June–September
Cymbalaria aequitriloba (toadflax)	13	Lavender, bright green foliage	April–June
Frankenia hirsuta	25	Pink, bronzy-green foliage	June–July
Gypsophila cerastioides	75	White, purple-veined	May–September
*Nierembergia repens (cup flower)	130	White	June–August
Sedum dasyphyllum	50	Blush-pink, grey foliage	June–July
*Selliera radicans	13	Pink	summer
Stachys corsica	25	Pale pink, light green foliage	summer
Thymus serpyllum	25	Rosy purple	June–September
Thymus serpyllum Albus	25	White	June–September
Thymus serpyllum Coccineus	25	Crimson	June–September
Thymus serpyllum lanuginosus	13	Pink, grey foliage	June–September
Thymus serpyllum 'Pink Chintz'	25	Pink	June–September

*Thrives best in damp shady positions.

rammed well back, using a blunt-ended tool, such as a trowel handle (not a sharp or pointed dibber), to prevent damage to the roots. The soil should be placed around each plant to form a shallow cup, about 25 mm deep, to act as a rain trap. Although this eventually fills up with soil it serves a very useful role during the first few months when the plant is establishing itself, by collecting water for the plant and preventing the soil around it from being washed away.

The aim should be to plant those species capable of establishing a ground cover with good root systems to prevent the soil from washing down the bank. To achieve this the rate of planting should be about fourteen plants to each square metre; on more gentle slopes and richer soils a lesser density of planting may be adopted provided that the plants are spaced so that their growth produces a solid mass by the autumn of the first season. On steep banks, plants suitable for incorporating in dry walling are likely to thrive, and on the lesser slopes, those at home in the alpine lawn.

The latter does not fulfil the same function as grass, since it cannot withstand heavy foot-traffic, but it has the advantage of requiring very little attention once established: maintenance consists of an annual trim with shears. Care must be taken with plant selection in order to avoid planting a quick-growing species adjacent to one of much slower growth. It does not matter whether slow or quick-growing alpines are chosen provided that the selection is made from the same class.

Paths are notorious for collecting weeds but there is no reason why weeds should not be replaced by carpeting plants. A path catering for light foot-traffic may incorporate a series of stepping stones set amid tough carpeting plants capable of ousting the indigenous weeds. If gravel is used as the surfacing material, provision must be made during the construction of the path for the plants to be able to root down into the soil.

The plants selected need to be fairly tough because they may have to withstand over-watering during the winter months. A list of carpeting plants is given in Table 83.

Alpines in paved areas

Gaps between individual paving flags vary according to the type of material and the pattern in which it is laid, but most of them afford sufficient space to permit the roots of alpine plants to establish themselves.

The easier, although not necessarily the more successful, way to establish alpines in paved areas is by sowing seed. Sifted sterilised soil is first swept into the crevices, the seed is sown onto it and then covered with a little more soil firmed in place and watered with a fine spray. The tougher alpines, able to withstand treading, may be planted directly in their positions. Soil should be swept into the crevices between the paving flags and the rooted fragments of the plants carefully set in place by means of a dibber, well-firmed with more soil on top and then watered.

Table 84 lists those plants which may be incorporated in paved areas.

Table 84
Alpines suitable for planting in paving

	Height (mm)	Colour	Period of maximum interest
Achillea 'King Edward' (yarrow)	150	Creamy yellow	June–August
Anthyllis montana Rubra	75	Crimson	June–September
Armeria maritima Corsica	100	Brick red	May–June
Armeria maritima 'Vindictive'	150	Bright crimson	June–July
Campanula fenestrellata	100	Light blue	May–September
Campanula garganica	100	Light blue	June–August
Campanula pulla	100	Deep violet	June–July
Dianthus 'Baker'	150	Deep pink	June–July
Dianthus 'Little Jock'	100	Rose pink	July–September
Erinus alpinus Albus	150	White	April–June
Erinus alpinus 'Dr Haenaele'	50	Carmine	April–June
Erinus alpinus 'Mrs Boyle'	50	Deep pink	May–July
Erodium chamaedryoides Roseum	50	Pink	May–October
*Geranium sanguineum lancastriense	150	Salmon pink	June–October
Gypsophila repens	100	Pink	June–August
Hippocrepis comosa (horseshoe vetch)	75	Yellow	June–August
Hypericum olympicum	150	Yellow	July–August
Hypericum polyphyllum	150	Yellow	July–August
Linaria alpina (toadflax)	75	Violet	June–August
Linum salsaloides Nanum	50	White	May–October
*Mimulus cupreus 'Whitecroft Scarlet'	100	Vermilion	June–September
Oenothera perennis (sundrops)	150	Yellow	June–August
Saxifraga caespitosa	75	White	April–June
Silene schafta	100	Rosy-red	August–September
Thymus serpyllum	13	Rosy-purple	June–July

*Thrives best in moist shady places.

Screes for alpine plants

Natural screes are found on mountain and hillsides and are composed of debris and parts of unstable rocks that have become dislodged higher up the mountainside and have scattered down it, finally coming to rest in the form of a fan-shaped scree. Because of the gradual slipping down of the surface stones and the addition of fresh falls of those from above, the scree is a very unstable habitat and the growth of plants there is hindered. A man-made scree, however, is obviously of a more stable nature and affords greater scope in the range of plant material it is able to support; it is also one of the cheapest methods of growing alpines (other than shade- or moisture-loving species).

A scree may alternatively be constructed using boiler ash in place of stone chippings. The ash, with the dust removed through a 3 mm sieve and with large clinkers excluded, must first be allowed to weather for at least six months. During this time it should be watered and turned at intervals, and it can then be used safely in the same way as stone chippings.

Alpines suitable for planting in screes constructed with either stone chippings or boiler ash are listed in Table 85.

Table 85
Alpines suitable for planting in a scree

	Height (mm)	Colour	Period of maximum interest
Androsace sarmentosa	100	Soft pink	May–June
Androsace sempervivoides	50	Pink, crimson eye	April–May
Asperula suberosa (woodruff)	75	Rosy pink	June–July
Boykinia jamesii	150	Crimson	May–June
Campanula pilosa Superba	100	Pale blue	May–June
Dianthus haematocalyx	100	Pink	July
Edraianthus pumilo	50	Lavender blue	June
Erigeron leiomerus	75	Light blue	June
Erigeron trifidus	50	Pale lavender	June
Erodium chamaedryoides Roseum	50	Pink	May–October
Globularia incanescens	75	Blue	June–July
Helichrysum milfordiae	75	White	June–July
Morisia monantha	13	Yellow	May–July
Saxifraga apiculata	75	Yellow	March–April
Saxifraga burseriana 'Gloria'	75	White	March–April
Saxifraga Haagii	75	Yellow	March–April
Saxifraga oppositifolia Splendens	25	Rosy-crimson	March–April
Silene acaulis (moss campion)	25	Pink	May–June

Ten Aquatics and Bog Plants

Aquatic gardens and the value of water in the landscape

During the middle of the nineteenth century a craze developed for cultivating the giant water-lily Victoria Regia from seeds of the plant raised at Chatsworth, one of the earliest water gardens of repute in England, and gave rise to a spate of aquatic garden development. This enthusiasm has continued up to the present day and in addition to the wealth of aquatic plants now available the construction of pools has been made simpler by the use of modern materials and fabrication methods.

Water is an asset in any layout since it has the ability to create a variety of moods, sounds and movement. Loudon observed in his *Encyclopaedia of Gardening*: '. . . water is a material of so captivating and interesting a description in the different characters in which it occurs in nature that no view can be reckoned complete in which it does not compose a feature' (Loudon, 1859: Part 2, Bk.III, 466). One of the delights of water is its charm in reflecting the surrounding scene, especially at night when floodlighting or coloured lights are used. Still water induces a sense of tranquility, particularly when set in the midst of grassland sweeping down to the water's edge. In woodland, water is seen at its best as a fast-flowing stream, swirling around obstacles in its path and cascad-

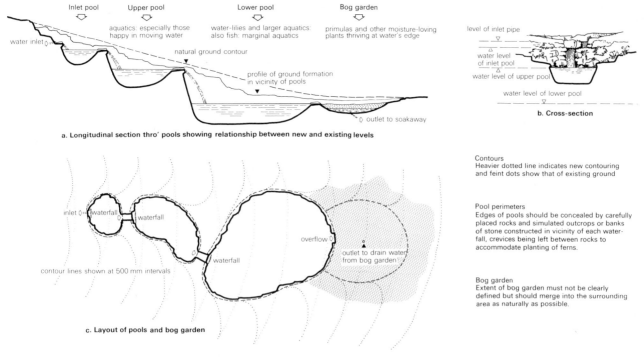

a. Longitudinal section thro' pools showing relationship between new and existing levels

Inlet pool

Upper pool
aquatics: especially those happy in moving water

Lower pool
water-lilies and larger aquatics: also fish: marginal aquatics

Bog garden
primulas and other moisture-loving plants thriving at water's edge

water inlet

natural ground contour

profile of ground formation in vicinity of pools

outlet to soakaway

b. Cross-section

level of inlet pipe

water level of inlet pool

water level of upper pool

water level of lower pool

inlet — waterfall — waterfall

overflow

waterfall

outlet to drain water from bog garden

contour lines shown at 500 mm intervals

c. Layout of pools and bog garden

Contours
Heavier dotted line indicates new contouring and feint dots show that of existing ground

Pool perimeters
Edges of pools should be concealed by carefully placed rocks and simulated outcrops or banks of stone constructed in vicinity of each waterfall, crevices being left between rocks to accommodate planting of ferns.

Bog garden
Extent of bog garden must not be clearly defined but should merge into the surrounding area as naturally as possible.

Fig. 60 Water garden layout

ing over rocks, creating miniature waterfalls and producing delightful sounds; even in the smallest shaft of sunlight it sparkles like diamonds.

Water has a place in almost any kind of environment, amid rocks, grassland, woodland, aquatic or bog garden, paved terrace or town square, each setting requiring a different collection of plant material (Fig. 60).

The use of aquatics and bog plants

Aquatics are non-woody plants, growing in or under water, which may be classed into three principal groups:

Rooted — Growing in the soil base but with many of their leaves standing above or floating on the surface of the water.

Floating — Floating freely at or just below the water surface but not rooted in the soil base.

Submerged — Entirely submerged and rooted in the soil base.

Bog plants enjoy moist conditions, thriving in permanently wet soils, and are found in the margins of pools and low-lying wetter areas.

Rooted aquatics

This group of plants includes the water-lily (*Nymphaea*) which holds pride of place among aquatics and ranges in size from miniature plants thriving in shallow pools to those of large and vigorous habit occupying a spacious surface area in lakes.

Although water-lilies provide the most interesting and colourful display in a pool there are other aquatics that also serve to provide cover for the pond life and create decorative interest on the water's surface. These are included in Tables 86–90 (pages 243–245).

Floating aquatics

The roots of these plants hang in the water, the plant itself providing food and natural shelter for the occupants of the pool. Some floating aquatics are also important aerators and help to keep the water sweet by means of the oxygen which they give off; they need to be kept under control since, in some cases, their growth is rapid and is liable ultimately to choke nearby plants.

A list of floating aquatics is given in Table 91 (page 246).

Submerged aquatics
These plants, a selection of which is given in Table 92, (page 247), play a vital role in helping to keep the pool in a perfect state of balance by liberating oxygen and absorbing the carbon dioxide. In addition, by competing for light and food they keep the pool reasonably free from algae (suspended microscopic organisms). The leaves of both submerged and floating aquatics also serve as a refuge for the young fry.

Bog plants
In nature there is no demarcation line between the pool itself and the ground surrounding it, the transitional zone being a swampy area where those moisture-loving plants, referred to as 'bog plants', thrive. The edge of the informal man-made pool needs to be camouflaged if it is to blend in with the immediate environment and it is here that the bog plants may be usefully employed. As these plants need a constant supply of moisture it is important that the bog garden should be sited at a low level to allow the ground to be flooded and the moisture retained.

A selection of hardy bog plants is given in Table 93 (page 248).

Aquatics and bog plants in their natural habitats

The natural habitat of aquatics and bog plants is areas having a high water-table: marshland and fenland.

Marshland
On gently sloping ground where there is a high water-table three fairly well defined zones of vegetation occur, related to the water-table heights: open water, swamp and marsh proper. Each zone is characterised by its own type of plants although there is a certain amount of overlapping between zones. The soil is either neutral or alkaline.

(i) *Open water zone.* The water-table may vary from a few millimetres to several metres above the ground level. The aquatics living here may be rooted in the mud with their foliage at or above the surface of the water or completely submerged. Some may not be rooted in the mud but float freely at or just below the surface.

Rooted aquatics obtain mineral salts from the mud via their roots and submerged parts. The upper surfaces of their leaves, which are at or above the water surface level, absorb carbon dioxide and oxygen from the air, some of which, dissolved in water, also passes into submerged parts of the plants.

The leaf-blades of the water-lilies are on long stalks which are held at an angle; when floods raise the water level these take on a vertical position, thereby enabling the leaves to remain resting on the water instead of becoming submerged. If the water level continues to rise the stalks are capable of elongating fairly quickly. The submerged leaves of many aquatics are very finely dissected, presenting a large total surface area capable of absorbing the dissolved salts and gases in the water.

Native plants in this category include:
Nuphar lutea (yellow water-lily or brandy bottle)
Nymphaea alba (white water-lily)
Ranunculus spp. (water crowfoot)
Sagittaria sagittifolia (arrowhead)

Floating aquatics are generally to be found where there is a fair depth of water. Their roots, where developed, hang suspended in the water and serve as balancing organs, absorbing dissolved salts and gases.

Native plants include:
Hydrocharis morsus-ranae (frog-bit)
Lemna spp. (duckweed)
Utricularia vulgaris (bladderwort)

Submerged aquatics also grow in deeper water but root in the mud with their leaves totally submerged although, in most cases, their flowering shoots rise above the surface. Their delicate cell structures enable them to absorb quite rapidly the salts and gases dissolved in water.

In this group are found:
Potamogeton spp. (pondweed)
Elodea canadensis (Canadian pondweed)
Hottonia palustris (water violet)
Myriophyllum verticillatum (whorled water milfoil)
Callitriche spp. (water starwort)

(ii) *Swamp zone.* This is the intermediate zone in which some parts lie above the ground level. It is characterised by tall reed-like plants of upright growth and sufficient flexibility to allow them to bend without breaking when subjected to wind. Their long creeping rhizomes penetrate the soil, spreading in all directions; a fairly large community may arise from a single plant and push out into the open water zone, ultimately transforming it into a swamp zone as a result of silting and the accumulation of plant debris.

Native plants found in the swamp zone include :

Phragmites australis (common reed)
Sparganum spp. (bur reed)
Phalaris arundinacea (reed canary-grass)
Butomus umbellatus (flowering rush)
Typha latifolia (reed mace or bulrush)
Alisma plantago-aquatica (water plantain)
Lythrum salicaria (purple loosestrife)
Lysimachia vulgaris (yellow loosestrife)
Ranunculus lingua (great spearwort)

In the less wet parts may be found some of the plants thriving in the marsh proper zone.

(iii) *Marsh proper zone.* The water-table in this highest part of the marshland is almost at ground level and the soil waterlogged. Standing water may occur in a few local areas but is of small significance. The plants growing in this zone are capable of thriving in a waterlogged soil which is deficient in oxygen ; they range from tiny mosses to tall herbs and typical of them is *Caltha palustris* (marsh marigold). Other native plants of this habitat include :

Mentha spp. (mint)
Lychnis flos-cuculi (ragged Robin)
Cirsium palustre (marsh thistle)
Filipendula ulmaria (meadowsweet)
Iris pseudacorus (yellow flag)
Veronica beccabunga (brooklime)
Equisetum spp. (horsetails)
Pedicularis sylvatica (lousewort)
Myosotis scorpioides (water forget-me-not)
Oenanthe crocata (hemlock water dropwort)
Hypericum tetrapterum (square-stalked St John's wort)
Hydrocotyle vulgaris (marsh pennywort)
Equilobium palustre (marsh willowherb)
Various sedges and rushes

The driest areas may support small woods (marsh carrs) of the following :

Alnus glutinosa (alder)
Salix viminalis (common osier)
S. cineria oleifolia (common sallow)
S. fragilis (crack willow)
S. caprea (goat willow)

and among them an undergrowth of marsh plants.

Fenland

Although fenland vegetation closely resembles that of marshland it is supported by a peaty soil and may be classified into three zones : open water, reed swamp and fen proper. Fenland occurs mainly at the head of silted-up estuaries where organic plant remains accumulate ; the water-table varies from just below ground level to a few metres above it.

(i) *Open water zone.* Aquatic plants typical of marsh open water occur in this zone.

(ii) *Reed swamp zone.* The same characteristics as are found in the marshland swamp zone are found here. Native plants such as :

Phalaris arundinacea (reed canary grass)
Phragmites australis (common reed)
Typha spp. (reed mace)
Scirpus lacustris (bulrush)

invade the open water zone and as the ground level rises, due to accumulated silt, further plants establish themselves so that the open water is transformed eventually into reed swamp.

(iii) *Fen proper zone.* The succession of plants in this zone depends, basically, upon the height of the soil above water level and its degree of moisture. Typical plants growing in this zone include :

Juncus subnodulosus (blunt-flowered rush)
Lychnis flos-cuculi (ragged Robin)
Glyceria maxima (reed sweet grass)
Filipendula ulmaria (meadowsweet)
Hypericum elodes (marsh St John's wort)
Valeriana officinalis (valerian)
Caltha palustris (marsh marigold)
Lythrum salicaria (purple loosestrife)
Angelica sylvestris (wild angelica)
Oenanthe fistulosa (water dropwort)
Orchis latifolia (marsh orchid)

Plants of the fen proper invade the reed swamp providing a succession of plants, according to the soil level above water, and peat from the accumulation of plant debris. On the higher, more dry areas scrub may develop in which isolated specimens of the following are to be found :

Rhamnus catharticus (buckthorn)
Alnus glutinosa (alder)
Salix herbacea (least willow)
Myrica gale (sweet gale)

A progressive scrub may develop into a small wood (fen carr) with alder as the dominant plant accompanied by :

Fraxinus excelsior (ash)
Rhamnus catharticus (buckthorn)
Salix cineria oleifolia (common sallow)
Viburnum opulus (guelder rose)
and an undergrowth containing :
Urtica dioica (stinging nettle)
Caltha palustris (marsh marigold)
Thelypteris palustris (marsh fern)
and various kinds of sedge.

Plants for the waterside

Among those plants usually found alongside water are the moisture-loving species of tree, shrub, ornamental grass, bamboo and fern. The larger specimens serve as a background, screen or windbreak while the smaller plants help to create interest at the water's edge.

Trees
For a single specimen there is none that can surpass the weeping willow (Salix babylonica) in a waterside setting, but it should be planted where there is a sufficient expanse of water to give the right scale. Other trees at home beside water include :
Acer rubrum (swamp or red maple)
A. saccharinum (silver maple)
Alnus glutinosa (common alder)
Betula pubescens (white birch)
B. nigra (river or red birch)
Populus marilandica (black poplar hybrid)
P. tremula (aspen)
Quercus bicolor (swamp white oak)
Q. phellos (willow oak)
Salix caprea (goat willow)
S. coerulea (cricket-bat willow)
Taxodium distichum (bog cypress)

Shrubs
Near the water's edge the moisture-loving dogwoods provide a very useful group of plants with their brightly coloured stems in winter and attractive foliage in summer. Other shrubs associated with an aquatic environment are shown in Table 94 (page 249).

Hardy ornamental grasses and bamboos
The slender, graceful habit of the ornamental grasses and bamboos is in marked contrast to the foliage of trees and shrubs. Many of the bamboos require shelter from east and north-east winds and therefore should be planted in protected locations such as in the foreground to a group of trees or shrubs. A selection, by no means exhaustive, is given in Table 95 (page 249).

Hardy ferns
Ferns prefer a moist shady situation in a cool, moist soil, sheltered from the cold spring winds ; the water's edge and the bog garden are ideal places in which to plant them although several species will grow in ordinary soil.
Planting is best done in the dormant season, between October and March, using a planting mixture comprising one part each of loam, fibrous peat and silver sand to which decayed leaf-mould is added. Care must be taken when transplanting to ensure that the mixture is not packed too tightly around the roots. Hardy ferns for the waterside are listed in Table 96 (page 250).

Preparation and planting of the pool

Rooted aquatics, including water-lilies, may be planted either directly into the soil base of the pool or in special containers (Fig. 61). The preparation of the pool depends upon which method of planting is to be employed. Before any work is put in hand a newly constructed concrete pool must be allowed to mature to prevent the pond life suffering any ill effects from the toxic elements present in the concrete. This may be effected by filling the pool with water and leaving it to stand throughout the winter months, after which time it is emptied and thoroughly rinsed out with clear water. Alternatively, the pool may be filled with water and a sufficient quantity of permanganate of potash crystals stirred into it to colour the water a wine-red. If allowed to stand for several days the liquid clears, leaving a sludge at the bottom ; the pool should then be emptied and well rinsed out. Although planting may be carried out afterwards, the introduction of livestock should be delayed for at least six weeks.
A much quicker method is to apply bituminous paint to the concrete surface to seal the pores of the material and so prevent the toxic substances from seeping through into the water in the pool.

Direct planting
Some aquatics, such as water-lilies, make a good deal of growth in a season and require a rich soil to ensure strong healthy plants. The planting compost, comprising one part cow manure to six parts turfy loam, should be prepared

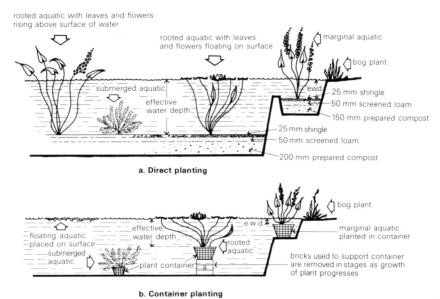

rooted aquatic with leaves and flowers
rising above surface of water

rooted aquatic with leaves
and flowers floating on surface

marginal aquatic

bog plant

submerged aquatic

effective
water depth

e.w.d.

25 mm shingle
50 mm screened loam
150 mm prepared compost

25 mm shingle
50 mm screened loam
200 mm prepared compost

a. Direct planting

bog plant

floating aquatic
placed on surface

effective
water depth

e.w.d.

marginal aquatic
planted in container

submerged
aquatic

rooted
aquatic

plant container

bricks used to support container
are removed in stages as growth
of plant progresses

b. Container planting

Fig. 61   Planting of pools

well in advance. On no account must any other animal manure be incorporated in the compost since it may either be too rich or cause fermentation, resulting in discolouration of the water. Peat, leaf-mould and organic substitutes have a similar effect and should not be used.

Where the compost cannot be prepared well in advance, a coarsely screened loam (the fibrous and root material removed) should be mixed with bonemeal in the proportions of four parts loam to one part bonemeal.

A 200 mm layer of compost should be spread on the bottom of the pool and a 150 mm layer along the marginal planting troughs. To prevent any cow manure from rising to the surface, so fouling the water, a layer of approximately 50 mm of screened loam should be applied and well firmed to prevent any disturbance by the addition of water to the pool. As a further precaution, a 25 mm layer of shingle may be laid carefully on top of the loam.

Planting should take place during April, May or June, the half-hardy aquatics being the last to be planted. The compost must be in a much wetter state than that normally employed for planting in garden soil so that it binds sufficiently well to prevent the plant roots from floating to the surface. Care is needed to ensure that the aquatics are firmly set because the action of running water into the pool may loosen or displace any that are not properly planted. Dead and broken foliage should be removed and the roots slightly trimmed beforehand. Quantities of plant material required for pools of various

size and depth are given in Table 97 (page 250).

Actual planting methods differ according to the type of aquatic, as described below.

Water-lilies. The rootstocks of the various groups must be set in their correct positions, as follows:

(a) *Odorata and tuberosa groups:* the long, fleshy rhizomes should be placed horizontally and covered with 25 mm of soil leaving only the growing point (crown) and top of the rhizome exposed.

(b) *Marliacea group:* the large rounded tubers should be set in a vertical position with the roots spread out and only the crown exposed. The plants grow from a collar, their rootstock going straight down into the soil.

When planting water-lilies the soil depth should be not less than 200 mm, with an area of 300×300 mm allowed for each plant. The roots need to be temporarily secured by placing a few large stones around the crowns until such time as they establish themselves.

Lotus (Nelumbo). The long tubers should be placed in a horizontal position and barely covered with soil. Great care must be taken to protect the growing point from damage, otherwise the plant will not survive.

Nuphars. These hardy, strong-growing aquatics are cultivated in the same way as water-lilies. The coarse rhizomatous roots must be planted firmly to prevent them from floating to the surface when water is added to the pool.

Submerged aquatics. These and other submerged plants must be set up to their crowns in soil or inserted as cuttings at the same time as the water-lilies and other aquatics are planted.

Floating aquatics. These require no planting preparation but are simply placed upon the surface of the water.

Marginal aquatics. Where the plants are to be set directly into the soil in planting troughs they may be planted at the same time as the other aquatics; they require 150 mm depth of soil submerged in (up to) 100 mm of water. Where there is no shelf for planting at the pool perimeter, the marginal aquatics require 150–460 mm depth of water.

If the plants are to be set in containers on a shelf, planting should be delayed until the water in the pool is at the shelf height.

Container planting

There are several kinds of container on the market but those having solid sides should be avoided because they prevent the plant roots from coming into contact with the water. Baskets or aquatic pans with regularly spaced holes in the sides are ideal; wooden crates may also be used.

The containers are lined with turf, so that soil is prevented from sifting out of them, and then filled with the prepared compost in which the aquatics are set in their correct positions. Each container is then carefully lowered into position with the plants set just below the water surface. In some cases it may be necessary to raise the containers by placing underneath them bricks, which may then be removed as necessary when the plants have grown in size.

Although a simple method, adopted where the pool is already in existence or the expanse of water is large, container planting has its drawbacks—partcularly in the case of the more vigorous water-lilies which may soon exhaust the supply of food material in the comparatively small containers. Aquatics planted this way require repotting every third year, otherwise they are liable to become weak and starved.

Adding water to the pool

Once planting is completed, water may gradually be added to the pool over a period of six to eight weeks, but initially the amount introduced must be sufficient only to cover the crowns of the plants. More water may be added a few days later and thereafter at intervals, the quantity being in direct proportion to the growth of the plants so that they are able to acclimatise themselves to their new environment.

Soon after planting has been carried out a chemical change takes place within the pool causing the water to become cloudy and discoloured. This natural phenomenon is due to the biological activities of the plant and animal life there; as soon as these achieve a balance the water becomes clear again. This may take several weeks, but if the cloudiness persists it is an indication that some additions are necessary; the introduction of a few more oxygenating aquatics should rectify this. Although chemical rectifiers may be a temporary remedy, the pool is best left alone to achieve its balance naturally.

Livestock in the pool

Livestock, although not essential to pool life, provides an interest and, in some cases, serves a useful purpose. It is wise to delay its introduction until the plant life is established so that the fish have some shady spots to which they may resort if the sun is hot. The incorporation of plenty of submerged aquatics provides a place for the eggs during the spawning stage and a sanctuary for the fry. Snails may also be introduced with the fish; being natural scavengers, they help to keep the pool clean by consuming the unwanted food and other waste matter. The two best varieties for still or slow-running water are the black ramshorn or trumpet snail (*Planorbis corneus*), which multiplies rapidly, and the freshwater winkle (*Paludina vivipara*). Although the freshwater whelk (*Limnea stagnalis*) is also a useful scavenger and a prolific breeder, it is known to attack the leaves of water-lilies.

When calculating the number of fish, 350 mm² of water surface area should be allowed for every 150 mm length of fish (including tail). During the initial stages of creating the pool, only approximately half the final quantity of fish should be introduced in order to allow for further growth of both fish and plants.

Fish for the medium-sized ornamental pool

GOLDFISH (*Carassius auratus*) 250–300 mm. The most popular fish for ornamental pools because of its hardiness and longevity. It breeds freely and ranges in colour between red, gold, yellow and white. Varieties of goldfish include:

Comet longtail goldfish	Similar to the common goldfish but has long flowing fins and tail and is usually a bright red colour.
Shubunkin	Considered to be the best fancy breed of goldfish for ornamental pools. Mistakenly described as nearly scaleless, it is found in a wide range of colours: reds, browns, yellows, blues and mottled.
Comet longtail shubunkin	A variety having long flowing fins and tail.

CARP (*Carassius* and *Cyprinus*)

Crucian or bronze carp (*Carassius*) 150–250 mm	Very similar to the goldfish but of less attractive colouring—generally a greenish-brown or bronze with a brassy-coloured belly. It lives for about seven years.
Gibel or Prussian carp	A variety of the crucian carp having a slimmer body.
Common carp (*Cyprinus carpio*) 250–500 mm	Similar in appearance to the crucian carp, but has four barbels on the upper lip. Its elongated body has a bluish-green or brownish-green back and sides of bluish-green to golden-yellow. Its life span is twice that of the crucian carp.
Red carp 600 mm or more	An oriental variety of the common carp bred under the name of *hi-goi* in colours mostly of rose- and grey-flecked black. Some specimens appear to be 'scaleless', like the shubunkin. The highly-coloured and spangled forms of the *koi* are thought to be superior to the *hi-goi* because they are more adaptable and easier to keep.

TENCH (*Tinca tinca*)

Common or green tench 200–300 mm	A small-scaled handsome fish varying considerably in colour according to locality; usually the back and sides range from dark to a light olive-green, often with a golden tint. It is a useful scavenger in the pool but, because it is a bottom feeder, is seldom seen.
Golden tench or schlei	A variety of the green tench, rich bronze in colour.

ORFE (*Idus idus*) 300–500 mm or more. An attractive fish for display in the pool since it swims near the surface; more suited to the larger pool.

Golden orfe	A fast-swimming fish with a pale gold back and a silvery pink belly. A shoal of golden orfe make a fine display in the pool. An excellent fish for keeping flies and other insects under control.
Silver orfe	A silvery-coloured variety similar to the golden orfe.

RUDD (*Scardinius erythrophthalmus*) 200–300 mm. Although sometimes mistaken for the roach, it is more attractive; in habit it is similar to the orfe, being an excellent fish for devouring mosquito larvae.

Generally, brassy-green back with brassy-yellow sides and a silvery-white belly. It has a life span of about five years.

Golden rudd	A variety with reddish-gold body and bright red fins.
Silver rudd	A similar variety having a silver-coloured body.

GUDGEON (*Gobio gobia*) 150 mm. In habit the gudgeon is similar to the tench, being a great scavenger which seldom rises to the surface. It has a greyish-green back with dark spots and streaks and a silvery-pink belly.

Fish for the smaller pool

Two varieties of fish, whose natural habitat is clear shallow water with a gravel bed, are the minnow and the loach. Both are able to adapt to the conditions of the small pool.

MINNOW (*Phoxinus phoxinus*) 75–125 mm. The minnow should not be kept in the same pool as larger fish, which are its predators. Because minnows are active shoalers and gregarious fish they need to be stocked in fair numbers.

LOACH. Although the loach in nature is found in fast-flowing shallow water, it will adapt itself to the conditions of the deeper pond where there is a shallow trough in which it can lie among the aquatics growing there.

Stone loach (*Nemacheilus barbatulus*) 100–125 mm	Generally dark olive to a muddy-yellow back; paler sides and belly with dark brown irregular markings.
Spined loach (*Cobitis taenia*) 75–100 mm	Pale yellow body with brownish coloured spots.

Fish for the larger pool or stream

PIKE (*Esox lucius*) 400–1000 mm. Because it is an extremely active predator the pike should not be kept with any other fish. The colour of the pike varies according to locality; it generally has a dark olive-green back and paler coloured sides with dark markings and a whitish belly. Its life-span is approximately fifteen years.

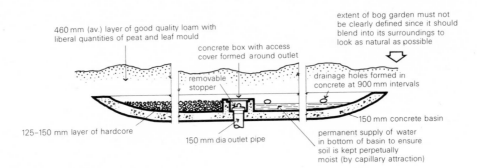

460 mm (av.) layer of good quality loam with liberal quantities of peat and leaf mould

concrete box with access cover formed around outlet

extent of bog garden must not be clearly defined since it should blend into its surroundings to look as natural as possible

removable stopper

drainage holes formed in concrete at 900 mm intervals

150 mm concrete basin

125–150 mm layer of hardcore

150 mm dia outlet pipe

permanent supply of water in bottom of basin to ensure soil is kept perpetually moist (by capillary attraction)

Fig. 62   Bog garden construction

Construction and planting of the bog garden

Ideally, the water garden should include a bog garden. This is the swampy area surrounding a pool or lake and is equivalent to the swamp zone of fenland or the reed swamp zone of marshland described earlier. The plants grown here must be those moisture-loving species which flourish close to water. If a natural site for the bog garden cannot be found it must be constructed in a low-lying area so that it appears as natural as possible. The area should be excavated to a depth of approximately 380 mm and a shallow reinforced concrete basin constructed, 150 mm thick, with drainage holes at 900 mm intervals around the sides, 125–150 mm from the top, to allow surplus water to be carried away. A drainage hole should also be incorporated at the bottom of the basin, fitted with a suitable plug, and provision made for easy access to it. A 125–150 mm layer of hardcore is then placed over the floor of the basin, taking care to see that the drainage plug is suitably protected but readily accessible. Over this is spread a 460 mm layer of good quality loam, into which a liberal quantity of peat and leaf mould has been incorporated; this acts as a sponge, conserving moisture and food for the plants in their new home. The addition of a little

coarse sand may be necessary to assist some plants, such as bog orchids, in the formation of new roots; it also helps to prevent decay. Lime is added only where required, to suit individual plant requirements (Fig.62).

The finished ground levels need not be even and it is better if the area is made to look more natural by creating mounds and hillocks. Stepping stones are necessary to give access to the more swampy parts of the bog garden. They also provide a home for those plants which thrive better in crevices between individual stones than in more open situations. The stones should be reasonably flat, large enough to stand upon with both feet and positioned an easy stride apart.

Water in the bottom of the basin is necessary in order for the soil to be kept in a perpetually moist condition (by capillary attraction). In order to maintain this supply a tap should be provided, suitably positioned nearby, to replenish the water when required. Any overflow from the pool should also be allowed to pass into the bog garden. Success depends upon the presence of constant moisture and only plants known to thrive in these conditions should be planted (Table 93). The plants are best set in large groups to create bold colour effects, rather than dotted about the garden as individual specimens.

Table 86
Hardy water-lilies for large pools or lakes 600–900 mm deep

Nymphaea alba	White. Native plant bearing flowers 75–100 mm across.
N. 'Attraction'	Garnet-red, flecked white. 175–200 mm across.
N. 'Charles de Meurville'	Wine-red. Vigorous variety, often flowering. 250 mm across.
N. 'Col. Welch'	Canary yellow star-shaped flowers, 75–100 mm above surface of water. Mottled foliage.
N. Colossea	Enormous flowers, pale pink passing to cream. Retains its character from early spring until the frosts.
N. 'Escarboucle'	Vermilion crimson with conspicuous crimson anthers. Unequalled for richness of colour. Free-flowering and prolific, 250 mm across.
N. 'Gladstoniana'	White. Large flowers 250 mm across with yellow stamens. Dark green foliage stands well out of water.
N. Marliacea Albida	White. Flowers stand just above surface of water and are freely produced.
N. Marliacea Carnea	Blush white with rosy tinge. Similar to above variety.
N. Marliacea Rosea	Soft pink. Golden stamens. Large fragrant flowers are long-lasting.
N. Picciola	Amaranth crimson. Abundance of large open star-shaped flowers often 230–250 mm across. Reddish-green leaves, splashed maroon.
N. tuberosa Richardsonii	White. Globular flowers with conspicuous green sepals.
N. Virginalis	White. Shell-shaped fragrant flowers, in bloom throughout the summer.

Table 87
Hardy water-lilies for medium-sized pools 450–600 mm deep

Nymphaea Brackleyi Rosea	Deep rose pink. Sweetly scented flowers stand just above water level. Green foliage.
N. 'Conqueror'	Rose crimson, flecked white. Cup-shaped flowers with white inside to sepals. Prolific bloomer.
N. 'Escarboucle'	See Table 86.
N. 'Formosa'	Rose pink passing to rich rose with age. Golden-yellow stamens.
N. Gloriosa	Dark crimson. Sweetly scented flowers 150–175 mm across.
N. Indiana	Orange-red turning to copper-red. Foliage heavily spotted maroon.
N. 'James Brydon'	Rose crimson. Large paeony-shaped flowers ; free-flowering and one of the finest of the hardy water-lilies. Succeeds in shady situations.
N. Mansaniello	Carmine rose. Sweet-scented large paeony-shaped flowers ; orange-yellow stamens.
N. 'Mary Exquisita'	Soft pink. Sweet-scented flowers 125–150 mm across. Continuous bloomer.
N. Moorei	Canary yellow. Bright yellow stamens. Green foliage heavily spotted brown.
N. odorata Alba	White. Sweetly scented flowers are freely produced from early June to October.
N. odorata Turicensis	Soft rose. Sweetly scented star-like blooms.
N. 'René Gerard'	Rich rose flecked crimson. Stellate flowers are often 230 mm across. Very free-flowering.
N. 'Rose Magnolia'	Soft pink. Flowers usually 100–125 mm across stand well out of the water. Handsome foliage.
N. 'Rose Nymph'	Deep rose. Large open fragrant flowers 150–175 mm float gracefully on the surface of the water and are produced in abundance from early spring until late autumn.
N. 'Sunrise'	Sulphur yellow. Large fragrant blooms with golden filaments. Green foliage, with a red under-surface, flecked with brown.
N. Virginalis	See Table 86.
N. 'Wm. Falconer'	Deep blood-red. Flowers are 150–175 mm across with yellow stamens. Dark red foliage passes to green with prominent red veining. Darkest red hardy water-lily (apart from *Atropurpurea*).

Table 88
Hardy water-lilies for small pools 300–450 mm deep

Nymphaea 'Albatross'	White. Large, star-shaped flowers with conspicuous golden-yellow anthers. Rich purple young foliage changes to deep green at maturity.
N. caroliniana	Rose pink. Sweetly scented flowers have yellow stamens.
N. 'Conqueror'	See Table 87.
N. 'Eugenia de Land'	Rich pink. Medium-sized stellate flowers with golden-yellow stamens stand above the water.
N. 'Firecrest'	Deep pink. Fragrant flowers, widely opened, reveal erect red-tipped stamens.
N. Froebeli	Wine red. Fragrant flowers ; first-rate variety for small pools and tubs. Free flowering.
N. Graziella	Coppery orange. Flowers tend to become lighter with age and have bright orange stamens. Excellent for tubs and very shallow pools.
N. 'Hermine'	White, star-shaped flowers have green sepals and stand well erect 75–100 mm from the water. Bright green foliage.
N. Laydekeri Fulgens	Crimson carmine. Bold clusters of orange-red stamens.
N. Laydekeri Lilacea	Rose lilac. Flowers deepen to bright carmine with age. Yellow stamens.
N. Laydekeri Purpurata	Rosy crimson. Flowers slightly spotted and flecked with white. Bright orange-red stamens. Best free-flowering form of the group.
N. odorata Sulphurea	Sulphur yellow. Star-shaped blooms stand above water-level and tend to darken with age. Green foliage blotched with dark brown markings. *N. grandiflora* has larger flowers and leaves.
N. odorata Turicensis	See Table 87.
N. 'Paul Hariot'	Apricot yellow turning to orange-pink and finally to brilliant copper-red with age. Green foliage mottled with maroon. Very free-flowering.
N. 'Pink Opal'	Coral pink. Stellate flowers stand above the water. Ideal for cutting.
N. Sanguinea	Crimson carmine. Bold clusters of orange-red stamens. Olive green foliage blotched with brown.
N. 'Sioux'	Rich yellow turning to reddish-copper with age. Foliage mottled brown and purple.
N. Somptuosa	Rose pink. Fragrant globular flowers with orange stamens. Dark foliage.
N. 'Sunrise'	See Table 87.

Table 89
Hardy water-lilies for miniature pools 100–250 mm deep

N. Laydekeri Fulgens	See Table 88.
N. Laydekeri Lilacea	See Table 88.
N. odorata minor	White. Sweetly scented star-shaped flowers. Soft green foliage with reddish under-surface. Early flowering.
N. 'Paul Hariot'	See Table 88.
N. pygmaea Alba	White. Smallest white water-lily. Ideal for very shallow water.
N. pygmaea Helvola	Soft sulphur yellow. Star-shaped flowers produced in abundance throughout the season. Olive green foliage streaked and marked with brown and maroon blotches.
N. Sanguinea	See Table 88.

Table 90
Hardy aquatic plants
(*figures denote average heights*)

Acorus calamus (sweet flag)	Sweetly scented reed-like plant with sedge habit ; broad strap-like leaves resembling flag iris ; greenish flowers. 750 mm. Suitable for margin of pool.
A. c. Variegatus	More desirable plant than the type. Variegated green and cream foliage. 750 mm.
Alisma lanceolatum (water plantain)	Slender lanceolate foliage, sharply pointed at tip. Pinkish-white flowers. 300–450 mm.
A. plantago-aquatica (great water plantain or mad dog weed)	Native aquatic. Large-stalked leaves and panicles of small rose-coloured flowers. 600–900 mm.
Aponogeton distachyum (water hawthorn)	Dainty, sweet-scented white flower with conspicuous black anthers. Broad strap-shaped leaves float on the surface. There are several varieties.
Baldellia ranunculoides (lesser water plantain)	Native plant, narrow leaves tapering both ends. Rosy-white flowers. 300 mm.
Butomus umbellatus (native flowering rush or water gladiole)	Sword-shaped leaves ; bold stems with umbels of rose-pink flowers. Suitable for shallow water. 600–1200 mm.
Calla palustris (bog arum)	Heart-shaped leaves ; white arum-like flowers, followed by red berries in autumn. Plant is fertilised by snails. 300–450 mm.
Caltha polypetala (giant marsh marigold)	Profusion of large golden-yellow flowers and bold dark green leaves up to 300 mm across. 600–900 mm.
C. p. Flore Pleno (double marsh marigold)	Masses of full double golden-yellow flowers. 300–450 mm. A later-flowering double type is *C. p. Monstrosa Plena*.
Cotula coronopifolia (brass buttons)	Masses of small golden flowers throughout the summer. Ideal for small pools and tubs. 230 mm.
Damasonium alisma (star fruit)	Rare native aquatic ; small glaucous leaves float on surface of shallow water. White flowers grow in whorls. 150 mm.
Decodon verticillatus (swamp loosestrife or water willow)	Very showy in autumn when bright green foliage turns to brilliant red shades. 750 mm.
Houttuynia cordata	Metallic blue-green heart-shaped leaves, bright red stems. Dainty cone-shaped flowers with four snow-white bracts. 450 mm.
Hypericum elodes (marsh St John's wort)	Clusters of soft yellow flowers and attractive woolly foliage. Useful for concealing the pool edge. 150 mm.
Iris laevigata vars.	Thrives equally well in moist soil or shallow water. 450 mm.
Juncus effusus spiralis (corkscrew rush)	Stems twisted in the manner of a corkscrew. Not invasive like the other *Juncus* and equally suitable for small pools or lakes. 450 mm.
J. inflexus (hard rush)	Stiff blue-grey furrowed stems. 600 mm.
J. subuliflorus (common rush)	Dark green stems and brown inflorescence. 300–1200 mm.
Limnanthemum peltatum (water fringe)	Native plant with heart-shaped mottled foliage which lies on surface of water. Golden-yellow flowers stand above water. Grows in 150–450 mm of water.
Ludwigia uruguayensis (floating jussieua or primrose willow)	Masses of creeping or floating stems. 300–900 mm. Covers surface of water. Golden flowers stand above the water.
Mentha aquatica (water mint or fish mint)	Native plant with aromatic foliage and whorls of lilac flowers. Useful for keeping water pure and clear. 300–1200 mm.
Menyanthes trifoliata (bog bean)	Native aquatic. Olive green three-leaved foliage with compound clusters of dainty white flowers. 300 mm.
Myosotis scorpioides	Clusters of bright blue florets. Free-flowering in shady positions, it grows to 230–300 mm. *M. s. Semperflorens* is a dwarf variety reaching 150–200 mm.
Orontium aquaticum (golden club)	Grows at pond edge or in deep water, leaves float on the surface like water-lilies. Small yellow florets 300–450 mm.
Peltandra virginica (green arrow arum)	Bright green shield-shaped leaves 100–750 mm long. White arum-like flowers succeeded by green berries.
Pontederia cordata (pickerel weed)	Shiny olive green foliage. Small delphinium-like pale blue flowers. 600 mm.
Ranunculus lingua (great spearwort)	Native aquatic with erect dark green foliage and large buttercup flowers. 600–750 mm. *R. l. Grandiflora* differs only in its greater size. *R. flammula* is similar but much smaller.

continued

Table 90 *Continued*

Rumex hydrolapathum (great water dock)	Bold, dark green dock-like leaves which assume crimson tints in autumn. Suitable only for planting to create bold effects along water courses. 1200–1800 mm.
Sagittaria latifolia (duck potato)	Broadly arrow-shaped leaves vary considerably in size and have long basal lobes. White flowers. 300–1200 mm.
S. sagittifolia (common arrowhead)	Whorls of snow-white flowers on erect stems. Arrowhead leaves. 450 mm.
S. s. Flore Pleno	Double-flowered form resembling giant double stock. One of the finest hardy aquatics.
Saururus cernus (American swamp lily or lizard's tail)	Dense spikes of nodding fragrant cream flowers. Bright green heart-shaped leaves. 300–600 mm.
Scutellaria galericulata (skull cap)	Bright blue snapdragon-like flowers; oblong tapering downy leaves. 300–400 mm.
Sonchus palustris (marsh sow thistle)	Native plant. Dandelion flower-heads and long narrow leaves. 1500–2400 mm.
Sparganium angustifolium (floating bur reed)	Native aquatic. Long transparent floating leaves and a solitary flower-head. Like the other species this plant is only suitable for the wild garden or as cover for wild fowl.
S. erectum (branched bur reed)	Similar in flower to *Iris pseudacorus*. Sword-shaped leaves triangular at base. 600 mm.
Teucrium scordium (water germander)	Native plant with whorls of purplish-red flowers and oblong serrated leaves. 100–150 mm.
Typha angustifolia (lesser reed mace)	Numerous cat's tail spikes of dark brown inflorescence; narrow glaucous foliage. 1200–2400 mm.
T. latifolia (bulrush or great reed mace)	Large rusty brown cat's tail spikes and long grassy leaves. Ideal for naturalising in large stretches of water. 1200–2400 mm.
Veronica beccabunga (brooklime)	Native creeping aquatic with clusters of bright blue flowers and shiny dark green foliage. 230–300 mm.

Table 91
Hardy floating aquatics

Azolla caroliniana (fairy moss)	Pale green moss-like foliage which assumes bright reddish tint in autumn.
Hydrocharis morsus-ranae (frogbit)	Small, bright green, kidney-shaped leaves and small three-petalled snow-white flowers resembling a tiny water-lily. Best native floating aquatic but snails tend to spoil leaves by feeding on them.
Limnobium boscii (American frogbit)	Similar to native plant but lighter in colour with larger, more pointed foliage. It retains its character throughout winter.
Riccia fluitans (crystal wort)	A good surface oxygenator; masses of pale green, tightly packed, segmented foliage provides sanctuary for fry.
Stratiotes aloides (water soldier)	Native plant. Foliage resembles that of the pineapple. White flowers. The plant roots in mud, rising to the surface to flower and sinking to bottom in autumn.
Trapa natans (water chestnut)	Huge rosettes of olive green foliage and small white flowers on thin stems.

Table 92
Submerged oxygenating aquatics

Callitriche autumnalis (autumnal starwort)	Excellent oxygenator and one of the few active during winter months. Tiny, dark green foliage.
Ceratophyllum demersum (hornwort)	Completely submerged aquatic ; dense whorls of spiny foliage (*C. muricatum* is very similar) ; first class oxygenator and suitable for soil-less pools.
Chara aspera (stonewort)	Slender branched stems with a tangled mass of bright green foliage.
C. vulgaris	Common in a number of localities in Britain. Ash-coloured branching stems.
Crassula recurva (pigmy weed)	Tufted or creeping habit in shallow water but becomes elongated in deeper water.
Egeria densa (*Elodea densa*)	Excellent pond oxygenator. Small three-petalled flowers appear just above water level. Whorls of linear leaves.
Eleocharis acicularis (slender spike rush)	Dense mats of hair-like foliage giving a graceful underwater effect.
Elodea canadensis (Canadian pondweed)	Excellent oxygenator. Brittle stem thickly clotted with whorls of minutely serrated oval leaves.
Fontinalis antipyretica (willow moss)	Very long branching stems covered with moss-like foliage. Excellent oxygenator, usually grown in running water.
Hottonia palustris (water violet)	Native aquatic bearing whorls of lilac flowers standing 150–300 mm above the surface.
Isoetes lacustris (quillwort or Merlin's grass)	Tufts of narrow rush-like foliage on which fish feed.
Lobelia dortmanna (water lobelia or water gladiole)	Dwarf tufts of bright green succulent foliage. Dainty light blue flower borne in loose terminal racemes above surface of water.
Myriophyllum verticillatum (whorled water milfoil)	Whorls of finely divided rich green foliage with small greenish flowers.
Oenanthe fluviatilis (river water dropwort)	Strong-growing submerged aquatic with only the flowers standing out of water. Good plant for running water.
Potamogeton crispus (curled pondweed)	Dense, crinkled, semi-translucent foliage which creates a rosy glow in bright sunlight.
P. lucens (shining pondweed)	Broad translucent leaves which tightly clasp the stem. Good plant for running water.
P. natans (floating pondweed)	Submerged narrow foliage (not always present) and elliptical leaves ; cylindrical spikes of small green flowers above water level. Useful for early spawning fish, e.g. carp and goldfish.
P. pectinatus (fennel-leaved pondweed)	Many-branching hair-like stems and foliage. Good oxygenator if kept within bounds.
Ranunculus aquatilis (water crowfoot)	Submerged leaves divided into numerous hair-like segments and three-lobed leaves floating on the surface. Small white flowers.

Table 93
Hardy plants for the bog garden
(*figures denote average heights*)

Aconitum anglicum (monkshood)	Native plant found in S. and S.W. England ; deep blue flowers—pleasing contrast with *Rudbeckia, Hemerocallis* and *Hosta.*. 900 mm.
Ajuga reptans (common bugle)	Found in woodlands. 150 mm.
Anagallis tenella (bog pimpernel)	Creeping native plant, rosy-pink flowers. 300 mm.
Anemone rivularis (wind flower)	Waterside plant with loose umbels of snow-white flowers and violet anthers. 600 mm.
Aruncus dioicus (goat's beard)	Dark, divided foliage and heavy plumes of creamy-white flowers. 900 mm.
Aster nemoralis (bog aster)	Violet/rose-pink flowers. 450 mm.
Astilbe arendsii vars. *'Fanal'*	Brilliant red. 750 mm.
'Granat'	Dark crimson. 1070 mm.
Caltha palustris Flore Pleno (marsh marigold)	Native plant with rich golden flowers. 300 mm.
Campanula rotundifolia (harebell)	Native plant with blue bell-shaped flowers. 450 mm.
Cardamine pratensis (lady's smock)	Native plant with rosy-lilac flowers. 150 mm.
Chrysanthemum lacustre (marsh ox-eye daisy)	White flowers. 600 mm.
Cimicifuga racemosa (snakeroot)	Fragrant white flowers from August to end September. 1200 mm.
Clintonia borealis	Light green plantain-like foliage, greenish-yellow flowers followed by oval, blue berries. 300 mm.
Cornus canadensis (creeping dogwood)	Carpeting plant, light green foliage. Silver-white flowers followed by scarlet berries. 150 mm.
Dodecatheon meadia var. *'Brilliant'* (shooting star or American cowslip)	Long green leaves spotted purple, deep rose-crimson flowers turned back as in the cyclamen. 300 mm.
Filipendula purpurea (*Spiraea palmata*) (meadow-sweet)	Dark green foliage and crimson-pink flowers. 1200 mm.
Gentiana pneumonanthe (marsh gentian)	Native species, rich blue flowers. 230 mm.
Gillenia trifoliata (bowman's root or Indian physic)	Sprays of white flowers and green spiraea-like foliage. 900 mm.
Hemerocallis vars. (day lily)	Colours range from yellow, apricot, orange, bronze through to rose. Associate well with *Hosta, Osmunda* and *Astilbe*. 600 mm.
Hosta sieboldiana (plantain lily)	Most ornamental member of the genus ; large cordate leaves, pale lilac flowers densely clustered on stems. 600 mm.
Iris kaempferi vars. (clematis iris)	Japanese irises with a wide range of colours. 900 mm.
Ligularia wilsonianus (giant groundsel)	Tall flower stems carry a rich profusion of rich golden-yellow flowers. Large heart-shaped leaves. 1500 mm.
Lythrum salicaria (purple loosestrife)	Handsome native plant with reddish-purple flowers. Surpassed in bloom by a number of hybrids. 750 mm.
Macleaya cordata (plume poppy)	Large, rounded grey-green leaves, numerous creamy-white starry flowers.
Physostegia virginiana 'Vivid' (obedient plant)	Rich dark lilac-pink flowers in September. 300 mm.
Podophyllum emodi (May apple)	Three-lobed umbrella-like leaves, bronze-red in spring turning to light green with black blotches later. White flowers followed by scarlet fruits. 450 mm.
Primula denticulata (Himalayan primrose)	Bold tufts of foliage and mauve globular flowers. 300 mm.
P. vulgaris and vars. (primrose)	A bright, colourful genus with many varieties. 150 mm.
Ranunculus aconitifolius Flore Pleno (Fair Maids of France or Kent)	Dark green buttercup leaves and double white flowers. 600 mm.
Rodgersia pinnata Superba	Deeply divided bronzy leaves and rich rose-coloured flowers. 900 mm.
Senecio aquaticus (marsh ragwort)	Native plant suitable for wild garden. Golden yellow flowers. 600 mm.
Smilacina racemosa (false spikenard)	Sprays of white blossoms followed by rosy-purple berries. 750 mm.
Tradescantia virginiana and vars. (flower of a day)	Erect plant with violet flowers freely produced throughout summer. 600 mm.
Trillium grandiflorum (wake Robin or ground lily)	White blooms. 300 mm.
Trollius ledebourii 'Golden Queen'	Saucer-shaped rich orange flowers. 750 mm.
Uvularia grandiflora (bellwort)	Bell-shaped yellow flowers. 300 mm.
Veronica gentianoides (speedwell)	Pale blue flowers with darker streaks. Useful ground cover plant. 450 mm.
Viola canina (dog violet)	Native plant. Small blue flowers. 100 mm.

Table 94
Shrubs for planting near the water's edge

Azalea	Spring blooms.
Clethra alnifolia (sweet pepper bush)	Handsome spikes of white flowers in late autumn.
Cornus alba vars. (dogwood)	Variegated leaves ; bright red or purple stems in winter.
C. florida (flowering dogwood)	Large white/pinkish flowers ; autumn leaf colours and scarlet fruits.
C. sericea (dogwood)	Yellow stems in winter.
Holodiscus discolor aeriaefolius	Spring flowers.
Rhododendron spp.	Spring and early summer blooms.
Rubus chamoemorus (cloudberry)	Flowers and fruits.
R. chloocladus	Useful cover plant in bog garden.
Salix daphnoides (violet willow)	Violet-purple stems with a bluish bloom in winter.
Sorbaria aitchisonii (false spiraee)	Bright red young stems ; attractive fern-like foliage, huge panicles of white flowers.
Spiraea arguta (bridal wreath)	Mass of small white blooms in spring.
S. canascens	Spring flowers.
S. japonica	Spring flowers.
S. salicifolia	Spring flowers.
Vaccinium myrtillus (bilberry or whortleberry)	Black berries with bluish bloom.

Table 95
Bamboos and grasses for the waterside
(*figures denote average heights*)

Arundo donax vars. (reed)	Large glaucous ornamental leaves ; large panicles of white flowers. 3 m.
Carex pseudocyperus	Bright green grassy leaves ; many drooping dark green spikelets. 600 mm.
C. riparia 'Bowles Golden'	Decorative sedge for shallow water. 300 mm.
Cortaderia argentea 'Suningale Silver' (pampas grass)	Silver-white plumes. 1·2–1·5 m.
C. rudiuscula	Lavender-coloured plumes more feathery than *C. argentea*. 1·2 m.
Cyperus eragrostis (galingale)	Grows in shallow water. 600 mm.
C. longus (sweet or English galingale)	Native species suitable for pond margin. 900 mm.
Eriophorum angustifolium (cotton grass)	Neat clumps of rush-like foliage.
Glyceria canadensis (rattlesnake grass)	The most handsome plant of this genus. Provides grain for wild fowl. 600 mm.
Miscanthus sacchariflorus (hardy sugar cane)	Best planted singly. Japanese species. 2·4 m.
M. sinensis	Deep green leaves with prominent white stripe down centre, each 600–900 mm long. 1·82 m.
Phragmites communis (common reed)	Broad glossy leaves and violet plumes of flowers. Useful for wild fowl cover in intensive lakeside plantings. 2·4 m.
Pleioblastus chino	Extremely hardy and one of the tallest bamboos of this genus. 4·6 m.
P. pumilus (dwarf bamboo)	Thin flexible canes and small leaves. 600 mm.
Polygonum amphibium (willow grass)	Lanceolate leaves, pink flower-spikes. Autumn foliage tints. 600–900 mm.
Pseudosasa japonica (bamboo)	Commonest variety of hardy bamboos. 1·82 m.
Sasa senanensis nebulosa	Bright green serrated leaves. 900 mm.
Scirpus lacustris (bulrush)	Fat, dark green rushes and umbels of dark brown flowers. 1·2 m.
Sinarundinaria nitida	One of the daintiest bamboos of this genus. 1·82 m.
Zizania aquatica (water or Indian rice)	One of the most handsome of aquatic grasses with broad, flat leaves and reedy stem. Grain useful for fish and water fowl (especially duck, widgeon and teal). 2·4 m.

Table 96
Hardy ferns for the waterside
(*figures denote average heights*)

Adiantum pedatum (hardy maidenhair)	Glistening black stems and soft green fronds. 450 mm.
Athyrium filix-foemina (lady fern)	Native fern with finely-cut vivid green fronds. 900 mm.
Cystopteris fragilis (brittle bladder fern)	Useful for growing in rock fissures near a waterfall. 100–200 mm.
Dryopteris filix mas var. *Bollandae* (buckler fern)	Imposing fern with conspicuous dark green fronds. 750 mm.
Matteuccia struthiopteris (ostrich feather fern)	Graceful plant with erect, pale green fronds which droop and spread to the form of a giant shuttlecock. 900 mm.
Onoclea sensibilis (sensitive fern)	Pale green fronds ; can grow in shallow water. 600 mm.
Osmunda regalis (royal fern)	Finest fern for planting near water ; pale green fronds in spring gradually change to assume deep russet hues in autumn. 1·2 m.
Phyllitis scolopendrium (common hart's tongue)	Shining bright green fronds ; evergreen. 450 mm.
Polypodium vulgare (common polypody or adder's fern)	Suitable for wild gardens or similar situations where it can be left undisturbed and allowed to take possession. 600 mm.
Thelypteris palustris (marsh fern)	Native fern with dainty erect fronts. 450 mm.

Table 97
Quantities of plant material required for pools of various sizes

Depth of water (*mm*)	Surface area (*m²*)	Water-lilies	Submerged oxygenators	Floating aquatics	Marginal aquatics
less than 380	1	1*	4	2	3
	2	1*	10	3	5
	3	2*	16	4	5
380–450	1	1	6	2	3
	2	1	10	3	5
	3	2	16	4	5
450–900	4	2	24	5	7
	5	3	27	5	7
	6	3	30	6	9
	7	4	34	7	9
	8	4	40	9	10
	9	5	46	11	11
	10	5	53	14	14

*Miniature varieties

Eleven Outdoor Furniture

Selection and specification

The term 'outdoor furniture' covers a wide range of goods and includes items such as lamp posts, bollards, road signs, etc. (generally classed under the heading of 'street furniture'); garden furniture, e.g. seats, tables, plant containers; and a host of miscellaneous items ranging from flagpoles and weather vanes to sports and play equipment. Some of these may be fixed in permanent positions, others are movable, depending upon their particular function and type of design. The materials used for their manufacture are equally wide in range and include timber, concrete, steel, aluminium, asbestos cement, plastics, etc., often two or more materials being used in combination. In practice, many of these items are usually specified under the relevant trade heading, e.g. a concrete litter bin under 'Concretor' or a timber seat under 'Carpenter and Joiner'. Where the contract is a relatively small one, however, it is sometimes more convenient to group all the outdoor furniture under the separate heading of 'Miscellaneous'.

Whatever type of feature is introduced into the outdoor scene, its choice and siting, as well as its functional and physical properties, must be given careful thought if it is to enhance rather than detract from its surroundings. Some items, e.g. street furniture, are governed by statutory or technical needs as to their size and location. However well designed an item of furniture, in itself, may be, it is likely to strike a discordant note if out of scale with the rest of the layout or if the materials used in its construction are not in sympathy with those of its setting. Outdoor furniture that is ideally suited to the urban scene does not necessarily achieve a similar result if sited in a rural location; town design philosophy must not be extended to include the countryside where materials need to be chosen for their natural or rugged appearance.

Probably one of the most important aspects often overlooked when selecting outdoor items is that of maintenance. Newly manufactured things look fresh and bright when first set in position but the effects of sun and rain can soon result in shabbiness, rust and early deterioration if the wrong selection is made. The risk of vandalism is another problem; one must never underestimate the rough treatment or misuse which some members of the public can inflict on anything within their reach; this applies particularly to any free-standing object or one that has movable parts.

Bollards, buffers and other 'controlled access' barriers

Walls, fences, hedges, etc., are a means of creating a barrier between two differing uses or ownerships of land. Where limited access is required, a gap is left and a gate or other type of movable barrier installed. A gate, however, does not always fulfil the purpose and may even be detrimental if improperly used (a gate left open so that animals can stray soon defeats the object of placing it there). Restricted access can be achieved by other, and sometimes more effective, means, e.g. the erection of bollards. In rural areas the problem is more likely to be one of deterring farm animals from straying without restricting pedestrian or vehicular access, and the solution may be the use of stiles or cattle-grids.

Segregation of traffic and pedestrians and the restriction of parked vehicles are ever-increasing problems in town and countryside alike, but need to be dealt with sympathetically within their differing environments so that neither design nor materials create obtrusive features in the landscape. The use of bollards may be the right solution in the town, but not necessarily in open countryside. Wandering pedestrians also present difficulties; means of restricting them can never be foolproof, since some folk are always determined to stray beyond barriers and may thereby unwittingly encounter danger. There is a limit, of course, to the extent and type of protection that can be provided consistent with common sense, and no hard and fast rules can be laid down to cover every circumstance. Much depends upon the location and its individual problems, but in all cases every endeavour should be made to employ local materials and traditional skills.

Bollards

The function of a bollard (or series of bollards) is generally to act as an obstruction to wheeled traffic, usually segregating it from foot traffic. Traditionally, stone or cast iron bollards were used as a means of protecting the plinths of buildings, particularly the corners where these abutted the street frontage, from damage by the wheels of passing carriages. Nowadays the use of bollards has considerably widened and their siting is governed by the function which they are intended to serve. Restriction of vehicular access is dictated by car widths; the distance between bollards should not exceed 1·40 m except where commercial vehicles only are to be excluded. Spacing to permit pedestrian access only should be not less than 760 mm in order to allow prams and wheelchairs to pass between the bollards.

With few exceptions bollards are commercially manufactured; those constructed in-situ either form part of a building structure or serve a special kind of function. Unless a large quantity is to be incorporated in a layout it is usually a more economical proposition to select a marketed product than to specify a set of purpose-made units. Heights of fixed bollards range from 330 to 990 mm with diameters of 150–305 mm. Designs vary according to the materials used in their manufacture. At one time granite was widely used; it is no longer an economical proposition (except in granite areas) and has been supplanted by cheaper materials. If granite is specified the type of finish required must be stated, i.e. smooth, polished or finished to any degree of rough texture desired. Other types of stone selected must be hard, durable and capable of withstanding sudden impact. The materials used for reconstructed stone bollards should meet the requirements laid down in BS 1217:1945 and those employed for both cast stone and reinforced concrete should comply with BS 12:Part 2:1971, BS 882:Part 2:1973, BS 4449:1969 and BS 4482:1969. Methods of manufacture for reinforced concrete and reconstructed stone are practically the same and both products can be made with a wide variety of finishes. Where a bollard is intended as a protection to the corner of a building, a timber quadrant is inserted in the mould at the time of casting and removed after the concrete has cured: the resultant void allows the bollard to be fixed directly onto the corner.

Once a traditional material for bollards, cast iron is still to be found in the older parts of many towns and cities. There is a limited demand for such products and nowadays they are cast to order but, depending upon the type of design chosen, their cost need not be prohibitive.

On quaysides and wharfs and similar structures constructed of stone or concrete, good quality cast iron bollards should be specified. These are similar to those fitted on ships for towing and mooring and range in size from 100 to 450 mm nominal diameter and 190–857 mm in height. They may be sited singly or in pairs.

Where strength coupled with comparative lightness in weight is required, mild steel is often employed in the form of steel hollow tubes or rectangular sections. The units may be fixed in a permanent position or be removable or collapsible, depending upon the particular purpose they serve.

(a) *Fixed*. These are manufactured from heavy-gauge steel tubes or rectangular sections provided with a plate, whose diameter is twice that of the tube, welded onto the bottom for fixing purposes.

Boundary posts, approximately 50 mm diameter and 770 mm high, used to indicate the limits of a parking area, are supplied with a fishtail end for setting in concrete.

(b) *Removable*. Intended more often as 'guard posts', these bollards are designed so that they can readily be dropped into a socket in the ground when required for use; a hinged cover plate seals the hole once the bollard is removed. When in the open position, the cover plate serves as a fixing device to which the post is secured by means of a locking pin. Locking the post in position is achieved by hooking a padlock through a hole in the fixing-pin. The top of the post may be provided with a hole, if required, through which a horizontal barrier chain or rod can be passed.

(c) *Collapsible*. Two types fall into this category: telescopic and hinged bollards. Both have a similar purpose and design to that of the removable bollard. When not in use the telescopic tube can be dropped into a socket in the ground, the cap of the post being the only part visible at ground level.

The hinged bollard is able to rotate in one plane through 180° and is fixed at its lower end to a mild steel angle base plate which is securely bolted into the ground. To alleviate the risk of damage through rough usage when in the unlocked position, a small rubber buffer is fixed to the top of the post on the side nearest to the ground (when in the 'down' position).

Traffic bollards are generally constructed of coated pressed steel and plastic and are illuminated internally. BS 873: Part 3:1970 specifies their materials, construction, finish and performance. A smaller bollard, useful for both car parks and pedestrian routes, consists of a 140 mm diameter rustproofed steel tube having a 450 mm root which can be set in concrete. The lighting unit is mounted 860 mm high on top of the tube and has an internally sandblasted dioptric lens which prevents the risk of glare.

Cast aluminium bollards are generally designed to incorporate lamps so that they can be used for illumination purposes. Many of them are purpose-made products and may be more expensive than other types.

Although not in common use, timber bollards are ideally suited to marine or waterside settings. Hardwoods such as ekki, greenheart, jarrah or makore should be specified.

Unless removable, all bollards must be securely positioned in the ground to a depth sufficient to prevent their collapse or removal. Stone, reinforced concrete and cast iron bollards should be set not less than 300–450 mm below ground surface level on a concrete base (1:2:4 mix) of at least 100 mm depth, and surrounded by concrete of the same mix, not less than 200 mm on all sides, up to the level of the underside of the paving material. The latter should be taken right up to and finished flush with the bollard itself. Fixed metal bollards may be provided with either a fixing plate, to allow them to be bolted down into position on a concrete base, or fishtail ends so that they can be set in not less than 230 mm of concrete. Timber bollards should be set into a cast iron shoe bedded in concrete and should either be secured to the shoe itself or be removable.

Buffers

Buffers serve a similar purpose to that of bollards but are of horizontal form. One of their main uses is as crash barriers, and for this purpose they need to be of fairly substantial construction (but not completely rigid) in order to minimise the force of impact caused by any colliding vehicle. Where used at the back of parking bays the height of the rails should correspond with that of vehicle bumpers; additional higher rails are necessary where they are used as crash barriers (see page 65).

'Controlled access' barriers

(i) *Vehicular use.* In certain situations it may be necessary to limit vehicular access to an area by erecting a movable barrier other than a gate. Although the erection of a 'No Entry' sign is the simplest and cheapest substitute it is of little use unless legally enforceable. The alternative is to provide a boom, cattlegrid or drawbridge, depending upon the need and economic circumstances.

(a) *Boom.* A boom is a simple, cheap substitute for a field gate. Depending upon the width to be spanned the boom may consist of a simply supported pole, set on V-notched timber uprights, for widths up to 2·45 m. The 50–80 mm diameter pole can easily be lifted off its supports and then replaced. Larger spans require the boom to be secured at one end so that it pivots on its support when moved through an angle of 90 degrees. Sometimes it may be more convenient for the boom to be fixed so that it pivots vertically; in this case the pivoted end should be weighted sufficiently to act as a counterbalance to the boom. Automatically operated booms are commonly found in official car parks. Because it is somewhat expensive to install, the automatic boom is usually employed in situations where fairly strict access-control is needed and payment is demanded before a vehicle is permitted to enter (or leave) the site.

(b) *Cattlegrid.* Materials and constructional requirements are set out in BS 4008 : 1973, which defines a cattlegrid as ' . . . a device, set in a roadway, consisting of a number of transverse bars supported over a pit (the tops of the bars being level with the surface of the road) over which wheeled traffic may pass but which forms a barrier against animals'.

In order to minimise costs, cattlegrids are usually designed to take single-line traffic, catering for axle loads of 10 tonnes maximum. If loads in excess of this amount are expected, a by-pass gate should also be provided. Generally, grids need to be at least 2·13 m long and preferably 2·6 m wide; where intended to repel deer, a greater length is necessary. Circular, rather than flat-topped, bars are a better deterrent to straying animals. Spacing of the bars is important; a gap of 130 mm is sufficient to enable a man to stand between the bars with his feet resting on the pit floor (in order to carry out maintenance) and permits a smooth ride to vehicles but, at the same time, discourages animal escape. If flat-topped bars are specified, the gap between them should be increased to 150 mm. The grid itself is set over a shallow concrete pit, the floor of which should be not less than 250 mm below the bottom level of the transverse bars.

Guard fences, constructed of metal or timber, need to be erected on each side of the grid to prevent animals from scrambling around terminal posts.

(c) *Drawbridge.* The idea of using a ditch (or stream) spanned by a drawbridge as a means of restricting access is reminiscent of the moated castle; it is nevertheless an effective device and one with a number of possible variations, according to needs. Basically, all that is required is support for the wheel-tracks of vehicles; depending upon the span and size of track supports, these may either be manually set in position or lowered mechanically.

(ii) *Pedestrian use.* Designs for structures which enable pedestrians to enter or leave a 'controlled' area probably offer more scope than those allowing the passage of vehicles. Means of giving pedestrian access without the use of gates (apart from wicket gates and turnstiles) include bollards and booms (described above), stiles and, in the case of water, stepping stones.

(a) *Stiles.* The material principally employed in the construction of stiles is timber, although in stone districts indigenous material is more likely to be used. These structures should be of rugged design and capable of withstanding rough usage. Steps should be provided, where necessary, to facilitate easy negotiation of the stile; on waterlogged ground, duckboards may also be required.

(b) *Stepping stones.* There are many kinds of bridge. Stepping stones are probably the simplest form. They should preferably be of natural stone; where economics prohibit this, concrete or a combination of brickwork and concrete may be used. It is essential that the stones should be firmly bedded and set so that the surface is just clear of the water when it is running at its (generally accepted) highest level.

Seating

To achieve its purpose a seat must be comfortable, stable and situated away from draughts and cold spots. Seats set in parks and other public places are often objects of abuse and, if vandalism is to be deterred, their construction must be robust and durable. Materials used in their manufacture include concrete, timber, metal or plastic, or a combination of two (or more). In the past, seats of classical design were carved from stone but, due to the high cost of labour and materials, stone has been superseded by either concrete or reconstructed stone.

Plate 20
Arena seating : Midlands Arts
Centre for Young People,
Cannon Hill, Birmingham. A
relatively cheap and simple
form of construction
incorporating standard precast
concrete paving flags for the
seats ; road kerbs serve as
back-rests. The work was
carried out by young volunteers
at International Work Camps
held there during several
summers.
Photo: Henry Southwell Eades.

Concrete benches*

A concrete (including precast stone) bench must be reasonably simple in shape. Concrete offers all sorts of design opportunities but it must be remembered that cost is closely related to the intricacy of the formwork needed for the execution of the finished product.

Finishes may be similar to those used for bollards, but the actual seating part of a simple all-concrete bench should have a reasonably smooth surface so that it is comfortable to sit upon. Where timber seating is used in conjunction with concrete supports the latter may, if desired, be of a much rougher texture (e.g. exposed aggregate). Although they may be freestanding designs the concrete supports are usually set into the ground to a minimum depth of 230 mm.

Where timber is incorporated to form the backrest and seating, good quality close-grained hardwoods such as teak or afrormosia are the most suitable for standing up to hard wear in situations requiring exceptional toughness and exposure to the elements. Screws and other fastenings should be of non-ferrous metal to avoid risk of corrosion.

Metal benches

The typical park bench of the last century, constructed with cast iron of elaborate design and mild steel flats that formed the actual seating, has largely been superseded by benches of aluminium alloy, tubular steel or other fabricated materials. Selection may be made from manufacturers' catalogues or advice sought from the Design Council, which has a system of awards for outstanding industrial design.

Timber benches

The design of timber benches is governed largely by the properties of the material used. Teak and other similar close-grained hardwoods provide a tough, sturdy product which is able to withstand weather and a fair amount of rough usage. Because the sun has a tendency to bleach the colour out of the wood, periodic treatment with linseed oil is necessary in order to preserve a good colour. Varnish may also be applied as a protective finish, but involves maintenance.

Plastic benches

The advent of various kinds of plastic has opened up new horizons in many design fields. So far as the design of seats

*The term *bench* avoids confusion with *seat*, i.e. that part of the structure for sitting upon.

is concerned, however, there appear to be few attempts to manufacture plastic benches on a large scale for outdoor purposes, although quite a range of individual seats is available on the market. The high cost of forming the necessary moulds tends to deter the specification of small quantities or one-off projects.

Asbestos cement benches

The design possibilities of this material are somewhat akin to those of plastics and in recent years new ideas have been conceived for both individual and public seating.

Miscellaneous types of seating

In some cases the design of a layout calls for something a little less conventional than the traditional type of bench, or lack of funds dictates the need for improvisation. A very simple, cheap and successful type of arena seating has been developed using standard concrete paving slabs in conjunction with road kerbs.

Another economic form of seating is the use of concrete or asbestos pipes as supports onto which are placed planks or simple round timber seats.

Picnic and garden furniture

Planned picnic sites are comparatively new to Britain, although on the Continent and in North America such amenities are taken for granted by motorists. Furniture for this purpose can be either fixed or portable (see Beazley, 1969, 100–104).

Fixed furniture generally comprises benches and tables, securely set into the ground in a permanent position, designed to meet the needs of a particular situation. Construction should be simple and robust, using indigenous materials wherever possible. In some cases, e.g. for picnic sites, seating need be nothing more elaborate than logs from locally felled trees or a series of old tree stumps.

Where tables are included, these, too, should be simple in character and of robust construction, especially where they are not fixed in permanent positions. They can be of any length, depending upon the materials available, but their width generally should not be less than 0·76 m. Table and benches may be constructed as a complete unit, without backrests in order to allow easy access to the table.

In districts of natural stone, picnic furniture need comprise little more than informally grouped large boulders around a 'table', the scale and siting of which require careful consideration. The composition of such a group must not appear too small in scale otherwise it is more likely to give the impression of being the Seven Dwarfs' dining-room! Sculptural forms are most important and, if boulders of the right size are unobtainable (or the cost of transporting them to the site is prohibitive), it is a far better proposition to erect free-shaped concrete structures with exposed aggregate surfaces, using local stone (nominal size not less than 38–50 mm), thus allowing both designer and user adequate scope for the exercise of imagination.

Obviously it is impossible to lay down hard-and-fast rules as to what should be used and where; much depends upon the local terrain, access to the site and the materials available, but items provided must be in harmony with their surroundings.

Portable furniture is usually lightweight and often readily dismantled for easy transport and storage. It is much smaller in scale than fixed furniture, with constructional emphasis on lightness coupled with strength. Height of tables is usually 355–685 mm and that of seats ranges from 355–430 mm.

Materials used include hardwoods, aluminium alloy, cane, tubular steel, plastic, etc., producing a variety of designs. Unless purpose-made items are specially request-ed (this is unusual because of cost) selection is usually made from a manufacturer's range. The specification should refer to the manufacturer, his address and the respective catalogue numbers, with an indication, where applicable, of the colours and finishes required.

Plant containers

Vases, urns, flower-boxes and other containers of various kinds are particularly useful in paved areas such as precincts and patios. A wide range of sizes and shapes is manufactured in a variety of materials: stone, concrete, asbestos cement and glassfibre.

Planting-bowls

Selection of planting-bowls (Table 98) depends upon the following factors:

(i) *Function*. The bowls may serve as obstacles in order to channel pedestrians along a particular route, may be required to enclose a seating area, or to hide duct covers, manholes or ugly paving junctions. Function of the bowls is likely to dictate their size, particularly height.

Table 98
Sizes of various types of plant container (mm)

Concrete			Glassfibre		Rectangular			Asbestos cement				
Rectangular			Circular tubs					Circular tubs		Window boxes		
length	width	height	diameter	height	length	width	height	diameter	height	length	width	height
911	657	381	450	300	1220	400	400	300	150	760	146	150
Hexagonal			610	400	1220	610	400	300	200	1780	190	230
760	760	150	610	530	1220	610	530	380	183	1650	300	250
in multiple heights of 150 mm			910	400	1830	610	400	380	250	1830	280	234
			910	530	1830	610	530	460	230			
Circular tubs					*Eliptical*			460	300			
diameter	height		*Glassfibre reinforced cement*		1220	450	400	530	260			
610	203		*Rectangular*		1220	450	530	530	360			
864	610		length	width	height	*Square*		600	300			
914	254		3000	1000	600	610	610	400	600	410		
914	286		*Square*			610	610	530	*Shallow bowls*			
914	305		2000	2000	605	910	910	400	460	106		
914	457		*Circular*			910	910	530	760	180		
914	572		diameter	height		*Hexagonal*			1070	250		
1219	356		2000	605		900	450	400	1220	250		
Circular containers			*Hexagonal*			1220	610	530	*Conical tubs*			
with pedestals			1980	445					610	280		
710	150		1220	460					760	300		
710	230											
890	150											
890	230											
in multiple heights of 150 or 230 mm												

(ii) *Floorscape pattern*. The scale and treatment of the floorscape dictates shape, size and material of the bowls.

(iii) *Siting*. Positioning of the bowls may be permanent or temporary. If the latter, they must be of a reasonably manageable size so that they may be moved, bearing in mind the weight of soil contained.

(iv) *Planting*. The size and habit of the plants intended for the bowls may dictate the particular type of container, where planting is of predominant importance.

Planting-troughs and flower-boxes

Planting-troughs are usually larger than flower-boxes and may be either free-standing or set directly upon the ground. Materials used in their construction vary according to whether they are built in-situ or fabricated. Most of the manufactured troughs on the market are made of timber, asbestos cement or glassfibre in order to facilitate easy handling, especially where intended as window-boxes. For this latter purpose a length of about 1·22 m is generally sufficient; anything larger tends to be somewhat cumbersome to handle and causes complication of fixing methods. Where requirements dictate a greater length it is better to install two shorter troughs.

It is essential that adequate fixing is provided for window-boxes. The average weight of moist topsoil is 1602 kg/m³; the weight contained in a box 1220 × 280 × 250 mm is likely to be in the region of 137 kg, and to this must be added the weight of the box itself. Fixing should consist of substantial wall brackets spaced at not more than 300 mm centres. If the box is on top of a brick wall, steel dowel pins should be built into the brickwork so that they project a minimum of 50 mm above the top of it, to correspond with drainage holes in the bottom of the box.

One of the disadvantages of window-boxes is the nuisance caused by soil splashing up over the windows in heavy rain. This can be prevented by spreading peat moss over the soil surface. The box itself may be filled with a mixture of:

> 3 parts good quality top soil (to BS 3882 : 1965)
> 1 part leaf mould
> 1 part clean coarse sand

This is placed on top of a layer of crocks or stones spread at the bottom of the box (to assist drainage) together with several pieces of charcoal which help to keep the soil sweet. This mixture is also suitable for other types of plant container.

Litter receptacles

Wherever the public are allowed access some means of disposing of their litter must be provided. To fulfil its purpose a litter receptacle needs to be placed strategically where it will readily be seen, but it should not obtrude on the landscape or create an obstruction.

The general principles of design and the materials suitable for the construction of litter-bins are contained in BS 4324 : 1968. The most substantially constructed are those of precast concrete, reinforced as necessary, and fitted with a removable lining of galvanised wire mesh. They may be either free-standing or fixed into the ground by means of rag bolts. The shape selected should be such that it blends in with the character of the layout; care must be taken to site the litter bin well clear of any plant containers in order to avoid confusion of use.

Other materials employed include stainless steel, pressed steel, plastic and galvanised wire mesh, all in a variety of designs and sizes. The open wire mesh receptacle, as such, is aesthetically undesirable and is best used as a liner so that the litter remains concealed from view. In exposed positions and in open country provision should be made for lids or hoods on the bins to prevent the wind from scattering the contents. If economics dictate the use of wire mesh for the container (with a plastic or paper sack liner), a small mesh should be specified since this looks much neater than a large open mesh. On exposed sites paper or plastic sacks suspended from open frames (or only partially protected by wire mesh) are of little use because the sack is liable to be blown about and torn, and its contents scattered.

As with much other outdoor furniture, the selection of litter-bins depends not only upon cost but also on a number of other factors such as location, scale, setting, etc. The choice of standard designs is fairly wide and several good products are marketed.

Advertisement display panels

Advertising is part of everyday living and in towns may take the form of posters, neon lights, shop window stickers or printed paper bags and carriers.

Paper posters are printed on sheets of standard size in accordance with BS 3047 : 1974, which allows some sort of co-ordination where a number are displayed together. The basic size of poster is 508 mm wide by 762 mm high and is known as the 'double crown' sheet. Multiples of this size are produced, the most commonly used being the '16 double crown sheet' which is 2 m wide by 3 m high. In shopping precincts and other pedestrian areas the standard poster size used for free-standing display units is the '4 sheet'–1 m wide by 1·5 m high. A larger but less popular size is the '32 sheet', which is 4 m wide by 3 m high. The largest multiple of the basic sheet is the '48 sheet', 6 m wide by 3 m high, which is ideally suitable for bold displays (intended to convey their message at a swift glance).

The double crown sheet is useful for small displays and public notices; the 'quad crown' sheet is of the same height but twice the width. Other standard poster sizes used for similar purposes include the 'double demy' sheet, 570 mm wide by 890 mm high, and the 'quad demy' sheet, 1140 mm wide by 890 mm high.

Advertisements not only serve as message conveyors but also provide a useful means of screening unsightly areas and unoccupied sites from view. 'Bulletin boards' are ideal for this purpose. These are painted boards (as opposed to paper posters) with a net height of advertising surface of 2·90 m. The widths are usually made up of 900 mm panels in multiples of 9, 12 or 15, giving overall widths of 8·22 m, 11 m and 13·72 m respectively. In some cases these widths are considerably increased and may exceed 22·86 m, depending upon the scale of the surroundings. The advertisement is painted directly onto the panels in the display artist's studio and, after assembly and erection on site, the entire board is given a finishing treatment. Usually, advertisement boards of this nature are illuminated.

A summary of poster and bulletin board sizes and their uses is given in Table 99.

Flags and flagpoles

Flying of flags

To fly a flag (i.e. to wear a flag) is a form of identification. Flags convey a meaning, or message, not only by their pattern or design but also by their position. When, for example, a flag is flown at half mast it is a recognised sign of mourning. If one national flag is flown over another in peace time it is an insult to the country represented by the lower flag; to honour another country without belittling one's own the flags of both countries should be of equal size and flown side by side at the same height, a procedure adopted at exhibitions, etc., where several countries are represented.

The flying of flags has always been associated primarily with shipping and it was natural that admiralty buildings and those associated with maritime activities should also adopt the practice. Inevitably the idea spread and today flags can be seen flying in a variety of places. Town halls and other official buildings honour representatives of other countries by flying the flag of the particular country throughout the duration of their visit.

Materials and sizes

Traditionally flags were of 'bunting', a strong woollen cloth made in Yorkshire and woven in strips 230 mm wide and 36·5 m long. Nowadays many flags are made from nylon-worsted material, but the original method of specifying the size of the flag, i.e. so many breadths, is retained; for example, a flag 900 mm wide is specified as a 'four breadths' flag. Flags are of different shapes: a long tapering one is referred to as a 'pendant', while a 'burgee'

Table 99
Sizes of posters and bulletin boards

Description of sheet (or board)	Width	Height	Use
Double crown	508 mm	760 mm	Small displays and public notice boards
Quad crown	1016 mm	760 mm	
Double demy	570 mm	890 mm	
Quad demy	1140 mm	890 mm	
4 double crown	1 m	1·5 m	Commercial advertisements
16 double crown	2 m	3 m	Various campaigns
32 double crown	4 m	3 m	Charity appeals
48 double crown	6 m	3 m	Political appeals
9-panel	8·22 m	2·90 m	Main thoroughfares, stations, airports, industrial
12-panel	10·97 m	2·90 m	estates, etc.
15-panel	13·71 m	2·90 m	
25-panel (or more)	22·86 m	2·90 m	

is a flag ending in a swallow-tail. The size of flag is determined by the wind load which the flagstaff is designed to resist and may range from 900 mm for a flagpole with an overall height of 3·65 m to 6 m for one not exceeding 21·33 m overall. These are maximum flag sizes for winds up to gale force 10 (Beaufort scale) ; where winds exceed this speed the flag should be hauled down.

Flagpoles

Timber or metal is commonly used in the manufacture of flagpoles. The most suitable woods are Columbian pine (Oregon), pitch pine, Scandinavian fir and ash, the latter being suitable only for shorter poles, up to about 4·5 m high. Because of the difficulties of selection to meet the grading requirements set out in CP 112 : Part 2 : 1971, it is not always possible to obtain the desired quality of wood for the larger flagpoles ; either mild steel or aluminium alloy is preferred, although the cost is likely to be anything up to twice that of timber flagpoles. Aluminium alloy has the advantage of lightness in weight which is easier for erection purposes. Another lightweight material sometimes adopted is glassfibre reinforced plastic (grp).

There are four standard methods of mounting :

> Spigot
> Stayed poles
> Wall
> Tabernacle

Flagpoles, like any other structure, are subject to the effect of wind which varies according to exposure. Four degrees of exposure are defined in Appendix C of CP 3 : Chap. V : Part 2 : 1972, summarised below :

Exposure A. Exceptionally small amount of exposure to wind, usually because of natural protection from surroundings. (Warning ! although the location is protected there may be a risk of wind funnel effects in some directions.)

Exposure B. General grading for most situations other than those near the coast or estuaries or at altitudes exceeding 152 m above sea level.

Exposure C. Open country where altitudes do not exceed 243 m above sea level, except in coastal areas or estuaries.

Exposure D. Exposed locations within 8 km of a coast or estuary or in areas exceeding 243 m above sea level.

These gradings represent the following wind velocities, measured at a standard 'effective' height of 12 m :

A	72 km/h
B	87 km/h
C	95 km/h
D	116 km/h

Since the siting of a flagpole is usually at the top of a building or in an open area of ground it is likely to be exposed to the full effects of the wind. It is important, therefore, that the design of the flagpole should conform to the wind loading requirements laid down in CP 3 referred to above. Wall-mounted flagpoles generally should not exceed an overall height of 15 m because of the weight of the supporting wall brackets required for fixing.

Miscellaneous poles and posts

What constitutes a pole or a post cannot be given a precise architectural definition since both terms are often applied to the same object. Generally, the term 'post' is applied to a stout stake or pillar ; a 'pole' is regarded as a shaft whose cross-sectional area in proportion to its length is considerably less than that of a post.

Materials used in their manufacture and the sizes and requirements for particular products are contained in the following British standards :

BS 607 : Part 2 : 1970	Poles used to support electrical overhead lines.
BS 1775 : 1964 ; BS 1471 : 1972	Steel and aluminium alloy tubes.
BS 1373 : 1967	Timber, steel and concrete clothes-line posts. (See also BS 4107 : 1967 which deals with rotating driers set on top of posts.)
BS 1990 : Part 2 : 1971	Wood poles for overhead power and telecommunication lines.
BS 3191 : Part 3A : 1961	Tubular steel assault poles for school playground equipment and climbing apparatus.
BS 3470 : 1962	Wood, concrete, tubular and rolled steel posts used in conjunction with field gates.

Children's play equipment

The wide variety of equipment provided in children's play areas may be classified broadly as (a) static and (b) swinging (or rotating) apparatus. BS 3178 specifies the materials, construction and dimensional requirements for various types of play apparatus designed for outdoor use.

Static play equipment
The two principal types of structure in this group are climbing frames, etc., and slides.

Climbing frames, horizontal bars, ladders, etc. Mild steel 32–38 mm diameter, or 38–50 mm square hollow sections, provide the basic materials for climbing frames fabricated to form a wide range of designs in a variety of sizes. The principal supporting members should be provided with base plates for fixing purposes. BS 3178 : Part 2A : 1959 gives recommendations for various items of equipment.

Slides. Slides are probably the most popular features of all playground equipment and are manufactured either as free-standing structures or as slide slopes designed to follow the contours of the ground.

The length of the chute itself may be anything from 3·65 m to 12 m or more, depending upon the height and slope. It may be fabricated as a simple straight run or shaped around a circular framework to form a 'helter-skelter'. In free-standing structures, tubular or hollow section mild steel framework is employed to support the chute. A ladder with hand-rails on each side and forming part of the structure provides access to the chute itself, which is usually made from mild steel sheet with a galvanised or stainless steel liner.

Safety rails must be provided on each side of the chute at the top for at least 3 m. In some designs a comparatively short slide is incorporated as part of a climbing frame (Junglegym). The design of slides is specified in BS 3178 : Part 2B : 1960.

Swinging or rotating play equipment
Three principal means of motivation comprise this group of structures, whose requirements are set out in BS 3178 : Part 3.

Pendulum swinging apparatus. This equipment consists of a variety of swings and pendulum seesaws.

Swings may be designed as individual swings, or for use by a group of children.

(i) Medium duty : primarily intended for younger children, these usually include from two to six seats and should be allotted a space of 42–84 m², according to the number provided. Height from ground level to centre of top bar = 2·45 m.

(ii) Heavy duty : for use by older children, these swings are often in bays of three swings each. Heights range from 2·45 to 3·65 m. Examples of space requirements are given in Table 100.

Table 100
Space requirements for play swings

Height (m)	No. of seats	Bays	Area (m²)
2·45	3	1	45
	4	2	52
	6	2	67
3	3	1	58
	4	2	67
	6	2	83
3·65	3	1	80
	4	2	90
	6	2	120

In both types of swing the timber seats are suspended on swing chains. *

(a) Plane swings : the design principle is similar to that of the ordinary swing, the individual seat being replaced by a short plank, set parallel to the direction of swing, which is suspended by six spring steel rods from three overhead bars (see BS 3178 : Part 3B : 1962).

(b) Plank swings : these can be used simultaneously by several children. Plank seats 3·65 or 4·26 m long are suspended on spring steel rods from heights of 2·28 m or 2·75 m and require a clearance space of 30–70 m² respectively. Footboards must be provided on the higher type of swing (see BS 3178 : Section 3C : 1964).

Pendulum see-saws are similar in size to the plank swing described above. This apparatus requires a clearance space of approximately 50 m² (see BS 3178 : Part 3A : 1960).

Rotating equipment. Two principal types of apparatus are classified under this heading : whirling platforms and rotating heads (see BS 3178 : Part 4 : 1965).

*Timber seats constitute a potential hazard and are better replaced by discarded car tyres.

Whirling platforms can be for either sitting or standing upon, depending upon the design. They require plenty of clearance space.

(a) Merry-go-round: consists of a circular metal base which supports an octagonal timber superstructure with metal grab-rails. The smaller size is 2·43 m diameter and requires a safety clearance space of 6 m diameter. The larger is 3 m diameter and requires a clearance space of 6·7 m diameter (approximately).

(b) Joy wheel: circular in shape, with grab-handles spaced at regular intervals around the perimeters. Diameters range from 2·75 to 3·8 m, with a corresponding safety clearance space of approximately 6·4–7·3 m, diameter according to the size selected.

Rotating heads comprise a centrally supported rotating mechanism from which is suspended either a rigid frame or a series of chains. In the former case ('Ocean waves') the safety clearance must be not less than 7·4 m diameter and for the suspended chains ('Giant stride') a space of at least 11 m diameter should be allotted. BS 3178 : Part 4 : 1965 lays down the dimensions and requirements for the design and construction of both types of apparatus.

Balancing equipment. The principal apparatus under this heading is the well-known seesaw. A 200 mm wide plank 3·65–4·87 m long is fixed so that it is balanced on a central support. A safety clearance space of 6–7·5 m² should be provided, according to the length of plank specified.

Sports equipment

Some of the items required for various sporting activities are only in use during the playing season. When specifying equipment such as posts and nets, durability and maintenance of the material used in their manufacture must be borne in mind. The list below is not complete but it indicates the requirements of various sporting activities.

Goal posts and nets

The goalmouths of playing pitches for the different team games should conform to the regulation size as laid down by the respective sporting associations. Timber or tubular steel is used for the goalposts which support the synthetic netting. Two sets must be specified for each pitch; the requirements set out below relate to one goalmouth.

Football. Regulation size goalmouth : 7·3 m wide × 2·45 m high.

Timber posts (painted white)	Two 100 mm × 75 mm × 2·9 m long set 450 mm into the ground in permanent sockets. One 100 mm × 75 mm × 7·3 m long top bar.
Steel posts	Two 60 mm or 75 mm overall diameter mild steel tubes (lengths as above) fitted with 150 × 150 × 6 mm sole-plates for fixing into concrete base set in the ground. One 60 mm or 75 mm top bar (length as above).
Net	Supported by two 2·45 m poles with guys and a cross-straining steel headline threaded under the meshes.

Hockey. Regulation size goalmouth : 3·65 m × 2·13 m.
Two 75 × 50 mm timber uprights 2·45m long set 450 mm into the ground.
One 75 × 50 mm cross bar 3·65 m long.
All timber to be painted white.

Rugby football. Regulation size goalmouth : 5·65 m wide × 3 m high to cross bar.

Timber posts	Two poles approximately 8 m long set into the ground to a depth of 600 mm. Cross bar 5·65 m long set at a height of 3 m above ground level.
Steel posts	The uprights may be in two telescopic tube sections, one 75 mm overall diameter and the other 75 mm inside diameter.

Tennis court equipment

Tennis equipment comprises a net, two posts and sundry items to each court.

Hard court posts. The posts may be either 75 mm square hollow section or 60 mm diameter tubular mild steel, capped and set in cast iron sockets in the ground. Several grades are manufactured, selection being according to the class of play intended (i.e. match tournaments or general educational use).

Nets. The choice of net also is dictated by class of play; 'best quality nylon stout thread, tarred, single twine throughout and fitted pre-shrunk head-band and galvanised steel headline' should be specified for tournament and first-class club use. Other nets are manufactured from heavy braid corded fibre similar in strength to nylon and available in several qualities. A centre guide adjuster, to prevent movement of the net, is hooked onto a ring at the top of the centre guide post which is set flush with the court surface.

Grass court posts. Steel or timber may be used for the manufacture of these posts; generally the former are specified for match tournament courts. Steel posts may be either square hollow section 75 × 75 mm, or tubular 75 mm or 88 mm diameter; timber, 75 × 75 mm or 88 × 88 mm. Posts are supplied in pairs: one anchor post, which is set into the ground in a fixed position, and one winder post complete with winding handle, set in a portable socket.

Miscellaneous items. On grass courts marking pins (L's and T's) should be provided. Tournament courts should be equipped with an umpire's chair.

Tennis practice equipment. Although not part of the actual court equipment, ancillary items may be required for practice. These include practice boards and tennis trainers.

Practice boards are fixed units, each of which is 2·4 m high by 1·22 m wide, supported by two vertical posts and back stays. Several units, in multiples of 1·22 m, may be erected at the end of a tennis court to form a tennis wall 2·4 m high.

A tennis trainer consists of two metal posts held in a rigid position by stay wires and a horizontal strainer. A practice ball is suspended at the end of a nylon cord centrally between the two uprights. Another type of trainer consists of a single steel post, set into the ground, at the top of which a helical spring provides anchorage for a 4·5 m length of cord with a tennis ball attached to its free end.

Cricket equipment

Sight screens, scoreboards (or boxes) and ground covers are part of the equipment required.

Sight screens. Three sizes are available:

3 × 3 m   4 × 3 m   4·5 × 3 m

The screen consists of timber framing, suitably braced, covered with 168 mm boards spaced 150 mm apart and painted white. Struts should be provided together with two sets of wheels to allow the screen to be wheeled into various positions.

Score recording mechanisms. The method adopted for displaying the scores, etc., may range from the simple type of portable scoreboard to a fabricated purpose-made scorebox. Whichever method of display is selected, its main function is to relay information that is easily discernible; to achieve this, the height of any individual figure should be not less than 75 mm. This is an ideal size for portable cricket (or bowls) scoreboards suitable for small clubs.

Cricket practice equipment. Practice nets can be erected singly or as a series of units, depending upon intensity of use. The equipment consists of four poles per unit (or eight per three bays, etc.) with double guy ropes, pegs and runners. Sizes of poles generally are:

50 mm diameter, 1·8, 2·1, 2·4 and 2·7 m long.
57 mm diameter, 3·0, 3·3 and 3·6 m long.

Nylon tarred netting is available to suit the height of pole specified and is attached to a top straining-wire and to each pole.

Posts for ball games

Posts are required for netball, volley ball and basket ball and may be either fixed or portable. Generally, tubular steel posts, 38–50 mm diameter, are employed for this purpose. Timber is also suitable but, in this case, the minimum cross-sectional dimension should be 75 mm.

Putting equipment

Items required for use on greens, clock golf and crazy golf courses include arrows, flags, golf-hole cases, roman numerals, etc. These are generally purchased as a set comprising either nine or eighteen units or holes. A golf-hole cutter should also be provided to facilitate the course installation.

Athletics equipment

Items required for the layout of a sports arena include:

Starting and finishing posts, distance indicators, flags, etc.
High-jump and pole-vault standards, crossbars and triple-jump measuring apparatus
Pole-vault troughs
Take-off boards
Throwing protection cage, etc.
Officials' stands, stools
Lap score-board, etc.

All items of equipment specified should conform to the

regulations and specifications laid down by IAAF, AAA and WAAA.

The layout and dimensions for an athletic track and arena should be in accordance with recommendations issued jointly by the National Playing Fields Association and the Amateur Athletic Association.

Plaques and plant labels

A plaque is usually provided to commemorate an event or person of note and should be placed in a fairly prominent position. Commemorative plaques are often sited beside trees planted by eminent persons. Since the idea of providing a plaque is to record an event for the benefit of posterity, it should be substantially made and of durable material. Bronze, bronzed metal, aluminium alloy and anodised metals have been employed in the past but plastic, of various sorts, is proving to be an equally acceptable material, particularly for smaller items such as plant labels. The type of lettering and content of commemorative plaques should be simple but compatible with the subject.

Plant labels for trees and shrubs should state the botanical name of the plant, that by which it is commonly known (if there is one), the plant's habitat and, in the case of trees, the year of planting. The size of label depends upon the amount of lettering required; wherever possible standard widths should be specified, the lengths varying to suit the extent of the lettering.

Appendix One   Glossary of Botanical Terms

ABORTIVE	Imperfectly developed
ACHENE	Small, one-seeded, dry indehiscent fruit
ACICULAR	Needle-shaped (usually applied to leaves)
ACUMINATE	Having a gradually tapered point
ACUTE	Sharp-pointed but less gradually tapered than acuminate
ADNATE	Whole or part fusion of different organs (e.g. fusion of a petal and a sepal). See also CONNATE
ADPRESSED	Description given to leaves which are closely pressed to the stem
ADVENTITIOUS BUDS	Buds which occur in places other than leaf axils
AERIAL ROOT	A root which appears above ground level (e.g. ivy growing on a wall)
ALPINE	A plant, generally of dwarf, compact habit, which grows naturally on mountains. The term is more generally applied to almost any plant which is adaptable to rock-garden conditions and is synonymous with 'rock plant'
ALTERNATE LEAVES	Leaves placed singly on a stem at different intervals (in contrast to leaves set in pairs, opposite one another or in whorls of several leaves)
ANDROECIUM	Male parts of a flower (stamens)
ANNUAL	A plant which completes its life cycle within a year (not necessarily a calendar year)—germinating, flowering, setting seed and dying
ANTERIOR	In front or turned away from the axis
ANTHER	The terminal and pollen-bearing part of a stamen
APETALOUS	Flowers having no petals
APEX	The termination of leaf or petal, etc.
APICAL	At the apex or tip of a structure
APICULATE	Coming to a small sharp point (applied to leaves)
AQUATIC	Any plant which lives wholly or partly in water
ARMED	A plant having spines, thorns or prickles
ASCENDING	Rising obliquely at first, becoming erect (description given to habit of some plants)

AURICLE	Ear-shaped lobe or appendage
AWL-SHAPED	Tapering to a fine, narrow or needle-like point (applied to leaves)
AWN	Thread-like attachment to a fruit or seed (applied to 'beard' of some grasses)
AXIL	Angle formed between upper side of leaf-stalk and stem or between midrib and chief veins of a leaf
AXILLARY	Springing from an axil (refers to a flower borne in axil of a leaf)
AXIS	The main line of development (main stem)
BARK	Corky outer layer of a tree or shrub, branch, stem or trunk
BASE	That part of a leaf blade nearest the point of attachment
BEARDED	Dense growth of long hairs, e.g. those on the lower petals (falls) of some irises
BEDDING PLANTS	Plants used for temporary display (bedding out). They may be annuals, biennials or perennials and hardy or half-hardy
BERRY	An indehiscent fruit of a fleshy nature containing several seeds
BIENNIAL	A plant whose life cycle is completed in two years
BI-PINNATE	Twice pinnate. Leaves composed of separate segments which, in turn, are also similarly divided
BI-TERNATE	Consisting of three main divisions, each having three leaflets (i.e. nine in all)
BRACT	A modified, reduced leaf found at the base of a flower stalk and from whose axil the flower is borne. It is often scale-like and sometimes highly coloured
BRACTEOLE	A small bract, produced on a secondary axis
BUD	End of the shoot, containing a leaf or flower (or both)
BULB	A storage organ, usually formed underground, with fleshy scales or swollen leaf bases which store food for a resting period. The term is loosely applied to all types of fleshy growth which store food and are able to produce new plants
BULLATE	Leaves having a naturally irregular surface, e.g. *Rhododendron bullatum*
BUSH	A low, dense shrub branching at or near ground level
CADUCOUS	Falling off early
CALCIFUGE	Lime-hating plant
CALLUS	Natural growth which forms over a wound made in a plant
CALYX	Outer whorl of a flower formed of sepals, in contrast to inner whorl formed of petals
CAMPANULATE	Bell-shaped flower
CAPSULE	A dry dehiscent fruit comprising two or more cells
CARPEL	Female unit of a flower (stigma, style and ovary) ; ovule-bearing structure which, after fertilisation, develops into the fruit
CARPETING PLANT	A plant of low-growing, wide-spreading habit suitable for providing ground cover
CATKIN	A type of inflorescence ; slender, tail-like and pendulous with stalkless flowers
CILIATE	Fringed with hairs (generally applied to leaf or petal margins)
CLADODE	A stem which has the function of a leaf (e.g. 'leaf' of butcher's broom)
CLONE	A group of plants propagated vegetatively from one parent
CLUSTER	Two or more leaves, flowers or fruits arising from the same point at the end of a main stem or of a side-shoot. See UMBEL
COMPOUND	Leaves, flowers or fruits composed of two or more similar parts
CONE	Fruit of a conifer, e.g. pine, spruce, fir, etc.
CONIFEROUS	A tree, not necessarily evergreen, which bears cones
CONNATE	Whole or part fusion of similar organs, e.g. fusion of two petals. See also ADNATE
CORDATE	Heart-shaped. Generally applied to leaves
CORIACEOUS	Of leathery texture
CORM	Underground storage organ comprising a thickened solid stem and, unlike the true bulb, having no fleshy scales but only papery ones which serve as a protective tunic (e.g. crocus, gladiolus, etc.)

CORMELS	Tiny corms or cormlets which form around the parent corm
COROLLA	Collective name given to the petals forming the inner whorl of the flower which, in most cases, provide the colourful display
CORONA	Usually applied to the cup, crown or trumpet of a narcissus (daffodil) but botanically refers to any appendage which separates the corolla from the anthers of a flower
CORYMB	A flat-topped (or nearly so) flower cluster in which the outer flowers open first. The stalks of the individual flowers do not start from a common point
CRENATE	Leaf margins which are scalloped or have shallow, more-or-less rounded teeth
CRENULATE	Minutely crenate
CROTCH	Point at which main trunk of a tree divides into branches
CROWN	Upper part of a rootstock from which shoots grow. Also refers to head of foliage
CULTIVAR	Cultivated variety
CUNEATE	Wedge-shaped ; the narrow end is at the point of attachment
CYME	Of similar shape to a corymb but with the flowers in the centre opening first
CYMOSE	Cyme-like
DECIDUOUS	A plant (particularly a tree or shrub) which loses its leaves in winter
DECUMBENT	Stem lying on the ground but with its ends ascending
DECUSSATE	Leaves in opposite pairs but with one pair at right angles to the next pair (cross-like)
DEHISCENT	Anther or seed pod which opens at maturity to release the contents (seeds)
DELTOID	Triangular in shape
DENTATE	Leaves with coarsely-toothed edges
DENTICULATE	Minutely dentate
DIGITATE	Hand-like ; compound leaves in which the leaflets are borne at the end of a common stalk (e.g. horsechestnut)
DIMORPHIC	Occurring in two forms on the same plant (e.g. leaves of many junipers)
DIOECIOUS	Plants in which flowers on any one plant are entirely male or female (e.g. *Skimmia japonica*)
DISSECTED	Cut into a number of narrow segments
DISTICHOUS	Leaves arranged opposite in two ranks
DISTINCT	Separate ; not fused
DIVIDED	Separated virtually to the base
DOT PLANT	A plant of taller growth set among lower growing plants to provide a point of interest or break up a monotonous line of plants of similar height
DRUPE	A fleshy indehiscent fruit containing a stone (hard endocarp) in which is (usually) one seed
DRUPELET	A small drupe (in a fruit composed of a number of drupelets)
DWARF CONIFER	A miniature form of a coniferous tree
EMARGINATE	Notched at the tip
ENDOCARP	Inner layer of the fruit wall
ENTIRE	Leaf margin even ; not toothed or lobed
ERICACEOUS	Belonging to the heath family (*Ericaceae*)
EVERGREEN	A plant (particularly a tree or shrub) which retains its leaves throughout the year. Although it sheds its leaves and produces new ones, the process is continuous so that at no time is the plant devoid of foliage
EXOTIC	A plant, not necessarily tender, which is not a native of the country
EXSERTED	Protruding ; sticking out. Applied to stamens or pistils which project beyond the other parts of a flower
FALCATE	Sickle-shaped
FALLS	Sepals of certain irises which hang down, in contrast to petals which stand up, forming that part of flower described as the 'standard'
FASTIGIATE	Of erect habit. Applied generally to trees and shrubs having branches erect and close together

FEMALE FLOWER	A flower bearing pistils but no stamens, in contrast to a male flower which bears stamens but no pistils or a hermaphrodite flower which has both pistils and stamens
FILAMENT	The slender stalk which bears an anther
FIMBRIATE	Having a fringed edge
FLACCID	Not stiff or rigid
FLORET	Each of the individual flowers which make up the head of a composite flower
FLORIFEROUS	Bearing flowers freely
FOLIACEOUS	Leaf-like
FOLIAGE PLANTS	Plants grown principally for their foliage
FOLLICLE	A dry dehiscent fruit which opens along one suture only
GAMOPETALOUS	Having the petals more or less joined together
GAMOSEPALOUS	Having the sepals more or less joined together
GENUS	Plural : genera ; adjective : generic. The first word of the Latin name of a plant
GLABROUS	Without hairs or down. Frequently wrongly used to describe 'smooth'
GLAND	A secreting organ on leaves, young shoots or parts of flowers
GLANDULAR	Bearing glands or gland-like structures
GLAUCOUS	Bluish-grey ; covered with a 'bloom' (like a plum). Used to describe the colour of leaves or stems
GYNOECIUM	Female parts of a flower (ovaries, styles and stigmas)
HABIT	Form and manner of growth of a plant
HASTATE	Shaped in the form of an arrow-head. Applied to leaves
HEAD	Dense cluster or short dense spike of flowers or fruits
HERB	A plant having soft growth (adjective : herbaceous). Also applied to those plants grown principally for seasoning food (e.g. sage, thyme, parsley, etc.)
HERBACEOUS	See HERB
HERMAPHRODITE	A flower in which both gynoecium and androecium are present
HIRSUTE	Hairy ; refers to coarse hairs found on leaves or stems of some plants
HISPID	Bristly ; refers to bristles or stiff hairs found on leaves or stems of some plants
HOARY	Frosted ; refers to dense, short, whitish hairs which cover the leaves or stems of some plants, giving them a frosted appearance
HYBRID	A plant bred from more or less unlike parents ; the result of 'crossing' two species
IMBRICATE	Overlapping ; leaves or bud scales overlap one another in a manner similar to roof tiling
INCISED	Leaves having rather deeply cut margins
INDEHISCENT	Not opening along any regular sutures
INFLORESCENCE	Mode of flowering of a plant or its flowering region
INFRUCTESCENCE	Fruiting region of a plant
INTERNODE	That part of a stem between two joints or nodes
INVOLUCRE	Whorl of bracts close beneath a flower or cluster
JUVENILE GROWTH	Distinct type of early growth which occurs in conifers, as distinct from later type or adult growth
LACINIATE	Leaves cut into narrow segments
LAMINA	Blade of a leaf
LANCEOLATE	Lance-shaped ; narrow and tapering towards the base
LANCEOLATE-OVAL	Lance-shaped in outline and broadest in the middle of the leaf, tapering towards both ends
LANCEOLATE-OVATE	Lance-shaped in outline and broadest below the middle of the leaf
LATERAL	At the side, as opposed to terminal
LENTICEL	A corky or wart-like protuberance on young bark
LEPIDATE	Leaves covered with small, scurf-like scales
LIGULATE	Strap-like

LINEAR	Leaves that are long and narrow with nearly parallel margins
LINEAR-OBOVATE	Elongated egg-shaped in outline and broadest above the middle of the leaf
LOBE	Segment or division (usually applied to leaves)
MIDRIB	Main vein or rib of a leaf, usually running lengthwise along the axis
MONOCARPIC	A plant which dies after flowering but takes a long period to attain flowering age
MONOECIOUS	A plant bearing flowers of two sexes (e.g. common hazel)
MUCRO	A small abrupt point or tip
MUCRONATE	Ending in a short, stiff point (refers to leaves)
NERVES	Chief veins
NODE	Joint of a branchlet at which a leaf is borne
OBCORDATE	Heart-shaped, the broad indented part furthest from the stalk
OBLANCEOLATE	Lance-shaped in outline and broadest above the middle of the leaf
OBLATE	Flattened (applied to leaves much wider than long)
OBLONG	Leaves that are ovate or lance-shaped with sides nearly parallel, except at their base and apex. Also describes fruits that are neither pear-shaped nor egg-shaped
OBOVATE	Egg-shaped in outline and broadest above the middle of the leaf
OBOVOID	Shaped like an egg, the thickest end uppermost
OBTUSE	Blunt or rounded leaf
OFFSET	A vegetatively-produced young plant growing alongside a parent plant but easily detached from it (applied to bulbs and corms or fibrous-rooted plants which produce several separate but loosely connected crowns)
OPPOSITE	Leaves which arise in pairs from the same level on opposite sides of the stem
OVARY	Part of the flower which ultimately develops the seeds
OVATE	Shaped like an egg and broadest below the middle
OVOID	Egg-shaped (commonly refers to fruits)
OVULE	Tiny seed-like body from which, after fertilisation, the seed develops
PALMATE	Leaves arranged like the fingers of a hand, arising from approximately the same point and spreading outwards
PALMATELY LOBED	Leaves having midribs of lobes palmately arranged
PANICLE	A branched inflorescence having numerous stalked flowers (with the youngest at the top) carried by each branchlet
PAPILIONACEOUS	Type of flower characteristic of the pea family
PAPPUS	Tuft of hairs or bristles on the calyx of some members of the daisy family (*Compositae*) which assist in seed disposal by wind
PEDICEL	The stalk of an individual flower in a compound inflorescence
PEDUNCLE	Main stalk of a flower cluster or the stalk of a single flower
PELTATE	Leaves attached to the stalk by the centre of the lower surface, not at the margin (e.g. common nasturtium)
PERENNIAL	A plant that lives for a number of years and produces flowers time and again
PERFECT	Flowers having effective male and female organs, as opposed to unisexual or sterile
PERFOLIATE	Stem which is apparently encircled by the leaf
PERIANTH	Outermost floral parts (floral envelope). Generally refers to flowers composed of only calyx or corolla or where the two are not distinguishable
PERICARP	The fruit or ovary wall
PERPETUAL	Plants which continue to bloom more or less continually for a long period
PERSISTENT	Remaining attached, as opposed to falling off
PETAL	A division of the corolla ; one of the separate and distinct leaves of the corolla of a flower
PETALOID	Resembling a petal, i.e. parts of a flower which are not true petals but resemble petals
PETIOLE	Leaf-stalk

PILOSE	Leaves or stems having long, soft hairs
PINNATE	Feather-like ; leaves composed of several leaflets arising from opposite sides of a common stalk
PINNATELY LOBED	Midribs of lobes pinnately arranged (applied to leaves)
PINNATELY VEINED	Principal side veins of a leaf arising at intervals from opposite sides of the midrib
PINNATIFID	Leaves that are cut or notched pinnate-like but are not composed of separate leaflets
PINNATISECT	See PINNATIFID
PISTIL	Female part of a flower, i.e. seed-producing (ovary, style and stigma)
PISTILLATE	Having pistils but no stamens (applied to flowers which have female organs only)
PLACENTA	That part of the ovary which bears the ovules
PLACENTATION	Arrangement of ovules in the ovary
PLUMOSE	Feathery or plumed (used to describe flower or seed parts)
POLLEN	Yellow dust-like grains (spores), produced by the stamens (male organs), which are conveyed by wind or insects to the pistil (female organs)
POLYGAMOUS	Plants that bear unisexual and bisexual flowers
POLYPETALOUS	Having the petals separate, i.e. not joined
POLYSEPALOUS	Having the sepals separate
POME	A fruit comprising several carpels surrounded by a thick fleshy layer (e.g. apple)
PRICKLE	A sharp outgrowth from the bark
PROCUMBENT	Lying on or near the ground
PROSTRATE	See PROCUMBENT
PUBERULENT	Minutely pubescent
PUBESCENT	Downy ; leaves or stems covered with soft short hairs
PYRIFORM	Pear-shaped (used to describe fruits)
RACEME	A group of flowers, more or less equally stalked, borne on an elongated stalk, the lower one opening first (the youngest are at the tip)
RACEMOSE	Raceme-like
RACHIS	The common stalk of a raceme, compound leaf, etc.
RADIAL	Spreading outwards on all sides at more or less the same level, similar to the arrangement of wheel spokes
RADICAL	Belonging to the root of a plant
RECEPTACLE	The swollen part at the top of a stem from which the floral organs arise
RECURVED	Curved or bent downwards or backwards (used to describe leaves or petals)
REFLEXED	Sharply or abruptly curved or bent downwards
RENIFORM	Leaves that are kidney-shaped
RETICULATE	A network of veins
RHIZOME	An underground stem, growing horizontally, which produces shoots at a distance from the parent plant
RHOMBOIDAL	Diamond or lozenge-shaped
RUGOSE	Leaves having a wrinkled surface (e.g. *Rosa rugosa*)
SAGITTATE	Leaves that are arrow-shaped
SAMARA	A winged achene
SCABRID	Rough to the touch
SCABROUS	See SCABRID
SCALE	A small leaf or bract
SCAPE	A flower stem which bears no leaves
SCION	A bud or shoot separated from its parent plant and joined to another plant by budding or grafting. The scion provides the aerial shoots or branches
SEED	A fertilised ovule
SELF	Flowers that are of one colour throughout

SELF-FERTILE	A plant capable of producing seeds as a result of fertilisation with its own pollen
SEMI-DOUBLE	Applied loosely to a flower which bears a greater number of petals than normal, but not having all its stamens and pistils transformed into petals as in a double flower
SEPAL	One of the separate segments forming the calyx of the flower
SERRATE	Saw-toothed ; the teeth pointing forwards
SERRULATE	Minutely serrate
SESSILE	Leaves or flowers having no stalks
SHRUB	Plant with woody stems which branch at or near ground level
SIMPLE	Not compound ; applied to leaves which are not divided into leaflets
SINGLE	A flower bearing the normal number of petals, as opposed to double
SINUS	The space, variously shaped according to the leaf design, between the lobes of a leaf
SOLITARY	One flower only occurring at the end of a shoot or in a leaf axil
SPATHULATE	Leaves or petals shaped like a spoon or paddle
SPECIES	Plants of similar structure which show no difference when given the same conditions of growth
SPIKE	A flower cluster resembling a raceme but with the individual flowers stalkless
SPINE	A sharp-pointed woody outgrowth
SPUR	A short shoot
STAMEN	Pollen-bearing (male) organ of a flower, generally consisting of many thread-like bodies each bearing an anther which contains pollen
STAMINODE	A sterile stamen or stamen-like structure
STANDARD	Broad upper petal of a papilionaceous flower
STELLATE	Star-like ; generally applied to a number of hairs radiating from one point
STERILE	A plant or flower incapable of either producing or taking part in the production of seed
STIGMA	The end of the pistil or female organ which receives the pollen
STIPULE	A scaly or leafy outgrowth at the base of a leaf stalk
STOLON	A sucker-like shoot which runs along the surface of the soil and forms roots as it goes
STOMATA	Breathing pores in leaves, generally on their undersurfaces
STROBILUS	A cone or cone-like inflorescence
STYLE	That part of the pistil which connects the stigma and ovary
SUB	Nearly but not quite, e.g. sub-opposite
SUB-SHRUB	A perennial plant which has a woody lower part and a soft and herbaceous upper part
SUBULATE	Awl-like
SUCKER	A shoot growing directly from the root of a plant (usually refers to shoots arising from the roots of grafted or budded plants)
SUFFRUTICOSE	See SUB-SHRUB
SUTURE	A line of splitting
SYNONYM	An alternative Latin name by which a plant is known
TAP ROOT	The first root, usually undivided, produced by a seedling which reaches straight down into the soil
TENDRIL	A coiled thread (which may be a modified leaf, leaflet or shoot) by which a climbing plant attaches itself to an object
TEPAL	Individual segment of a flower not clearly distinguished as either a petal or sepal
TERMINAL	At the end, as opposed to lateral
TERNATE	Leaves arranged in threes
TOMENTOSE	Leaves or stems covered with dense, woolly hairs
TOMENTUM	A covering of dense, woolly hairs
TOOTHED	The edge of a leaf which resembles the teeth of a saw. It may be finely, coarsely, unevenly, closely, distantly, minutely, sharp, blunt, double or round-toothed
TREE	A woody plant having a distinct trunk or main stem, usually taller than a shrub

TRIFOLIATE	A compound leaf comprising three leaflets
TRUNCATE	A plant which terminates abruptly, as if cut off at tip or base
TUBER	A thickened underground stem or root, the difference being that a stem tuber has eyes whereas the root tuber does not
UMBEL	A flower cluster in which all the flower stalks (pedicels) arise from a common point at the top of a main flower stem and resemble the formation of an umbrella
UMBELLATE	Borne in umbels
UNDULATING	The outline of a leaf which is curved (in a horizontal plane) in a manner not sufficiently pronounced to be described as either toothed or lobed
UNISEXUAL	Single sexed. A flower which produces stamens but no pistils is male; where there are pistils but no stamens it is female. (A flower possessing both is bisexual)
URCEOLATE	Urn-shaped
VARIEGATED	A leaf, stem or flower of two or more colours
VENATION	Arrangement or pattern of veins in a leaf
VILLOUS	Covered with soft, curly hairs (but not matted)
WAVY	The margin of a leaf which is folded or crinkled in a vertical plane, as distinct from undulating
WHORL	The arrangement of three or more leaves or flowers in a circle like wheel spokes, arising from the same level on all sides of the main axis

Appendix Two List of Tables
Appearing in the Text

Bibliography

Introduction

COLVIN, B. *Land and Landscape*, revised edition. London: John Murray, 1970.

DUTTON, R. *The English Garden*, 2nd edition. London: Batsford, 1950.

FAIRBROTHER, N. *New Lives. New Landscapes*. London: Architectural Press, 1970.

FAIRBROTHER, N. *The Nature of Landscape Design*. London: Architectural Press, 1974.

FEARNSIDES, W. G. and BULMAN, O. M. B. *Geology in the Service of Man* (Part One), 2nd edition, revised. Harmondsworth: Penguin Books, 1950.

JELLICOE, G. A. *Studies in Landscape Design*, vols 1 and 2. London: Oxford University Press, 1960–66.

MITCHELL, J. B. *Historical Geography*. London: English Universities Press, 1954.

NICHOLSON, N. *The Environmental Revolution*. London: Hodder & Stoughton, 1970.

SAVAGE, W. *The Making of our Towns*. London: Eyre & Spottiswoode, 1952.

SHARP, T. *English Panorama*. London: Architectural Press, 1950.

STAMP, L. Dudley. *Britain's Structure and Scenery*. New Naturalist Series No. 4. London: Collins, 1955.

STEWART, C. *A Prospect of Cities: Being Studies Towards a History of Town Planning*. London: Longmans, Green, 1952.

TANSLEY, A. G. *The British Islands and their Vegetation*, vols 1 and 2 (Chapter VIII). London: Cambridge University Press, 1950.

Chapter 1   Site clearance

Tree felling and removal

Arboricultural Association. *The Care of Trees on Development Sites*. Leaflet No.3. London: Arboricultural Association, 1968.

HART, C. E. *Practical Forestry for the Agent and Surveyor*. (Outlines methods of harvesting timber crops.) London: Estates Gazette, 1967.

HILEY, W. H. *Woodland Management*, revised edition (Part 2: Production, felling and conversion of woodland products). London: Faber & Faber, 1967.

JAMES, N. D. G. *The Forester's Companion*. Oxford: Blackwell, 1955.

MELLOWS, A. R. *The Preservation and Felling of Trees*. Oyez Practice Note No.54. (Written for the legal profession: useful reference work.) London: Solicitors' Law Stationery Society, 1964.

Ministry of Agriculture, Fisheries and Food. *Tree, Bush and Stump Clearance*. Fixed Equipment of the Farm Leaflet No.37. London: HMSO, 1959.

Ministry of Land and Natural Resources. *Memorandum on the Preservation of Trees and Woodlands*, 2nd edition. London: HMSO, 1966.

POLLARD, R. S. W. *Trees and the Law*. London: Arboricultural Association, 1973.

Hedging and ditching

ALDRIDGE, T. M. *Boundaries, Walls and Fences*. Oyez Practice Note No.46. (Written for the legal profession: useful reference work.) London: Solicitors' Law Stationery Society, 1963.

BAKER, M. *Discovering Topiary*. (Includes a list of gardens in the British Isles where examples may be seen.) Tring, Herts: Shire Publications, 1969.

BEDDALL, J. L. *Hedges for Farm and Garden*. London: Faber & Faber, 1950.

CABORN, J. M. *Shelterbelts and Microclimate*. Forestry Commission Bulletin No.29. London: HMSO, 1957.

CABORN, J. M. *Shelterbelts and Windbreaks*. London: Faber & Faber, 1965.

EDLIN, H. J. *Woodland Crafts in Britain*. (Chapter 10, Hawthorns and hedgecraft). London: Batsford, 1949.

EIMERN, J. van (Ed.) *Windbreaks and Shelterbelts*. Technical Note No.59. Geneva: World Meteorological Association, 1964.

LE SUEUR, A. D. *Hedges, Shelterbelts and Screens*. London: Country Life, 1951.

Ministry of Agriculture, Fisheries and Food. *Farm and Estate Hedges*. Fixed Equipment of the Farm Leaflet No.11. London: HMSO, 1960.

Ministry of Agriculture, Fisheries and Food. *Shelterbelts for Farmland*. London: HMSO, 1969.

OSBORNE, A. *Shrubs and Trees for the Garden*. London: Ward, Lock, 1963.

PROCKTER, N. S. *Garden Hedges*. London: Collingridge, 1960.

Demolition and clearing the site

NICHOLS, H. L. *Modern Techniques of Excavation*. London: Odhams Press, 1956.

Chapter 2 Ground contouring and soil preparation

The soils of Britain and their influence on plants

BRADE-BIRKS, S. G. *Good Soil*, revised edition (Teach Yourself Books). London: English Universities Press, 1966.
CLARKE, G. R. and BECKETT, P. *The Study of Soil in the Field*, 5th edition. London: Oxford University Press, 1971.
COKER, E. G. *Horticultural Science and Soils*. Vol.1, Horticultural Science; vol.2, Soils and Fertilisers. MacDonald Horticultural Series. London: BPC Publishing, 1971.
COOK, J. G. *Your Guide to the Soil*, 2nd edition. Science for Everyone Series. Watford, Herts: Merrow, 1965.
CRUIKSHANK, J. G. *Soil Geography*. Newton Abbot: David & Charles, 1972.
DONAHUE, R. L., SHICKLUNA, J. C. and ROBERTSON, L. S. *Soils: An Introduction to Soils and Plant Growth*, 3rd edition. Englewood Cliffs, NJ: Prentice-Hall, 1958.
DRABBLE, H. *Plant Ecology* (Chapters I and II). London: Edward Arnold, 1951.
Ministry of Agriculture, Fisheries and Food. *Modern Farming and the Soil: Report of the Advisory Council on Soil Structure and Soil Fertility*. London: HMSO, 1970.
Ministry of Agriculture, Fisheries and Food. *Soil Analysis for Advisory Purposes*. Advisory Leaflet No.270, revised edition. London: HMSO, 1973.
SHEWELL-COOPER, W. E. *Horticultural Notebooks, Section 6*. London: Technical Press, 1960.
TANSLEY, A. G. *The British Islands and their Vegetation*, vols 1 and 2 (Chapters IV and V). London: Cambridge University Press, 1950.
TOWNSEND, W. N. *An Introduction to the Scientific Study of Soil*, 5th edition. London: Edward Arnold, 1973.
VOYSEY, A. *Landscape and Soil*. Rural Education Series. (Simple approach, written for young people.) London: Longmans, 1963.

Treatment of derelict land

BEAVER, S. H. Land reclamation after surface mineral working. *Journal of the Town Planning Institute*, **41** 146–154, 1955.
COLLINS, W. G. and BUSH, P. W. The definition and classification of derelict land. *Journal of the Town Planning Institute*, **55,** 111 and 115, 1969.
COLLINS, W. G. and BUSH, P. W. The use of aerial photographs in the study of derelict land. *Journal of the Town Planning Institute*, **55,** 246–255, 1969.
DAVIES, W. Morley. Land restoration following mineral extraction and deposition of waste materials. *Journal of the Royal Agricultural Society*, **122,** 26–38, 1961.
HOLFORD, W. The reclamation of land disfigured by industrial uses. *Journal of the Royal Society of Arts*, **106,** 149–173, 1958.
KNOWLES, A. S. and COOK, T. L. *Reclamation for Recreation: Levelling and Reinstatement*. London: National Playing Fields Association, 1972.
Ministry of Housing and Local Government. *Restoration of Land*. Report of the Committee (Lord Kennet, Chairman). London: HMSO, 1939.
Ministry of Housing and Local Government. *Derelict Land and its Reclamation*. Technical Memorandum No.7. London: HMSO, 1956.
Ministry of Housing and Local Government. *New Life for Dead Lands: Derelict Areas Reclaimed*. London: HMSO, 1963.
Nature Conservancy. *The Countryside in 1970*. Proceedings of the Study Conference on the Countryside, 1963 (Paper No.2 and Annex to Paper No.2, 106–151). London: HMSO, 1964.
OXENHAM, J. R. The Restoration of Derelict Land. *Final Report of the Public Works and Municipal Services Congress, 1952*. (494–526.) London: The Congress and Exhibition Council, 1953.
OXENHAM, J. R. *Reclaiming Derelict Land*. London: Faber & Faber, 1972.
REES, W. J. and SIDRAK, G. H. Plant growth on fly ash. *Nature*, **176,** 352, 1955.
REES, W. J. and SKELDING, A. D. Grass establishment on power station waste. *Agriculture*, **59,** 586, 1953.
Sand and Gravel Association of Great Britain (London). Pamphlet No.1 *Gravel Pits and Agriculture* (undated). Pamphlet No.2 *Gravel Pits and Building*. 1959. Pamphlet No.3 *Gravel Pits and Nature*. 1961. Pamphlet No.4 *Gravel Pits and Water Sports*. 1961. Pamphlet No.5 *Gravel Pits and Recreation*. 1963. *Landfall*. (Pamphlet containing a map showing locations of award-winning schemes involving landscape reclamation and rehabilitation.) 1974.
University of Newcastle upon Tyne. *Landscape Reclamation*, vols 1 and 2. London: Iliffe Science Technical Publications, 1972.

WHYTE, R. O. and SISAM, J. W. B. *The Establishment of Vegetation on Industrial Waste Land*. Oxford : Commonwealth Agricultural Bureau, 1949.

WOOD, R. F. and THIRGOOD, J. V. *Tree Planting on Colliery Spoil Heaps*. Forest Research Branch Paper No.17. London : Forestry Commission, 1955.

Earth-moving and excavating operations

Building Research Establishment Digest No.64 (2nd Series). *Soils and Foundations: 2*. London : HMSO, 1965.

HAMMOND, R. *Earthmoving and Excavating Plant*. London : Maclaren, 1964.

KNOWLES, A. S. and COOK, T. L. *Reclamation for Recreation: Levelling and Reinstatement*. London : National Playing Fields Association, 1972.

NICHOLS, H. L. *Modern Techniques of Excavation*. London : Odhams Press, 1956.

NICHOLS, H. L. *Mining the Earth: The Workbook of Excavation*, 2nd edition. London : Van Nostrand Reinhold, 1962.

Surface grading and cultivating

FAULKNER, R. P. *Garden Manures and Fertilizers*. London : Collingridge, 1955.

HAWKINS, J. C. *Tractor Ploughing*, 4th edition. Ministry of Agriculture, Fisheries and Food. London : HMSO, 1962.

Ministry of Agriculture, Fisheries and Food. *Lime and Liming*, 7th edition. Bulletin No.35. London : HMSO, 1973.

ROBINSON, D. H. (Ed.) *Fream's Elements of Agriculture*, 15th edition. (Chapter 6 deals with farm machinery.) London : John Murray, 1972.

Chapter 3 Structures in the landscape

ALDRIDGE, T. M. *Boundaries, Walls and Fences*. Oyez Practice Note No.46. (Written for the legal profession : useful reference work.) London : Solicitors' Law Stationery Society, 1963.

Building Research Establishment Digests (2nd Series) (London : HMSO).
No.58 *Mortars for Jointing*. 1965.
No.63. *Soils and Foundations: 1*. 1965.
No.67. *Soils and Foundations: 3*. 1966.
No.70. *Painting Iron and Steel: 1*. 1973.
No.71. *Painting Iron and Steel: 2*. 1973.
No.95. *Choosing a Type of Pile*. 1968.
No.132. *Wilful Damage on Housing Estates*. 1971.
No.156. *Specifying Timber*. 1973.
No.164. *Clay Brickwork: 1*. 1974.
No.165. *Clay Brickwork: 2*. 1974.
No.175. *Choice of Glues for Wood*. 1975.
No.177. *Decay and Conservation of Stone Masonry*. 1975.

CROWE, S. *Garden Design*. London : Country Life, 1958.

DÄUMEL, G. (transl. Van Amerongen, C.) *Concrete in the Garden*. London and Amsterdam : Elsevier, 1971.

EDLIN, H. L. *Woodland Crafts in Britain*. (Chapter XII deals with hurdles). London : Batsford, 1949.

FOSTER, J. S. *Mitchell's Building Construction*. London : Batsford, 1973.

LINDLEY, K. *Landscape and Buildings*. Oxford : Pergamon, 1970.

MARTIN, L. and MARCH, L. *Urban Space and Structures*. London : Cambridge University Press, 1972.

Ministry of Agriculture, Fisheries and Food. *Construction and Heating of Commercial Glasshouses*, 3rd edition. Bulletin No.115. London : HMSO, 1960.

Ministry of Agriculture, Fisheries and Food. *Beehives*, 4th edition. Bulletin No.144. London : HMSO, 1968.

Ministry of Agriculture, Fisheries and Food. *Horticultural Buildings Pocketbook*. London : HMSO, 1968.

Ministry of Agriculture, Fisheries and Food. Fixed Equipment of the Farm Leaflets (London : HMSO).
No.6. *Permanent Farm Fences*. 1962.
No.8. *Farm Gates*. 1973.
No.17. *Preservation of Timber and Metal*. 1968.
No.42. *Round Timber from the Farm*. 1971.
No.52. *The Appearance of Farm Buildings in the Landscape*. 1972.
Ministry of Housing and Local Government. *Caravan Parks: Location, Layout, Landscape*. London : HMSO, 1962.
National Federation of Clay Industries. Brick Information Sheets (London : undated).
Nos. 1–8. *Bricks and Bond*.
No.12. *Mortar and Jointing*.

PENNINGTON, A. M. *Concrete Fences*. London : Concrete Publications, 1950.
SUDELL, R. and WATERS, D. T. *Sports Buildings and Playing Fields*. London : Batsford, 1957.
TANDY, C. (Ed.) *Handbook of Urban Landscape*. London : Architectural Press, 1972.
Timber Research and Development Association. *Timber Fencing and Gates for Agriculture and Open Space Purposes*. London : TRADA, 1956.
Timber Research and Development Association. *Timber Fencing and Gates for Housing and Other Buildings*. London : TRADA, 1956.
WARD, M. Gates and fences. *Architectural Review*, **688**, 277–281, 1954.

Chapter 4   The use and disposal of water

The use of water

BRIGGS, R. T. *The Environment and Water Sports*. Monograph No.6. London : Institution of Municipal Engineers, 1972.
Cement and Concrete Association. *Design and Construction of Open-air Swimming Pools*. London : Cement and Concrete Association, 1960.
CROWE, S. *Garden Design* (Chapter 2). London : Country Life, 1958.
FALCONER, P. Small swimming pools. *Architects Journal*, **129**, 3350, 735–738, 1959.
FEARNSIDES, W. G. and BULMAN, O. M. B. *Geology in the Service of Man* (Part One), 2nd edition, revised (Chapter VI). Harmondsworth : Penguin Books, 1950.
JELLICOE, S. and JELLICOE, G. *Water: The Use of Water in Landscape Architecture*. London : A. & C. Black, 1971.
LAVERTON, S. *Irrigation: Its Profitable Use for Agricultural and Horticultural Crops*. (Costs given in Chapter 7 are out of date, but a useful, practical guide.) London : Oxford University Press, 1964.
MANN, R. *Rivers in the City*. Newton Abbot : David & Charles, 1972.
Ministry of Agriculture, Fisheries and Food. *Calculation of Irrigation Need*. Advisory Bulletin No.4. London : HMSO, 1962.
Ministry of Agriculture, Fisheries and Food. *Introducing Outdoor Irrigation*. Advisory Leaflet No.487. London : HMSO, 1961.
Ministry of Agriculture, Fisheries and Food. *Irrigation*, 3rd edition. Advisory Bulletin No.138. London : HMSO, 1962.
Ministry of Agriculture, Fisheries and Food. *Water for Irrigation*. Bulletin No.202. London : HMSO, 1967.
US Department of Agriculture Forest Service. *How to Build a Farm Pond*. Washington, DC : US Department of Agriculture, 1949.
Water Resources Board with the Scottish Development Department. (London : HMSO).
Surface Water Year Book of Great Britain, 1965–1966. Hydrometric statistics for British rivers, together with related rainfalls and river water temperatures for the year ended 30 September 1966, 1967.
Supplement 1965. Description of gauging stations, information as to presentation and computation, and notes for use with the *Surface Water Year Book* (with correction). 1968.

The disposal of water

Building Research Establishment Digests (2nd Series) (London : HMSO).
   No. 6. *Drainage for Housing.* 1961.
   No.130. *Drainage Pipelines: 1.* 1971.
   No.131. *Drainage Pipelines: 2.* 1971.
COOPER, T. *Practical Land Drainage.* London : Leonard Hill, 1965.
LIVESLEY, M. C. *Field Drainage.* London : E. & F. Spon, 1960.
Ministry of Agriculture, Fisheries and Food. Fixed Equipment on the Farm Leaflets (London : HMSO).
   No.21. *Drainage of the Farm Homestead.* 1964 (new edition in preparation 1975).
   No.44. *Mole Drainage for Heavy Land.* 1960.
Ministry of Housing and Local Government. *Small Sewage Works Operators' Handbook.* London : HMSO, 1965.
ROBINSON, D. H. (Ed.) *Fream's Elements of Agriculture*, 15th edition. (Chapter 3 deals with field drainage.) London : John Murray, 1972.

Chapter 5   Electricity in the landscape

The application of electric power out of doors

Building Research Establishment Digest No.179 (2nd Series). *Electricity Distribution on Sites.* London : HMSO, 1975.
CANHAM, A. E. *Electricity in Horticulture.* Technical and Craft Series. London : MacDonald, 1964.
Council for the Preservation of Rural England. *Electricity Installations and the Landscape.* London : CPRE, 1971.
CROWE, S. *The Landscape of Power.* London : Architectural Press, 1958.
DE BOER, J. B. *Public Lighting* (Chapters 3, 6 and 10). Eindhoven : Philips Technical Library, 1967.
GOULTY, G. A. *The Landscape Problems Associated with the Development of Electricity Substations.* Paper read to the Institute of Landscape Architects, 1963. (Believed to have been circulated to public authorities by the CEGB : available ILA Library.)
HEBBLETHWAITE, R. L. *Landscape Maintenance: A Report on Landscape Maintenance at Power Station and Substation Sites.* London : Central Electricity Generating Board, 1969.
HINTON, Sir Christopher and HOLFORD, Sir William. *Power Production and Transmission in the Countryside: Preserving Amenities.* Two papers read to the Royal Society of Arts, November 1959. London : Central Electricity Generating Board, 1960.
JONES, D. (Ed.) Communications and energy in changing urban environments. *Proceedings of the 21st Symposium of the Colston Research Society.* London : Butterworth, 1970.
Ministry of Agriculture, Fisheries and Food. *Electric Fencing*, 4th edition, revised. Bulletin No.147. London : HMSO, 1972.
Ministry of Housing and Local Government. *Planning Control of Signs and Posters.* London : HMSO, 1966.

Chapter 6   Hard paved surfaces

Asphalt and Coated Macadam Association (London)
Model Specification for Roads and Footways on Housing Estates. 1949.
Dense Road Bases and Basecourses. 1968.
Recommendations for the Construction and Surfacing of Paved Areas for Recreation and Sport. (Deals with games pitches, cycling tracks, motor and motor-cycle tracks.) 1969.
Recommendations for the Construction and Surfacing of Vehicle Parking Areas. 1969.
Recommendations for the Surfacing of Playgrounds and Recreation Areas. 1969.
Types and Scope of Coated Macadam. 1970.
Modern Flexible Road Construction. 1971.
Hot Process Asphalts, metric edition. 1975.
BEAZLEY, E. *Space Between Buildings*. London : Architectural Press, 1960.
British Granite and Whinstone Federation (London)
Dense Bitumen Macadam Wearing Course. 1963.
Lightly Coated Chippings for Surface Dressing, 2nd edition. 1963.
Road Bases: Wet-mix and Lean Concrete. 1964.
Dense Bituminous Road Bases and Basecourse. 1966.
British Road Federation. *Landscaping of Motorways*. Report of a conference, May 1962. London : British Road Federation, 1962.
British Tar Industry Association (London).
Dense Tar Surfacing Wearing Course and Hot-laid Tarmacadam Basecourse. 1962.
Road Construction with Tar: A Guide to the Choice of Specifications, 2nd edition. 1966.
Tarmacadam. 1966.
Oil-resistant Surfaces for Car Parks: A Guide to the Choice of Specifications, Dense Tar Surface Wearing Courses. 1967.
Cement and Concrete Association (London).
Housing Estate Roads. 1961.
Specification for Housing Estate and Other Minor Roads in Concrete, revised edition. 1961.
Lean Concrete Bases for Roads. 1962.
Concrete Car Parks for Private Vehicles. 1963.
Bay Layout for Concrete Roads. 1964.
Specification for Laying Precast Concrete Flags. 1964.
CROWE, S. *The Landscape of Roads*. London : Architectural Press, 1950.

GAGE, M. *Hard Landscaping in Concrete*. London : Architectural Press, 1973.
HADFIELD, W. *Design for Service and Off-street Loading Areas*. Research Report No.1. Croydon : Freight Transport Association Limited, 1972.
LIVERSEDGE, F. and BULLOCK, G. Tar-bitumen blends in road construction and maintenance, *Road Tar*, **26,** 3, 4–7, 1972.
MAGUIRE, R. External paving. *Architectural Review*, **121,** 722, 141–146 and 723, 282–288, 1957.
Ministry of Transport. *Specification of Road and Bridge Works*. London : HMSO, 1969.
National Playing Fields Association (London).
Cricket on Non-turf Pitches. NPFA and MCC Joint Committee 2nd Report. 1954.
Pitch and Court Markings Suitable for Games with a Playleader. Technical drawing No.26. 1959.
Cinder Running Tracks to a Simplified Specification. NPFA and Amateur Athletic Association Joint Committee. 1961.
Facilities for Athletics (*Track and Field*). 1972.
Notes on Hard, Porous and All-weather Playing Surfaces for Athletics, Children's Playgrounds, General Play Areas, Cricket, Golf, Roller Skating, Synthetic Grass, Ski-ing and Tennis. 1974.
Sports Ground Construction–Specifications, 2nd edition. 1975.
Road Research Laboratory (London : HMSO).
Road Note No.1. *Recommendations for Tar Surface Dressings*, 4th edition. Ministry of Transport. 1965.
Road Note No.19. *The Design Thickness of Concrete Roads*. Department of Scientific and Industrial Research. 1955 (new edition in preparation).
Road Note No.25. *Sources of White and Coloured Aggregates in Great Britain*, 2nd edition. Ministry of Transport. 1966.
Road Note No.29. *A Guide to the Structural Design of Pavements for New Roads*, 3rd edition. Department of the Environment. 1970.
Road Note No.39. *Recommendations for Road Surface Dressing*. Department of the Environment. 1972.
Sources of Road Aggregate in Great Britain, 3rd edition. Ministry of Transport in collaboration with Geological Survey and Museum. 1960.

ROBINSON, J. R. *Highways and our Environment*. New York : McGraw Hill, 1971.

Society of Motor Manufacturers and Traders. *British Commercial Vehicles for the World*. (Gives details of sizes, etc. of individual vehicles.) London : IPC Press in conjunction with *Commercial Motor*, 1974.

TANDY, C. (Ed.) *Handbook of Urban Landscape*. London : Architectural Press, 1972.

WILLIAMS-ELLIS, C. *Roads in the Landscape*. Ministry of Transport. London : HMSO, 1967.

Chapter 7   Soft landscaped surfaces

CAVE, L. W. *Cave's Guide to Turf Culture*. London : Pelham Books, 1967.

GILL, N. T. and VEAR, K. C. *Agricultural Botany*, 2nd edition (Chapters XVI and XVII). London : Duckworth, 1966.

GOOCH, R. G. *Selection and Layout of Land for Playing Fields and Playgrounds*. London : National Playing Fields Association, 1959.

GREENFIELD, I. *Turf Culture*. London : Leonard Hill, 1962.

HAWTHORN, R. (Ed.) *Dawson's Practical Lawncraft*, 7th edition. London : Crosby Lockwood Staples, 1977.

HOPPER, H. T. *The Provision and Maintenance of Playing Fields and Churchyards*. Morden, Surrey : Trade & Technical Press, 1971.

LINDLEY, K. *Graves and Graveyards*. London : Routledge & Kegan Paul, 1972.

Ministry of Transport. *Instructions on the Establishment and Maintenance of Grass Slopes, Verges and Central Reservations*. Technical Memorandum T2/65. London : HMSO, 1965.

MUSSER, H. B. *Turf Management*. New York : McGraw-Hill, 1962.

ROBINSON, D. H. *Good Grassland*. Teach Yourself Farming series. London : English Universities Press, 1947.

ROBINSON, D. H. (Ed.) *Fream's Elements of Agriculture*, 15th edition. (Chapter 11 deals with grassland.) London : John Murray, 1972.

SMITH, P. W. *Planning, Construction and Maintenance of Playing Fields*. London : Oxford University Press, 1950.

SUDELL, R. and WATERS, D. T. *Sports Buildings and Playing Fields*. London : Batsford, 1957.

SUTTON, M. A. *Lawns and Sports Grounds*, 7th edition. Reading : Sutton & Sons, 1962.

Sutton & Sons. *Golf Courses: Design, Construction and Upkeep*. Reading : Sutton & Sons, 1950.

WATSON, S. J. *Grassland and Grassland Products*. London : Edward Arnold, 1951.

Chapter 8   Trees: Planting, care and protection

Tree planting

Arboricultural Association (London).
Leaflet No.1. *Tree Preservation Orders*. 1967.
Leaflet No.2. *Site Preparation and Planting*. 1970.
Leaflet No.3. *A Tree for Every Site*. 1971.
BEAN, W. J. *Trees and Shrubs Hardy in the British Isles*, 8th edition, vols 1, 2 and 3. (Standard work: comprehensive, but sparsely illustrated.) London: John Murray, 1967.
BEDFORD FRANKLIN, T. *Climates in Miniature*. London: Faber & Faber, 1960.
BOWE, W. H. *Tree and Shrub Growing*. London: Faber & Faber, 1949.
CABORN, J. M. *Shelterbelts and Windbreaks*. London: Faber & Faber, 1965.
CABORN, J. M. *Shelterbelts and Microclimate*. Forestry Commission Bulletin No.29. London: HMSO, 1957.
Civic Trust (London).
Moving Big Trees. 1967.
Street Improvement Schemes. Practice notes for co-ordinating architects. 1967.
Tree Planting. 1967.
COLVIN, B. *Trees for Town and Country*, 3rd edition. London: Lund Humphries, 1965.
EDLIN, H. L. *Guide to Tree Planting and Cultivation*. London: Collins, 1970.
EIMERN, J. van (Ed.) *Windbreaks and Shelterbelts*. Technical Note No.59. Geneva: World Meteorological Organisation, 1964.
Forestry Commission. *Forestry in the Landscape*. Forestry Practice Bulletin No.14. London: HMSO, 1964.
GARTHWAITE, P. *The Forester and the Landscape*. Forestry Commission Research and Development Paper No.53. London: HMSO, 1967.
GORER, R. *Multi-season Shrubs and Trees*. London: Faber & Faber, 1971.
HADFIELD, M. *Landscape with Trees*. London: Country Life, 1967.
HARRISON, S. G. *Garden Shrubs and Trees*. The Kew Series. London: Eyre & Spottiswoode, 1960.
HART, C. E. *Practical Forestry for the Agent and Surveyor*. London: Estates Gazette, 1967.
HAY, R. and SYNGE, P. M. *Dictionary of Garden Plants in Colour*. London: Ebury Press and Michael Joseph, 1969.

HILEY, W. E. *Woodland Management*. London: Faber & Faber, 1967.
Hillier & Sons. *A Manual of Trees and Shrubs*, revised edition. Winchester: Hillier & Sons, 1974.
JAMES, N. D. G. *The Arboriculturist's Companion*. Oxford: Blackwell, 1972.
JENSEN, M. *Shelter Effect*. Copenhagen: Danish Technical Press, 1954.
JOHNSON, D. R., GRAYSON, A. J. and BRADLEY, R.T. *Forest Planning*. London: Faber & Faber, 1967.
MAKINS, F. K. *British Trees in Winter*. London: J. M. Dent, 1945.
MAKINS, F. K. *The Identification of Trees and Shrubs*, 2nd edition. London: J. M. Dent, 1952.
MCHARG, I. L. *Design with Nature*. American Museum of Natural History. New York: Natural History Press, 1972.
MEIKLE, R. D. *British Trees and Shrubs*. The Kew Series. London: Eyre & Spottiswoode, 1958.
MILES, R. *Forestry in the English Landscape*. London: Faber & Faber, 1967.
Ministry of Agriculture, Fisheries and Food. *Shelterbelts for Farmland*. London: HMSO, 1969.
Ministry of Housing and Local Government. *Trees in Town and City*. London: HMSO, 1958.
MORLING, R. J. *Trees in Towns*. London: Estates Gazette, 1954.
MORLING, R. J. *Trees, including Preservation, Planting, Law, Highways*, revised edition. London: Estates Gazette, 1963.
OSBORN, A. *Shrubs and Trees for the Garden*. London: Ward, Lock, 1963.
REID, D. *Elementary Ecology*. (Simple introduction with clear diagrams.) London: Allman, 1959.
ROGER, M. *Forestry in the English Landscape*. London: Faber & Faber, 1967
ROWE, W. H. *Tree and Shrub Growing*. (A practical guide.) London: Faber & Faber, 1949.
SCHWANKL, A. (Transl. Edlin, H. L.). *Bark*. (Illustrations and descriptions of the bark of common species.) Open Air Guides. London: Thames & Hudson, 1956.
SEARLE, S. A. *Environment and Plant Life*. London: Faber & Faber, 1973.
SOMERVILLE, W. *How a Tree Grows*. London: Oxford University Press, 1927.
STEP, E. *Wayside and Woodland Trees: A Guide to the British Sylva*. London: Frederick Warne, 1959.
STOKOE, W. J. (Ed.) *The Observer's Book of Trees and Shrubs*, 2nd edition. London: Frederick Warne, 1960.

TANSLEY, A. G. *The British Islands and their Vegetation*, vols 1 and 2. London : Cambridge University Press, 1950.

TANSLEY, A. G. *Introduction to Plant Ecology*. London : Allen & Unwin, 1958.

VEDEL, H. and LANGE, J. (Transl. Hillman, C.H.R.) *Trees and Bushes in Wood and Hedgerow*. London : Methuen, 1960.

WEDDLE, A. E. *Techniques of Landscape Architecture*. London : Heinemann, 1967.

WRIGHT, S. (Ed.) *Aspects of Landscape Ecology and Maintenance*. Ashford, Kent : Wye College, 1972.

ZION, R. L. *Trees for Architecture*. London : Van Nostrand Reinhold, 1968.

Tree surgery and protection

Arboricultural Association. *Guide to Tree Pruning*. Leaflet No.2. London : Arboricultural Association, 1966.

BROWN, G. E. *The Pruning of Trees, Shrubs and Conifers*. (Gives alphabetical list of genera and pruning required.) London : Faber & Faber, 1972.

GIBBS, J. N. *Dutch Elm Disease*. Forestry Commission. London : HMSO, 1971.

JAMES, N. D. G. *The Arboriculturist's Companion*. Oxford : Blackwell, 1972.

LE SUEUR, A. D. *The Care and Repair of Ornamental Trees*. London : Country Life, 1949.

PEACE, T. R. *Pathology of Trees and Shrubs*. (The standard scientific work on tree diseases.) Oxford : Clarendon Press, 1962.

PIRONE, P. P. *Tree Maintenance*. (The standard American work on tree surgery.) New York : Oxford University Press, 1959.

Chapter 9   Shrubs, herbaceous and alpine plants

Shrubs

BEAN, W. J. *Trees and Shrubs Hardy in the British Isles*, 8th edition, vols 1, 2 and 3. London : John Murray, 1967.

BROOKES, J. *Garden Design and Layout*. Garden Centre. London : Queen Anne Press, 1970.

CANE, P. S. *The Creative Art of Garden Design*. London : Country Life, 1967.

DOBER, R. P. *Environmental Design*. London : Van Nostrand Reinhold, 1970.

GORER, R. *Hardy Foliage Plants*. London : Collingridge, 1966.

GORER, R. *Multi-season Shrubs and Trees*. London : Faber & Faber, 1971.

HACKETT, B. *Landscape Planning: An Introduction to Theory and Practice*. Newcastle : Oriel Press, 1971.

HACKETT, B. *Landscape Development of Steep Slopes*. Newcastle : Oriel Press, 1972.

HARRISON, S. G. *Garden Shrubs and Trees*. The Kew Series. London : Eyre & Spottiswoode, 1960.

HELLYER, A. G. L. *Garden Plants in Colour*. London : Collingridge, 1958.

Hillier & Sons. *A Manual of Trees and Shrubs*, revised edition. Winchester : Hillier & Sons, 1974.

KENFIELD, W. G. *The Wild Gardener in the Wild Landscape. The Art of Naturalistic Landscaping*. New York : Hafner, 1967.

MAKINS, F. K. *The Identification of Trees and Shrubs*, 2nd edition. London : J. M. Dent, 1952.

MCHARG, I. L. *Design with Nature*. American Museum of Natural History. New York : Natural History Press, 1972.

MEIKLE, R. D. *British Trees and Shrubs*. The Kew Series. London : Eyre & Spottiswoode, 1958.

OSBORN, A. *Shrubs and Trees for the Garden*. London : Ward, Lock, 1963.

MORRIS, H. V. *Planning a Nature Trail*. Monograph No.9. London : Institution of Municipal Engineers, 1972.

TANSLEY, A. G. *The British Islands and their Vegetation*, vols 1 and 2. London : Cambridge University Press, 1950.

WEDDLE, A. E. *Techniques of Landscape Architecture*. London : Heinemann, 1967.

WRIGHT, S. (Ed.) *Aspects of Landscape Ecology and Maintenance*. Ashford, Kent : Wye College, 1972.

Bulbous plants

ANDERSON, E. B. *Dwarf Bulbs for the Rock Garden*. London: Thos. Nelson, 1959.

GENDERS, R. *Miniature Bulbs*. London: Faber & Faber, 1961.

HAES, E. C. M. *Winter Colour in the Garden*. (Chapter 4 deals with winter-flowering bulbs). London: C. Arthur Pearson, 1965.

HAY, R. and SYNGE, P. M. *Dictionary of Garden Plants in Colour*. London: Ebury Press and Michael Joseph, 1969.

MOORE, W. C. *Diseases of Bulbs*. Ministry of Agriculture, Fisheries and Food. London: HMSO, 1939.

SYNGE, P. M. *Collins's Guide to Bulbs*. London: Collins, 1961.

Herbaceous and alpine plants

BODDY, F. A. *Foliage Plants*. Newton Abbot: David & Charles, 1973.

GORER, R. *Hardy Foliage Plants*. London: Collingridge, 1966.

HUNT, P. R. S. *Herbaceous Plants*, vols 1 and 2. London: Ebury Press, 1965.

LLOYD, C. *Foliage Plants*. London: Collins, 1973.

SHEWELL-COOPER, W. E. *ABC of the Herbaceous Border*. London: English Universities Press, 1959.

THOMAS, G. S. *Plants for Ground Cover*. London: Dent, 1970.

UNDERWOOD, D. *Grey and Silver Plants*. London: Collins, 1971.

Chapter 10 Aquatics and bog plants

BEEDELL, S. *Water in the Garden*. Newton Abbot: David & Charles, 1973.

BURSCHE, E. M. *A Handbook of Water Plants*. (Includes keys for identification.) London: Frederick Warne, 1971.

LOUDON, J. C. *An Encyclopaedia of Gardening*, 2nd edition. London: Longman, Brown, Green, Longmans & Roberts, 1859.

Ministry of Agriculture, Fisheries and Food. *Identification of Common Water Weeds*. Bulletin No.183. London: HMSO, 1962.

Ministry of Agriculture, Fisheries and Food. *Control of Aquatic Weeds*, 2nd edition. Bulletin No.194. London: HMSO, 1973.

PERRY, F. *Water Gardening*, 3rd edition. London: Country Life, 1961.

PERRY, F. *The Garden Pool*, revised edition. London: Collingridge, 1971.

Chapter 11   Outdoor furniture

ALLEN OF HURTWOOD, Lady. *Design for Play*. London: The Housing Centre Trust, 1962.

ALLEN OF HURTWOOD, Lady. *Planning for Play*. London: Thames & Hudson, 1968.

BEAZLEY, E. *Designed for Recreation*. London: Faber & Faber, 1969.

BENGTSSON, A. *Adventure Playgrounds*. London: Crosby Lockwood Staples, 1972.

BROOKES, J. *Room Outside: A Plan for the Garden*. London: Thames & Hudson, 1968.

DATTNER, R. *Design for Play*. New York: Van Nostrand Reinhold, 1969.

Design Council. *Street Furniture Design Index*. London: Design Council (perpetually updated).

DOUGLASS, R. W. *Forest Recreation*. New York: Pergamon Press, 1969.

GRAY, N. *Lettering on Buildings*. London: Architectural Press, 1960.

LEDERMANN, A. and TRACHSEL, A. *Playgrounds and Recreation Spaces*. London: Architectural Press, 1959.

Ministry of Agriculture, Fisheries and Food. *Cattle Grids for Private Roads*. Fixed Equipment of the Farm Leaflet No.7. London: HMSO, 1962.

Ministry of Housing and Local Government. *Planning Control of Signs and Posters*. London: HMSO, 1966.

National Playing Fields Association (London).
Adventure Playgrounds. (no date).
Sandpits: Construction and Maintenance. 1950.
Playgrounds for Blocks of Flats. 1961.
New Playgrounds. 1968.
Technical drawing No.3. *Space Requirements and Orientation for the More Popular Outdoor Games*. 1974.
Technical drawing No.9. *Hard Tennis Court Details*. 1974.
Technical drawing No.10. *Details of Tennis Stop Net Enclosure*. 1974.
Technical drawing No.13. *Athletic Arena: Standard Layout*. 1962.
Technical drawing No.26. *Pitch and Court Markings Suitable for Games with a Playleader*. 1959.
Technical drawing No.32. *Knock up Practice Walls for Children's Playgrounds*. 1974.

British Standards Institution: British Standards and Codes of Practice referred to in the text

BS 4: Part 1: 1972 *Hot-rolled structural steel sections*

BS 4: Part 2: 1969 *Hot-rolled hollow structural steel sections*

BS 12: Part 2: 1971 *Portland cement (ordinary and rapid-hardening). Metric units*

BS 65 & 540: Part 1: 1971 *Clay drain and sewer pipes including surface water pipes and fittings. Pipes and fittings*

BS 76: 1964 *Tars for road purposes*

BS 78: Part 1: 1961 *Cast iron spigot and socket pipes (vertically cast)*

BS 78: Part 2: 1965 *Cast iron spigot and socket fittings*

BS 146: Part 2: 1973 *Portland-blastfurnace cement*

BS 153: Parts 3B and 4: 1972 *Steel girder bridges*

BS 187: Part 2: 1970 *Calcium silicate (sandlime and flintlime) bricks. Metric units*

BS 368: 1971 *Precast concrete flags*

BS 434: 1973 *Bitumen road emulsion (anionic and cationic)*

BS 435: 1931 *Granite and whinstone kerbs, channels, quadrants, and setts*

BS 437: Part 1: 1970 *Cast iron spigot and socket drain pipes, bends, branches and access fittings*

BS 443: 1969 *Galvanized coatings on wire*

BS 486: 1973 *Asbestos-cement pressure pipes*

BS 556: Part 2: 1972 *Concrete cylindrical pipes and fittings including manholes, inspection chambers and street gullies. Metric units*

BS 559: 1955 *Electric signs and high-voltage luminous-discharge-tube installations*

BS 565: 1972 *Glossary of terms relating to timber and woodwork*

BS 594: 1973 *Rolled asphalt (hot process) for roads and other paved areas*

BS 607: Part 2: 1970 *Concrete poles for electrical transmission and traction systems. Metric units*

BS 706: 1936 *Sandstone kerbs, channels, quadrants and setts*

BS 729: 1971 *Hot dip galvanized coatings on iron and steel articles*

BS 802: 1967 *Tarmacadam with crushed rock or slag aggregate*

BS 812: 1967 *Methods for sampling and testing of mineral aggregates, sands and fillers*

BS 873: Part 3: 1970 *The construction of internally illuminated bollards*

BS 881,589 : 1955 *Nomenclature of commercial timber including sources of supply*

BS 882 : Part 2 : 1973 *Coarse and fine aggregates from natural sources for concrete*

BS 890 : 1972 *Building limes*

BS 892 : 1967 *Glossary of highway engineering terms*

BS 915 : Part 2 : 1972 *High alumina cement. Metric units*

BS 970 : Part 4 : 1970 *Stainless, heat resisting and valve steels*

BS 1014 : 1961 *Pigments for cement, magnesium oxy-chloride and concrete*

BS 1052 : 1942 *Mild steel wire for general engineering purposes*

BS 1180 : 1972 *Concrete bricks and fixing bricks*

BS 1186 : Part 1 : 1971 *Quality of timber in joinery*

BS 1194 : 1969 *Concrete porous pipes for under-drainage*

BS 1196 : 1971 *Clayware field drain pipes*

BS 1200 : 1955 *Building sands from natural sources*

BS 1204 : Part 2 : 1965 *Close-contact synthetic resin adhesives (phenolic and aminoplastic) for wood*

BS 1211 : 1958 *Centrifugally cast (spun) iron pressure pipes for water, gas and sewage*

BS 1217 : 1945 *Cast stone*

BS 1222 : 1945 *Battery-operated electric fences*

BS 1224 : 1970 *Electroplated coatings of nickel and chromium*

BS 1227 : Part 1A : 1967 *Hinges for general building purposes*

BS 1241 : 1959 *Tarmacadam and tar carpets (gravel aggregate)*

BS 1242 : 1960 *Tarmacadam 'tarpaving' for footpaths, playgrounds and similar works*

BS 1282 : 1959 *Classification of wood preservatives and their methods of application*

BS 1286 : 1945 *Clay tiles for flooring*

BS 1331 : 1954 *Builders' hardware for housing*

BS 1370 : Part 2 : 1974 *Low heat Portland cement*

BS 1373 : 1967 *Clothes-line posts*

BS 1377 : 1967 *Methods of testing soils for civil engineering purposes*

BS 1446 : 1973 *Mastic asphalt (natural rock asphalt fine aggregate) for roads and footways*

BS 1447 : 1973 *Mastic asphalt (limestone fine aggregate) for roads and footways*

BS 1449 : Part 4 : 1967 *Stainless and heat resisting plate, sheet and strip*

BS 1452 : 1961 *Grey iron castings*

BS 1471 : 1972 *Wrought aluminium and aluminium alloys for general engineering purposes – plate, sheet and strip*

BS 1494 : Part 2 : 1967 *Fixing accessories for building purposes. Sundry fixings*

BS 1521 : 1972 *Waterproof building papers*

BS 1579 : 1960 *Connectors for timber*

BS 1621 : 1961 *Bitumen macadam with crushed rock or slag aggregate*

BS 1690 : 1962 *Cold asphalt*

BS 1706 : 1960 *Electroplated coatings of cadmium and zinc on iron and steel*

BS 1722 : Part 1 : 1972 *Chain link fences*

BS 1722 : Part 2 : 1973 *Woven wire fences*

BS 1722 : Part 3 : 1973 *Strained wire fences*

BS 1722 : Part 4 : 1972 *Cleft chestnut pale fences*

BS 1722 : Part 5 : 1972 *Close-boarded fences including oak pale fences*

BS 1722 : Part 6 : 1972 *Wooden palisade fences*

BS 1722 : Part 7 : 1972 *Wooden post and rail fences*

BS 1722 : Part 8 : 1966 *Mild steel or wrought iron continuous bar fences*

BS 1722 : Part 9 : 1963 *Mild steel or wrought iron un-climbable fences with round or square verticals and flat standards and horizontals*

BS 1722 : Part 10 : 1972 *Anti-intruder chain link fences*

BS 1722 : Part 11 : 1972 *Woven wooden fences*

BS 1775 : 1964 *Steel tubes for mechanical, structural and general engineering purposes*

BS 1788 : 1964 *Street lighting lanterns for use with electric lamps*

BS 1881 : Part 1 : 1970 *Methods of sampling fresh concrete*

BS 1926 : 1962 *Ready-mixed concrete*

BS 1984 : 1967 *Gravel aggregates for surface treatment (including surface dressings) on roads*

BS 1990 : Part 2 : 1971 *Wood poles for overhead lines (power and telecommunication lines). Metric units*

BS 2028, 1364 : 1968 *Precast concrete blocks*

BS 2040 : 1953 *Bitumen macadam with gravel aggregate*

BS 2569 : Part 1 : 1964 *Sprayed metal coatings. Protection of iron and steel by aluminium and zinc against atmospheric corrosion*

BS 2632 : 1955 *Mains-operated electric fence controllers*

BS 2760 : 1973 *Pitch-impregnated fibre pipes and fittings for drainage below and above ground*

BS 2874 : 1969 *Copper and copper alloys. Rods and sections (other than forging stock)*

BS 2898 : 1970 *Wrought aluminium and aluminium alloys for electrical purposes. Bars, extruded round tube and sections*

BS 3047 : 1974 *Sizes of posters*

BS 3148 : 1959 *Tests for water for making concrete*
BS 3178 : Part 1 : 1959 *General requirements for playground equipment for parks*
BS 3178 : Part 2A : 1959 *Special requirements for static playground equipment for parks (except slides)*
BS 3178 : Part 2B : 1960 *Special requirements for slides for parks*
BS 3178 : Part 3A : 1960 *Pendulum see-saws for parks*
BS 3178 · Part 3B : 1962 *Plane swings for parks*
BS 3178 : Section 3C : 1964 *Plank swings for parks*
BS 3178 : Part 4 : 1965 *Rotating playground equipment for parks*
BS 3191 : Part 3A : 1961 *Fixed playground equipment for schools. Special requirements for steel tubular assault poles*
BS 3470 : 1962 *Field gates and posts*
BS 3656 : 1973 *Asbestos-cement pipes, joints and fittings for sewerage and drainage*
BS 3690 : 1970 *Bitumens for road purposes*
BS 3882 : 1965 *Recommendations and classification for top soil*
BS 3921 : : 1974 *Clay bricks and blocks*
BS 3936 : Part 1 : 1965 *Nursery stock. Trees and shrubs*
BS 3936 : Part 4 : 1966 *Nursery stock. Forest trees*
BS 3936 : Part 9 : 1968 *Nursery stock. Bulbs, corms and tubers*
BS 3969 : 1965 *Recommendations for turf for general landscape purposes*
BS 3975 : Part 4 : 1966 *Glossary for landscape work. Plant description*
BS 3975 : Part 5 : 1969 *Glossary for landscape work. Horticultural, arboricultural and forestry practice*
BS 3998 : 1966 *Recommendations for tree work*
BS 4008 : 1973 *Cattle grids on private roads*
BS 4043 : 1966 *Recommendations for transplanting semi-mature trees*
BS 4092 : 1966 *Domestic front entrance gates*
BS 4102 : 1971 *Steel wire for fences*
BS 4107 : 1967 *Fixed outdoor rotary clothes driers*
BS 4118 : 1967 *Glossary of sanitation terms*
BS 4132 : 1973 *Winkle clinker for landscape work*
BS 4324 : 1968 *Litter bins*
BS 4360 : 1972 *Weldable structural steels*
BS 4363 : 1968 *Distribution units for electricity supplies for construction and building sites*
BS 4428 : 1969 *Recommendations for general landscape operations (excluding hard surfaces)*
BS 4449 : 1969 *Hot rolled steel bars for the reinforcement of concrete*

BS 4471 : Part 1 : 1969 *Dimensions for softwood. Basic sections*
BS 4482 : 1969 *Hard drawn mild steel wire for the reinforcement of concrete*
BS 4483 : 1969 *Steel fabric for the reinforcement of concrete*
BS 4551 : 1970 *Methods of testing mortars and specification for mortar testing sand*
BS 4721 : 1971 *Ready-mixed lime: sand for mortar*
BS 4727 : Part 2 : Group 04 : 1973 *Glossary of transformer terminology*
BS 4727 : Part 2 : Group 05 : 1972 *Glossary of voltage fluctuation terminology*
BS 4921 : 1973 *Sherardized coatings on iron and steel articles*
BS 4987 : 1973 *Coated macadam for roads and other paved areas*

CP 3 : Chapter V : Part 2 : 1972 *Code of basic data for the design of buildings. Wind loads*
CP 3 : Chapter VII : 1950 *Engineering and utility services*
CP 94 : 1971 *Demolition*
CP 98 : 1964 *Preservative treatments for constructional timber*
CP 111 : Part 2 : 1970 *Structural recommendations for loadbearing walls. Metric units*
CP 112 : Part 2 : 1971 *The structural use of timber. Metric units*
CP 114 : Part 2 : 1969 *Structural use of reinforced concrete in buildings. Metric units*
CP 116 : Part 2 : 1969 *The structural use of precast concrete*
CP 121 : Part 1 : 1973 *Walling. Brick and block masonry*
CP 121.201 : 1951 *Masonry walls ashlared with natural stone or with cast stone*
CP 121.202 : 1951 *Masonry. Rubble walls*
CP 123.101 : 1951 *Dense concrete walls*
CP 231 : 1966 *Painting of buildings*
CP 301 : 1971 *Building drainage*
CP 326 : 1965 *The protection of structures against lightning*
CP 1004 : Part 1 : 1973 *Street lighting. General principles*
CP 1017 : 1969 *Distribution of electricity on construction and building sites*
CP 2001 : 1957 *Site investigations*
CP 2004 : 1972 *Foundations*
CP 2005 : 1968 *Sewerage*
CP 2007 : Part 2 : 1970 *Design and construction of reinforced and prestressed concrete structure for the storage of water and other aqueous liquids. Metric units*
CP 2008 : 1966 *Protection of iron and steel structures from corrosion*

Index

Bold type denotes illustrations